*So You Want to Be a
Garden Designer*

So You Want to Be a Garden Designer

HOW TO GET STARTED,
GROW, AND THRIVE
IN THE
LANDSCAPE DESIGN
BUSINESS

Love Albrecht Howard

TIMBER PRESS
Portland · London

Photos and illustrations by Love Albrecht Howard unless otherwise credited.

Frontispiece: A tiny shade garden offers a welcome
respite from the heat and noise of the city.

Published in 2010 by Timber Press, Inc.

The Haseltine Building   2 The Quadrant
133 S.W. Second Avenue, Suite 450   135 Salusbury Road
Portland, Oregon 97204-3527   London NW6 6RJ
www.timberpress.com   www.timberpress.co.uk

Text designed by Susan Applegate
Printed in China

Library of Congress Cataloging-in-Publication Data

Howard, Love Albrecht.
    So you want to be a garden designer: how to get started, grow, and
thrive in the landscape design business/Love Albrecht Howard.
        p. cm.
    Includes bibliographical references and index.
    ISBN-13: 978-0-88192-904-1
    1. Landscape design—Vocational guidance. I. Title.
    SB472.45.H69 2010
    712.023—dc22   2009036879

A catalog record for this book is also available from the British Library.

To my husband, **Bruce Richard Howard,** my partner in all things, including the gardens in which we find so much joy (and, well, work). You are truly the most supportive friend in the world. This all started with your suggestion: "First you need to amend the soil." Who knew how far that remark would take us!

To my son, **Griffin Thomas Howard,** the most wonderful creation I have ever helped nurture and watch grow, and the single most significant element in my personal growth. You have been smothered with plants in the back of my car since the day you were born. Thanks for being such a good sport. You bless my life.

To my mother, **Janiece Fergeson Albrecht,** for instilling in me a spectacular work ethic, for encouraging me to think creatively, for letting me get dirty, for having both the individuality and the courage to name me Love, and for always reinforcing that I really can do anything I set my mind to.

To my father in-law, the late **Dr. Richard A. Howard,** who recognized my budding interest in plants, presented me with my first *Horticulture* magazine, and brought me on my first garden tour. Thank you for insisting my horticultural and botanical knowledge go beyond common names. I miss you.

And finally, to all the plants I killed as I was learning to be a gardener. Thanks to you, I now succeed far more than I fail!

CONTENTS

An old Underwood typewriter finds new life in the garden. You can, too.
Photo courtesy of Eric Roth, Eric Roth Photography.

PREFACE

THOUSANDS OF BOOKS OUT THERE endeavor to teach you how to plan space, design glorious gardens and landscapes, create captivating plant combinations, and be a better gardener. You will not learn any of that here. This is a handbook about starting and growing a garden design business. If you love gardening and playing with plants in your personal time, and if you have wondered repeatedly what it would be like to work in this world, this book is for you.

From identifying the first steps to walking you through retirement options, I share how to develop the knowledge, skills, and confidence to promote yourself, talk with clients, develop and present design recommendations, charge for your time, prepare estimates, work with subcontractors, implement construction, and integrate your new business with your life. You'll learn what a garden design business is and what it takes to succeed.

I love this business. I love being part of something that contributes to people's happiness, creates beautiful spaces, and lets me make a good living. I love working with other designers, some of whom are the most talented, dedicated, good-natured people I have ever met. If you are seriously considering becoming a garden designer, I hope that my own enthusiasm, experience, and knowledge will help you as you take those first brave steps.

I'm also here to tell you that you can do this. You can! All you need is a passion for plants and gardening, a desire to try something different, and a willingness to do more with your skills and your zeal. Most of the garden designers I know have a wide variety of professional backgrounds. Many of them entered this field in midlife when they were looking for something new. They wanted to work in a capacity that gave them more ownership and made the most of a personal interest. You can do it, too.

The joy of working with plants, the satisfaction of being your own boss—the life of a garden designer might be the perfect life for you. I can't promise you success or assure you riches, but I can guarantee you'll never be bored.

CHAPTER ONE

The Journey from Gardener to Designer

Aᴅᴍɪᴛ ɪᴛ, ʏᴏᴜ'ᴠᴇ ᴛᴏʏᴇᴅ ᴡɪᴛʜ ᴛʜᴇ ɪᴅᴇᴀ. As you commute to work do you look at landscapes and mentally redo them? Are you horrified by landscape crimes you see in the making? Did you pass the red house when they were planting the bright pink roses along the foundation and want to scream out the window, "Noooo!"? Have you watered and primped neglected plants in your doctor's office? Do you wander nurseries just to see what brand new, special plant varieties are available? Have you brought plants home that you knew you had no place for but just had to have? Do Mondays find you already yearning for the weekend so that you can have entire days to play in the soil?

How many times did you nod yes? You just might have the passion it takes to be a successful, satisfied garden design professional.

HOW I GOT HERE

"Wow, you design gardens? Really? That must be so much fun!" That is the usual response when someone finds out what I do for a living. I smile and reply, "Yes, it really is fun." I know I am truly fortunate to make a living by following my passion. I get to create beauty —how incredible is that? Even cooler, I get to wear jeans to work and get dirty every day, and I work with awesome people. Make no mistake: this is a real job. I have real-job problems to solve, challenges to face, and fears, fatigue, and worry to overcome. But I am constantly delighted by the thrill of creation and transformation, and I find great joy in the friendship and appreciation I receive from my coworkers and clients. I wouldn't trade this job for anything.

I haven't done this all my life. I started off in the corporate world in human resources, marketing, and advertising. My background was in engineering, mathematics, and science, and I had never thought of myself as creative. When I found gardening, it seemed to be a perfect convergence of science, nurturing, miracle, and creativity. It gave me tangible results I could hold in my hand or stand back and admire (or even eat!). Gardening became "it"—my hobby, my avenue for decompression, my outlet for inspiration. Fortunately my husband, Bruce, shares my passion, so gardening was how we spent evenings and weekends for many years. And whenever we went on vacation, we always checked out area nurseries and gardens.

Like many of my colleagues, I came to garden design a bit late and by a circuitous route. I was thirty-one before I even got into gardening as a hobby. One afternoon in the late 1980s I was at my childhood home in Massachusetts and saw the neighbor, Mr. Galvin, tacking up a "for sale" sign. The house was a Craftsman-style bungalow on a little more than 3 acres, with about a third of the land wooded and the rest open fields and lawn. My husband and I liquidated everything we had and bought the place.

On the late-winter day we moved in, we found a large fruit basket on the kitchen table with a note from the Galvins, which I read out loud: "We wish you all the best with the house, and we hope you'll keep up the tradition of the vegetable garden, since we fed five children out of it for twenty-five years." I remember snorting to Bruce, "I'm good with houseplants, but everything I've ever planted outside has died." "Really?" he replied. "Well, first you need to amend the soil." This phrase had no meaning for me at the time, but I said, "Okay, sure. We'll try."

Up to this point I had no idea that Bruce's earlier experience at Harvard's Arnold Arboretum would end up being so valuable. His dad, Dr. Richard A. Howard, had been the director of the arboretum for about twenty-five years, and the family had lived in a marvelous old farmhouse on the Case Estates in Weston, Massachusetts, part of the property holdings of the arboretum. When Bruce was old enough, he worked summers as a laborer on the grounds of the Case Estates, plowing, mowing, weeding, hoeing, preparing garden beds, cleaning up after the livestock. If a strong, young back could do it, he did it, and I guess by doing so, he learned a thing or two (or twenty).

At the end of our first May in the Galvins' house, we headed for the little 16-foot-square vestige of the vegetable garden. We raked out the winter detritus and pulled the few weeds that had sprouted up in the warm soil. We had purchased composted cow manure, which we broadcast thickly over the surface and lightly forked in. I had never touched this kind of soil. It was like crumbly chocolate cake.

We planted flats of tomatoes, cabbages, broccoli, and lettuce. We direct-sowed zucchini, winter squash, corn, and beans. That's quite a lot to cram into 250 square feet, but we were optimistic and had no experience to tell us to do otherwise. We even included some flowering annuals because Bruce had remembered they would attract pollinators. I remembered how Mrs. Galvin had always asked for grass clippings for her garden, so we also used clippings as mulch. Finally we watered and stood back.

The vegetable garden was a phenomenal success, and I was hooked. I started devouring every gardening book and magazine I could get my

Our farmette. Photo courtesy of Bruce R. Howard.

hands on. PBS's *Victory Garden* became the single half-hour each week during which no one was allowed to disturb me. I began to query my father-in-law about plants and growing. The following year we started playing with perennials, then bulbs, and soon all bets were off. If it was green and it looked like it would grow, we bought it. The garden had been minimal when we moved in, but no more. We began to create borders, foundation plantings, colorful beds, and planting pots. We added hundreds of trees and flowering shrubs, and people started referring to our place as "the house with the flowers." Within a few short years I was the one answering, not asking, the gardening questions.

And that, my friends, is how I became a gardener.

So how did I get from planting my own place to designing for others? In the fall of 1994 I was expecting our first child. It was a hard-won pregnancy, so Bruce was supportive when I said I wanted to take a few years off and just be a mother.

The following spring, friends started asking me gardening and design questions, and I casually offered my opinions and advice. No big deal, just talking.

Summer found my friend Marianne and I strolling along the coast in Scituate with our baby boys. She suggested we stop in to say hi to her husband, John, who managed a waterfront hotel. During the visit I made a casual comment about the hotel's gardens, which I felt detracted from the beautiful location and view: "Gee, this place could be so lovely— too bad the gardens are so overgrown." John asked what I meant, and I offered a few suggestions.

A few days later he called me. "Love, if you want to redo the hotel's gardens, I want you to do it. My budget will be bare bones, so I can't pay you, but I can buy all the plants and pay for all the help you need."

Wow. A chance to design professionally, and at this great seaside location? Yes, yes, yes! I didn't know how to begin but forged ahead with research, plans, and sketches. I wanted the hotel to have waves of color from early spring through November. John approved my design, and we ordered shrubs, grasses, flowering perennials, and lots of bulbs. Early that fall we gutted and renovated the gardens. We exposed the great bones of the hillside and let the hotel breathe again. (Two years later, "the perennial gardens at the Clipper Ship" won the town's beautification award. Success!)

Around the same time I met Mike Walsh, president of Horticultural Concepts, following a lecture he gave for a local garden club. After I introduced myself, he asked if I had any particular passions when it came to garden design. I replied, "Actually, yes. I love shade gardens." He looked a little surprised, then suggested we collaborate on a project some time. Figuring this was a polite brush-off I never gave his comment another thought. A couple of months later he called and asked if I would be interested in working on a shade garden design with one of the other landscape designers in his firm.

This was the beginning of my "grand education" and transition from gardener to designer. The client was a woman from England who was an amazing horticulturist herself. We decided to create what I called a "discovery garden," in which there would be something new for her to discover every day, nearly year-round. The garden would surround a patio Mike was constructing in the shade of two towering maples located just off of their sunroom. Knowing that the client was a major plant

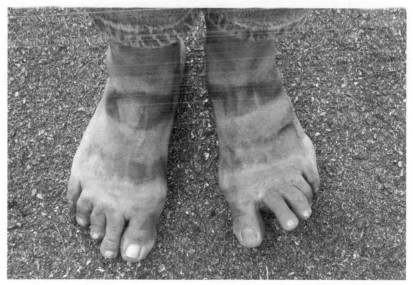

My feet after a day of work.

aficionado, we worked to find all kinds of special plant varieties to tickle her fancy. She was thrilled with the results, and the collaboration was a tremendous success.

A few months later found me measuring and photographing new job sites for Mike. Ultimately I learned to use the computer-aided design (CAD) technology his company employed, and I started preparing all the base maps of existing conditions for his firm. Before long I was working preliminary designs and setting up planting plans.

At some point, probably in desperation, Mike threw me onto a few projects to manage the construction. I ran those jobs by the seat of my pants, but they finished well. As I took on more for Mike, my own jobs were also becoming more substantive, and suddenly—poof!—I was designing dramatic flowering borders, masonry and driveways, swimming pools and spas, a summerhouse, sheds, conservation plantings, just about everything. Of course, that "poof" took years, but I loved the steep learning curve, as well as being in the dirt with the crews and collaborating with the clients.

WHAT IS A GARDEN DESIGNER?

A garden designer is generally described as a person who knows horticulture and designs the combinations and layout of plants for a particular garden. A landscape designer modifies the use of space and designs changes in landscapes by recommending design treatments that may include regrading, masonry, carpentry, and other disciplines. A landscape designer may or may not design the plantings.

Those are not my definitions, however. I feel a garden designer can function as a landscape designer, and a landscape designer can function as a garden designer. There used to be an implied hierarchy to the titles, with a garden designer being somehow less skilled than a landscape designer, but the terms have become more interchangeable. Some of the greatest "land and garden designers" I know consider themselves garden designers rather than landscape designers. Wayne Winterrowd and Joe Eck of North Hill Garden Design Associates in Readsboro, Vermont, are a perfect case in point. This greatly respected duo refer to themselves as garden designers, and they design some of the most amazing land and space transformations you could imagine.

Another category in the industry, landscape contractor, is generally someone who works to maintain an established landscape. Landscape contractors mow, blow, feed, and treat lawns, sometimes do snow removal and gutter cleaning, and less frequently carry out perennial garden maintenance. When I hear "landscape contractor" I mostly think maintenance, although many of these professionals also offer design install services.

Finally, a landscape architect (LA) is a design professional who has an accredited four-year degree and has passed a licensing exam. Many of them have an advanced degree and have completed an apprenticeship under a registered landscape architect. It is illegal to call yourself a landscape architect unless you hold the degree and license; on occasion a client will introduce me as their landscape architect, and I always correct them.

Sometimes garden designers, landscape designers, and landscape architects work in concert. Particularly in large design shops, projects come forward that are initially conceived by landscape architects, who devise the big picture for the space, after which the full design and construction specifications are worked out by landscape designers and garden designers.

I call myself a garden designer. When people don't get it (although, really, how can you misinterpret that?), I explain that I "design and build landscapes and gardens." Ohhh. A woman I once met finally summed it up by saying (and you must say this with an edgy Boston accent for full effect), "Oh, okay. So you, like, go to someone's house and say, 'Okay, you put the yellow flowahs ovah theyah, and the red flowahs ovah theyah.' Right?" Smiling, I replied, "Well, yes, I suppose you could sum it up that way."

WHY BE A GARDEN DESIGNER?

When I ask other garden and landscape designers why they do what they do, I often get a shrug and the quick answer, "I love plants." That's my answer, too: plant madness. I was the houseplant queen in each of my previous jobs, and my office was always a small jungle. It wasn't until much later that I learned I could enjoy even more success and enjoyment by taking my plant passion outdoors.

There is also joy in being your own boss. The choice is yours when it

17

comes to working with a particular client or subcontractor, or buying from this or that supplier. There is a great deal of freedom in this, which you will particularly appreciate if you have ever worked for a punishing or suffocating manager. You can choose to flow your business around your life, or if you tend to be a workaholic, your life can flow around your business. Whatever works best for you is what you strive for.

Working for myself has been a particular blessing since I started my business when our only child, Griffin, was six months old. I was fortunate to never have to leave him to work in this field. Packed on my back or plopped on a blanket, he was happy, and I could do just about anything I needed to do on the job site. By the time I was working larger jobs that required more hours, he was in school and I worked around his schedule. Griff is now in high school, and I still work around his schedule. This gives me both the time to make a living and the freedom to be a mom. I tend to work too much, and I have to fight that, so having a child to remind me of what is really important is a tremendous benefit.

Of course, even though I am my own boss, I still answer to someone else. Certainly I answer to my clients. Every client is effectively my boss, even though I prefer to see the relationship as a collaboration. I also answer to my subcontractors. They may work for me, but I still have to provide them with information and direction.

When you're the boss, you get the credit for a job well done. Sometimes clients gush over a new installation and tell me what a talent I am. That's wonderful, and I'm grateful for any and all appreciation, but I always credit my team of subcontractors and workers. "Didn't Joe do a tremendous job on the walls?" "Wasn't the slope beautifully planted by Al, Angel, and José?" "Greg and his crew really transformed the house with the new paint."

Needless to say, when you're the boss the fault is equally yours, too. The buck most assuredly stops with me, and it is my responsibility to make things right. That said, I firmly believe that the advantages to being your own boss greatly outweigh the liabilities.

And then there is the satisfaction of creating something significant. Many years ago, during an interview for an internal-hire position at Polaroid, I was asked what I found frustrating about my current job. After thinking about it, it hit me that what I didn't like was that my work was nearly the same every day. Since my position revolved around constant updates, nothing was ever really finished. The interviewer smiled and said, "I think you'd like a position in which you can create something meaningful, grasp the finished product, and have finite results and completion."

This was a serendipitous moment, because he was right. He taught me an important lesson about myself: I need a start, a middle, and an end. I did not know then what I know now, that the part of the job I love most is the process of working with a team to create and execute a campaign—or a construction project.

As a garden designer, I create something nearly every day. Whether I am mentally ruminating on a new landscape, designing on the computer, or laying out plants in a new garden, I am creating something concrete that is beautiful and meaningful. The satisfaction is incredible. One of the things I love most is meeting with clients at the end of a construction project. I like to sit with them in the newly completed space, and walk them through the "existing conditions" photos I took when we first met. Usually they have forgotten by then exactly what their place originally looked like, and they are astonished and delighted anew by the transformation.

BROAD KNOWLEDGE, MANY TALENTS

To become a professional garden designer, you will grow to have knowledge in many different areas: horticulture, space alteration, masonry, drainage, lighting, irrigation, soil characteristics, architecture, drafting, design, water features, furnishings, integrated pest management, safety issues, color theory. If you enjoy constant learning and stimulation, this may be the field for you.

After my first couple of projects with Mike Walsh, he told me I had "a rare combination of talents and interests." I was like, uh, really? "I can find the people with the horticultural knowledge," he said, "and I can find the people who can work with the technology. But I rarely find anyone with the capacity for both." Today I think Mike would have less trouble finding that combination, primarily because almost everyone now uses a computer, from ten-year-olds to people in their seventies. Fear of technology has mostly evaporated.

In fact I would bet that you use a computer daily or nearly so. And even if you don't end up creating your designs using a CAD program, you'll use a computer to run your business. This is a huge leg up considering where we were not so many years ago, and it only goes to prove we can all learn new things.

Other ways your varied talents will come into play are many. Can you swing a hammer? Repair a simple light fixture? Use a power drill? Decorate a Christmas tree? Believe it or not, this knowledge can help you design and install landscape lighting. Can you choose plants that will bloom in waves of pinks and whites from March to November in a shade garden? Assess tree health? Know the difference between sandy and clay soils? Can you wield a paintbrush? Use a power washer? Clean a gutter? Sure you can! Well, if you can't do it today, you can learn enough to try it by, say, tomorrow. Yes, tomorrow. Ask for advice wherever you buy supplies; people who know their stuff are generally happy to share tips.

You're asking, this is part of garden design? It is for me. I started with gardens but have grown to be able to take care of just about everything on the outside of a home. I just keep learning and marching boldly forward.

An old adage in the education of medical professionals is "Learn one, do one, teach one." Someone shows us how something is done, then we practice it either under supervision or on our own. When we have reached a certain level of proficiency, we can show someone else how to do the task. Obviously the "learn one, do one" time for, say, practicing neurosurgery is longer than for learning how to paint window trim. Still, you will be amazed by what you'll learn to do when you embark on this profession. I have learned to do many things simply because waiting for another professional to come and do it would have taken too long or cost too much. You simply learn how to do it, then do it—there's no wait, the clients are happy, other construction phases are not held up, and *you* get paid for doing the job. The beauty is that the education never stops.

WILL IT BE A GOOD FIT?

This profession is not just about horticulture. Starting your own business makes you an entrepreneur, and you need to take a look at your skills and honestly assess your personality to see if there is a fit. Yes, you absolutely need horticultural knowledge, but the business of garden design is about flexibility, responsiveness, leadership, and working with people.

Are you personally motivated by all levels of challenge? Garden design involves problem solving, and every day is different. Even if I think I know how my day will run, unexpected things happen. I love the stimulation and the challenges. How do you feel about taking risks? Every new assignment—every foray into working with a new site, new material, new type of installation—involves risk. It is never "same old, same old." To me, the new is really cool; the learning is steep and incredibly gratifying.

Do you shift gears well? Can you respond to a crisis and give it your full attention, then shift back to tending to something mundane? You can be checking in on a masonry job in one town, and then get a phone call telling you that an excavator at another site in another town just dug up and cut a gas line. You need to respond calmly, act quickly, and then return to your regularly scheduled program as if almost nothing happened. Your mind may be screaming in horror, but your mouth will be calmly saying, "Okay, Danny, relax. Here's what you do. Make certain no one is smoking. Get everyone out of the house. Be sure the broken gas line is venting up out of the ground. Tell James to call 911 immediately, and tell them the site is 38 Notting Road. Repeat that back to me: 38 Notting Road. Turn off the machinery. Go to the bottom of the driveway, wait for the emergency vehicles, and point them in." During this conversation, of course, you will have gotten into your car and started quickly making your way to Danny's site. Then you'll phone 911 to make sure Danny made the call and gave them the correct address, and you'll give them your own name and number. When it's all over, back to the mundane: you call the mason you just abandoned and give him the feedback you'd started when the phone call came in.

This scenario actually happened to me (although the names have been changed to protect the guilty, and yes, we had called Dig Safe, our local dig hotline). Fortunately no one was hurt, the lines were repaired quickly, and in retrospect I was pretty satisfied with how I reacted to the call.

Do you work well alone? Designing can be lonely. It's usually just you, your mind, your opinions and creativity, and your computer or drafting table. I confer and design with other designers on occasion, and the camaraderie is tremendous, but most of my design work is done alone. I enjoy the peace and quiet of working on a new design, and relish the days I get to submerge myself and totally Zen into my work. This is a luxury for me.

Conversely, you'll need to work well on a team. Site work can be twenty people at once going in twelve different directions. Masons putting in the driveway are asking what to do about butting up the new stone to the cobble collar, carpenters replacing windows are looking for an answer about fixing the sill rot they just uncovered, landscape contractors are yelling that they found a 3-foot stump in the drainage path they're digging out in the rear, the electrician needs to move where you wanted the lines to come out for the low-voltage transformer, your client is telling you she's not sure she likes the three hundred annuals that just arrived, and you need to give her the great news about the sill rot. Meanwhile it's hot and humid, and your phone keeps ringing. When this kind of thing happens to me, I love it. In the moment I might be thinking, "Oy!" but to be honest I thrive on it. Don't get freaked out—this does not happen every day by any means. But it helps if you can enjoy those times when it's a perfect storm and everyone is cranking and grooving on a site. To quote Mr. Rogers, "It's a beautiful day in the neighborhood."

Can you lead and inspire others to do their best? Taking a team approach works beautifully when you're managing crews. Everyone likes to be thanked and praised for a job well done, and constructive feedback makes us all better at what we do.

Can you take someone else's desires and needs and create an environment for their enjoyment? As designers we do not design for ourselves; we step into the minds and lives of our clients and design for them. Could you build something a client specifically asked for even if you thought it wasn't the right thing to do? I have done this, as long as it didn't negatively impact the neighbors or the environment. After all, it is the client's property.

I have also said no. For example, potential clients once asked for a great deal of fencing to stop neighborhood children from using their side yard to get to the skating pond in the woods behind their house. The cut-through had been accessible to the neighborhood for more than fifty years, and the kids would have to walk over a mile if access were cut off. Since foot traffic was only a concern for about two weeks each winter, I suggested fencing the yard while still leaving an access corridor. They disagreed. I turned down the job.

Understand, too, going into this profession, that working outdoors isn't always a walk in the park. You'll have to deal with adverse weather and biting insects, to name just a couple of challenges. And since garden design involves physical work, you'll need to guard against injury. Still, despite all of that (maybe even because of all that—you know, wounds and all), we designers love what we do.

All of these skills and characteristics are personal elements that you will refine as you go along, but you do need to take a look at yourself at the outset and determine whether this type of business will suit you. There is no right or wrong response, it's just what is right for you.

A friend of mine, Mike Saganich, is a superb hobbyist. He has a phenomenal wealth of horticultural knowledge, gives delightful lectures, writes beautifully, is a master propagator and seed starter, and can grow anything. A couple of years ago I suggested he try working on some garden designs, just something small to start out as a way to get into the professional end of this industry.

Mike told me how a local nursery had once connected him with a potential client. He called the client and asked a few questions designed to elicit some information about his needs and tastes in plants and landscaping. It only took a few moments for Mike to discover that the gentleman's knowledge of plants was virtually nil, and that the amount of time he wished to spend maintaining his proposed garden was extremely modest. The client essentially wanted, in his own words, "something to look at."

Mike told the man that he'd get back to him, then debated briefly with himself before calling back to say that he couldn't take the job. Since then, he's been leery of going into the garden design business.

What my friend realized was that having a passion for plants and gardening is only part of the equation. You also have to be able to meet clients at their own level of knowledge and enthusiasm. At its core, this job isn't about dealing with plants; it's about dealing with people and meeting their needs.

"Garden designers face the same demand that the administrators of public gardens face," he wrote me. "Sophisticated aesthetics aren't the priority. Rare and unusual plants aren't the priority. The brief to you seems much simpler: make it look pretty. But of course they mean make it look pretty *all the time*. Oh, and we need to screen the view of the neighbor's shed and incorporate Aunt Sally's urn. And do you have any plants that match our school colors?"

"That can all be very rewarding," Mike concluded, "but if your real passion is educating people about special plants, realize that most clients are not going to pay you to do it in their backyards."

ARE YOU A GARDEN DESIGNER?

My father-in-law originally thought I should propagate *Asarum europaeum*, wild European ginger. He knew I loved plants, and from what he could see around our place, we were really good at growing ginger. European ginger grows beautifully for me—it self-sows everywhere— and at nurseries it is much more expensive than other groundcovers. He suggested that filling a narrow niche by propagating a specialized, in-demand perennial would be a satisfying and lucrative career. I'm sure it would be, for the right person. I love plants and growing them, but what I really love doing is tucking the little babies here and there in order to accent other plants. See? What I love most is the art of mixing plants in the garden.

Ultimately the decision to be a garden designer has to come from your heart. When you leverage a passion into a career, it is the best career choice in the world. Your love becomes your life. I'll be honest. Although most of us make a good living, unless you are among the very famous and talented few, you will not become wealthy doing this work. You won't have a pension. Paid vacations, sick days, and holidays will all be things of the past. In the heat of the season, calls will start coming in from subs and suppliers at 5:30 a.m. Sometimes you'll be laboring on a design layout or completing plant orders until midnight. You'll work many spring and summer weekends, particularly when you're first getting established, and the truth is you won't have nearly as much time or energy for your own garden. But you will be living something you love, learning constantly, creating beauty, and making people happy.

I started out with just my passion in my pocket in 1995, and now I have a thriving design-build business. I still attend as many lectures, seminars, and courses as I can. I keep abreast of industry trends. I continue to voraciously read and learn, and my skills continue to grow. In the beginning I planted container gardens. Now I design and build walls, walkways, driveways, decks, patios, pergolas, fire pits, outdoor kitchens, waterfalls, pools, ponds, fencing, lighting, and, of course, gardens, gardens, gardens! In each of the last five years my business grossed between $600,000 and $1,000,000, and there's no end in sight. The only thing that limits me is being one person.

Few garden designers would choose to do anything different from what they do. For me, 'tis a great life.

Am I saying you'll love it? Not necessarily. But I am saying that for those of us who try garden design and find it a good fit, it is a very satisfying profession. If you think you might give it a try, I want you to walk into it with your eyes wide open. It will take a while to build up your skills, and it will take time to develop a critical mass of clients. As in so many things, what you put into it will be what you'll get out of it.

CHAPTER TWO

Turning Your Passion into Your Profession

THE TRANSITION FROM GARDENER to designer is easily accomplished once you know what you're in for. There is a shift in mindset when you move from designing gardens and space for yourself to designing for other people. You know your plants and your climate. So what is involved in the transition? How do you look at things with the eye of a designer?

I am a major hort-head, and I started out thinking that every client would be impressed and delighted by my considerable horticultural knowledge. I knew they'd love to learn the background of every tree and flower. I thought they'd want unique, exotic specimens that had come to their backyard all the way from China and Turkey. I figured they'd revel in species bulbs, precious varieties, and perhaps a rare clematis scrambling over their new trellis. But no. With the teensiest of exceptions, my clients—and yours—want their landscapes to function well, they want them to be low maintenance, and they want it all to be pretty. Period.

When I first look at a new property, I do not think, "What would I do if this were mine?" Well, okay, sometimes I do, just because I can't help myself. But for the client, I try to focus on what is right for them. I learn how they are currently using their property and how they dream of using it. At the very beginning, ask what kinds of landscapes or gardens your clients have seen that are telling them that this is the time to hire a professional and effect changes. Why now? What is the inspiration? Ask if they have any photographs of gardens that have turned them on, or pictures from magazines. If they have, terrific. This will be the exception, though. Most people find it difficult to articulate what they're looking for, and many don't really know what they need, just that what they have right now is not doing it for them. As you get to know people and familiarize yourself with their property, you'll begin to identify changes that could increase the beauty and functionality of the landscape and make it more enjoyable for your clients. When it is time for the design presentation, you'll articulate your thoughts back to them. That is the shift in mindset. We stop focusing on what we would do to make ourselves happy, and focus instead on what works for someone else's property and lifestyle.

What do you say when someone asks, "What would you do if this were your yard?" This happens a lot, and I have a pat answer about it being their yard, not mine. Sometimes a client pushes for an answer, and if I'm feeling really comfortable, and a little playful, my response might go something like this (with accompanying gestures): "Okay, if you really want to know, if this were all mine, I would clean off the ledge at the far left and construct a waterfall to cascade over the outcropping to a large pool at the base. A rill would connect to another larger pool down at the center there. I would leave all the trees, and flood the rear area with hundreds of shade lovers in long, dramatic swaths of green. Here I'd build a large, raised patio with generous fieldstone walls forming terraced planters that would layer down from the patio to the lower gardens. Huge steps of native stone would also carry a dozen large Mexican-style pots stuffed with brilliant tropical plants. I'd remove this window and put in a wall of glass with French doors leading out to the new patio. I'd have a large bird station right over there, with multiple feeders, a dripping bath and water area, and a series of birdhouses." At this point, with the client gaping at me wondering what kind of monster has been unleashed, I would add, "That's what I'd do if this were my property. But this is your yard, and we are going to design it for you."

On the few occasions I've risked it and gone off like this, my clients have actually been delighted. This lets them know that I work creatively, that I'm not afraid to make some wild suggestions uniquely suited to their property, that I'm going to design with their goals in mind, and that together we will realize their vision (even if they don't really have a vision).

LEARNING DESIGN PRINCIPLES

I am not going to even remotely attempt to teach garden design principles here. Learning the basics of good design—how to look at and reformat space, how to combine plants—is both science and art, and there is no magic pill. Gaining this knowledge requires genuine interest coupled with commitment. Attend seminars. Take courses. Explore garden design shows. Study magazine articles and immerse yourself in design books. Each activity has something to teach you. You've been gardening and playing with this for years—trust and use your natural instincts. Design is objective and subjective. As in most things, you'll learn most by doing.

Apprentice with someone. Call several landscape design firms in your area, tell them about your passion and background, and ask to meet with them for fifteen minutes. Suggest that you would appreciate the opportunity to pick their brain about how to enter this profession. You just might be hired. If not, you've at least added to your network, and perhaps made a friend or two you could call on in the future. One caveat, though: it might not be best to call in the spring or early summer. This is the crazed period for designers, and they'll barely have time to eat, never mind meet with someone who wants to go information fishing. (On the other hand, they might be crazed enough to hire you to help out for a few weeks!)

There are design rules. Once you learn the rules, you can break them. I do have steadfast rules I use with space planning: minimum widths for walkways and driveways, dimensions for decks, staircase riser and tread depths, how deep to make a border. And I'll admit I break these rules, too. Then there are the more subjective "rules" of composition and color. My one hard and fast color rule: sulfur yellow blooming next to Pepto pink is gas station gardening and should be avoided at all costs. There are nonnegotiable state and local construction rules as well. You need to work within those parameters for permitting, and for safety. These rules and guidelines quickly become second nature, and you'll use them in just about every garden, in nearly every design.

TALKING THE TALK

There is a lingo. Learn what design terms mean and become fluent in their use. In addition to gaining confidence in your own knowledge and ability to articulate what you know, you will inspire confidence in your clients. For starters the word is *soil*, not *dirt*, and we don't plant *bushes*, we plant *shrubs*. Pronounce all three syllables of *foliage*, and understand that *loam* rhymes with *home*.

I have a friend who entered "landscape design" via the nursery trade. Long in the business of growing annuals with his family business, he decided to branch out and do landscape renovations. He calls them "rip-outs." When he meets with a client, he talks about what he's going to "trash" and what "bushes" he'll "throw in." It's a wonder that anyone would hire him, except that he's fairly cheap. So what does his work look like when he's done? Well, unfortunately you often get what you pay for, and his installations look like very poorly executed do-it-yourself jobs. I love the guy as a person, but in just a year I've been called twice to fix landscapes he's done. This approach doesn't help our industry gain credibility.

On the other hand, if you meet with a client and can discuss privacy

Long rows of container-grown shrubs. Photo courtesy of Veronica Wordell, Sylvan Nursery, Westport, Massachusetts.

screenings, focal points, view lines, curb appeal, safe footing, and property transformation, you will come across as the design professional you are.

COMMUNICATION

A key component of success—in fact, a key component of business survival—is communication. In any service industry communication is critical. Communication with clients, subcontractors, suppliers, everyone. If you are not a natural communicator, you can train yourself to communicate sufficiently. I consider myself to be a fairly good communicator, but I am most definitely not a phone person, preferring to respond in writing. Still, because it is part of my job, I force myself to return phone calls. The easiest way to get over these hurdles is to just do it. Don't wait, don't agonize, don't procrastinate—slap yourself into submission and do it.

Learning to deal with all types of people in a multitude of settings will also help you accomplish your goals. You'll need to be able to relate to wealthy clients as well as uneducated laborers, and you'll discover how to find common ground with both stay-at-home mothers and never-home professionals. If you're female, you'll learn how to communicate with men's men who aren't used to taking direction from a woman. And you'll learn to develop good relationships with town officials to grease the wheels for permitting you might need.

ETHICS

How you behave, how you operate in this new business, will be even more important than how well you lay out plant combinations and design. Your ethics will make or break you.

In his amazing book *The Last Lecture*, the late Randy Pausch talks about the importance of not only realizing your own dreams but also enabling the dreams of others along the way. He warns against becoming arrogant and talks about conducting yourself with sincerity, saying thank you, telling the truth, and apologizing when you make a mistake. He points out that there are no shortcuts; you need to put in the time necessary to learn your craft well. Having a sense of humor is essential, too, as is enjoying yourself along the way.

One of my former corporate jobs was working for a marketing agency in the Boston area. It was a marvelous company, and the founders never ceased to inspire us to do our best, grow, innovate, take the ball and run with it. The agency's corporate goals really spoke to the employees, as well as the clients:

- Focus on the customer.
- Do things right the first time.
- Be innovative.
- Make a profit.
- Have fun.

These are great business directives whether you're talking about a marketing company, car manufacturer, pancake house, or garden design business. They are timeless, universal, and as applicable to your personal life as to your company. (Yes, you can make a profit on your spouse. It's called love.)

Whatever business you end up in, if you always focus on your customer and conduct yourself with the highest ethics, you will be doing it better than the other guy. And not only will you be a better business person, you'll also be a better parent, spouse, son, daughter, or friend. Best yet, you'll always sleep at night.

WHAT HAPPENED TO MY HOBBY?

Once you make the metamorphosis from amateur in the dirt to professional in the soil, your behavior in your own garden will never be quite the same. Although I once practically leaped out of bed at dawn on a Saturday to weed, mulch, schlep, plant, trim, and primp for twelve or fourteen hours, it is no longer so delightful. Now it's work. I still enjoy the beauty and fruits of our gardens, still love transforming the spaces, planting the pots, and installing seasonal garden art, and still appreciate the ever-changing palette. But I have little time to linger. I'm also still delighted with those perfect gardening moments, the rare days when everything comes together as an exquisite frozen moment in time, but since becoming a designer, I haven't quite relaxed into my own gardens the way I once did. Now I forgive no flaws. There is always more perfection to be attained, one more change to make, a little more attention needed to reach satisfaction.

I'm also a little lazier. One of the things you quickly appreciate when you enter this business is the sheer joy of having a cadre of burly dudes clean out the gardens, spread twenty yards of mulch, and edge all the beds in a single day—tasks that would take my husband, my son, and me a month of weekends to complete. For the past couple of years I've cut us some slack, bitten my lip, and hired my favorite crew to work in our own gardens for a day or two. My friend and fellow landscape designer Mike Walsh is right when he says, "The most powerful tool in the landscape is the pen. Write the check."

TAKING THE PLUNGE

First things first, don't quit your day job. Okay, I take that back. If you really want to do this, your goal should be to quit your day job, but only do it now if you have the means to stay afloat for a year or two with little income. Yes, if you launch a design business, you'll quickly gain clients and you'll make some money the first year. But trust me, at first it won't be enough to pay your mortgage. That said, only you can determine when it is time to quit your day job and move ahead bravely into this new world. You will need to assess your own situation and determine whether you want to jump in or ease in.

Because I was raised with little money, I am not a financial risk taker by nature. It was a huge leap of faith for me to go from working for someone else (regular paycheck, familiarity, security) to working for myself (ambiguous income, unknowns, lack of certainty). Admittedly at the outset there was little risk involved, since I had already left my corporate job when I had our son. And the upfront costs required to launch yourself as a garden designer can be minimal. But there is still that personal, internal hurdle to overcome. "Can I build this type of business? Can I sell myself, attract clients, and lead teams of workers? Can I live month to month not knowing what my income will be?" You are the only person who can answer these questions.

Joseph Campbell famously pointed out the value of following your bliss. I believe he was right and have tried to abide by his advice. It's also often true that when you pursue what makes you happy, money follows (even though, despite popular belief, it wasn't Campbell who said that). Here is a case in point. One of my landscape design friends left a good job in the publishing industry. She was about forty, an accomplished gardener, and had taken a number of courses on landscape design, drafting, and site engineering. She had knowledge but little insider experience, and she really wanted to do this type of work. She was single and without much of a financial cushion, but she was determined. Through friends, she met another accomplished designer with a small firm and boldly said to him, "I want to learn the business, and I'd like to learn it from you. I'll work for you for x dollars per hour [a paltry sum] doing anything you want me to learn." Initially she made just enough to keep herself from sinking, but as her skills grew, her hours expanded, she became a more valuable employee, and her hourly rate increased. Within a few years she grew into an accomplished designer and project manager. She jumped in and remained afloat while her skills were being honed and her client base grew, and she now makes a healthy living with her own design, installation, and maintenance company.

JUMPING IN

If you have a spouse or partner whose income can pay the bills while you spend a couple of years getting started, then by all means, once you have good working knowledge of gardening and design and you feel you're ready to jump in, do it. But before you do, assess your financial situation and ensure that you can remain solvent during the two or three years it will take to gain a critical mass of clients. Your partner and family need to be supportive of your decision.

You also need to think about location. To build a successful garden design business, you need clients, suppliers, and workers. Are you situated in a fairly populous area? Is there enough affluence in your locale to support a garden design business? It is hard to manage this type of business if you need to drive 75 miles one way for a client or two, although I know people who do it. Within many metropolitan areas and most suburbs, you should be able to find enough clients to build and support your business. You'll also need suppliers that are within about an hour's drive, including wholesale nurseries, landscape supply yards, and purveyors of stone and masonry supplies. And you'll need a source of workers. Of course, if your area has the wholesalers and the potential for clients, you know you will be able to find the workers and artisans needed to keep building your business.

You'll need a healthy dose of chutzpah to get out there and sell yourself, but overall jumping right in is a great way to submerge yourself in your new business. If you're inclined to go this route and have weighed the pros and cons, if you can look yourself in the mirror and say, "Just do it," then you might be ready. Know, however, that it will take some time to ramp up your skills and develop a cadre of paying clients.

EASING IN

If you're not ready to give up your day job, cannot be solvent without your current steady income, or don't have the support of family and friends, you will need to ease into this business. Offer to do small jobs, window boxes, foundation planting refurbs, pots at the front door, vignettes on patios. My friend Kate ran a business called Vessels that consisted entirely of container plantings. Another friend has been operating a successful organic vegetable garden business for years. Working collaboratively with her clients, she chooses a sunny spot in the yard, sets up a raised bed out of untreated cedar right on top of the lawn, brings in certified organic soil, adds rabbit fencing, installs trellising for tomatoes, cucumbers, and pole beans, plants the entire garden with vegetables and herbs of the client's choice, and provides care and harvest information. For additional fees, she can set up automatic drip irrigation, maintain the garden and replant as things bolt or wither, or even harvest the vegetables, leaving a basket of produce on the client's steps each week. She offers three sizes of garden, each for a published price. This is a brilliant, turnkey business.

You could offer herb pots and small theme-food gardens. How about a tomato, basil, mini-pepper, and oregano creation—"the Italiano pot," anyone? Provide information about care and use, plus a few recipes. Or offer an herb garden as a gift for Mother's or Father's Day. Package an offering so that you can crank out the product. Offer to deliver!

Ask a local nursery if you could create packaged gardens for them. Of course, they could say no, then turn around and decide to sell their own garden-in-a-pot, but it might be the start of a beautiful relationship.

Do you know any maintenance contractors? Ask if you can use their client list and send a quick mailing out to offer front door bling. You could do container plantings that the maintenance company's workers could then charge to maintain—a mutually beneficial proposal.

Speaking of maintenance, talk with some of the better maintenance companies about the possibility of you providing garden maintenance for their larger clients. Perennial garden maintenance is a dying art, but there is a great need out there. As you maintain the gardens, you'll get to know the clients, and they'll start asking for this or that—a pot here, a little refurb there, maybe a pool installed next year (grin!). This will get you going. Do any installations using the maintenance company you partnered with, or offer them a finder's fee type of arrangement if you are hired by one of their clients. If you make it beneficial for them as well, the relationship could blossom for years.

As you start, work on projects you know you can accomplish well in a day or two, and spend your weekends working this "side" business. If you'll need an extra pair of hands for a particular job, know where you can get them. (My husband has always been helpful in these situations.) You're not going to get rich doing this, but you'll get your name out there and begin to establish yourself in the industry and with local suppliers. This is a solid spot from which to launch.

One way you can ease into the garden design business
is by focusing on container plantings.

DEFINING SUCCESS

How will you know whether you are successful? Success means different things to different people. I am a person who needs external validation. I like hearing "Great job!" even if I already know I've done a great job. Some people might think that qualifies me for a few sessions with a shrink, but I don't think I'm alone in this regard.

To me, success is a mosaic of things, some tangible, others not. It is making my clients happy, working well with my subcontractors, designing and managing transformations, completing a job well done, and earning a living. Honestly, there are weeks when success means getting through the week in one piece. But overall it's knowing that my contribution is greatly valued by my clients. Several years ago I was strolling with a client through her completed landscape. "So," I said, "overall you're really pleased." She turned, took a big breath, and replied, "I never thought it could be as pretty as I'd hoped. Instead, it's more beautiful than I ever imagined."

A friend of mine defines success as making enough money to have to pay taxes. Having struggled for many years before finally making good money, he felt grateful to earn enough to owe the government a cut. Hey! This is success, for sure.

Part of success is achieving a particular quality of life. I wanted to be able to stay home to raise my son, and I still want to make his needs and schedule a top priority. Looking back, I am so grateful I could work on my budding business and also be there for my child.

For some people, success might be the joy of being their own boss. Still others may just love physical labor or working outside. Lots of people like feeling connected to something they've created and being able to see the fruits of their labor. For me, it is all that and more.

CHAPTER THREE

Beyond Horticulture 101

WHAT EXACTLY IS horticulture? *Merriam-Webster's* defines it as "the science and art of growing fruits, vegetables, flowers, or ornamental plants." Horticulture is growing plants, growing plants is gardening, and good gardening is the foundation of any successful garden design. Knowledge of horticulture is the foundation of any successful garden designer.

Ironically, a huge number of people making a comfortable living doing landscape or garden design know little about horticulture. If you really know your plants, how they grow in your region and the conditions they prefer, you will distinguish yourself as a professional who is above the rest. You will also help to ensure the success of the gardens and landscapes you design. When we guarantee plants, we want them to live in order to minimize the expense and labor costs (not to mention embarrassment) of needing to install replacements. Our work is our calling card to all the potential clients out there, so the plants we use in our designs have to look terrific.

But how do you develop horticultural knowledge? What kind of background do you need? Some designers have advanced degrees, while others are completely self-taught. If you belong to the latter group, this overview will help guide you in the right direction. Here's a rough ranking of the activities and resources that have given me the best working horticultural knowledge to apply to my trade.

Gardening, getting dirty, killing a lot of plants. Yup, if you garden and garden to the extreme (pushing zones, attempting to grow challenging specimens, trying novel approaches), you're going to kill a lot of plants, and if you pay attention, you'll learn from each mistake you make. The trials and errors have made me a much better gardener than I would be if everything I ever planted had thrived. Sure, I lament the loss of certain unusual plants that cost me dearly. Some of those really challenging sweeties limp along for a year or two. Others disappear their first winter, or the first time they're allowed to go dry. Still others are amazing successes. I learn from each mistake, whatever the cause, and take time to celebrate each victory, as should you. I encourage you to keep pairing the tried and true with the new and wonderful, because nearly every day in the garden teaches you something. (Note that I'm referring to plants in your own gardens, however; it's best not to take risks with your clients' properties.)

Books. Ah, how I love books: design books, gardening books, business books, philosophy books. All add to your growing base of knowledge. Soak them up. Also choose books for their gorgeous photography. Not only will the images be incredibly inspiring, you can also use them to elicit feedback from clients. "You like this garden?" "What about this combination?" And you can use the photographs to sell the concepts of what you're aiming for in the landscape. "Here's the type of patio treatment I'm recommending for your side yard." If a book contains one photograph that sells a concept, one idea you can incorporate into a design, one pearl of wisdom that speaks to you, it is well worth buying. A well-stocked library of gardening books will serve your business immeasurably.

Magazines. I spend half the winter reading through the magazines that I have almost no time to open during the gardening season. I rip out articles and images, how-to sections, great ideas, advertisements for intriguing products. I keep file upon file, and refer to these files repeatedly. Industry luminaries write a significant portion of the articles; you can keep up with what's happening in design, horticulture, etymology, disease and pest outbreaks, and regulations. You'll stay abreast of industry trends and developments, learning about cutting-edge design techniques, new selections of natives, and ecological gardening practices. As a garden designer you should be among the first to be able to converse intelligently on trends like meadow gardening, green roofs, rain gardens, Xeriscaping, and the "no lawn" movement. I spend $400 to $500 a year on magazine subscriptions, from *Architectural Digest* to *Horticulture* and *Organic Gardening*, and I review them all. Magazines like *Smithsonian* and *Audubon* let you know what's happening in the natural world around the United States and the globe. This has a bearing on our work. Shelter magazines are a great way to see what's happening in interior and exterior design-scaping, and to learn how to integrate gardens with the homes and lifestyles of your clients. As your gardening skills mature, you'll need the how-to information less and less, but there are always gems to be found between the pages of even beginner-targeted periodicals.

Catalogs. There is a huge amount of knowledge and inspiration to be had from plant and seed catalogs. Not only will you learn what plants are hot and available in the marketplace, you'll also get cultural tips, design ideas, and great photographs of inspiring plant combinations. I keep some catalogs for years just because the photography is so good. Once you start getting one catalog, a host of others will follow as the plant purveyors share lists. This is a good thing, as far as I'm concerned, since I can never get enough plant catalogs.

Volunteering. To get a breadth of gardening experience beyond your own parcel of land, volunteer. Friends are often delighted to have a pal to garden alongside. Find three friends who garden and offer one to two hours in each of their gardens every week or so. You don't even have to tell them you're thinking about a profession in the dirt, just that you're looking for more experience. Stick with it for at least one season, and you will be surprised what you'll learn. You'll be exposed to other gardening conditions, like different soil types, sun and wind exposures, and microclimates. You'll also see how other people relate to and use their outdoor spaces, how they plan their plant combinations, beds, and borders. You'll also have fun!

Outside of friends, a variety of volunteer opportunities can be found. Greenhouse operations often need extra seasonal help. Just call around and find a grower who could use you. This is learning the business from the ground—and roots!—up.

Community gardens. These gardens often need volunteers to work with the gardeners, help keep the common areas tidy, or water plants when gardeners are away. This is also a great way to gain more gardening friends and get your name spread around. You'll bank a lot of good will.

Master gardener programs. You can complete one of these programs through a local horticultural society or arboretum. It usually requires classroom study paired with out-of-classroom experience, and a number of hours volunteering to help other gardeners (help lines, open garden days, and so forth) and work in the society gardens.

Local garden clubs. Attending garden clubs is a great way to learn from and schmooze with other gardeners. They're often involved in town or city projects where you can volunteer time doing design, installation, and maintenance. In my little New England town, one of our garden clubs requires you to spend a significant number of hours working in the period gardens outside the headquarters of the town historic society. This is required for advancement from junior member to full-fledged member. Volunteering in this capacity builds knowledge, encourages gardening friendships, and keeps the historical society's gardens looking wonderful to boot.

Plant-an-island programs. If your town doesn't have this type of program, where they plant and maintain traffic islands, start one. Simply stop by the Department of Public Works for your town or a neighboring town, and offer to plant one island. Ask if you can put a small sign on it, like "Island planted by Budding Gardeners." With a minimal investment in time and money, you'll learn a lot about planting something for the public, you'll be building name recognition in your community, and your name will be associated with gardening in exactly the place you'll want to be mining clients. Plant the garden simply and maintain it beautifully (keep safety strictly in mind, since you'll be working around moving traffic).

Plantings around town. Might one of the buildings in your municipality need beautification? Go to your town clerk's office and offer to purchase, plant, and maintain pots for the entry. A no-brainer for them. Yes, you'll be out a couple of hundred dollars or so. And you'll need to come by to water the pots frequently, and keep them in tip-top shape. But you can also ask to include signage: "A gift to the town of Meredith from Budding Gardeners." Again, you're learning more, building name recognition, and making your name synonymous with gardening.

Seminars and courses. There is a wealth of knowledge available in virtually every corner: agricultural schools; adult education courses; extension courses at local colleges and universities; courses at area gardening societies and arboreta; seminars at local wholesalers; lectures at green-industry trade shows, local nurseries, watershed associations, and wetlands protection organizations. Ask your local conservation commission if they know of upcoming seminars and lectures. Attend as many as you can. Most are inexpensive; some are even free.

Colleges and universities. Many schools of higher learning offer degrees in ornamental horticulture, public horticulture, landscape architecture and design, even turf management. Look in the yellow pages, use the Internet, call local public gardens and plant societies. Pick their brains. Usually plant people are delighted to talk with other plant people. There are a myriad of online courses—so many, in fact, that before you write a check you should speak with several graduates and check them out through the local Better Business Bureau. If you're feeling ready to dedicate 100% of your efforts to getting an "official" background in garden and landscape design, you can certainly go back to school for a number of years and get a degree in ornamental horticulture or landscape architecture. That is a noble goal. But you will still need to couple your classroom training with field experience. Get out there and get dirty!

Local nurseries. From mom-and-pop nurseries to big-box stores, these businesses often need extra help during the gardening season and to cover weekends. This is one of those things you can do to get more experience while keeping your day job. Working retail is a great place to get hands-on knowledge of the plants that work well in your area, bone up on plant culture and nomenclature, learn from other area gardeners, and get a feel for the types of questions you'll encounter once you start a business. You'll also see which wholesalers are supplying the retailers. You'll meet landscape contractors, designers and architects, masons, lighting people, and maintenance specialists. Collect their cards. Go see their work.

This experience can be a valuable entrée to the industry, and you can even leverage your work at a retail nursery against your future design business. Be a valuable employee and make friends. When you are eventually ready to leave, tell them you'll be opening a design business. In exchange for their referrals, offer to purchase plants from them. This can be a great way to start your business while having the benefit of friends who operate as your suppliers and subcontractors.

Garden tours and open garden days. Go see other gardens. Take photos. Talk to the owners and designers. Find out why they did what they did. Ask about what has worked particularly well, as well as what didn't work and what they did to remedy it. What would they do differently if they had it to do over, and why? Gardeners and designers love to talk the talk. Take advantage of this and learn from them. Study the photos when you get home. Look for what you like and don't like. Mentally see what you might have done differently. This is a terrific way to complement your other forays into horticulture and garden design.

Gardening television shows. Okay, I love and hate these. Design shows: I love them for showing how transformations can occur. I love the ones that pit several designers against each other for a job, because it's fun to see how each of them interprets the client's wants and needs. I love seeing how designers present their design, what tools they use, how their layouts look, the process of the design presentation, the materials they share. I love the "reveal," seeing homeowners delighted with the new use of space in their gardens. I love seeing new products and techniques. But I hate the shows that say, "We did this entire backyard makeover for $1200!" Many times, numbers like this don't consider design or labor costs. In lots of instances the materials have even been donated. So this sets up an expectation with potential clients that garden design costs next to nothing. I also resent it when shows present a transformation taking place in one or two days that in the real world would take several days, weeks, or even months. Some designs are also often clearly unsustainable—in a couple of weeks they'll begin to look shabby unless the owners are really, really into garden maintenance. Lastly, I am horrified when the designs do not take safety into consideration, when there are potential fire or water hazards, or places to fall off the deck or snap an ankle on the walkways. Nevertheless, despite the flaws, I do encourage you to watch these shows, because when you're watching with a critical eye there is much information to be had, in terms of both what to do and what not to do. How-to shows: I have to say that gardening how-to shows are usually pretty terrific, and even though I've been gardening crazily for more than twenty years, I still hear good tips here and there. From *The Victory Garden* on PBS to the offerings on HGTV, TLC, and the DIY networks, there is such a plethora of gardening television out there that you can almost watch only gardening shows from morning till night.

WORKHORSE PLANTS

Of course, there's a lot more to plants than Latin names, and much more to learn than what looks pretty. Plants are not just ornamental. We use different plants for different purposes, and to make them work for us and our clients, our horticultural knowledge needs to go beyond the conventional.

Plant materials are used for increased privacy, visual screening, wind diversion, shade cover, erosion control, soil enrichment, water absorption, groundcover. We use plants to attract wildlife (nectar producers for butterflies) and repel wildlife (thorny hedges to divert deer). The selections will be different depending on the climate and conditions, but whether you are in Key West or Westchester, you will address similar problems and challenges with your landscape designs. You will need to know the four-season performance characteristics of a wide variety of plants.

Take screening, for example. The first item that comes to mind might be the ubiquitous arborvitae. How I tire of seeing the relentless soldier-straight lines of arbs tracing the property boundaries across America. I do greatly appreciate arborvitae, it's just that designers need to know that an arb is not an arb is not an arb. Or more pointedly, a *Thuja* is not a *Thuja* is not a *Thuja*. The nature of some varieties is to grow wide and rather bloblike. Others quickly grow tall and slender. Some turn bronze in winter, others stay green. Still others grow in a globe form and never top 6 feet. Learn the best materials for screening in your area. Me, I prefer tapestry hedges, an intermingling of deciduous and evergreen trees and shrubs that looks more natural and ages better than the fortifications of *Thuja*. Learn the attributes of the evergreens that grow well in your area, and develop a short list of the plants that work best to screen unsightly views and provide privacy. You will find that privacy screening is one of the key reasons you get calls from potential clients.

PLANTS TO AVOID

Some plants are desirable, others not so much. As a garden designer you need to know which plants in your area are toxic, irritating to the skin, invasive, or prohibited.

Many common plants are highly toxic if ingested, and others cause contact dermatitis or other reactions. Foxglove (*Digitalis*) is one example. If your clients request it, let them know that it is poisonous. If they still want it, fine, but stress that small children and pets must be kept away.

QUICK GLOSSARY OF HORTICULTURE TERMS

Accent plant. Plant that provides special interest through its form, texture, color, and so forth, usually as part of a larger planting.

Annual. Plant that completes its life cycle within one year.

Annual garden. Garden that requires replanting each year because the plants selected are annuals or are tender (not cold hardy).

B&B. Balled and burlapped, referring to field-grown tree and shrub materials whose root balls have been wrapped in burlap and securely tied for transport.

Bed. Planted area that is generally freestanding or surrounded by lawn or hardscape, and is not on an edge of the property nor against a building. In garden descriptions, all borders are beds, but not all beds are borders.

Bedding plants. Usually refers to flowering annuals used in masses, designed to be replaced seasonally.

Border planting. Planting that divides spaces in a landscape, or that borders an edge of the property or is next to a structure.

Caliper. Thickness of a tree, approximately 6 inches above the root flare, used for grading and pricing tree stock. If the caliper is 6 inches or more, the tree is measured at 4 feet above the root flare with the notation ABH (average breast height).

Entry garden. Landscaped area flanking or near the entry to a building. Attracts attention and provides a welcome.

Foundation planting. Planting located in beds surrounding the base of a structure.

Freestanding or island planting. Planting not linked to a structure or to the edges of the property.

Ditto the glorious monkshood (*Aconitum*), *Narcissus*, *Helleborus*, even the common yew (*Taxus baccata*). Castor plants are highly prized in the landscape, but eating two of the pretty seeds is all it takes to kill an adult. All parts of the oleander, used abundantly in landscapes throughout the warmer regions of the United States, are deadly. In fact this plant is so poisonous that you are discouraged from including it in your compost pile, on the chance the finished compost might be used to grow edible plants. Yikes!

I'm not suggesting you eliminate poisonous plants entirely from your garden designs. I use lots of *Aconitum*, *Caladium*, *Digitalis*, *Kalmia*, *Lupinus*, and other genera. But you should become familiar with any deleterious side effects from the plants you might specify, and keep poisonous

Height, width. Estimated size at maturity. Always select and space plants based on mature size.

Mass planting. Planting in which many plants of the same species are used in large swaths or groupings.

Mixed border. Border that mixes woody stock with herbaceous stock. Can include trees, shrubs, grasses, perennials, and annuals.

Nursery stock. Woody stock available at wholesale or retail nurseries.

Perennial garden. Herbaceous planting that can withstand the local climate and regrows the following spring.

Perennial stock. Herbaceous perennials available at wholesale or retail nurseries.

Seasonal interest. Continuing appeal created by the color, texture, and form of plants and by forms produced by hardscape and garden art.

Shrub. Multistemmed, woody plant that generally does not exceed 12 feet tall.

Specimen plant. Plant that provides an exclamation point in the landscape by exhibiting eye-catching color, flowers, fruit, or special characteristics.

Sustainable landscape. Landscape that has been designed and constructed in an environmentally sound manner and that is maintained without synthetic chemicals.

Texture. Coarseness or fineness of a plant, including the characteristics of leaves, bark, branches, and coloring.

Tree. Woody plant that usually has one main stem and reaches at least 12 feet tall. Trees are critical landscape elements considered early in the design process.

Zone creep. Effect of global warming on shifting plant hardiness zones.

plants out of landscapes where small children play. Nelson, Shih, and Balick's *Handbook of Poisonous and Injurious Plants* is great to keep on hand. Refer to it and know what you are including in the gardens you design.

Most of us are all too familiar with the consequence of a close encounter with poison ivy, poison oak, or poison sumac (the poison three—see chapter 10), but many other plants can irritate skin, some of which are still quite garden worthy. Stinging nettles (*Urtica dioica* and related subspecies) do just that: sting. Several plants, including gas plant (*Dictamnus*), cause bad skin irritation. Hogweed (*Heracleum*) is one of several plants that can cause nasty phytophototoxicity, a bizarre skin reaction. If your skin comes in contact with the active chemical, nothing happens until the area is exposed to sun, at which point the ultraviolet rays activate the chemical and cause redness, blistering, pain, and a darkening of the skin. Eventually the blisters heal and the dark patches flake off, revealing new skin. The summer of 2007, one of my crew members and I both had this happen, each of us showing up with long slashes of darkened skin and blisters on our hands and forearms. We had no idea what we had been exposed to, but it had obviously happened when we were clearing a small area of brush. Go figure.

Invasive plants, both native and exotic, make up another category. Learn what is prohibited in your state and avoid known thugs. Massachusetts no longer allows several rapacious growers to be sold or planted, including Norway maple (*Acer platanoides*), a ubiquitous street tree; Japanese barberry (*Berberis thunbergii*); and the bane of fresh waterways, purple loosestrife (*Lythrum salicaria*). Federally listed as a noxious weed, blue forget-me-nots (*Myosotis scorpioides*) are considered "likely invasive" in my state. Before they were identified as such by the Massachusetts Invasives Advisory Group, I purchased them nearly every spring, because they are darling when in bloom. I must admit that I could never get them to last a single year, never mind having a problem with them self-sowing. But now that I know they are potentially invasive, I have stopped buying and trying. Even if you're planting in an area that doesn't seem likely to encourage running (like installing purple loosestrife in an area far from water), life usually manages to find a way. So please resist the temptation, be a responsible steward of the land, and stay away from invasives altogether.

Many states prohibit certain species from being brought over state lines, and this includes mail order. These prohibited plants are not necessarily invasive, but they might have the potential to harbor a particular disease or pest. States known for their agricultural industry often prohibit certain plants from coming in. As you thumb through plant catalogs, you'll come across statements like, "Cannot ship to AZ, CA, FL, TX, LA or HI." Don't try to get around these laws; they exist to protect the state. You don't want to be the one who introduces lily beetle or some other scourge into your area.

PUSHING IT

I am a firm believer in matching the cultural and growth characteristics of the plant to the location and purpose (even if strictly for ornamentation), because the plant will be much happier in the long run. Matching a plant with its optimal cultural needs keeps maintenance to a minimum. It also helps guarantee success not only for the life expectancy of the plant but also for the long-term viability of the design. Sure, I push zones and cultural requirements for plants I'm babying in my own yard, but I recommend against doing this in your clients' gardens. Your clients want a sure bet. The more you provide it, the more success your plantings will have, and the more your credibility—and future work—will be assured.

VULNERABILITY TO PESTS AND DISEASES

Many pests and diseases race across the nation and devastate particular species. Learn about these problems and avoid using susceptible plants. Stands of the magnificent American beech (*Fagus grandifolia*), for example, have been crippled throughout the Northeast by beech bark disease. The hemlock wooly adelgid is destroying eastern hemlock (*Tsuga canadensis*) from Georgia to Maine, and there are other host-specific wooly adelgids that are affecting stands of larch (*Larix*) and spruce (*Picea*). The Asian longhorned beetle has infested parts of central Massachusetts; if eradication measures do not succeed, millions of hardwood trees will be lost. Dogwood anthracnose has been sweeping the nation and slowly destroying one of our loveliest native trees, the flowering dogwoods (*Cornus florida*). Other emerging scourges include viburnum leaf beetle, red lily leaf beetle, and hosta virus X. To avoid the temptation to resort to toxic chemicals, stay abreast of pestilence happenings via e-newsletters and popular horticultural press and don't use plants that could have shortened lives in the landscape.

YOUR FAVORITE THINGS

Nearly every designer and landscape architect that I know has their list of favorite trees, shrubs, and herbaceous perennials. I am no exception. As a plant lover, my favorites comprise a fairly long list, but I add—and delete—plants from my list just about every year. Climate conditions affect my favorites considerably (we have had some funky winters the last couple of years, resulting in a great deal of plant death), as does availability, of course. I like tried-and-true plants that give superior performance and have characteristics like long season of interest, good winter structure, supreme hardiness, excellent pest resistance. Over time you will learn which plants are sure bets for your area, which ones give the greatest pleasure to your clients, and which ones can be used in nearly every design.

When I get to the specifics of planting plans, I actually print out my current master list and read through it, selecting plants I know the site and the client will both like. My list is broken up by cultural requirements: sun versus shade, with moisture and exposure subcategories. I also have a list just for coastal (salt-exposed) locations, one for riparian areas, as well as a list of useful native plants. These references save me a great deal of pondering and researching time when I'm starting planting plans. I even have "Oh, yes!" moments when my list reminds me of a terrific combination, because I don't always remember every plant possibility off the top of my head for each area I'm designing.

I do go outside my list every year and frequently try new species or varieties. I won't make something untried (by me) the backbone of any design, however; instead I grow them in my own gardens first. As you start paying attention to happenings in this industry, you'll find that when a new plant is introduced it is heralded with all the marketing aplomb of a life-saving pharmaceutical. As in most sales pitches, the hype is often mostly that, hype, and new plants frequently perform less spectacularly than promised. Then again, sometimes they do outstandingly.

Here's a story about one of them. Blue mophead hydrangeas are iffy in my climate. Down on Cape Cod, no problem, spectacular, but once you leave the sandy soils and more moderate winters of the Cape, we're not so lucky. About four out of every five years we have erratic, very cold winter weather, and the buds of these hydrangeas—grown on old wood the year before—die and therefore don't blossom the following season. You don't know how many of my clients have said, "Well, we have these hydrangeas, but they never bloom." They lament that they fertilize and tweak pH and hand-water and kiss and coddle, to no avail. As I would explain to them, this is through no fault of their own, it's just the nature of growing a plant on the edge of its hardiness. Then, eureka. *Hydrangea* 'Endless Summer' was released with all the hoopla of a United Nations peace agreement. My response was, "Uh-huh, yeah, sure," but I purchased three plants, stuck them in three locations with different exposures in my mixed borders, watered them in well, and bid them good luck. As a gardener I tend to be cheap with water, I don't fertilize at all (I top-dress with compost yearly), and the plants need to mostly fend for themselves. Let me tell you that no one was more surprised than I when these plants not only lived but thrived. They blossomed in my borders until nearly Thanksgiving and were blooming again by the first of June. They truly bloom the entire summer. I now use 'Endless Summer' in many of my mixed borders, to the continuous delight of my clients. How can you not love something so gorgeous and reliable?

Hydrangea 'Endless Summer' makes good on the promise.

So, you will try new plants. Your list of favorites will ebb and flow. And it's all a good thing. But plant what you know at client properties; experiment in your own yard.

TURF MANAGEMENT

Lawns are simply a collection of plants, and turf management is a specialty unto itself. Know your soil types, learn what turf types grow best in what soils in your climate, and become educated on how to work with less-than-desirable soil to make it productive for the lawns in your designs. A couple of my friends in the industry are amazing turf specialists, and I call on them for any lawn issue that requires a diagnosis beyond what I can provide. Work to find resources who are educated and skilled at lawn maintenance. You can provide your clients with a valuable service by recommending lawn care by proven professionals. Or offer the service yourself and subcontract professionals to work through you, thereby augmenting your income.

Lawns are a major guy thing, and you need to know that lawn envy is real. If you are working with a traditional couple, chances are the man will

A coddled lawn makes a stunning emerald carpet. These beautiful results are obtainable without using toxic chemicals and synthetic fertilizers.

want a gorgeous lawn, and the woman will care less about the lawn while insisting on beautiful, colorful borders. Given that you design gardens, you'll be able to talk flowers with knowledge and enthusiasm. Become equally conversant on lawn issues, and both clients will be delighted.

I build new lawns so that they can be managed and kept beautiful without a host of chemicals. To me this is essential, and I go into detail on the whys and hows of organic lawn care in chapter 4.

When installing a new lawn, you can choose between sod and seed, including dry seed and hydroseed. Some designers only do sod, others only hydroseed. As much as I love the instant gratification of sod (really, you go from looking at a rather dismal, brown expanse to an immediate green carpet of turf magnificence), it is by far the most labor-intensive, expensive lawn solution, both short term and in the long run, and I feel that seeding ultimately creates a healthier, more sustainable lawn. If I have a tiny gem of a lawn area that is going to be kissed daily and tucked in at night, I might use sod, but for larger projects I almost always seed.

For the entire first year, any new lawn should be treated with great care. It's still a baby until year two.

SOD

Sod is grown on a sod farm specifically for lawn installations and is harvested in strips. You can usually choose from several turf mixtures, ordering the square footage you need a couple of days ahead. Sod is delivered on a flatbed, the strips rolled soil side out, stacked on pallets. The strips do not keep well on the pallet, and in fact will rot, dry out, or cook if left rolled more than twenty-four hours (or forty-eight hours in cooler weather). Sod should be delivered the day you are going to lay it; have the pallets put in the shade if possible. Laying sod is a little like installing carpet squares. We prepare the soil well, amend it with compost, and till it to a depth of about 8 or 9 inches. Then we hand-grade and roll it. The irrigation system should already be installed (watch the irrigation lines when you are tilling!). Then the sod goes down. Stagger seams and push the edges up towards each other, then push down gently. Your goal is to have tight seams with no gaps, so the edges don't dry out. Cut openings for the irrigation heads, and trim the edges around beds, walks, trees, and so forth. Now water, water, water.

Water is the key to getting sod off to a good start, because if it dries out it dies. Water well in the morning and again late in the afternoon; and keep up this twice-daily schedule for several weeks. Warn your clients: do not walk on new sod that is wet. They may carefully walk on new sod between waterings, but walking on new wet sod generally causes pieces to slide, opening up gaps and ripping away the little feeder roots that are making their way from the sod layer into the soil beneath. Ideally no one should play on new sod for about a month; this gives the roots a chance to take hold. Having been raised on a perfect diet of chemicals, constant moisture, and perfect sunlight, the sod will also need fertilizer. I recommend adding a time-release organic fertilizer about three weeks after installation. An application of manure tea works beautifully, too. Watch that the sod doesn't become chlorotic (turn yellow).

I prefer to lay sod only in the spring and fall, and only on smaller installations. Summer installations of sod are difficult to keep from burning out from the heat of midday alone.

For the first four to six weeks, mow sod with a hand mower rather than a riding mower. The weight of the ride-on can rip away delicate roots, extending the time it will take for the sod to become established. Don't let the grass grow long before cutting it, as this will cause browning and burning. Cut less length and mow with greater frequency, and let the blades of the grass grow to at least 3 to 3½ inches tall. This will create a healthier, more resilient lawn environment.

SEED

I really like to seed new lawns. This gives me greater control over the turf mix, as I can choose seed mixes best suited for my site conditions (soil, exposure) or even have custom seed mixes blended. Your local cooperative agricultural researchers will have recommendations for seed mixes that are optimal for your area, and I have found them to be most willing to share their knowledge. They are "cooperative," indeed.

Seeding a new lawn requires the same prep needed for sod, but after my crew rolls the newly prepared soil, I have them run a spring rake over the surface to fluff up the top ¼ inch. Then, if we are dry-seeding, we either hand-broadcast or use a spreader to drop the seed. In either case, to get the most even seed distribution, the seeding is done in two directions: east to west, then north to south, or left to right, then front to back. Then we use the back of the spring rake and drag that through the seed on the soil surface. We sometimes use a "seed starter mix"—it comes bagged and looks green and cottony—which we hand-broadcast over the new seed. This contains a synthetic fertilizer (yes, the only time

COMMON LAWN SEED TYPES

Many varieties are available beyond those in this abbreviated list, and your particular locale and use will determine the seed varieties and mixes that are optimal for your application. A state-by-state guide can also be found at lawngrass.com. Cool-season grasses are used in areas with cold winters, while warm-season grasses are appropriate for the southern tier of the United States where freezing weather is infrequent.

COOL-SEASON GRASSES:
Fescue. Includes turf-type tall fescues and fine, shorter fescues. Easily seeded. Shade tolerant. Green year-round. Drought resistant.

Ryegrass. Annual and perennial ryegrasses were originally introduced from Europe. Annual ryes grow fast and green up quickly so are good for short-term seasonal use. They can help establish a new lawn rapidly when used as a fill-in grass. Perennial ryegrasses are low maintenance and provide a tough, wearable turf cover. Ryegrass germinates quickly, has a shiny green color, is finely textured, and forms a dense sod. Highly disease and insect resistant.

Bentgrass. Beautiful and finely textured. Used for putting greens, since it can be cut very short. Shallow rooted, and needs a cooler climate and adequate water to perform well.

Bluegrass. Bright green to deep bluish green, bluegrasses make the lawn of champions here in New England. Beautiful and finely textured, great to walk on. Relatively high maintenance, and needs plenty of fertilizer and water to look good. Slower growing but very long lived.

WARM-SEASON GRASSES:
Bermuda grass. This sun-loving grass is considered the "South's grass." A favorite in the tropics and subtropics for its texture and color. Medium maintenance. Salt tolerant. Goes brown when temperatures dip below 60°F.

Zoysia. Originally from Asia, this low-growing, heat-resistant, wiry grass forms a dense sod that wears well and is resistant to weeds, disease, pests, and drought. Slow to establish but aggressive in the face of competition. Turns golden brown during dormancy.

I will opt to use a synthetic fertilizer), and it also helps to hold moisture at the surface. The green color gives us an indication as to what the finished lawn will look like. Then we set up the watering.

You will want to water every morning and evening, enough to really dampen the soil but not enough to cause runoff. Seed takes about a week to germinate, and once you have "little green mouse fur" growing, you cannot let the top of the soil dry out. Regular, light watering is critical for success. Climate and soil conditions, coupled with time of year, will drive your watering schedule.

Hydroseeding is another way to seed a lawn. Seed is mixed into a slurry with water, fertilizer, a mulch-type substance, often a tackifier (a substance that helps bind the mix together to help avert runoff), and a colorant (usually green, but I have seen orange!). Any hydroseeding should be done by a reputable company who knows what they are doing. Initial soil prep is the same for hydroseeding as for sod or hand-seeding. Adhering to a watering schedule is equally necessary.

Any seeded lawn benefits from an overseeding the following fall or spring. This will fill in any bare spots and thicken everything up. We usually start by broadcasting and raking fine compost into the lawn surface. This gives the new seed a nice medium to settle into. I always hand-seed when we overseed, but you can also hire someone to slice seed. This involves using a machine that makes teensy cuts in the soil and pushes seed mix down into those cuts. It is effective but works best on existing lawns that are cut very short or that have lots of open, bare spots. I am an advocate for never cutting a lawn lower than 3 or 3½ inches tall, so using a seed spreader works best on the lawns I have installed.

THE DIRT ON DIRT

It ain't dirt, it's soil, and you will deal with different soil types in every town and on every property where you work. Any soil can be made better by loosening it up and adding amendments, but you can also choose plants that work beautifully with the soil types you find. I personally garden in two locations: at our home, in magnificent, deep, rich loam (with no rocks!), and at our cabin 30 miles away, in what is basically sugar sand. Though some plants will thrive in both gardens, there are things I will not be able to grow in one place that will grow like weeds in the other.

I'm not fighting it. I'm working with what nature doles out, and beautiful gardens exist in both locations.

About 90% of the time I can accurately tell what type of soil someone has just by driving up to their property. But that other 10% often gives me a big surprise. Some friends recently built their dream home high on a cliff overlooking a sandy beach and the ocean. So their soil is loose, granular sand, right? Wrong! The lot is comprised of much heavy clay, and it is wet where it slopes away in the rear. It goes to show, you can't really know what soil conditions each property has until you plunge a shovel into the ground.

Because I amend most garden beds with compost, and compost takes care of a multitude of soil sins, I rarely do much soil testing. This is true unless I'm designing a vegetable garden, in which case I have the soil tested by our local agricultural extension office. This will tell me not only what soil type and nutrient deficiencies we're dealing with, but also if any heavy metals or contaminants are in the soil. We don't want to grow food plants where substances like lead, cadmium, or mercury can be taken up into their edible parts.

MULCH

Volcanoes? Breasts? Whatever you call them, mulch mounds are bad. Never do this! Mulch should be applied 1 to 2 inches deep and kept 4 to 6 inches away from the trunks of trees or base of shrubs. Mulch up against the bark of woody plant materials can rot bark, encourage places for pests to enter, cause the tree to send out small rootlets into the smothering mulch, and impede healthy growth. If applied deeply around herbaceous plants, mulch can cause crown rot and encourage various fungi. This is bad horticultural practice. It also just plain looks stupid.

Whether it's called cypress mulch, orange mulch, hemlock mulch, cedar mulch, or designer mulch, this stuff does not belong on this planet, never mind in a garden. Bald cypress (*Taxodium*) is a wonderful, enigmatic tree native to the wetlands of the American South. It produces magnificent wood and for centuries was the preferred choice for greenhouses for its ability to stand up to moisture and weathering without splitting, checking, or rotting. But cypress swamps are now being clearcut and the venerable trees shredded into garden mulch. This is a huge waste of a limited resource and an insult to such a magnificent species. Boycott cypress mulch.

CARE OF PLANTS

When you plant large nursery stock, remove whatever it is growing in, whether cage, twine, plastic, or container. Leaving the container on the shrub or tree almost always causes a problem down the road. Yes, burlap is fine to leave tucked way down in the soil—it will decompose quickly. But anything else should be removed and disposed of properly. You would not believe the stuff we dig up when renovating an existing land-scape, and you should see the mess we find the roots in, snarled around cages and caught up in plastic. When you are planting, you are giving a plant a new home. Make it a comfortable one.

Another thing: you wouldn't wear a sweater with the tag hanging off the sleeve, would you? Please remove all plant tags. Don't leave them on the branches or bury them. Take them off and dispose of them properly. If your client wants to save the tags, remove them, clean them off, and bag them. If they insist on labeling everything, use visually quiet copper or zinc plant ID stakes.

When it comes to pruning, natural is better. Unless shrubs are grow-ing in a very formal garden, they're not meant to resemble cubes, trian-gles, light bulbs, gumdrops, or trapezoids. Similarly, let trees do their own thing. Do not head back, do not prune, do not lollipop, do not mul-let. Leave them alone except to cut out dead or damaged and crossing branches. If you do have to prune, make a carefully considered, healthy cut just beyond the branch collar. And if you don't know what that means, immediately back away from the pruning saw and hire a certified arborist.

CHAPTER FOUR

The Green Industry:
A Greener Shade of Green

O NCE YOU HAVE A FOUNDATION of horticultural knowledge, it's time to embrace another kind of green. Professional garden and landscape designers are increasingly committing themselves to more sustainable practices, and I urge you to learn about these practices as you begin your journey in this industry.

Becoming a professional garden and landscape designer will bring you closer to the natural world than you have ever been. If you are coming from a traditional type of job where you work indoors and focus on the world at the end of your fingertips, you will delight in becoming more simpatico with nature and the wider world outside your door. You will develop a heightened awareness of what is going on outside, from the weather and the seasons to the birds and bees.

Besides global warming—which, though very real, is so big it's hard to get your brain around—we humans are affecting nature in a gazillion other ways, from the macro (oil spills) to the micro (pharmaceuticals in our waterways). The good news is that working in a green industry gives us a unique opportunity to educate our clients and coworkers about the beauty and perfection in our environment, and to reinforce the obligation that we have to work responsibly with nature. We are all stewards of our environment, and each of us—yes, even acting individually—can have a huge impact on each other and the world at large.

ENVIRONMENTAL STEWARDSHIP

Why bother? First off, it's the right thing to do. Everyone talks about being green, "green" being the catchword for acting in an environmentally responsible way. But in our industry we have the ability to work truly green, beyond recycling plastics and glass, worrying about gas mileage, and composting kitchen scraps.

Second, it will benefit your bottom line. Most people working in the green industry do not work green. Chemical use is rampant and even considered an absolute necessity by many of my colleagues. Those of us who design in concert with nature and build landscapes that are sustainable can set ourselves apart from the professionals who rely on an arsenal of chemicals. What it will take is for us to educate our clients and let them know why truly green methods of sustainable landscape construction and maintenance are superior to what the other guys are offering.

Make sure the only thing she is exposed to is the scent of lavender and the wonders of nature. Photo courtesy of Heather D. Jarnot.

Reinforce to them that with their own family's health at stake, this is the only way to go. It is a powerful, positive message.

Pesticides are intentionally toxic substances. For emphasis, I repeat: pesticides are intentionally toxic substances. The gritty truth is that the fertilizers, herbicides, pesticides, and fungicides that make up the average chemical soup for the average landscape are full of heavy metals and toxic chemicals; they are designed to chemically maim, disable, and kill. Human exposure to these biocides can cause many short- and long-term problems and diseases. They have been linked to ADD, ADHD, Parkinson's disease, chronic fatigue syndrome, anxiety, depression, male and female infertility, birth defects, and the ever increasing numbers of childhood and adult cancers. And death of pets from cancers and various neurological disorders is rising significantly. Oh, but you have no pets or children? You don't go out into your yard? These toxins don't just stay on the lawn. They are air-carried and foot-tracked into our homes, where they reside (and build up) for years in our carpets and upholstery. Additionally, very little is known about the safety of secondary compounds that can occur when these applied chemicals bond with naturally occurring compounds in our environment.

When you say no to chemicals, you let beautiful species flourish, like the monarch butterfly. Photo courtesy of Griffin T. Howard.

Toxin-filled lawn chemicals just do not mix well with humans (especially children), pets, or wildlife. As large-scale agriculture is learning to cut back on these biocide and fertilization chemicals, the one area of the pesticide industry that continues to grow is residential use. Homeowners use up to ten times more chemical pesticides per acre on their properties than farmers use on crops. The EPA permits more than two hundred different pesticides to be used for lawn care, often mixed together and sold as chemical combinations. Lawn care pesticides are not tested for their chronic health effects unless they are also licensed for use on food crops. As of 2002 the EPA had only tested 9 of the 750 registered pesticides for their effects on the developing nervous system, and 6 of the 9 tested were more harmful to young animals than adult animals, showing that children, developing fetuses, and young pets are more at risk. Lastly, pesticides are composed of active ingredients and inert ingredients. Some inert ingredients may be more toxic than the active ingredients and can comprise 90% to 95% of the product. Inert ingredients are not required to be tested, and their identity is, in fact, protected as a trade secret under the Federal Insecticide, Fungicide, and Rodenticide Act. Some inert ingredients are suspected carcinogens, while others have been linked to central nervous system disorders, liver and kidney damage, birth defects, and negative short-term health effects.

That's motivation enough for me, but the information I've given you so far doesn't even start to address the reality of downstream toxicity to birds, bees, aquatic life, other wildlife, and soil microorganisms, and the poisoning of our groundwater supplies.

Pesticides are intentionally toxic substances. Our landscapes do not need them. Reasons enough for me to want to avoid all use of them.

Even if I weren't able to uncover all of this damning evidence about the toxicity of lawn and garden chemicals, I choose to believe that lawn and garden pesticides are potentially toxic until proven innocent. I subscribe to the precautionary principle, a decision-making approach that says if clear evidence of harm or safety is missing, we should choose the least harmful way to meet the goal. In other words, if it might cause harm, either don't do it or choose another option. Precaution serves as the default decision. The precautionary principle has gained international acceptance as the code for environmental decision-making.

THE BIGGER PICTURE—WE ARE THE FROGS

You might say I'm a bit of an evangelist for the environment, but our environment is what sustains us and we are killing it. My friend Mike Walsh likes to say, "We are the frogs." As the story goes, if you put a frog into a pot of cool water over a low flame, the frog will remain complacent and not jump out, even as the water slowly warms to boiling and boils him to death. What a fitting analogy for our own predicament. Honeybees are dying in droves from Colony Collapse Disorder, and scientists still don't know why. North American bats are perishing in huge numbers for unknown reasons. Some songbird populations are down 75% since the mid-1990s— certainly the action at my own feeders has dropped measurably. Monarch butterfly populations have plunged due to loss of winter habitat and chemical pesticide poisoning in their summer territories. Whales arrive in Baja in starvation mode. Ocean experts have seen a decline in fish species of up to 90% since the mid-1990s. Native ladybug species and fireflies are disappearing. Coral reefs are bleaching. Deserts are expanding. Pretty sobering.

Are we the frogs? We humans are not immune to the planetary woes— only seems natural that we'd be next. This is way beyond an inconvenient truth. It seems to be an incontrovertible truth, and it's terrifying.

It does make a difference when each of us does our part. Act locally, work responsibly with nature, educate others, and continue to keep your eye on the big blue ball that we call home.

A GREENER GREEN

So how do you build a greener green business? What knowledge and skills do you need? Here are ten simple steps:

1. Stop using chemicals in the landscape. Period.
2. Learn sustainable or organic techniques by reading and taking courses. Google "organic gardening" plus "courses" plus your state's name. Understand how to transition a chemical-dependant landscape to a healthy, sustainable landscape. Find where to purchase and how to use certified organic fertilizers and control products.
3. Work with your local conservation commission. They are generally very reasonable people trying to do the right thing for your

community and for the earth. If you work with them, you might even net yourself some excellent referrals.

4. Healthy soil is the basis for all life. Prepare planting beds and lawn areas appropriately.

5. Plants want to grow. Learn your horticulture, match plants to the cultural conditions they prefer, give them a healthy soil environment, and then get out of their way.

6. Use compost to top-dress and even to mulch. Compost builds the soil, encouraging healthy microorganisms to thrive, which translates to healthier, more resilient plants that grow beautifully and are able to elude diseases and handle pests.

7. Use water wisely. Design landscapes that will need virtually no supplemental water after two or three years.

8. Protect neighboring wetlands during landscape construction. Whether or not local ordinances require it, you are a steward of the environment and should install a temporary silt fence and hay bales to catch any erosion that may run into a storm drain or foul a nearby wetland.

9. Dispose of all refuse and detritus properly. Recycle everything you possibly can. Think about the products you are putting into the new landscape and consider the cradle-to-grave implications of their components.

10. Walk the walk. Practice sustainable gardening in your own gardens.

You can start to find information and coursework on organic and sustainable gardening practices in the same places you used as resources to bone up on your general horticultural knowledge. In addition to local resources, there is a wealth of knowledge on the Internet, on television, in books, and through magazines. Having never gardened with chemicals, it was easy for me to transition to being truly green. When I started gardening more than twenty years ago, I immediately eschewed chemicals, for two simple reasons: they smelled horrible and scary, so I figured they couldn't be good; and I knew they would be injurious to the bees, ladybugs, praying mantids, and other happy creatures I liked to see in my garden. Rodale's *Organic Gardening* magazine became essential reading, and I devoured many copies of Rodale's books. You can start there—it will give you a great foundation of understanding sustainable concepts.

I like to educate my clients, but I try not to cram my no-chemical approach down their throats, particularly at the beginning. My marketing materials state that I use "an organic approach that is safe for people, pets, and wildlife," and I always mention that I like to guide my clients in the direction of a healthy, chemical-free property. That sows the seed. As we work together on their property transformation, I gain credibility and their trust. They come to see me as a source of knowledge in many areas and recognize that I'm not a tree-hugging whack job. That's when they are receptive to this message.

THE LAWN DEBATE

We have been brainwashed by the fertilizer and pesticide industries to believe you cannot have a nice lawn without a host of chemicals. I've had clients say that, well, sure, their garden can be chemical free, but they can't have a nice-looking lawn without their six-step program. "But it will not grow." "But it will be weedy." "But it won't be green." "But it will get grubs." I beg to differ. Lawns can be both beautiful and chemical free, and your clients can maintain them using a completely sustainable approach. They can even hire a lawn service if they prefer, since some now offer sustainable or organic maintenance —a wonderful shift in the industry.

I developed a lawn care protocol that identifies how to get from here (chemical dependence) to there (chemical freedom). It started with an innocent inquiry from two of my friends' husbands: "Come on, are lawn chemicals really so bad?" My gut instinct (and nose) told me that yes, they are bad, but I knew that answer wouldn't be enough for these analytical guys, so I started doing research. Within several months I had produced a packet of information on sustainable lawn care. More than the "what" and "how," I felt I really needed to explain the "why."

Garden TV host and national lecturer Paul Tukey developed the nonprofit organization SafeLawns to educate both homeowners and professionals and change the way Americans care for their lawns. The Web site, safelawns.org, pictures glorious, chemical-free lawns growing from Maine to Texas that were built using SafeLawns principles. The organization has launched various initiatives, such as the SafeLawns Million Acre Challenge, which aims to convert one million of the more than forty million acres of turf growing in the United States to safe lawns. Tukey's *Organic Lawn Care Manual* is also full of sound advice and has been lauded as the most extensive guide to natural lawn care yet.

As designers and specifiers, we can help by committing to build and care for lawns and gardens in an ecofriendly way, by eliminating synthetic fertilizers and pesticides, using push or electric mowers, and planting and watering responsibly. Convert your own yard, convert a client's yard, spread the compost, and spread the word!

CHILDREN, PETS, AND LAWN CHEMICALS

A few years ago I was working with new clients who had a gorgeous lawn. It was a perfect turf monoculture, a green carpet that was doused with chemical after chemical by their lawn maintenance company, and that received additional lawn treatments from a service that came about every month and sprayed something. In this green but barren landscape there were no earthworms, ants, or grubs. Basically nothing in the soil looked alive. When we were getting ready to do construction, I said, "Let's work to move your lawn and gardens to a chemical-free diet. It'll be healthier for the lawn, and for you, and will save you time and money over the long haul. Game?" These educated, affluent people in their early forties looked at each other, then back at me, and asked, "Why?" I gestured to their three small children playing on the lawn with their dogs and said, "Well, primarily, *them*." When I went on to describe some of the toxins in chemical fertilizers and treatments, they were horrified. They had no idea that any of this stuff wasn't completely safe. My message hit home big time. I later learned that they had lost dogs to cancer and had assumed it was just bad luck. Had it actually been the fault of the lawn chemicals? Hard to say, but I can assure you, the lawn chemicals certainly didn't help.

When construction was done and the clients saw their new lawn and gardens doing beautifully without all those chemicals, they became converts to chemical-free landscapes and shared this information with their friends. The good news multiplied, and I received referrals.

Inasmuch as any living thing can be negatively affected by lawn chemicals, children are particularly vulnerable. First is their size. An adult exposed to a given amount of a neurotoxin will be less affected than a 40-pound child. The timing of exposure also matters, since developing nervous systems are considerably more sensitive to chemical tampering than mature ones. Lastly, children are closer to the ground. They roll on the lawn and have much higher incidences of hand-to-mouth behaviors. Children playing on a treated lawn receive dermal, oral, and respiratory exposure to chemicals that are linked to infertility, neurological diseases, and childhood cancers. Reason enough to get pesticides and herbicides out of the areas where our children play.

Pets are also at risk. Introduced to raise awareness about the threats that lawn chemicals pose to our pets, *The Truth About Cats, Dogs, and Lawn Chemicals* is an entertaining and informative eighteen-minute documentary that every homeowner and landscape professional should see (you can find it on the Internet). Using humor, investigative journalism,

Bart can frolic without fear—no chemicals are used on the lawn or gardens at his home. Photo courtesy of Heather D. Jarnot.

and reality television techniques, it illustrates the profound connections between animals and humans, and exposes the collision between big chemicals and our front yards.

In a nationwide study of 9282 people, the U.S. Centers for Disease Control and Prevention found pesticides in 100% of the people who had their blood and urine tested. Unfortunately, we do not have similar data for pets, but we know that lawn chemicals pose a health threat to them. Pets are closer to the ground and consequently closer to the chemicals. When they roll on the lawn, they are rolling in chemicals and inhaling them. When they munch on the grass, they get a chemical snack. When they lick their paws and their coats, they ingest chemicals. And they track these toxins into the home. And die from them.

You won't always be able to move your clients away from chemicals. But even if you don't change their mindset, trust that you have given them something to consider. You've planted the seed. Sometimes all it takes is a little time.

WATER EQUALS LIFE

Water is a precious resource, as anyone from Atlanta would tell you after the drought of 2007. Frankly, the entire East Coast of the United States was affected that year—in my locale we had a mandatory and complete water ban for the first time in more than twenty-five years. That is pretty scary for a garden designer. I had to postpone several plantings for clients until spring of 2008, and ended up losing several mature trees on my own property. But unlike Atlanta, we still had water for showers, laundry, and drinking.

The clash between the constant demand for water and a dwindling water supply is by no means just a domestic crisis involving California and the American Southwest. Australia is facing an epic drought, and increasing heat and continued drought are devastating Africa, South America, the Middle East, Southeast Asia, and India. Global warming is already exacerbating dry areas and creating new pockets of desert, and this phenomenon has only just begun. Persisting droughts and increasing water demands are a recipe for global disaster.

WaterPartners International is a U.S.-based nonprofit organization working to provide safe, accessible water supplies to communities in developing countries. Their "water is life" education module explains that although our planet is approximately 71% water, clean, fresh sources of water are incredibly rare. The worldwide fresh water supply is only 0.003% of the total water on Earth. Geography, climate, and weather all affect water supply. As does how we use it. In the United States, many of us shamelessly take our plentiful water supply for granted.

Water *is* life. If you don't have it, water is the most precious resource in the world.

Wherever you live, using water with intent and consideration is a crucial part of working green in garden and landscape design. Appropriate horticultural planning coupled with water-wise irrigation practices can result in considerably less water use while providing a beautiful residential landscape.

One of the greatest ways to reduce water usage is to reduce the size of the lawn. Lawns are one of the most water-intensive creations of our society, mostly because we insist on growing them where they are not meant to grow (the arid Southwest, for example), and because rampant chemical fertilization forces growth, which requires copious amounts of water, at a time when the turf grasses would normally slow down their growth or go dormant (summer). You could even eliminate some—or all!—of the lawn areas from your designs and end up with a beautiful landscape that requires considerably less water to maintain. Lawns are basically good for two things: providing recreational play areas (if they're not maintained with poisonous chemicals) and serving as a pretty foil for other areas, like flowering borders. Reduce the lawn, reduce the water usage. It's a simple equation.

Gray water is another consideration. Why do we water our landscapes with 100% clean, potable water, when the waste water from our showers and laundry would work beautifully? This makes no sense. When we renovated our home in 2003, I tried to get a gray-water system tied into our house, but plumbing code in Massachusetts wasn't there yet, and I got a huge thumbs-down from both my plumber and the local board of health. I even tried to bribe one of the plumbers I knew to plumb a secret gray-water system for me after all of the other inspections had been completed. He said, "Uh, no." Fast-forward to the present. Water is at such a premium that municipalities and states are finally realizing it doesn't make sense to use pristine water for flushing toilets and irrigating gardens. On behalf of all of your future clients, investigate and stay abreast of what is allowed in your state. Push local authorities to allow and promote gray-water systems. Using the same water twice to accomplish two tasks just makes so much sense.

DISPOSAL

Nearly everything that comes off of a landscaping job site is recyclable. It's either compostable yard waste; chippable brush, tree detritus, and wood fencing (if it is not pressure-treated); recyclable plastics; reusable concrete, asphalt, and stone products; or useful scrap metal. There is so little that we cannot recycle. Part of working truly green is disposing of all construction waste appropriately. Do not dump it or bury it in your client's yard or in the neighboring woods. Do not dump it illegally off-property. Do not let the debris from your job become someone else's burden. Work within the letter of the law, and recycle all you can. Let your subcontractors know that you expect them to work with you to make sure everything that leaves the job site goes where it should.

If there is any question about anything you have that you need to get rid of, call the local public works department, who will be more than happy to tell you about the closest locations for properly disposing construction waste. If you have clean fill from grading or excavation work, the local municipality may be happy to use it if you can get it to them. Since dumping fees can be pretty steep in some places, it's great if you can off-load waste and benefit someone who can use it, for just the cost of getting it there.

Whenever you uncover a hazardous waste, make sure you dispose of it correctly. Things like old oil barrels can be a particular nuisance, but these do not belong in landfills, nor should they be dumped at the side of the road. Learn your local ordinances for getting rid of various types of waste. Illegal dumping is not only wrong, it can result in hefty fines. Burying waste on-site is really bush league. Okay, worse than that, it's sleazy. You wouldn't believe the things we have dug up that don't belong there. This stuff then becomes *our* waste to manage. Truly working green means making sure all of your construction and site waste is taken care of properly.

THE DARK OF NIGHT

One of the quieter, yet still quite startling, side effects of our modern society is that in much of the developed world we no longer see the true night sky. Sure, we can see the moon and pick out the North Star or the three stars that make up Orion's Belt. But have you ever seen the night sky peppered with the billions of stars that we're told are out there? Have you ever turned your eyes up on a clear night and been able to actually see our galaxy, the Milky Way? For most of us, the answer is no. Electricity, particularly the overwhelming preponderance of electric lights shining up into our skies, has blacked out the night. Or more accurately, it has whited it out. This is light pollution. It comes in lots of forms and is attributed to the relentless lighting from shopping plazas, gas stations, commercial signage, office buildings, parking areas, night games, street lights, and, of course, from our own homes.

Residential landscape lighting has become ubiquitous and has gone way past the single sconce light at the front door that most of us grew up with. Much of it is, well, way too much. No one needs Disney World on their front lawn.

Here on Long Pond, away from some of the glare just 40 miles from Boston, we can see so many more stars in the night sky, yet it is still a miniscule percentage of what we should be able to see.

Beyond the aesthetics and waste of electricity, should we care? I mean, what's the big deal? Don't we need lots of lighting for security? The answer may surprise you.

For most of history, the only light on Earth came from naturally radiant sources: sun, moon, stars. From the first fires, humans have used artificial light to extend the day. But modern man has taken the use of artificial light to new extremes, and we are now faced with the possibility that within a generation or two, the only view we will have of the night sky will be simulated on a computer or broadcast on a television screen. Urban sky glow will have replaced the brilliant night sky with a sad and muddied view.

How do we save our night sky? Lack of awareness, rather than resistance, is the leading problem. People just don't know what light pollution is, how damaging it can be, and how simple it can be to implement solutions. As garden designers, we can learn the right way to design exterior

CONSEQUENCES OF LIGHT POLLUTION

Urban sky glow. The bright, hazy glow seen around cities from many miles away, caused by excessive and unshielded light reflected or pointing up, is obliterating the stars for most of the world's population and is a particular problem for astronomers.

Night glare. Excessive brightness causes physical discomfort and is often blinding, reducing visibility for both pedestrians and drivers.

Light trespass. Outdoor light frequently falls where it is not intended, needed, or desired.

Wildlife disturbance. Excessive outdoor lighting contributes to the widespread death of migratory birds, fish, sea turtles, amphibians, insects, bats, and other animals.

Energy waste. The International Dark-Sky Association estimates that the waste of electricity from excessive lighting in the United States alone represents an annual cost of $1.7 billion per year. Additionally, the fossil fuels burned to provide the wasted electricity release 38 million tons of carbon dioxide, contributing to global warming.

Human cancers. A growing body of evidence links the lack of nighttime darkness to negative impacts on human health and the human immune system, including increased incidences of cancer.

lighting to avoid contributing to light pollution. We can also educate others and advocate for darker skies.

Where I live in the Northeast, we have one of the highest levels of exterior night illumination. This is not a good thing. At my home, 11 miles as the crow flies from Boston, our night sky is a dim, murky brownish color, even when the weather is clear. But I have had the good fortune to see the night sky as it was intended to be seen. On a visit to Flagstaff a few years ago, on a wonderfully clear, cold February night we went to the Lowell Observatory, bringing our ten-year-old son with us. There we saw not only our galaxy with the unaided eye, but also Saturn—and its rings!—and other celestial bodies. I was blown away. No wonder the ancients worshipped the sky. That night we also learned about the Dark Sky Initiative. The people of Flagstaff, one of the first Dark Sky cities, have passed ordinances to control light waste and light pollution in an effort to keep their glorious night sky. I became an instant convert and have since worked to design lighting in concert with the mission of the Dark Sky proponents.

As outdoor lighting designers, we are in a perfect position to help raise awareness about saving our view of the night sky. We can easily work to design and install outdoor lighting in cooperation with Dark Sky protocol. It's a greener approach to lighting the way. (For specifics on designing appropriate outdoor lighting, see chapter 9.)

GREENER GREEN EQUALS PEACE OF MIND

Operating a truly green business is a great way to feel good about your work and yourself. Picture yourself, thumbs hooked in your suspenders, lookin' purty proud. Though cliché, this image is fitting, because you'll know you are heading up a business that is helping the environment one property at a time. When you do your best for the planet, your clients, and your workers, you earn a great side benefit: peace of mind.

As you practice chemical-free, sustainable landscape design and construction, you and your subcontractors will not be exposed to the toxins that standard landscape workers are regularly exposed to. Your clients and their children and pets will be able to roll around in their new landscape without worrying about inhaling carcinogens and heavy metals, and marinating in neurological toxins and endocrine disruptors. All in all, nature will thrive and the world will smile. Alright, that reads a bit glib, but it's true. In all sincerity, I take such pleasure in walking through a client's lush, flowering, chemical-free landscape and encountering all kinds of critters, including toads, butterflies, songbirds, hummingbirds, turtles, and bees. I was tickled to see a huge green katydid recently, just a few hours after spying a stunning 5-inch-long praying mantis. These are all indicators of a healthy ecosystem. The fact that I have had a hand in creating these environments is greatly satisfying. The knowledge that I can wander through these landscapes and know that I don't need to take a shower to scrub off toxins before I enter my home—well, that peace of mind is a really good thing.

I keep repeating that we as garden and landscape designers are in a unique position to create beauty and earn a great living doing it. But when we also work in harmony with nature, we are actively educating everyone within our reach. Our clients, subcontractors, and workers, and even our suppliers, catch the message.

Recently I was talking to a lighting contractor about our plans for lighting a client's backyard. He had been hired directly by the homeowners, so

One sign of a healthy ecosystem.

he had done the design. He planned to put small spots at the front of this rear border planting to shine up and into the backdrop of trees. Knowing that this was a Dark Sky no-no, I talked with him. He said he'd never even thought about the night sky this way before. (Remember, raising awareness is often the largest part of the solution.) I suggested we use smaller fixtures with a narrower beam and lower wattage, and install them up in the trees to gently shine down into the planting. He got it. He understood. It was like Helen Keller at the well. That one little touchpoint might just eventually affect thousands of light installations for the better.

Sometimes all it takes is one conversation.

CHAPTER FIVE

Pathways, Walls, and Fences

WHEN YOU BEGIN DESIGNING professionally, unless you strictly offer garden work only, you'll quickly be pulled into areas where you have less knowledge, and you'll need to ramp up fast. The good news is you'll never stop learning. Clients ask for all sorts of "other" work. One asks for a walkway—time to ramp up on masonry knowledge and choose materials and a contractor. Another wants a fence—you'll need to think about styles, materials, purveyors. Oh, howzabout a flagpole? I had this request myself. It got me to learn about flags, poles, and the codes around their installation. We did such a nice job that the flagpole company wanted our team to become their regular installers. The knee bone is connected to the hip bone in all things, including garden design.

WORKING WITH STONE

Many paths and boundaries involve stone, a huge subject in itself. To become knowledgeable about working with this material, study the stone work at stone yards. Better ones will have display areas with good signage that will help educate you. Many stone yards offer packets of information that clearly show wall styles, stone types, brick types, brick patterns, paver options, and so on. Many wonderful books cover masonry and stonework as well, and lots of design books will walk you through the basics. All of these can help you quickly develop a good, general base of knowledge.

The variety of stone available from almost any stone yard is phenomenal. Yes, actual stone offerings will shift due to your locale, but the range of stone out there is still mind-boggling. And thrilling! Go to several of your local stone purveyors and look at their sample walls and flat work. Not all will offer the same products. Check out what types of stone they offer and what each type is used for. See how it is packaged. Ask how buyers generally choose the stone (can you pick through a pile, or do you have to take whole pallets?), and ask how it's delivered (do you need to have a machine on-site or can the stone yard deliver and spider it in?). I love stone, so a visit to a stone yard is a complete pleasure, even when I have to rush in and rush out.

Stone is purchased by the ton. It is usually stacked on pallets and held together for transport with shrink wrap or chicken wire. Each type of stone will give you a different running length of wall, or square footage of flat application, per ton. Your masonry subcontractors will know how to estimate and price all of your stone walls. As you become more familiar with estimating and pricing jobs, you'll be able to provide client estimates without getting quotes from all of your subcontractors. Note, however, that masonry is one area where you'll always need to be very careful about pricing. Before I provide final pricing to any client, I always get estimates from my masons. Between the cost of stone, materials, delivery, and labor, you cannot afford to make even a slight mistake in pricing masonry. It could bury the entire profit of your project.

No matter what the project, you can never go wrong if you opt to use natural stone for much of your hardscaping. Stone gives a permanence and solidity unmatched by other materials, and stone work done well is truly a beautiful thing to behold.

Wall stone comes in hundreds of varieties but only several basic shapes. *Fieldstone* is rounded and can range from the size of a baseball to the size of a watermelon. *Stacking stone* or *ledgestone* is irregularly shaped but relatively flat, particularly as compared to fieldstone. *Dressed stone* is carefully cut to be uniform and flat. As you start to design a stone wall, you will select the type of stone based on the look you and your clients want for the application, and the price. *Ashlar* is a style of dressed stone that provides rectangular blocks of masonry sculpted to have square edges

Small fieldstones make a charming wall with a rustic or country feel.

The large fieldstones in this wall have raked-back mortar joints to give the illusion of a dry-laid wall.

In the hands of a talented craftsperson, stacked ledgestone can be used to make a wall that appeals to many.

Dressed stone has been further worked by a mason to soften the revealed edges, creating a more time-worn look.

Naturally flat fieldstone that has been laid perpendicular to the ground makes a handsome wall.

Ashlar stones are sculpted to have square edges and even faces.

and even faces. Ashlar stones are roughly two times as wide as they are high, which makes them easier to work with than irregular wall stones. Dressed stones give a wall a more formal appearance than irregular stones or fieldstones and tend to be more expensive because of the labor involved to create a more uniform product.

Typical flat stone tends to be, well, flat. Certainly it is flatter than wall stone, which is more often than not shaped like what it is: rocks! Flat work requires fairly level stones. Even rustic patios and walkways need a relatively flat surface if people are to walk on them and furniture is to sit properly.

The stone used for flat work falls into four categories: stone pavers, stone flagging, brick pavers, and concrete pavers. Concrete pavers are a relatively new product. Their uniformity of size, interlocking shapes, and moderately low cost make them a desirable alternative to brick or stone. They can be used for driveways, walkways, patios, stoops, and wall work. Brick, also called brick pavers, can be used in all the same types of applications. Make sure you choose brick pavers, however, and not brick designed to be used in wall work. Wall brick is not meant to hold up to the same extremes as brick pavers. Know that there is a difference.

The stone used in flat applications is a natural product that can be laid in intricate formal patterns or rough and rustic designs. It is available as either flagging or paving. Flagging is any flat stone that is irregular. It is usually a natural-cleft stone, which means it is split along natural seams in the rock, leaving a somewhat irregular stepping surface. Paving is any flat stone that is cut into a regular shape (square or rectangular). It can also be natural-cleft, or it can be a cut or sawn product. Sawn bluestone, for example, has a smooth stepping surface created by diamond-blade saws, whereas natural-cleft bluestone paving is square or rectangular but has a relatively textured stepping surface.

The types of natural stone for flat work that are available to you will depend on your local stone purveyor, as well as your location, but it is now possible to obtain stone from just about all over the world. The kinds of stone commonly used for flat or horizontal work include cobblestone, flagstone, granite, bluestone, slate, sandstone, limestone, brownstone, marble, and granite.

Brick is stone, too. And like other stone, it can be installed with mortar, or it can be dry-laid. Brick is classic, and a multitude of different types of bricks and different brick patterns can be used for virtually any stone application. Brickwork can provide a traditional, formal look or a homey, relaxed, country feel. Used extensively throughout the United States, it is a time-honored medium for home construction in the Southeast and the Midwest, and makes a classic walkway in New England. The things to keep in mind when specifying brick in your designs is to choose brick suited to both your climate and the particular application. Different types of brick have greatly different performance characteristics. A brick that is suited for an exterior patio in Florida may not work at all in the icy winters of Vermont. Your local stone yard will know which brick types are right for each of your applications.

Brick comes in a variety of subtle colors, from the traditional brick red to burgundy, aubergine, orange, brown, mocha, tan, and combinations. Nearly white is also available, although I'm hard pressed to think of a wall or patio installation where I would want to use that particular color. This is probably a testament to prejudicial thinking, not to the limitations of the brick!

Some brick types are uniform in color and size. These are particularly preferred for use in formal applications. Other types of brick offer quite a range in color shifts through your average pallet of product, as well as imperfect sizing. This makes for a more country-style wall, patio, or walkway.

About a hundred years ago, clinker bricks—misshapen bricks that were originally discarded—became sought-after accents for Craftsman-style construction. They're used in walls, fireplaces, and patios as well as on home structures themselves. Original clinker bricks now cost upwards of $40 apiece, although an Internet search will quickly show where you can get "new" clinkers. At the right installation, I think it would be a blast to design an outdoor fireplace or kitchen that included some of these bricks as accents.

Brick patterns for flat work can be simple or complex. Almost any stone yard that sells brick will have copies of brick patterns with anywhere from eight or ten to several dozen examples. When you are

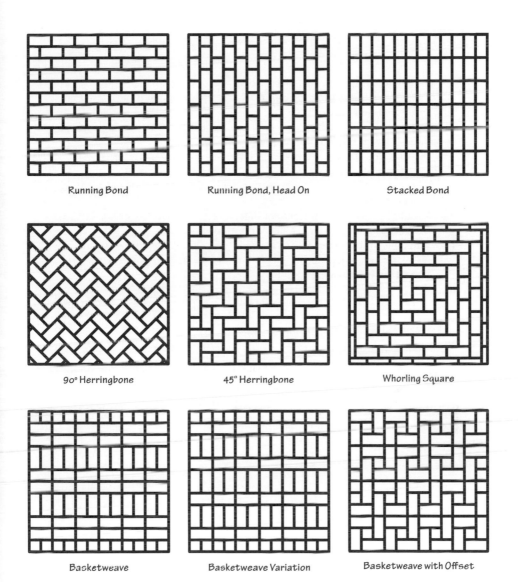

Running Bond

Running Bond, Head On

Stacked Bond

90° Herringbone

45° Herringbone

Whorling Square

Basketweave

Basketweave Variation

Basketweave with Offset

Nine common brick patterns. There are many
more, and you can even make up your own.

QUICK GLOSSARY OF MASONRY TERMS

Batter. Inclined outer slope of a masonry wall or hedge.

Capstone. Stone used at the top of a wall or arch to protect the stacked or mortared stone below.

Coping. Top course of brick or stone that forms a protective cap on a wall. Also the edge around the perimeter of a swimming pool.

Dry-laid, dry-stacked. Constructed without cementitious mortar.

Jointing. Treatment of mortar in masonry. Can be thick, thin, or variable.

Mortar. Bonding material, generally a mixture of sand, cement, and water, that hardens.

Raked-back. Said of a mortar joint that is "dug out" before it sets up to make the masonry resemble dry-laid materials.

Veneer. Thin stone mortared or glued onto a backing, primarily used on homes, outdoor kitchen installations, or any application where we want to maximize the veneering material.

recommending patterns for a brick patio or walk, remember that a complex pattern will cost more to install than a simple pattern. More labor will be involved, and since more brick cuts will be required, particularly along the edges of a complex pattern, more product will be discarded, so there will be more waste. This is another time that I highly suggest you get an estimate from your masons.

If the home at the property you are designing is constructed of brick, be cautious about using this material in the landscape. Brick "everything" can end up being daunting and hard edged. Consider building the patio or walkway using another stone that will complement the brick and not overwhelm the people in the space.

DRIVEWAYS

Most driveways in America are ugly black tongues lolling across the front yard to the street. Lovely description, eh? It's true. Take a long, critical look at driveways. Most are ugly, and many point you into the property at the worst angle, never allowing you to see the prettiest face of the house. Many driveways are positioned with minimal regard for view lines and safety. You can fix these things.

Most driveways are left over from the home builder, even if the home was built fifty or seventy-five years ago. At the end of construction, builders are out of time and money, so the shortest route from street to garage is usually what they do. Pave it to sell it. I have even seen multimillion-dollar homes with hideous drives and—shudder!—asphalt walkways. The quick and dirty way rarely offers optimal results.

I frequently change the driveway, not because I want to spend people's money, but because doing so can bring dramatic change to both the aesthetics and functionality of the home. Arrival and departure dynamics can be greatly enhanced, safety concerns can be addressed, and even if you opt for standard black asphalt surfacing, a new layout and complementary walkways and plantings can allow a driveway to beautify a landscape.

I only use driveway contractors for driveway construction, and I suggest you do the same. Hit the yellow pages or Internet to find contractors in your area. They know what works in your climate and are formulaic in their approach. This gives the most consistent, reliable results, and when we're talking driveways, consistency and reliability are critical.

One of the first questions I ask myself when looking at a client's driveway is, does it work for this family? This spawns a whole list of other questions. Does it allow safe access into the property? As a car turns in, they should be able to continue along the drive without hidden spots where they could hit a child on a bike, or a pet that is lounging in the shade. Can you exit the drive onto the roadway with good visibility? Optimally, exiting a driveway nose first is the safest way. Can you see up and down the street for oncoming traffic? How does this work in all seasons? Shrubs may preclude a clear view in the summer but allow for good visibility in the colder months. Or there could be a clear view in the summer, while snow pileup in the winter makes exiting dangerous. This problem can be resolved. How could the layout be tweaked for maximum safety? Are there obvious places to push and pile up snow? Herbaceous beds that give 3 to 6 feet of room for snow load are critical in snowy climates. Is there room for parking all of the family cars, and can cars get in and out without playing musical vehicles? Is there adequate parking for guests? Is it easy to drop off or pick up a child? Aesthetics are important, too. Does the drive approach give you a good view to the front door (for

This drive was too small to allow for guest parking, and the asphalt detracted from the setting.

A new layout provides generous space for parking, and the new drive surface complements the house and landscape.

me, a must) or at least a good view towards it? Lots of driveways present a great view of . . . the garage doors. Ugh. Designers, we can do better.

Link any new drive layout to a walkway that firmly directs guests to the front door. Many driveways and parking areas are confusing, often so much so that guests have no idea where to go, particularly if there is no view to the front door. Our job is to give the flow of traffic and people a direction, and to make it all look beautiful.

As you drive around, start noticing details about materials, construction, and layout of driveways. What is the surfacing made of? How did they lay the pattern? What about this installation do I love? What would I change? How could it be more functional? You will learn a lot just by active observation.

Measurements for driveways and parking areas follow some general rules. The average parking space should be 10 feet wide by 20 feet long, wider and longer if your clients drive large pickup trucks or SUVs. To allow for turning out of a parking space or the garage, allow a backup of 20 feet before the turn, and allow the turn to be 20 feet deep for adequate clearance. If the parking area or drive is going to be surrounded by walls, allow an extra 2 feet for turning and parking. You want people to be able to open their car doors.

Driveway widths are usually no narrower than 10 feet, although I like a 12- or 14-foot-wide drive if there is much curve in it. This permits drivers to negotiate the driveway easily without worrying about running over bordering lawn or gardens.

Parking circles are areas where we cannot skimp. Turning circles should be no smaller than 45 feet in diameter, larger if you can comfortably accommodate it on the property, and larger still by several feet if there will be walls around the perimeter, or around a central planting or feature. With many people driving trucks and SUVs, the larger diameter leaves a margin for turning error and driving comfort. If you find you really don't have the space for a good turning circle, use a modified T instead.

No matter what climate you'll be working in, there will be many different options for driveway surfaces. From gravel to granite, drives can be as simple or as exotic as you and your clients would like. Four of my clients brought me in specifically to design and install driveways of concrete pavers. Each lives in a high-end neighborhood in an affluent town, so high-end driveway treatments are appropriate for the area. In each case the driveway redesigns maximized the space, delivered greater functionality and ease of use, and were considerably more beautiful. They also inspired additional changes to the properties: new walkways, new plantings, new lighting. Does this mean I recommend paver driveways all of the time? Of course not. Far too many surfacing options are available to pigeonhole just one.

Asphalt is *the* driveway material of North America: tried and true, relatively inexpensive, formulaic in its installation, with many contractors available to install on short notice. Over 90% of all paving in the United States is asphalt, and there are many reasons for this. Over time, asphalt is fairly forgiving and ages well. It can be used in any climate. When

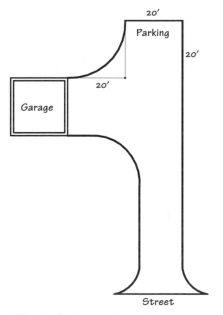

This simple driveway layout incorporates a modified T structure to allow for turns and parking. Note the measurements for the garage approach, turnaround area, and two parking spaces (10 feet by 20 feet each).

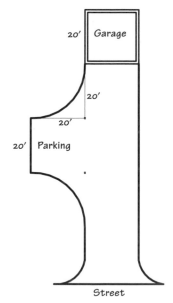

Another modified T structure, this one with a straight approach to the garage.

well prepped, it can handle a great deal of weight. Edges can be straight or curved, surfaces can be flat or follow the undulations of the terrain. In residential applications it's a great surface for kids to play on—bike riding, hoops, hopscotch, chalk art. You can maintain the black-tongue look by sealing the surface frequently, or you can leave it alone without deleterious effect. I actually prefer the color of a traditional asphalt driveway when it has had time to age to a quieter, less visually imposing, weathered gray. When we had our driveway replaced, we used asphalt, but we didn't want it to look new. We asked for just the (rougher) binder coat to be installed, and then had the driveway company cover the surface with coarse builders' sand and run their 12-ton roller over the whole thing. A few weeks later, after rain and traffic had worked most of the sand into the surface, we swept off the remaining sand. This gave us just we wanted: an older-looking driveway. Of course, this wouldn't be everyone's aesthetic, but it worked for us—we like antique homes, rusty metal, and old stone walls, too.

The cons to asphalt, besides the color (again, lolling black tongue), are that it heats up miserably in the summer sun, and most people feel the need to maintain it, sealing it every year or two and exposing themselves to some nasty chemicals in the process.

Colored asphalts are emerging in the industry. I'm not sure I'd personally want a kelly green or burgundy driveway, but there are gorgeous applications of textured colored asphalt throughout the United States. This type of surfacing is available even in cold winter climates, where the surfacing will be exposed to freezing weather, salting, and snowplowing.

An embellished form of asphalt paving, chip seal (or chip and seal), is becoming quite popular. The base is prepped and the first layer laid exactly like a normal asphalt driveway, but instead of a top coat of asphalt, a layer of liquid asphalt is poured onto the base, which is quickly topped with gravel. A 12-ton roller embeds much of the gravel into the liquid asphalt surface, and the rest of the gravel remains loose on top, effectively making the installation look like a gravel driveway, but performing much like asphalt.

Concrete is a terrific choice for driveways and even walks and patios. Long preferred for use in warmer climates, it is completely reliable in

A chip seal driveway looks rustic yet elegant, and provides that incomparable audible crunch as vehicles come and go.

the northern tier of the United States when prepped well and finished properly.

Driveways made of concrete can also be textured and colored to look like stone or brickwork, or laid to look like tile. To accomplish this, after the area is prepped well and a good base is laid, 4 or 5 inches of concrete is poured (I'd go with 5 inches—it will be able to take more compression from trucks and other heavy vehicles, and the additional cost is negligible), mats are laid on the wet concrete, and designs are stamped into the surface. Color can be added by either broadcasting dyes over the wet surface or adding colorants to the entire concrete load.

Concrete pavers have become very popular. Reliable, easy to work with, lovely results, relatively inexpensive—what's not to love? And they make not only glorious driveways but also attractive pool aprons, walkways, and patios. They are available in many sizes and several finishes, including smooth or regular, tumbled (to look aged), and dimpled.

Packed stone can make a gorgeous, easy-to-maintain driveway surface, even in areas where snow needs to be plowed. The basic prep is about the

Nothing says "country" quite like a gravel drive.

same as for asphalt or concrete—a well-prepared base (whatever is recommended for your climate) topped by the crushed stone, then rolled
with a large drive-roller or compacted with a plate compactor. Regular
maintenance usually consists of raking the odd piece of stray stone out of
the surrounding lawn or borders. Snow removal involves either shoveling,
snowblowing, or plowing, with the plow raised about an inch from normal plow height. I usually pair stone driveways with a cobblestone border,
or collar, where the drive meets the street. It provides a nice visual transition between the two surfaces, and helps to prevent any loose stone from
migrating into the roadway.

Gravel can make a glorious country-style driveway. Prepared much like
you would for packed stone, these driveways look friendly and homey.
That said, they are often used in high-end settings, because they are also
beautiful in the landscape. There is the lovely audible property of gravel,
which we don't get from solid drive surfacing. Gravel and packed stone
crunch under your tires, announcing a vehicle's arrival to those already at
home, and giving the homeowner both a sense of welcome and an aural

cue to decompress because they are home. Installation and snow care are the same as for packed stone.

Drive strips remind me of my grandmother's home in Oklahoma. I just love the look of them. They usually consist of two slices of concrete just wide enough for the tires to sit on, separated by a mown path or even a planted path. These work best for straight driveways, where one is not going to drive over the center strip—straight in, straight out. But they can connect to a solid area where there will be turning of vehicles. Drive strips are friendly, visually quiet in the landscape, and easy to maintain. Just plow in the winter as you would any surfacing. Strips with a planted center can be a feature unto themselves, beautifully adorned with sedums, short grasses, herbs, and other small steppable plants.

Other materials could be germane, depending on your location. Crushed shell is popular on Cape Cod and at other seaside locations. A mulched drive is soft and quiet; I saw one at a cabin in New Hampshire, and it was woodsy and nestled looking, although the cost to keep up the mulch

So retro, this drive strip could lead you right into the past.

might eventually become prohibitive. One of the most beautiful drive-ways I've ever seen was made of large slabs of granite. Cost would pre-clude most of us from having this type of driveway, but it was glorious. On a design show (they *are* of value), I saw an asphalt driveway resur-faced with a layer of "polymer cement" tinted a color and stamped with a cobble pattern. This was in a Midwestern neighborhood that gets snow, so the surface was made plowable. I have no idea how this treatment will hold up, but it was a quick, reasonably priced upgrade to the existing drive. Other materials I've seen used include beach pebbles, brick, mosa-ics, packed sand, and chunky fieldstone.

A lovely touch is to herald a transition in materials, function, or space with a collar of cobblestones. This treatment works well if you are transi-tioning from street to private drive, from drive to walkway, or even from parking spaces to active driving field. Whether you use antique cobbles or modern granite called Belgian block, this can make a beautiful accent in a driveway layout.

A cobblestone driveway collar provides a visible and audible transition from the public space to the private.

WALKWAYS

Walkways serve a purpose: they allow access to the house and to other landscaped areas. They show direction and give people a way to get from one area to another, usually on a solid surface that allows passage without getting shoes or feet dirty. A walkway can be a work of beauty, or it can be so ugly that it drags everything around it down. (Personally I detest, hate, loathe, and despise asphalt walkways. This is often a builder's quick and cheap way out, or a homeowner's solution when no one offered them a better alternative. No matter what the house looks like, or how beautiful the gardens, asphalt walkways are ugly, ugly, ugly. You can put a jewel on a wart, but when all is said and done, it's still a wart.)

In the category of walkways, I include pathways, but they are different animals. Walkways generally connect a source location (like the driveway) to a destination (the front door), and as a rule are considered public areas. Most are made of brick, natural stone, or concrete pavers. Pathways, on the other hand, bring to mind meandering routes and private spaces like backyards. They usually have a destination, but not always. A

This seldom-used front walkway is barely more than a path, but the stepping stones create a charming vignette at the front of the antique home.

path could just be a circuitous route through a woodland, for example, offering a nice place for a stroll. It could be little more than an opening in some groundcover, simple and unobtrusive, or a slender trail of pea-stone. It could even be as unexpected and delightful as a single mown strip through a grassy field. Pathways can be particularly fun to design, since they do not necessarily need the critical safety and functionality that walkways require. One tip, though, regarding stepping stones: these should not be dotted through any recreational lawn. This is done in TV design shows all the time, and it is just plain wrong. Stones positioned this way are difficult to mow around, hard to play around, and ankle snappers to boot.

Here are my self-imposed rules when designing walkways. I like walks to be wide enough to accommodate two people comfortably walking abreast. Most of my walkways are 4 feet wide or more, but some are as narrow as my bare minimum of 3 feet because of constrictions imposed by the site. If the walkway connects to a stoop, doorway, or landing, I make sure its end is at least as wide as whatever it is attached to. I do not want someone to step off a stoop expecting to hit a walkway and instead step onto "nothing" (a garden or lawn)—this makes for unsafe conditions.

Curviness for the sake of it in a walk is unnecessary, but this doesn't mean walks should be soldier-straight. I believe in simplicity and functionality. If you want visitors to slow down and look at the garden, add some curves or shifts in direction. Run the walk parallel or perpendicular to the house if you are looking to tie in strongly to the architecture. To make the design functionally successful, create a well-defined connection to the driveway or parking area, and a definite connection at the destination end.

Walkways have even more surfacing options than driveways. They can be made of natural stone, brick, concrete pavers, poured concrete, wood, fieldstone, gravel, river stone, peastone, rice stone, mosaics, tile, steppable plants, mulch, pine needles, crushed shells, stone slabs, corrugated steel plating (I saw this in a modernist setting—it was quite beautiful), railroad or landscape ties, or tree trunk cross sections. For safety, I like walkways to offer a solid, relatively even surface. But a clearly delineated walkway also shows intention: this is the way to the front door.

Brick is traditional across the United States, and I don't think anyone could go wrong with a brick walkway aesthetically or functionally. Make sure you choose brick pavers appropriate for your climate. Warn clients against deicing brick with salt, which can damage it and lead to an early demise. Clay-based kitty litter or sand are safer alternatives.

I generally choose natural stone for walkways. Bluestone, brownstone, slate, granite, sandstone, marble, regular, irregular, multiple size—I love all of it. Stone is solid and elegant in a way that no paver can match. Walkways should be prepped much like a driveway but do not require the same depth of packed base since they support considerably less weight. Lots of stone promises to tolerate deicing salts, but again, I encourage clients to stick with more innocuous products to guard against staining or shattering. Nontoxic, nonstaining kitty litter and sand are safe for children, pets, floors, and carpets, unlike deicing salts, which can burn mucous membranes and are highly toxic if ingested. Safe Paw is a good, nationally available deicer that will not harm pets or plants.

Concrete pavers can provide a serviceable and good-looking walkway. I don't like pavers as well as natural stone, but that's my personal bias. Pavers come in a phenomenal range of colors, sizes, textures, and mixes. They are easy to work with and quick to install, so square foot to square foot, pavers are usually a less expensive solution than natural stone. When installing, make sure your masons prep the area and install the base correctly. The pavers should be laid tight, and edge guards should always be used to prevent paver migration from use and from freeze-thaw cycles.

STAIRWAY TO HEAVEN

Stairs allow the landscape to change in grade, or give access to the inside of a building. Stairways that connect a walk to the house can be made of just about any masonry or decking product, including natural stone (both solid and veneer), concrete pavers, poured concrete, wood, and alternative decking materials (composites). How you design stairs (how many steps, how deep, and so forth) is somewhat formulaic. For safety reasons, you must adhere to local and statewide building codes, and there are practical considerations, too. Your climate comes into play (in cold winter climates you're going to need a railing, even if you're only going up two or three steps, simply because ice can make stairs treacherous). You'll consider the architecture of the house, the ages of your clients and their family, the design aesthetic (for example, formal versus contemporary versus country), what personally turns your clients on, and of course, what the budget allows.

A staircase is composed of treads, risers, and stringers. The stringer provides support to the treads in a stick (wood) stair installation. There are no stringers in masonry stair installations unless you count the base materials, which could be cinder block or poured concrete. The tread is the horizontal part of the stair, where you put your foot. The measurement of the tread is the depth of the stair. The riser is the vertical part

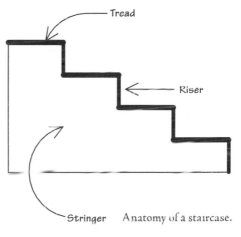

Anatomy of a staircase.

Antique granite treads are a solid complement to the large granite blocks that comprise the patio wall.

of the stair and is measured as the height from one tread to the next (the rise). Most risers range from 5 to 8 inches high. In Massachusetts the highest stair riser allowed by code is 8¼ inches, which makes for a fairly high step.

The formula for stair construction is 2R + T = 24–27. To translate, two times the riser height plus the tread depth (in inches) should be a number between 24 and 27. So if I have a 7-inch rise and a 12-inch tread, this gives me 7 × 2 + 12, which equals 26. Perfect. However, I prefer deeper treads and fairly low risers, so I sort of throw the formula out the window. This ends up taking more stairs for any given run, so it is slightly more costly, but it results in a more comfortable stair height for seniors and toddlers, and the treads provide a solid place for your foot and are deep enough to park your butt or hold a planted pot. Additionally, it gives any entry or deck approach a more elegant, gracious aesthetic than standard-sized stairs.

To calculate how many stairs you need for a given area, measure the distance from the finished height of the walk, drive, or whatever surface you are starting from, to the height you want to reach at the top of the staircase. Say we are going to build stairs that link the front walkway (the finished level we're starting from) to an entry stoop (the finished level at which we will end). The total height we are going to rise is 32 inches. Taking 7 inches as an average riser height, how many steps would we need? Divide 32 by 7 and you get 4.57, so roughly four and a half steps. Since we cannot do a partial step (well, we can, but it is not to code and would be dangerous, because each series of stairs needs to have an even rhythm of step heights for the people walking on them), we can either do five steps that are lower than 7 inches or four steps that are higher than 7 inches. Given that 32 divided by 5 is 6.4, if we go for five steps, each would be 6.4 inches high. And since 32 divided by 4 is 8, if we decided to use four steps, each would be 8 inches high.

An 8-inch step height is still within local building code parameters, but it adds 1.6 inches of height to each step over what we would need if we used five steps for this run. Understand that either four steps or five steps would work and be within code, but if we have the depth available, I would go with the lower steps and use a fairly deep tread—like 14 to 16 inches—for each stair. If we apply the stair construction formula, we

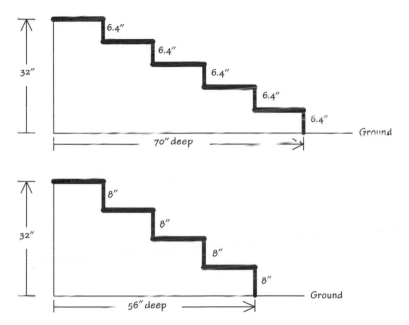

Two 32-inch-high staircases. The first contains five steps, each 6.4 inches high. The second contains four steps, each 8 inches high.

Low risers and deep treads not only provide a gracious ascent but are also generous enough to comfortably act as seating at this pond-side location.

would get 6.4 × 2 + 16 = 29, so this scenario is definitely outside the recommended parameters. But again, if we have the depth to work with, I would go with the five lower steps and a generous tread.

Tread depth can range from 9 inches (a bare minimum, in my opinion) to just about as deep as you'd like. I have seen fabulous staircases on the approach to municipal buildings with very low rises, like 4 inches, coupled with treads as deep as 24 or even 32 inches or more. I think when you get to 20 inches or deeper, things start looking estatelike, commercial, or institutional. That's not necessarily bad, but it could be overkill if you are working on an average American home. When I am designing stairs using either masonry or wood, I set a minimal stair tread depth of 12 inches, and I only use 12 inches if there are space constraints. I prefer a depth of 14 to 16 inches and rarely exceed 16. Note that the deeper the tread, the more space you need to run the stairs. If you are using five stairs with 12-inch treads, you will need 5 × 12 inches, or 60 inches, of depth to construct the stairs. If you are using those same five stairs, but are going with 16-inch treads, you will need 80 inches of depth to build the stairs. So as you design stairs, consider where you are starting from, where you will end up, and how much space you have to work with in the middle. This will all play into your thought process and final design recommendations.

As you work with designing and refining detailed layout instructions, you will quickly recognize how changes in something as seemingly simple as a set of stairs can dramatically affect the functionality, aesthetics, and human experience of the area being designed.

Stairs most often lead to another structure, like a deck, patio, entry, or stoop. When they connect to a front entry, I like designing a stoop or landing that is large enough for two people to comfortably stand on together. This gives visitors a sense of arrival when they reach the entry, and sure, solid footing as they wait. I also like to make entry landings deep enough so that visitors are not right up against the door, which is not only uncomfortable for visitors but also invades the homeowner's personal space as the door is opened. A comfortable minimum depth for most stoops or landings is about 4 feet, and the stoop should be at least as wide as the door plus the door trim. If it can be larger, all the better.

Then you can accommodate a planted pot or urn, a doormat, maybe even a little bench or chair.

So how much stair calculation will you need to do? Frankly, not a whole lot. But you need to understand what goes into the thinking behind any stair design, and how and what the stairs connect to, and you need to be able to articulate this to your clients as you discuss design, as well as to the masons or carpenters doing the construction.

STONE WALLS

Stone walls are scrumptious. Beautiful, substantive, timeless. I love using them to define space, determine property extents, accent or enclose an area, and of course to retain slopes. As a designer you do not need to know how to build a wall yourself, although if you get the chance, I certainly recommend participating in the process, since nothing teaches like doing. But you do need to be knowledgeable about wall styles, types of stone, the way good walls are constructed, some basic terminology, and how to use stone walls to best effect.

Walls, like all masonry, can be dry-laid or constructed with mortar. They can also be made of veneered stone, either natural or cultured (man-made). Veneering is done by applying thin slices of stone onto a formed, poured concrete structure, a properly prepped stick structure, or over mortared cinder block or concrete block. The substrate will vary based on your locale and the particular application. The veneering is applied using a mortar compound specified by the manufacturer of the stone product. Exterior veneers are designed to withstand the elements and last a lifetime.

There are two basic types of stone wall: freestanding (double-faced) and retaining (single-faced).

Freestanding walls, which can be viewed from both sides, can be used to denote a property line or the extent of a particular area, or can enclose space, like a patio or garden room. They can be virtually any height and made of any stone material. I usually call them double-faced walls because of the translation to cost: these walls take more than twice the labor and materials to create than a retaining wall of the same length and height.

Retaining walls hold back (retain) a slope, and only their front sides are visible. Given their raison d'être, stone retaining walls are built with a slight lean into the embankment they are holding. This is called the batter and is generally a lean of about 6 degrees. To visualize this, picture an analog clock with the hands showing a time of 12:01. The hour hand is straight up (90 degrees to the vertical plane), and the minute hand makes an angle of approximately 6 degrees. Retaining walls can retain almost any degree of slope, and as with freestanding walls, they can be built just about any height and are crafted from a wide variety of materials.

Stone walls can also be constructed of single-standing or slightly leaning (retaining) stones. These types of walls are pretty unusual these days, but my husband grew up with "the largest single-stone standing wall in New England" in his backyard. This particular wall is monolithic and an impressive sight.

As with any masonry project, wall aesthetics is key, but the integrity of the structure is paramount. Assure that the people you hire can deliver the look and the quality you need for your clients. Only partner with proven masons who know their craft well and who will not short the construction of the project.

A New England fieldstone farmer's wall, designed with holes to allow for air circulation.

DESIGNING FREESTANDING WALLS

Since these walls can be viewed from more than one direction, it takes a knowledgeable mason to create a sturdy wall with an even visual rhythm of stones. All walls need to be prepped correctly, and that usually involves creating a footing. A footing will provide a stable base for a stone wall, and will prevent moisture and icing from heaving or otherwise undermining the wall. For a stone wall in New England, footings are usually about 12 inches deep. (Note that footings for stone walls do not need to go below the frost line.) Constructing a footing is important but pretty easy. A trench is dug to the required depth and runs the entire length of the wall. The footing trench is usually just a bit larger than the width of the wall. Crushed gravel is laid in the bottom and lightly tamped. If the wall is to be mortared, masons will usually pour a 4- to 6-inch layer of concrete on top of the gravel and will let that set up before starting the wall. The first course of stones should sit at or just below final finished grade. If the wall is to be dry-laid, the first course of stone will start right on the gravel, with no concrete required.

To increase the integrity of a freestanding wall, through-stones are

A new fieldstone and rubble wall, with tremendous granite pillars punctuating the ends.

employed at regular intervals. A through-stone is long enough to show a face (a side of the rock) on both sides of the wall, so it helps to lock both faces of the wall together. Joints in the stones should be staggered and should not line up one above the other, as running joints will weaken the wall. The saying for how to set stone to avoid running joints is "two over one and one over two," referring to putting two stones on top of one stone, and one stone on top of two stones to act as a strengthening bridge. To finish a wall, capstones may or may not be employed.

I have used freestanding walls along front property lines. If they are kept relatively low, say 3 feet high or less, they define the space but do not block the view of the house. They are also a gorgeous foil for plantings. Given the beauty of these walls, make sure the plant material you specify is airy enough to allow some windows in to glimpse the stone. Freestanding walls also delineate side property lines beautifully. And I love them for defining a garden room or focal area within a client's property.

From the formal to the rustic, walls can have a profound impact on how people perceive the landscape. Even common New England fieldstone walls—originally made as farmers cleared their fields year after year and piled stones along the property borders—have a rusticity and timeless elegance that is unforgettable. Classic.

DESIGNING RETAINING WALLS

We often use these walls at the base of a slope to set off the gardens above or below the wall. Oftentimes a high foundation exposure will call for a retaining wall to run the length of the house (or even the entire perimeter), so we give additional "instant" height to the installed foundation plantings, and ground the home visually. The perimeter of a patio is another lovely place to put a retaining wall. If you design the wall to finish at about 18 inches tall, and instruct your mason to finish the top with generous-sized capstones, it can serve as a perfect "seating wall," significantly increasing the number of people who can be comfortably seated when your clients are entertaining. Raising the soil outside of this patio wall brings the plant height up, increasing a feeling of enclosure and privacy, and giving the plant materials more emphasis.

Most of the stone walls I design serve as retaining walls of one type or another, and most are less than 3 feet tall. If your retaining wall will be 3 feet tall or less, and the slope is not greater than 45 degrees, nor deeper than 10 feet, you generally will not need an engineer's help. However, if you are retaining a large or particularly steep slope, engineering may be required. This is a good thing, because you want the retaining walls you build for your clients to be structurally sound and hold for many years.

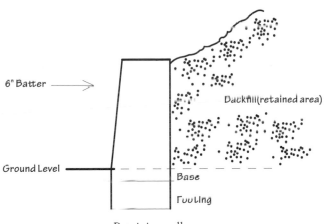

6° Batter

Backfill (retained area)

Ground Level

Base

Footing

Retaining wall.

Granite blocks create a beautiful and stable retaining wall along a front drive.

To retain a slope safely and effectively, the wall needs to be constructed to resist excessive settling or slipping, and to avoid collapsing or overturning under the pressure of the banking it is retaining. If you need to retain a large area, seek out the services of a structural or geotechnical engineer, or a mason who has a relationship with a structural expert. The engineer will take the finished height and depth of the area to be retained and augment this information with site data including soil conditions, local climate, plant materials to be retained on the slope, and materials for construction of the walls. Using this data, the engineer will determine the active earth pressure against the retaining wall, and will engineer the specifications for the wall footings, tiebacks (structural elements that tie the wall into the embankment), and other wall construction requirements.

FENCING

"Good fences make good neighbors." Most people mistakenly use this phrase from Robert Frost's "Mending Wall" to justify the erection of a fence or a wall. Frost, however, was suggesting that the walls between people—both literal and metaphorical—are a sad reality of our civilization, and he questioned the necessity of "walling in or walling out."

If Frost were around now, nearly a century after writing his poem, he might not question the need for fencing. Denser housing, busier roadways, relentless noise, constant stressors in our lives—people are looking for ways to create the illusion of security, privacy, and solitude. I can assure you that designing fencing will play a prominent role in your garden design business. You will quickly become conversant in the various uses for fencing, as well as the range of fencing styles and materials available.

Why a fence? Well, not all fences are ugly, nor are they all unappreciated by neighbors. Fencing done well can raise satisfaction on both sides of the fence. Fencing that blocks sight lines into a private area of your clients' yard can increase their sense of solitude. Screening a neighbor's overt view that looks onto a patio or deck can make your clients feel more secure and allow them to relax in their outdoor space. Privacy fencing can alleviate a sense of constant visual invasion between two neighbors and can help quiet simmering feuds. Privacy and screening fencing can even muffle noise.

Fences are by no means always for privacy. A low picket or split-rail fence across the front of a property can be a charming addition, creating just enough of a division between house and street to make the residents feel less exposed and more protected. Fences like this can even turn a front yard on a busy street into a safe place for children to play, and can keep other people's children and pets out.

A fence can be purely ornamental. I love creating charming "door yard" gardens by building simple picket enclosures around an entryway. With the right architecture, this greatly enhances the curb appeal of the house.

On the island of Nantucket, off the coast of Massachusetts, each home is required to have unique picket fencing on particular streets. Some of the design iterations are fabulous fancies created by the homeowner or their carpenter.

A well-designed fence can focus your client's view, screen out distracting sights, and direct sight lines and viewing angles. And remember, fences make great foils for glorious borders. They can give you a reason to design more gardens.

Fences come in a huge range of styles and are made with a wide variety of materials. Google "fencing types" and you'll have way more than

A mahogany-topped captain's fence creates a private space that offers a welcome to all.

enough reading for an afternoon. The fencing you recommend should be appropriate for the desired function (privacy, enclosure, accent, definition, ornamentation), complement the architectural style of the house, and work with the landscape. When presenting styles and materials, give the pros and cons of each, but recognize that some clients may feel overwhelmed by so many options. Make a solid recommendation. Your advice will help cut down the decision-making timeframe. And after all, you're the expert.

Get to know your local fence purveyors. Not all will carry the same products, so branch out a bit as you look to find key suppliers. Find out which companies build their own fencing, which ones install, which ones will design with you versus just taking orders. The key to having a beautiful, long-lasting fence is good construction, followed by proper installation. Look at finished jobs done by each company (I can see a schlock job half a mile away). In a well-installed fence, the panels will be plumb and square, posts will be plumb, and gates will operate well, with no rubbing, slumping, or catching.

A rustic wattle fence gives privacy to an entertaining area enclosed by a peeled-cedar pergola.

Prices for fencing vary dramatically, so know that there is "play" in most quotes. Large fencing companies with solid reputations probably won't work with you much on price, although some will give you a contractor's discount because you are in the trade. On the other hand, well-established companies will always stand by their product and their installation for years down the road.

Materials used for residential fencing include natural wood, pressure-treated wood, chain-link, aluminum, wrought iron, bamboo, electric, wire, and PVC or vinyl.

Wood is a lovely, classic choice, whether for a 6-foot stockade-style privacy fence or a rustic split-rail fence. Pressure-treated wood is used extensively, as are naturally rot-resistant woods. Here in New England much of our locally sourced fencing is made from eastern white cedar (*Thuja occidentalis*), a good wood for exterior application. The upside to wood fencing is that it is easy to work with, comes in zillions of styles, and can be made into a truly unique custom fence. Additionally, wood fencing

Solid fencing panels of stained cedar give privacy to the sanctuary in back, while English-lattice-topped panels provide a friendly screening along the property line.

almost always blends well with the house and gardens, quickly looking like a natural addition to the property. The downside is maintenance. Wood eventually decays, although a well-maintained fence, like a well-maintained natural wood deck, can last almost indefinitely. If painted, it will need repainting regularly. Wood fences take stain well, and stain or paint can increase the useful life of a wood fence, as well as customize it to the site with color. Periodically doing a light power washing of each wood fence, using a mild detergent, can get rid of moss, algae, and grime, and dislodge insects. Note, too, that wood posts that serve as uprights for fencing (or wood trellises, arbors, pergolas, vine posts, and so forth) should not be set into the ground in concrete, since invariably the post will rot where the two materials meet. Instead, dig the hole you need, set in the post, and add gravel around the post. Level, plumb, tamp, backfill. Done! This method is easier, the post will last far longer in the ground if not set in concrete, and when it's time to remove the post, you won't have a 100-pound blob of cement that requires a machine to urge out of the ground, nor will you need to pay to dispose of it. Overall my feeling is that you can never go wrong with wood fencing.

Chain-link is the security fence of choice around the United States (hey, probably around the world) and surrounds just about every junkyard, parking lot, lumberyard, garden center, and schoolyard. It is the least expensive option for metal fencing. I always think of chain-link as being serviceable, but it can give a very commercial or downscale look to areas where it is installed. In a residential setting, I have never specified chain-link for the front of a property, but I have used it in the back. It provides enclosure while allowing a view through to the surrounding area. The black-plastic-coated version tends to blend well with the surroundings if set back from people's gathering spots, like decks and patios. Sometimes chain-link is the obvious choice for securing an area or, say, fencing a dog. In its favor, it is durable, secure, not extremely costly, and graffiti resistant, and just about every fence company carries and installs it.

Aluminum fencing is attractive, low-key, secure, and easy to install. Many fencing companies in your area will carry aluminum, but it is also available online. Probably the most striking benefit of this fencing is its resistance to moisture. Aluminum does not rust like iron or steel, and will not swell, twist, or split like wood, even after years of exposure. Wood and vinyl expand and contract in extreme temperatures, causing premature aging, but aluminum remains virtually unaffected. Aluminum's main benefit over wood is greater durability and strength, but note that aluminum is not as strong as its iron and steel counterparts. If you are designing fencing that is going to be subject to heavy stresses, you need to take that into consideration. Ornamental gates, post caps, and balusters are great additions to an aluminum fence design, and any aluminum fencing is available in a variety of colors that can complement the house. While somewhat expensive, aluminum provides a beautiful and highly durable fencing solution.

Wrought iron makes glorious fencing. A wrought iron fence defines property lines in a classic manner while still allowing views of the landscape and architecture. Almost a relic of days gone by, iron is extremely strong, but it does need periodic maintenance. It rusts, so must be maintained to fight oxidation wherever it is exposed to the moisture in the air. Wrought iron is expensive, but the elegant look it delivers is the benchmark for estate-quality fencing.

Aluminum gates and fencing with substantial granite pillars resemble old-world wrought iron, and bring an estate-like feel to this striking entrance.

Bamboo fencing entered the market a number of years ago. I designed and installed a glorious bamboo fence in the mid-1990s, and it has weathered but still looks beautiful. Bamboo is a vital construction product in the tropics because it is easily obtainable and naturally resistant to rot, insects, and water. It is also highly renewable, so using bamboo means going green. Bamboo fences can give an Asian edge to any design. They blend in beautifully and become part of the backdrop for any mixed border.

Electric fencing is typically used to hold in livestock or keep out pesky critters like deer and raccoons. I have never recommended an electric fence to a client—there hasn't been any need—but I would not hesitate to do so. These can be fairly easily installed and use just the tiniest amount of electricity. To keep electric fences operating well, keep plant materials from growing high enough to touch the wires.

Invisible dog fencing has become popular in the suburbs. This consists of a transformer-base station, linked to a slender, subsurface wire that surrounds the area where the dogs are allowed. Each dog wears a special collar that beeps a warning when the dog gets within 6 feet of the underground wire. As the dog gets closer to the wire, the beeps get more insistent, until finally the collar delivers a small electric shock. It takes most dogs just a day or two to get used to the system. I highly recommend that anyone starting to use this system test it and feel the collar shock themselves before putting it on their pet. The shock setting should often be adjusted lower. I know many people feel this kind of fencing is cruel, but seeing your dog dead in the street is pretty horrid too. I have not recommended an invisible dog fence to anyone, but there are existing systems at many of my clients' homes. I will tell you that the main involvement I have with dog fences is repairing them. The surround wire is slender and usually only about 3 inches in the ground, so it is easily cut by even a trowel. When the wire is cut, the base unit gives an alarm. I keep a wire repair kit in my car (about the size of a little tin of cough drops) along with spare wire for splicing. We can fix a dog fence wire in about three minutes once we locate the break. A word to the wise: if you have been doing any digging at a property with a dog fence, check the status of the dog fence system before you leave. Better to fix it when you are right there than to get an irate call at 10:00 p.m.

PVC or vinyl fencing is fairly popular, but I am so horrified by the PVC industry that I would never specify any fencing made of this material. PVC is among the most environmentally hazardous products on the market. Its manufacture releases dioxin (the most potent carcinogen known to humankind) and other persistent pollutants into the air, water, and land. Randomly tested people who live in the general vicinity of PVC-manufacturing plants have been shown to have one hundred times the national average of dioxin in their bodies. No wonder the cancer rates in places like Mossville, Louisiana—located near four PVC plants in a region known as Cancer Alley—are many times the national average. In spite of these documented effects, the federal government has bowed to pressure to keep the PVC industry's air emissions largely unregulated.

But the active toxicity of PVC does not end with manufacturing. PVC is useless without the addition of a plethora of toxic chemical stabilizers, which leach, flake, and outgas from the PVC throughout its lifetime, raising rates of asthma, lead poisoning, infertility, and many cancers. When PVC burns, not only does it release yet more dioxin and other pollutants into the environment, but the fumes can kill you (and the firefighter coming to your rescue). PVC cannot be recycled, and when dumped in landfills further leaches toxic additives.

We can fight this industry by being conscientious consumers. A host of alternatives are available, and there is no need to purchase or specify PVC products of any kind, period.

My environmental objections aside, I just do not like PVC fencing. It's shiny. There, I said it. There is something about a shiny, reflective, white vinyl fence that screams "plastic" and "cheap." Are they cheap? Heck, no. Vinyl fencing will run you quite a bit more than wood. What brings people to want vinyl is its reputation for being almost maintenance free and highly weather resistant. However, vinyl fencing tends to get chalky as it breaks down, and moss eventually grows on the parts least exposed to sun. To keep it looking fresh, it needs periodic power washing or hand-scrubbing.

Have I ever used a vinyl fence in my installations? Yes, in three instances, twice when the clients insisted and once when I didn't yet know better.

CHAPTER SIX

Patios, Decks, and Other Living Spaces

THINK I'VE MADE IT CLEAR that being a garden designer will enable you to branch off into other areas of outdoor design. As I think about this, I find it ironic that I now spend considerably less time designing actual gardens than I do designing everything else. The design of gardens and plantings seems to have morphed from the entire basis of my business to what is now the icing on the cake, even though I still feel that the gardens are what allow the entire exterior design to become a cohesive whole.

Outdoor spaces fall into the important category of "everything else." As a garden designer you will aim to make your clients' landscapes not only more beautiful but also more functional. If, after working with you, your clients are getting better use and more enjoyment from their property, you are doing your job right. Much of their increased enjoyment will come from you designing outdoor spaces specifically for them and their family and friends. Designing a better outdoor living space, like a wonderful patio or deck, effectively enlarges their home, giving them another "room" in which to play. These are spaces for your clients to sit and enjoy the outdoors, delight in their gardens, dine, lounge, or just watch their children or pets play.

PATIOS AND OTHER FLAT-STONE DESIGNS

Much of the stone work you design will be flat. I build patios and other flat-stone creations three to one over wall work. Part of this is because walls are expensive, and part is because clients are often convinced they need a patio but may not be convinced they need a wall to define their side yard or surround the patio. Sometimes it comes down to money. Flat-stone creations take less stone and less labor to build per square foot, so they deliver more bang for your client's buck.

Patios are often used when there is minimal elevation change from the main floor of the house to the level of the outdoor space you are creating. A rough average in elevation change would be one to perhaps five steps down from the house to the patio level. Patios can be built several steps above ground level, but having a patio that is much higher than that means adding a lot of retaining walls around it, and lots and lots of fill to raise the patio space to the desired height. This starts to get costly.

Like walls, patios and other flat stone work can be constructed with mortar or can be dry-laid. Given our freeze-thaw cycles here in New England, nearly all the flat work I design for my clients is dry-laid. It just holds up better over time. I admit, though, to envying the types of detailed flat work, exterior tile, and mosaics that can be done in warmer climates. The work is glorious!

As with driveways and walkways, much of the secret to good flat work is preparation. If you make sure the foundation is prepped correctly for your climate and for the materials you are working with, your horizontal stone work should install easily and perform well for many years.

Styles of flat stone installations run the gamut from the formal to the rustic or funky. The only limit is your imagination.

Size does matter, particularly when crafting outdoor spaces. One of the most common mistakes I see when I come to talk with new clients is the size of their patio (or deck). Too small. Too small to function correctly, too small to be enjoyed, often even too small for the scale of the house or yard. Whether you are designing a patio that is free-form or formal, make room for a table and enough chairs for the homeowner's family, perhaps a chaise or two, maybe side chairs or benches if extra seating space is required, and space for moving around. To do this right, you need to think in three dimensions.

Here's a simplified example. It might look good on paper to have a 4-foot round outdoor table with four chairs positioned comfortably, centered on a round patio that is 12 feet in diameter. You'd allow a generous

Balcony. Platform projecting from the wall of a building, usually enclosed by a railing and balusters. Think Juliet.

Courtyard. Outdoor area surrounded by buildings on three or four sides, or enclosed by a building, or adjacent to a building and enclosed by walls.

Deck. A roofless area adjoining a house, generally constructed of wood or faux-wood materials.

Gallery. Balcony or passage running along the wall of a building.

Lanai. In Hawaii, an open-roofed porch or veranda, often used for outside living space.

Loggia. Covered, open-sided walkway running along one side of a building.

Patio. Paved recreation area, usually at the rear of the home.

Pergola. A framed structure consisting of upright columns or posts with a latticed roof, designed to support climbing plants and provide shade.

Porch. Raised platform covered by a roof that runs along the side of a house, or a covered shelter at the entrance.

Portico. Covered entrance or walkway.

Terrace. Flat roof used as living space, or a paved or grassy area immediately outside and on the same level as a building, used for sitting or eating outdoors. Can be used interchangeably with *patio*.

Veranda. Porch, usually with a roof, sometimes partially enclosed, that extends along the outside wall of a building.

This glorious rooftop patio uses bluestone in a very formal style. The drama of the space is accentuated by the beautiful pergola.

2 feet for each chair depth (the average chair is 18 to 20 inches deep), and then add 2 feet beyond that for scooching the chairs back and getting in and out of the table. Simple, yes? No. In reality, the chair when occupied or pushed back from the table (the usual position on a patio), needs nearly 3 to 4 feet of space for itself, even if the occupant of the chair has their knees under the table. Then, to allow movement *behind* an occupied chair—for people getting up for more food, answering the phone, whatever—another 3 feet is necessary, although 4 feet is better. Here's where we need to think in three dimensions. A person's butt can take up considerably more space than their feet (grin!), and butt and stomach height are just about the same height as a chair back; trying to push one around the other, well, we need enough room to do this comfortably. Allowing adequate space would tell us we need a patio that is 4 feet (the table) plus 3 feet on each side (for the chairs) plus 4 feet on each side (for the walk-around room). This is 4 + 3 + 3 + 4 + 4 or a patio that is 18 feet in diameter. Wow. Big difference. Remember geometry? The area of a circle is πR^2 where π is 3.14 and R is the radius of the circle. The square footage of a 12-foot-diameter (6-foot-radius) patio is 3.14 × 36 feet or 113 square feet. The square footage of an 18-foot-diameter (9-foot-radius) table is 3.14 × 81 feet or 254 square feet, or more than twice the area of the smaller patio layout. So you can see that an 18-foot patio gives us considerably more room than a 12-foot patio!

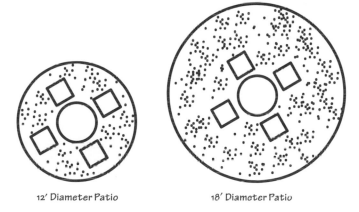

12′ Diameter Patio   18′ Diameter Patio

Two round patios. The 12-foot patio allows no room for
movement, while the 18-foot version offers plenty of space.

If we have a seating wall around said patio, I always increase the diameter by yet another foot or two. Seating walls can impinge on the available space, making it feel a little smaller than it is—you don't want your clients skinning their knees on stone! And the available move-around space really is smaller if you have someone sitting on the wall.

If there is a drop-off around the patio you are designing, or stairs that connect, add even more space to the dimensions. You don't want a person snapping an ankle, or a chair leg slipping over the edge.

I used a simple circle in my example, but there are as many forms for patios as there are homes in America. Free-form layouts of patios are organic and should follow the intended flow of people through the space. Have fun with them while making sure there is enough room to accommodate furnishings and people. Formal patio spaces are equally lovely to design, and there is great left-brain satisfaction to developing this kind of space, again, while keeping your eye on the functional space requirements.

DECKS

I probably design a deck as often as I design a patio. Decks can be just 6 inches off the ground, but most are higher. They can come off the house just a step or two down from house level, but they can be many feet off the ground. Decks usually allow people to access the grounds of the property. If you are designing a deck that will not be connected to the ground, I would probably call it a balcony or porch. If you are designing a deck that sits very high up and you want to link it to the ground below, add stairs with periodic landings and turns in direction. They are not only effective and beautiful but also safe, since if you fall on a staircase with periodic landings, you generally will not be falling more than five or so stairs.

Terracing the actual decking can give a spectacular effect, allowing you to design distinctly different functional spaces that step people down from the highest deck level to the ground plane. The eating area, the grilling deck, the chaise deck, the hot tub deck. Use your imagination! Deck terraces also beautifully integrate decking that comes off of a house fairly high up, so that it doesn't look like a space platform dangling off the side of the building.

So, where to begin? As you get to know your clients, you will develop valid reasons for suggesting a deck: more outdoor entertaining, another exit to the backyard, taking advantage of a great view, dining al fresco, easier access to grilling, sunbathing. The features you design into a deck should reflect the lifestyle your clients want to live. Whatever the reasons for this new deck, as you start to design it you need to keep several questions in mind: What are the options for locating the deck? How do your clients want to use it? What's the right size? What are the legal issues?

LOCATION, LOCATION, LOCATION

There may be one completely obvious place the deck should go, but not always. In many instances you might be building the client's first deck, or working on new construction that still has some "customizable" features. Maybe your clients already have a deck, but it looks over their neighbor's collection of rusty muscle cars. In those instances, there may be more than one location to consider.

This terraced section was added to an existing deck, so we used the same pressure-treated materials and stained it all to make the new resemble the old. A seating platform allows parents to watch their small children at play. Vertical boards were used to screen a storage area underneath the staircase for toys and gardening tools.

It's nice to have a deck come off a kitchen or family room. These rooms typically have a high degree of activity, which is a good reason to suggest they have access to the outside. You can always create access where there is none; you could add a doorway or a set of French doors to invite in more light and grandly open onto a deck. Or you could build a walkway that links to just the right detached deck location. There is no law stating that decks need to be attached to the house.

Does your client have a particularly nice view they could see better depending on the deck's location? Maybe there's a water view to one side of the house—we can exit onto a deck from many different rooms of the house, including bedrooms. However, unless you're designing a private deck or balcony, always make sure a deck has at least one "public" doorway into the house.

A deck on the north or east side of a house will be cooler in the afternoons. A deck on the south or west will be warm during the heat of day, but you can cool it down in the summer with an awning or pergola. If there is a great location to watch sunsets, design the deck with an open view to the west. Want quiet? Put the deck on the side of the house with the least amount of traffic. Are there bothersome winds? Locate the deck on the lee side of the house, or include a windscreen. Adding a hot tub? Privacy might be paramount. Locate the deck so that screening plantings can quickly provide the seclusion your clients want. Sometimes it is easier to design functionality when you see yourself in the space. Mentally walk through the house, exit to the new deck, and "use" the proposed space. What additional elements would make the experience more enjoyable?

FORM FOLLOWS FUNCTION

What will this new space allow your clients to do? This is a bit about making dreams come true. Grilling? Make sure the grill is located where it can be seen from the kitchen. Adding color and drama? Include pots of bodacious, bright tropicals. Maybe your clients would like to add a security gate and allow their children to play in this protected spot. If they will be dining outside, incorporate a lovely table and comfortable chairs. What about adding soft mood lighting to enjoy the deck well into the evenings?

Part of your job will be to suggest ways your clients can enjoy the outdoors more. Are they going to be entertaining? Do they need benches for seating and storage? Ask if they would prefer one large gathering area or several smaller spots for more intimate conversations. If they are either empty nesters or just starting out, perhaps they would rather have a cozy space for two or four people? She has always wanted an herb garden right off the kitchen. No problem. He wants a quiet spot to play his guitar. Design a bench that is wide enough to accommodate both guitarist and guitar, and build in a small music stand with clips to prevent the music from blowing away. These little touches matter. What about disguising traffic noise? Add a comfortably sized, plug-and-play bubbling fountain and an elegant wind chime. You can have such fun dreaming up ways for your clients to use their new outdoor space. If you build it, they will come.

FINDING THE RIGHT SIZE

The deck you design should be in balance with the size of the house. Simply put, scale is everything. A deck that is too small on a large house looks just as awkward as a huge deck on a tiny house. Study your photographs and measurements of the area. It's actually pretty rare to go too big. Also, the expanse of a large deck can be softened by well-designed plantings that integrate the deck with the larger landscape. Most homeowners and designers err on the side of designing too small a space, so the deck ends up being much less functional than it could be.

When first designing this kind of space, you might feel uncomfortable relating to the layout. At this point I see the space in my mind's eye: I sit on the benches, I know the view angles. If you don't see this at first, you'll get there. Until you do, you can lay out the proposed deck with stakes and string, and stand in the space to experience it. Okay, so this might be tough if the deck is coming off the second floor, but you can still mark out the same footprint on the ground and walk into the space. You might have to do this for your clients—few will be able to visualize as well as you do—so become comfortable with proposing space this way.

One of the things I see constantly are teensy 8-by-10-foot decks attached to three- to four-bedroom homes. What on earth can you do in 80 square feet? Not a whole lot. This wouldn't be a bad size for two

117

chaise lounges and a small cocktail table, maybe a pot or two of geraniums, but it doesn't provide room for much else. Any deck needs to allow room for furnishings, access to the furnishings, and room to get around and through all the furnishings, people, and accessories in the space.

The difference in cost between a deck that is too small and one that is the right size is often insignificant. Much of the labor that goes into a deck is in the structure built to support it. Going larger may take a few more supports and a little more decking, but the labor won't be considerably more. Another tip is to design decks in even-numbered, 2-foot increments (say, 16 feet by 12 feet). This allows your contractor to purchase and use standard lengths of wood, which minimizes waste and can save a little labor.

LEGAL CONSIDERATIONS

Check out the local zoning ordinances before sharing any proposed deck design with your clients. This is one of the first things I do when I'm

This deck looked huge when construction began, but once completed, it was a beautiful, functional size. A trio of small children and a fear of splinters made the homeowners choose a composite product for the floor. The pergola is Spanish cedar, which weathered to the same soft gray color as the decking. Photo courtesy of Heather D. Jarnot.

working on a new site where I know we'll be doing more than planting gardens. Local zoning ordinances will have building considerations for decks, the height and location of constructed privacy screening (fences, pergolas, arbors), and minimum distances from any structure (including decks) to the lot lines, which are called set-back requirements. For example, in my residential zone, we are required to keep any building or deck 40 feet from the front lot line, 50 feet from the rear lot line, and 20 feet from each of the side lot lines. We are allowed fencing no higher than 6 feet, or up to 8 feet with a zoning variance and no objections from abutters, and fencing is allowed to be installed right on the property boundary (some zoning bylaws require you to be 1 to 3 feet back from the property line).

Some municipalities limit the percentage of square footage you can cover on a lot. Say the house plus the garage plus the three-season room covers 40% of the 7000-square-foot lot size, and you want to add a 500-square-foot deck. This would bring the total lot coverage to 42%. If the statute allows up to 50% of the surface area to be covered, you're fine. If it only allows 38%, you either need to pare down the deck size, or go through the process of requesting a variance, which is a time-consuming and often costly process. If you feel the functionality of the deck will not be unduly affected by paring it down, go ahead and do it so you can move on. Another option is to design the deck so as to stay just under the maximum lot coverage, and then step down the deck to a stone patio (which for some bizarre reason doesn't count as lot coverage). Of course, acquiring this information before you present design options to clients will help to avoid disappointment and embarrassment.

Because safety is the paramount consideration in building codes, every building department has restrictions relative to height of railings, how far apart balusters may be placed, and how many inches the decking can be off the ground until railings are required. They will also have restrictions on stair construction, including allowable riser heights, step widths, railing requirements, and landings. In some towns, you are required to include landings after x number of stairs.

Make sure there are no easements in the area where you plan to put the deck. Easements are permanent allowances recorded on the deed for the property; they entitle someone use of real estate owned by another person. The type of easement you would be most concerned with would be an easement "in gross." This type of easement might have granted the right for a utility to place power lines through the area, or allow the gas company to run gas lines through. A drainage easement would allow storm drains on the street to drain through piping that has been laid within the easement area on the property. The homeowners should know if they have an easement on any area of their property, but if they've lived there a while, they could have forgotten. Certainly any easements will be indicated on a certified plot plan.

Assuredly, your local ordinances will be different from those in my area. After years in this business, I learned the hard way to always check out local code before finalizing any proposed design. I was working a design-build project with another designer. We had hired an architect to design an elegant pergola to stand off the client's sunroom. Design it he did, and we presented the design to the clients. They loved it! We specified all materials and then asked our general contractor to price it. He priced it, we presented pricing to the clients, and they approved and signed off. The contractor went to apply for the building permit and was promptly turned down. Nearly the entire pergola was going to sit within the side set-back requirement for this residential zone. The architect had not checked the set-back requirements. Nor had I or the other designer, assuming the architect had done so. Major egg on our faces, and the clients were furious. The potentially fatal side effect from something like this is that it undermines the confidence you've been working to build with your client. Our clients could have easily killed the project right then and there. Luckily the situation ultimately turned out well—beautifully, in fact—but there were some uncomfortable moments, and we were never allowed to build the pergola.

How do you avoid this type of situation? Pay a quick visit to the local building department and get the necessary information. Go in, introduce yourself as a landscape designer, and tell them you are designing a landscape that will include a deck in their town (I never give client names). They might ask for the street address, because each town usually has several different zones, each with their own specific limitations. Go ahead and give them the location. Let them know that you will be using a carpenter or general contractor who will be pulling a permit, and that you're looking for information in order to design the deck in concert with local code. I have always found building departments most helpful.

Building permits are required for many construction projects, particularly if they involve stick (wood) construction. Make sure your contractor or the homeowner pulls the required permits for any work you are doing. Playing nice with the local building departments assures that you will have a long and healthy working relationship with them. I have even received referrals from several building department inspectors.

Here is an irony. I consider stone walls and stone patios to be permanent additions to the landscape. I think of decks as being relatively temporary since they have to be replaced periodically (the life of decking is anywhere from ten to twenty years depending on several factors). In Massachusetts you need a building permit to construct a deck of any size, and there are several points at which your carpentry contractor will need inspections and signoffs on the permit. However, you do not need a building permit to construct a patio or most stone walls. Go figure.

MATERIALS

Until recently our choices for decking materials were limited to pressure-treated pine, cedar, redwood, or imported tropical hardwoods, but composite decking products have dramatically expanded the options, and even aluminum and PVC products have entered the decking realm. So how do you choose a decking product to recommend to your clients?

Just about all decks are framed using pressure-treated wood, so you will be deciding on material for the decking and the railing systems. The first question you need to answer is whether you are going to recommend real wood or a manmade product. There are pros and cons to both.

Natural wood decks continue to set the standard for aesthetics. They almost always complement the home and are a beautiful transition from house to yard. In my estimation, nothing else comes close to the beauty and warmth offered by real wood.

Wood decks can last several decades but do require more maintenance than decks made of composites or other manmade materials. They should be looked over annually for insect damage, warping, cracking or checking, loose fasteners, and water damage. Optimally they should be cleaned every year and treated with a UV-inhibiting stain or wood preservative. Any major splitting or raising of the grain should be lightly sanded down and stained or sealed. And of course, natural wood decks and railings can splinter, potentially hurting little hands and bare feet.

Pressure-treated southern yellow pine is an option, but it is not a product I recommend. Of course you can create a functional and good-looking deck out of pressure-treated wood, but when I'm dealing with well-designed and well-built homes, pressure-treated decking just doesn't cut it. That said, pressure-treated wood has some benefits. The cost is comparatively low, every carpenter knows how to work with it, and it can last just about indefinitely. These decks can be stained a variety of subtle colors. It's good to clean them annually to remove grime, algae, and moss, but this is not a requirement. Even though pressure-treated decking is very hard and durable, it is still wood and can check, warp, split, splinter, rot, and age poorly.

In 2004 the EPA took pressure-treated decking containing chromated copper arsenate (CCA) off the market for residential use because of the dangers inherent with leaching chromium and arsenic. CCA pressure-treated wood has been replaced with alkaline copper quat (ACQ types B and D) and copper azole (CBA-A and CA-B). Note that rot resistance is now offered in different levels; when you need a pressure-treated wood that will withstand ground contact, make sure your contractor is purchasing the ground-contact certified version. Plastic tags on each pressure-treated board indicate how the wood was preserved and for what level of rot resistance.

Redwood and western red cedar are domestic wood products that make beautiful decks. Both are naturally rot and insect resistant, and can withstand years of weathering. They can be treated with a stain or penetrating wood oil (with or without colorant), or be left to weather to a silvery gray. Annual cleaning is recommended, which will remove grime, moss, and any detritus that has collected. As with any deck, the integrity of the fasteners, support structure, and railings should be checked annually.

A number of tropical hardwoods are spectacular (though expensive) alternatives for decking. Considerably harder than domestic redwood or cedar, tropical hardwoods are phenomenally resistant to decay and insects, more resistant to scratching, and easier to clean. These woods soften in color over time, and like all wood, they swell and shrink as they continuously absorb moisture and dry out in an exterior environment. Ipe is a gorgeous wood; it is so hard it will quickly dull most saw blades, and every screw needs a pilot hole. Tigerwood is gorgeous, stable, and easier to install than most tropical wood species. Massaranduba is a deep red brown and even harder than ipe. Red tauari is reddish tan with a tight grain like mahogany. Cumaru is golden with strong grain lines like oak. Other tropical hardwoods used for decking include jarrah, ekki, azobe, teak, and mahogany, to name just a few.

Words of extreme caution: even as I sit here recommending wood for decking, I cringe. The increased demand for tropical hardwoods has expanded dramatically. This demand is helping to drive illegal and destructive logging in the rain forests of the Amazon, Africa, and Southeast Asia. In most of these areas, forestry industry practices are still unsustainable, although some countries are working towards managing timber farming in a more sustainable way. Many beautiful woods fall into this category, including teak, mahogany, Brazilian cherry, and others. What can we as designers do? One way to help is to recommend domestic wood decking products, or alternative products like composite or aluminum, to your clients and explain your reasoning. This can bite you in the proverbial arse, however, for some people want that which is the most rare or difficult to obtain. Or as one client retorted to me, "Love, I just want what I want. That's all."

If tropical hardwoods are the choice, know that it is now possible to purchase products that have been grown sustainably, often in plantations. Ask your lumber purveyor to show you that the wood has a certificate of sustainable forest management, such as accreditation from the Forest Stewardship Council (FSC). This helps to guarantee your project is not contributing to the destruction of tropical rain forests.

Composites and other decking materials can also be appropriate for certain lifestyles and locations. Open up any shelter magazine and you will see a myriad of advertisements for these kinds of products, which are revolutionizing the deck industry. Although alternative decking products can cost 50% to as much as 100% more than natural wood decks, many of your clients will have had a wood deck in the past and may be

Knowing the correct names for the major components of a deck will allow you to be more comfortable as you discuss deck projects with clients and contractors. Please remember that all lumber used in any decking project should be suitable for exterior use, and any materials touching the ground should be specifically rated for ground contact.

Arbor. Structure used to support vines or hanging plants. Can provide shade.

Awning. Overhead covering that provides shade and protection from the weather.

Baluster, spindle. Vertical member of a railing, in between the posts. Local building codes dictate the spacing.

Balustrade. Complete, assembled rail system.

Bridging. Blocking used between joists to add structural stability and prevent twisting.

Decking. Material that makes up the surface of the deck.

Deck post. Vertical lumber that sits on the footing and supports the girders and deck.

Fascia. Trim board used to cover the front and side rim joists.

Flashing. Material used to prevent water from entering the home. On a deck, often used where the ledger board bolts to the house. Required by code in some locales.

Footing. Below-grade concrete support that serves as the foundation on which the deck is built.

Girder, bearer. Lateral support beam that the deck joists sit on.

Joist. Any of the timbers that make the substructure of the floor. The decking is fastened to the decking joists. Joist spacing is determined by the length the deck is spanning and is subject to local code.

Joist hanger. Metal bracket used to secure the joist end to the ledger board.

Landing. Platform between flights of stairs or at the termination of a flight of stairs. Frequently used where stairs change direction.

Lattice. Framework of crossed, interwoven strips, usually used for privacy screening and to skirt decks. Lattice that crosses on the diagonal is American lattice; lattice on the straight is English lattice. With American lattice, the eye is drawn to the diagonal pattern, so the pattern advances and stands out. Conversely, the eye forgives the right angles of English lattice, so it is much quieter in the landscape and a nicer complement to any architecture.

Ledger board, ledger plate, stringer. Board bolted to the house to which the joist hangers will be fastened.

Post base. Metal brackets used to securely fasten the deck post to the footing.

Post top. Decorative top that can be added to a railing post.

Rail. Top or bottom horizontal member that balusters or spindles are attached to.

Rise. Vertical distance of one step.

Riser. Vertical board in back of a stair tread.

Skirt, skirting. Material (lattice, vertical boards, and so forth) used to screen the view into the area underneath a deck.

Stringer. Framing for treads and risers to be attached to in a staircase. Also can refer to the ledger board.

Tread. Horizontal part of the stair that is stepped on.

Trellis. Structure designed to support climbing plants. Can provide screening or shade.

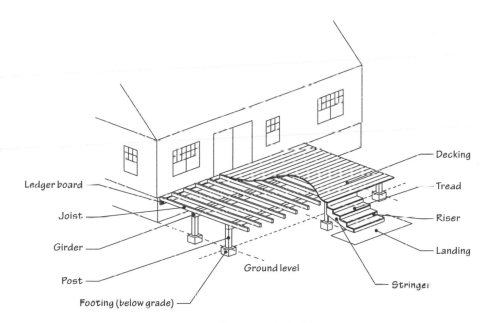

Anatomy of a deck.

well aware of the maintenance requirements and looking for an alternative. While none of the alternatives are yet able to replicate the beauty of real wood, they come pretty close. They are also easy to maintain, rot and insect resistant, nonsplintering, cool even in hot locations, and feature quickly installed, attractive railing systems.

Some of the decking systems available nationally go beyond just the decking surface. Many come with their own snap-and-lock railing systems, saving time and labor dollars and ensuring no splinters. I am a great fan of the invisible fasteners that many composite decking manufacturers have pioneered. This means that no screws or nails show, so the decking surface is unblemished. There's no dimpling to hold water, and no screw holes to invite rot. Of course, invisible fastening systems can be used for natural wood, too.

Before falling in love with a type of composite decking you've found in a magazine or online, learn what types of composite decking are being sold by the better lumberyards in your area. Doesn't pay to fall in love if there are no distributors in your state. Also, you need to see the actual product. You need to hold pieces in your hand and see an installed example before you can really judge the aesthetics.

Showing samples of composite decking to your clients gives them a wide range of colors, textures, and grain patterns to choose from. Note that there is a learning curve to working with composite decking products. Make sure the contractor you work with is knowledgeable about any product you are asking him or her to use.

Aluminum is a new entry in the decking products arena, heralded as easy to clean and maintain, with no need for sanding, staining, or sealing. This decking will not age as quickly as natural wood or composite decking; will not rot, decay, splinter, or be infested with insects; and is barefoot friendly, remaining cool on even the hottest days.

Aluminum offers a wide range of colors and textures. Some products are even watertight, allowing you to use them over a flat roof or to provide rain protection for an area underneath the constructed deck. Most aluminum decking systems offer matching railings and stairs, and some come with a twenty-year warrantee.

Although aluminum decking is more expensive initially, it may be worth it when you consider that the deck will need virtually no annual maintenance and will have a longer life. Further, every component of an aluminum deck can be recycled.

PVC or vinyl decking is also available, but I stand by my opinion to just say no. For more on the toxic qualities of every product manufactured by the PVC industry, see "Fencing" in chapter 5.

LEVERAGING A CONTINUED INCOME STREAM

The work associated with designing and building a deck doesn't have to stop with the end of the construction. Deck maintenance can become part of your business offering. Annual power washing, staining or oiling, inspection of fasteners and structural components—this can add up to a nice "spring start" business. It provides a good service to your clients, gives you a tidy jumpstart income, and puts you in your client's mind and face at the beginning of the season, which can prompt them to think about additional services you can provide. Pots, anyone? Another border along the edge of the woods? Water feature this year? You'd be surprised what that little "I'm here!" tickle can net you in additional work.

OUTDOOR KITCHENS

Outdoor kitchens are one of the hottest home improvement trends, and garden designers who are stretching themselves can hop right on the bandwagon. Nothing makes dining outside easier than a fully stocked kitchen. Most outdoor kitchens have a great grill, of course, but they also often include sinks, refrigerators, bars, serving or buffet areas, and even pizza ovens or fireplaces. These spaces are a blend of all the disciplines used in garden design: masonry, decking, water, patio, electricity, lighting, space utilization and enclosure, and seating. Plus, of course, cooking. Designing an outdoor kitchen should be fun and fairly easy for any good landscape designer.

Typically outdoor kitchens are built onto existing patios or decks right next to the house. This makes it fairly easy to tap into the home's electrical, gas, and plumbing systems. Having the outdoor kitchen within a few steps of the indoor kitchen also makes it easier for homeowners to zip inside to get another utensil or condiment. Design of the outdoor kitchen should be compatible with the architectural features, colors, and materials used on the house. To cover all details, check with the local building department to see if a building permit is required, or if there are fire codes that dictate clearance requirements for the grill or oven.

The layout should consider the relationship between the indoor and outdoor kitchens. Your design should allow for easy passage from the house to the outdoor kitchen work or preparation area, as well as from the cooking area to the outdoor serving area. I have seen wonderful outdoor kitchens organized by grouping all of the prep areas separately from the cooking and cleaning areas. Some kitchens are organized by traffic flow: first station, food enters and is stored; second, food is prepped; third, food is cooked; fourth, food is served. Still others are organized with the classic kitchen work triangles of splitting the distances between sink, fridge, and stove. I think outdoor kitchens require a little more elbow room than interior kitchens, so plan for generous counter space around the sink or cooking surfaces, and plenty of preparation and serving space.

I sometimes start by locating the optimal proximities to electric, water, waste, and gas hookups. If those work out well relative to the appliances we will be incorporating, and if I can see possibilities for good traffic flow, this can be a good starting point.

If you are planning an outdoor kitchen as part of a number of spaces that you are developing for a client, bring all of the elements together in a single, cohesive design. Cooking and dining areas, lounging areas, a pool or spa—all often coexist. Plan for smooth traffic flow between areas, and make sure the cook is not isolated from the rest of the outdoor activities.

Appliances and materials have to be able to take all types of weather, all year, so find those rated for outdoor use. Here in New England outdoor kitchens take some winterizing. We shut off the water to outdoor sinks and let the pipes drain, unplug refrigerators, and clean out any shelving or storage areas. My family grills all winter, as do most of my clients, so there is no need to turn off gas or shut down the grill.

When choosing materials, consider that stainless steel resists corrosion and is easy to keep clean. It is often the material of choice for appliances, and even countertops. Do think about how your countertop selection will perform in bright sunlight; many surfaces get hot to the touch, even to the point of burning skin. Also make sure the countertops and appliances will not cause irritatingly bright reflections back into the house. I've seen stainless steel appliances and glass surfaces reflect so much sunlight back into the house that the clients had to pull their shades on bright days. Countertops and decking or patio materials should be easy to clean and degrease. If you recommend the right materials to your clients, often dishwashing detergent, a little scrub brush, and a strong hose blast will be all the cleaning products they'll ever need.

Lighting should be designed for effective performance of tasks, like cooking and cleanup, and you should include fixtures that promote a nice dining experience after dark. I am a big fan of dimmers, which can make all the difference in how your clients and their guests experience the space. Of course, safety and path lighting should also be incorporated where necessary.

Add music to the mix. This can be the simplest, least expensive addition to the outside space that you are designing, but it can be the perfect finishing touch. Music helps mask ambient traffic and neighborhood noise, and can easily set a mood. Exterior speakers are available in a number of styles, and the addition of speakers and a small CD changing system certainly won't break the bank.

An outdoor kitchen can completely change how people use their homes. Nothing makes entertaining or dining outside easier than a beautifully equipped outdoor kitchen. And outdoor kitchens are so popular, they are usually a sound renovation investment—good information for your clients to know if they are pondering resale within a few years.

FIRE PITS AND OUTDOOR FIREPLACES

Outdoor fires are unbelievably hot. Yes, pun intended, but along with the lust for water features, there is an equal desire for fire. Call it a primal reaction, a cellular memory of sorts. We as a species have been using fire for tens of thousands of years. Fire resonates with the promise of warmth, food, light, comfort. To our ancestors, fire often meant the difference between survival and death. No wonder fire is such a compelling and captivating feature.

Fire pits and outdoor fireplaces have become a staple of outdoor living spaces. Backyard entertaining can continue when the sun goes down, even if there is a chill in the air. You can melt marshmallows and nibble s'mores while staying toasty warm by the dancing flames. From a rustic, stone-ringed pit to a glorious, two-story, fieldstone hearth, outdoor fires are the rage.

As you consider adding fire to a design, first call the local fire safety office and ask what the local fire prevention code is. In my area, fire pits or anything with an open flame must be a minimum of 20 feet away from any combustible surface. They should also not be sited under low-hanging tree branches or beneath a pergola or arbor. Safety is paramount when we're talking about fire features.

There are a zillion different portable fire pits on the market. These can be a lovely addition to an outdoor party or just to sit and relax nearby with a glass of wine. The benefits are that you can move the fire to where you want it, and it can be put out of the way for particular gatherings. If your clients would prefer a permanent structure, you can design a built-in fire pit or fireplace. Do remember that whether you build a custom fire pit or choose a portable one, always include drainage in the bottom so that rainwater does not collect.

A portable fire pit makes an instant gathering place, and the screen cover prevents embers from being blown into the surrounding gardens.

Fire pits can burn wood or compressed fiber logs, or can be plumbed to burn gas. Gas is easy, since one click of the remote and—poof!—instant ambiance. With wood you have the delightful crackling sounds and delicious scent, but wood needs to be purchased, schlepped, and tended, and the ashes need to be disposed. Let your clients know the pros and cons of wood versus gas, and ask which they prefer. In general I have found that the more affluent the client, the more they want gas.

Always have a screen. This helps prevent ashes or embers from being swept into the landscape by a gust of wind. It also helps protect people from falling into the fire pit if they trip, or catching any billowing clothes on fire as they walk by. These are all very real dangers, so position any fire pit with regard to safety, safety, safety, and caution your clients to never leave a fire pit unattended. Ever.

Outdoor fires should always have a source of water nearby. A hose bib and hose, with water turned on and nozzle turned off, should be available to douse any accident that may happen. Fires should also be soaked at the end of the evening to extinguish every last ember. Your clients will look to you for care and usage guidelines. Caution them about how to use an outdoor fire safely and instruct them on the safety precautions they should always take.

Fire pits and outdoor fireplaces can be made of a variety of materials: concrete, brick, pavers, natural stone. Make sure the lining materials are rated for fire and heat. Only use a mason who has experience with constructing fire pits or fireplaces. I have no problem using a relatively new mason on a walkway or small retaining wall, but when it comes to fire, your job is not the job they should be learning on.

Fire features can bring a unique drama to the landscape. Design, build, and operate with safety in mind, and these features can be a source of delight to your clients for many years.

THE EXTRAS

My designs provide a complete landscape transformation, right down to container plantings, furnishings, birdfeeders, and garden art. I have to admit, these finishing touches are almost what I love doing the most. It's like adding the final touches of jewelry to the landscape.

I enjoy few forays more than going to choose containers and pottery,

The addition of a simple bench and planted pot creates a charming vignette, providing a perfect resting spot, destination, or focal point in the garden.

Pots, pots, pots. I truly believe you can never have enough.

Birdbaths invite birds into the garden and add a certain sculptural beauty.

along with the bodacious plants to fill them. At the outset of my garden design business, about half my work was designing and installing patio plantings. You can find wholesale pottery and garden art suppliers right in your area, or talk to your larger local garden retailers. They will often extend a discount of 10% to 50% to designers for purchasing pottery and other garden accoutrements.

Purveyors of higher-end garden furnishings offer to-the-trade exclusivity and discounts. Landscape furniture should be well manufactured and substantive enough to withstand local weather conditions and some wind. Pots should be appropriate for all four seasons; otherwise, in areas with freezing winters, be prepared to empty and store your clients' ceramic or terracotta pots to prevent crazing, cracks, and breakage.

Bird-feeding areas are always a pleasure to site and install. We have always enjoyed feeding birds year-round at our home, and I am continually amazed by the reaction of clients I turn on to this. It's like they never noticed birds before, and now they have whole menageries right outside their windows. Remember to site these feeding areas where clients can see them, and where seed shells will not be a big nuisance. Also locate feeders so that bird poop will not be hitting windows, furniture, decking, or cars (birds frequently excrete just as they take off). Make sure to add water to your bird-feeding areas. This is enormously beneficial to birds, and their antics as they sip and bathe are always a delight. In cold-weather climates, I install birdbath heaters to provide a winter water source for songbirds.

Art can be as serious or whimsical as your clients want. I tend to not go too wild with my suggestions, but some gardens just beg for a bit of whimsy. Indulge them.

CHAPTER SEVEN

Water Features

EVERY SHELTER MAGAZINE, every gardening publication, every home and garden makeover seems to include a water feature. Whether it is a plug-and-play mini-fountain on a bistro table, or a 30-foot pond with a waterfall, wading area, bridge, and koi, water features are in demand. Just about every garden designer adds water to their design repertoire at some point, but creating water features is also a great niche business. The designers who specialize in creating waterfalls, rills, ponds, and fountains are in a burgeoning field. It seems that once the client's eye has been opened to the possibilities offered by a water feature, the more they want one. And then, kind of like having a boat, some people soon want a larger one. There is a fairly brisk business upgrading existing water features to larger, more complex iterations.

Nothing quite transforms a landscape like water. It can give your client's garden an irresistible, sparkling focal point, it can provide delightful background sounds to help muffle ambient noise, and it can be an instant stress reducer, effectively turning down the volume of life. Wherever I have added water features, my clients cannot imagine their gardens without them.

Oftentimes a new client will tell me they're looking for a fountain or waterfall, but there are certainly instances when I introduce the idea for a water feature at the design presentation. I'll admit, I have gotten blank stares. For some people, anything involving water sounds like a lot of work. But I have also seen that "Eureka!" moment as people's eyes light up—these are the clients who will really get into having a water feature.

By no means do I present ideas for a water feature only for the sake of adding water ("Let's throw a fountain over here") or to increase the project scope or revenue. As you go through the discovery phase with your client, and bond with the property, you'll see when the right combination of factors makes a water feature a really good possibility. First, the clients need to be open to new ideas and a little adventurous. They also need the kind of lifestyle that would welcome the addition of an "active" feature in their new outdoor space. And of course, the site must clearly benefit from adding some element of water. Although almost every site could take a water feature, it's the intersection of these dynamics that makes a water feature work.

You must consider a number of factors when designing a fountain, pond, or waterfall, including type of water feature, style, location, size, plantings, water plants, pump particulars, filtration, fish, regular maintenance, and annual maintenance. That's quite a list, but not many water features need all of these things. I have two modest water features in my yard. Both have small pumps and water plants but nothing else, and they just about take care of themselves.

From the simple to the sublime, water features are as limitless as your imagination. I have clients with three water plants in a whiskey barrel with a little clip-on, water-spouting fish. Simple. Makes them happy. Other clients have a small splash pool at the base of a large hill, with water that circulates up about 10 feet before splashily meandering down a rock-strewn creek the bottom. Yet another client has a 20,000-gallon pond with an upper pool, a granite bridge across a meandering creek, tiered waterfalls, and both a bog and a gravel beach for margin plants. They have koi that will eat out of your hand, and so many goldfish that they give them away in baggies. Sublime.

I know you've seen just-add-water-and-plug-it-in fountains at your local nursery. Don't dismiss these. Sited correctly and integrated in a garden or nestled next to a collection of planted pots, these fountains can work beautifully. They function particularly well in a small garden or as an accent in a garden room. Installation couldn't be easier. Set it down, plug it in, add water, turn on, enjoy.

A private retreat uses the burble of water to mask street noises.
Photo courtesy of Mike Walsh, Horticultural Concepts.

The water play from this bubbling pot and spouting fish create a reminder
to relax. The clients installed this water feature in just a couple of hours.

A burbling pot makes a charming addition to just about any garden or patio. Take a pot of your client's choice, from elegant to wildly rustic, perch it on a fountain base, set it up with a pump and some waterproofing around the intake, and—poof!—you have a very easy but glorious fountain. This will add the lovely sound and sparkle of moving water to the garden.

Ponds can be easy-to-build affairs that use a preformed plastic liner and a pump system, or they can be dozens of feet across, even acres in size. Some products now available permit the designer to work outside of liner limitations, effectively allowing ponds as large as the designer and client want to go.

Streams and waterfalls are compelling, their burbling and reflected, twinkling sunlight are delightful additions to any garden area. Any time you design this type of feature, think, "What would nature do?" Creeks or streambeds need to wind and curve just like they would in nature. Any rill or stream should be in scale with the pond, since nature would never allow a torrent of a waterfall to drop into a tiny basin. The source of the water that begins a natural-looking stream or waterfall should look like it has always been there. I like using locally sourced stone for most of the natural water features I design. This way they look more in keeping with the environment and more like we've uncovered a happy accident rather than contrived something fake. Use a large variety of stones, from boulders to gravel, just as you would find in a natural stream.

Formal water features are also stunning. The elegant lines of an English garden accented by a formal pond or graceful fountain can define the space and add drama. Similarly, a modern reflecting pool with clean lines of stone or metal against a plane of dark, still water can create a jaw-dropping feature in the landscape.

LOCATION AND SIZE

You can use a number of approaches to site a water feature in a landscape design. I place water features that create sound in a location where they can help mask whatever ambient noise is intruding, such as between the local street noise and the main recreational space. If I cannot do that, I try for a spot that gives the main patio or deck the most "water music."

Again, the sound of the water becomes foreground sound, and all of the other aural indignities soften to the background. Of course, how you view a water feature is important, too. Most clients like to see their water feature from both inside and outside the house, which makes perfect sense. Water features can be centered on a main view line, or a multiple-functioned water feature (for example, a mix of pond, stream, and waterfall elements) could begin from one view angle and terminate at the center of another view.

Many times I suggest a water garden of some kind to cover an unsightly feature in the landscape. An unattractive, rocky hillside could just be terraced with meadow plants, which could be lovely. Or we could go a step further and feature the hillside by having it hold a meandering dry creek bed with a small waterfall at the base, trickling into a shallow, rock-strewn pool. Flood the rest of the area with prairie grasses and rock garden plants that will enjoy the drainage and sun, as well as soften the edges of the "creek." Though entirely manmade, this creation can look as if it has always been there, making what was once an eyesore now something splendid.

Whether your client has acres of land or a single balcony, you can design a water feature that enhances their site. For city dwellers with a small backyard or a condo deck, an urn spilling over onto a contained base of river rock may be the perfect solution. This type of water feature can fit into an existing planting bed or be tucked into a corner, no matter what size the space. It can also be tied into a switched outlet, allowing the client to turn the water feature on from inside the house, or you can use a remote-driven outlet attachment—no messing with plugs each time you want the play of water. We have our little features on a timer, so they run for two hours in the morning and about three hours in the evening, when we are usually in that general area.

As you work to site a water feature, there are cultural and logistical considerations to remember. Water features in full sun can grow the largest number of plants, including water lilies, both tropical and hardy. Keeping the water feature away from overhanging trees will help keep leaf litter out. Leaf litter is not only unsightly, but as leaves decompose they can release gases that are harmful to the water garden. And pumps that recirculate water can be clogged by leaves, even with filtration.

Water features don't have to be in the backyard. One of my clients has a front yard facing a busy street and a backyard with views of a glorious natural pond. A water feature in the back would be redundant, and we decided that the sounds of a splashing urn fountain would enhance the entranceway and create a lovely sound diversion for the breakfast room.

Consider the refilling of the water feature and how this will be accomplished, either manually or through an automatic irrigation system. If the pond will be filled manually, it needs to be an easy hose-length away from a water source, or you could have a line with a sill-cock installed right next to the feature (but hidden, of course) for easy water access. If you are planning to have the pond tied into the irrigation system, a simple float valve can make refilling a completely automated task. Best for most clients, I assure you.

Proximity to electrical connections should also play into your siting, although it's usually pretty easy to run electricity to wherever you intend to put the water feature. Give some thought to including a rheostat. A rheostat on the electrical connection to your pump can enable you or your clients to turn the water volume of your waterfall or fountain up or down. This can change the ambiance dramatically, allowing you to choose anything from a playful trickle to a raging torrent.

PLANTS, FISH, MOSQUITOES

When you create a water feature, no matter what size, you are in effect creating a little ecosystem. The stability of the system depends on the interrelationships between the plants and creatures that live there. This sounds a little intimidating, but it really isn't. Much of the active "gardening" of water gardening is just waiting for the water ecosystem to find balance.

I always include some plants in my client's water features. When we add plants to a water feature, it becomes a water garden. If you have never tried water gardening, don't fret. It is really quite easy. In fact, some of my clients find their water gardens the easiest part of their landscapes. Know that you can design water features or water gardens, but you can subcontract out the construction and maintenance to a water gardening company. Still, you need to understand some of the basic principles of this type of gardening.

Plants make natural water features look more integrated into the greater landscape. Even a few floating water plants, had for about $10, can make the water feature look like a natural part of the landscape. A side benefit is that these same plants can help keep algae at bay and keep the water smelling sweet. Hardy water lilies are incredibly easy to grow, and the floating water plants are usually so happy that you have to keep pulling some out and throwing them into the compost (or selling them to another client!). Papyrus is gorgeous and incredibly easy to grow. You can even save a hunk and winter it over in a pot of water in your living room. In 2008 I had lemon grass, a tropical, winter over successfully in several locations outdoors. Weird.

Plants in the water garden are not only pretty but also work for you. They provide shade that helps cool the water and control algae growth, and they help with water balance, making it all easier to maintain. Water plants help to provide oxygen, and they give fish and frogs a place to hide.

Water plants fall into several categories. First are emergent plants, whose roots are just below the water surface while their shoots are above. Some water lilies and lotuses enjoy having their roots in several feet of water, but they send their leaves and blossoms up above the surface.

Hardy water lilies, so easy to grow, actually help the ecosystem of water features.

Second are completely submerged plants. These are usually the oxygen-ators; they help keep the pond healthy and are particularly beneficial if you are planning to add fish. Marginal or bog plants like to live in the saturated area at the water's edge. Some common garden plants are very comfortable in the margin zone, including daylilies (*Hemerocallis*), Siberian iris (*Iris sibirica*), *Lobelia* species and cultivars, some ferns, and many rushes and cattails (*Juncus* and *Typha* varieties). Last are the free-floating plants, which you just toss in to add a finishing touch to a natural-appearing water garden. These plants constantly change as they move with the breeze. They also help to oxygenate the pond and shade the water.

Watch your plant selections. Some common water plants are actually invasives, particularly in warmer parts of the United States. A prolific tropical plant that will not be winter-killed is not a good addition to a south Florida bog garden. The risk of the invasive plant making its way into the natural landscape by seed or by hitching a ride on a bird or animal is too risky. There are plenty of other options.

Water gardening is a popular pastime, so there are a multitude of books about designing, planting, and maintaining water gardens. There are books about water garden fish and water garden plants. There are mail-order water gardening suppliers with a wealth of knowledge to share and a plethora of products to purchase. Local nurseries are also in the game, and you can get great water garden plants for fairly short money. Your clients can take care of their water feature or water garden, or they can hire a water gardening professional. Or, once you feel knowledgeable enough, this could be a good side business to augment your design work.

Adding fish to a water garden will delight both children and adults. Fish quickly become acclimated to being fed and will come to the surface when they see people approaching. Koi, or Chinese ornamental carp, are the jewels of the water garden and can become like pets (I have friends who have named all their fish and hand-feed them). Goldfish, too, can be a lovely addition. Fish are beneficial in that they eat algae and mosquito larvae, but they can also become too much of a good thing when their excrement and uneaten food cloud the water. Again, balance is everything in an ecosystem.

If your client has a sizable pond full of fish, it can attract birds that prey on fish. Where I live, we have to particularly watch out for great blue herons. When a heron dines on an occasional $300 special baby, it is terribly distressing and quickly becomes expensive.

Every year I have leopard frogs in my water features. This is a mystery to me because the closest bodies of water are swamps, each located about 500 feet away. To reach one of my water features, a frog would need to come up a 100-foot hill through the woods, cross a busy street, and traverse a lot of open, sunny space. That's a lot of dry land for an amphibian to negotiate. All we know is, we clean the little ponds out in the early spring (these are very small ponds, and we not only empty them but also wash them thoroughly), and by June we have big ol' leopard frogs. It's wonderful. Strange, but wonderful.

Even a simple container with water in it becomes a little ecosystem, and they'll grow what you want them to grow. Of course, sometimes they'll grow what you don't want them to grow. Clients often ask whether water features invite or breed mosquitoes.

I have never had a mosquito problem with any of my own or my clients' water features. Mosquitoes need still water for eggs and larvae to mature, so keeping water moving is a great way to completely avoid them. And since fish eat mosquito larvae, having fish can be another simple solution.

Mosquito dunks, or briquettes, are one of the easiest, no-brainer solutions. These little donuts of peat or other material are impregnated with a biologic control, *Bacillus thuringiensis* subsp. *israelensis* (Bti), that will kill the larval stages of midges, mosquitoes, and no-see-ums without hurting children, pets, fish, frogs, or other insects. Pop a dunk into your client's water feature and for a month or more any mosquito larvae in the water will die. Dunks float, and I prefer them not to. For one of my own still water features, I tied half a dunk with a 2-inch rock in some netting from a bag of onions. I threw it into the water, where it fell to the bottom, and that piece of dunk lasted all season, roughly six months. I've had water features for years, and I'm still using my original $5 package of mosquito dunks.

SEVEN SIMPLE STEPS TO BUILDING A WATER FEATURE

As a designer you need to understand the process of building a pond, waterfall, stream, or other active water feature. Basically it involves using a container or creating a reservoir that can hold water, installing an appropriately sized pump to circulate water, including some type of filtration, and "naturalizing" the manmade components with a combination of installed stone and plants. These seven steps assume you are using a flexible pond liner, which is like a huge sheet of strong membrane. You drape this membrane into a hole you have excavated, then fit and tuck the liner, and it holds the water. You could also use a preformed pond liner, which simplifies the process, although it locks you into a particular size and shape.

1. Using paper, sketch the design for the water feature in the location you have chosen. Include notations for special elements such as a plant shelf, deep spot for fish, or area for a gravel beach.
2. On-site, use a hose to try different layouts before committing to the final shape. Outline this with landscape paint. (A note about liners: if you are using a flexible liner, make sure you have enough to cover the surface, the width and depth, and have 2 to 3 feet of excess liner around the entire perimeter. Make sure not to dig wider or deeper than your liner can cover, or the pond will leak. Only use liners that are rated "fish safe.")
3. Excavate the hole for your liner according to your design. As you dig, check the edges for level. The edges of the water feature need to be close to level to hold the water. Rake the bottom smooth and pick up *all* small stones that could cause a tear in the liner. A broom works well for this.
4. Install the underlayment (usually a spun polyester fabric designed to protect the liner from damage from rocks below, although a layer of peat moss or play sand also works well), and then lay in the liner. Gently tuck and shape into all corners of the pool, folding areas over when necessary. These folds will eventually be covered, so don't worry about them too much. (To avoid damaging the liner, I take my shoes off for this step and just muck around in my socks or bare feet. Other people tromp all over the liner, even in boots, but knowing how Murphy's Law can rule the day, I tend to be cautious. I'd rather replace a pair of socks than an $800 liner.)
5. When everything is laid in and tucked well, carefully cover the liner with rocks on the bottom, sides, and top. The rocks should

fit snugly but look natural. Check over each major rock to show its best face, particularly if it has beautiful colors or moss growing on it. Chunky fieldstones can be used along the bottom and sides, flat stones for the edges. Fill in between the rocks with smaller stones and then scatter gravel in the crevices. This is how water moves and positions rocks in nature, which you are attempting to emulate.

6. Install the pump and then add more rocks and gravel to disguise it. Add water and wash all the soil and grit off the rocks. Activate the pump, empty the dirty water out of the pond, and refill with clean water. This may take several cycles. Tuck in any liner that is visible around the edges.

7. Add the last of the gravel, and decorate with water and margin plants. Plug in, turn on the pump, and enjoy!

SAFETY

If not designed with safety in mind, water features can be drowning hazards to children, pets, and wildlife. I will not include a water feature more

The process of creating a pond is pretty gnarly, but the end results are so worth the effort and mess.

than 2 inches deep on any property where small children live or play unless it is securely fenced off from the general recreation area. Instead I'll design something with moving water splashing down into an inch or two of still water, so that if a child falls in, it will be like falling into a shallow puddle. I also always caution clients to never leave children or pets unattended around any water source. Ponds with slick, hard plastic liners can be a death trap for family cats and even dogs if there isn't a shallow place for them to get out. Wildlife can also dive or fall in and perish. I know it's not the end of the world for a client to find a dead chipmunk in their pond, but it's still distressing. A good rule is to incorporate some shallow areas into every water feature or water garden you create. Design water features that best suit the homeowner's family and lifestyle to make sure their new landscape is not only beautiful but also completely safe.

MAINTENANCE

My own water features are small and really take care of themselves. In the fall we clean out the lion's share of leaves and remove the pump. In the spring we empty the pools completely, take all the muck out of the bottom (smells like a swamp), and wipe down all sides of the liner. Then we refill the water, restock the plants, add a new filter to the pump, and plug her in. We do nothing else to maintain the ponds during the growing season, and they always look clear and smell sweet, and the plants grow beautifully.

Larger water features or those with fish or more plants will need more care. Pond filtration for large water features requires two main components: mechanical filtration and biofiltration. Mechanical filtration systems remove the suspended particles, leaves, and other debris that settle in the water feature. If these are not removed, the decomposing debris can cause ammonium and nitrite toxins to rise to levels that can kill aquatic life. Biofiltration systems use biologically active bacteria to break down ammonium and nitrites to harmless or beneficial chemicals like nitrates, oxygen, and nitrogen.

Algae can be a big nuisance. Submerged plants are good competitors for the light and nutrients algae needs to survive, and fish also eat algae. I have never had a problem with algae in the water features I have designed, but that might be because I tend to keep water moving, which keeps the water aerated and oxygenated, a great boon to water health and aquatic life. Then for the most part I stand back and let nature do its thing.

If your clients don't have the interest or motivation to take care of their water features, they might have the means to hire maintenance crews for both their property and their water gardens. I do think water feature or water garden maintenance would be a great side business for a designer. Personally, I have learned enough to design a beautiful and functional water feature, but I let my experts install and maintain them.

CHAPTER EIGHT

Spas, Pools, and Poolscaping

I F YOU KEEP EXPANDING YOUR SKILLS and offerings in garden and landscape design, you will inevitably design a swimming pool, and you'll most certainly landscape your share of them. Especially in warmer parts of the United States, nearly every large landscape job includes the addition or renovation of a pool or spa.

I have designed a number of pools over the past fifteen years. Again, this is an area where you need to understand the terminology, and what goes into the siting and design, and you need to be able to converse intelligently with subcontractors, but you do not need to know how to lay down gunite. Partner with a solid, proven pool design-build company, work collaboratively, and the partnership will benefit both of you as well as your client.

How do you search for a good pool-building partner? Use the Internet or phone book to find pool builders in your area. After googling "pools" plus my zip code, I uncovered eleven pool companies who build and service in my area of southeastern Massachusetts. After you get a fairly short list, go to the Web site of your Better Business Bureau and check out each company. If they are not BBB members, that's a red flag.

Have a look at each company's Web site. Find out how long they have been in business. Less than five years? I'd be very careful. More than ten years, they're probably a proven company with a fairly good track record. Check out the styles and designs of pools they have built that appeal to you. Look for professional certifications held by their owners and employees. Eventually pick five or six companies that you like the smell of, call them, and tell them you are a designer looking for a pool design-build partner for whatever town you're working in. Let them know you would like to meet with them at their office.

The pool company office should not look shabby but relatively organized and ready to receive clients. Bring your site notes and tell them about your preliminary design thoughts for your client. Ask how they have worked with outside landscape designers in the past. If they cannot immediately tell you about a good experience they've had doing this, you can probably write them off. The last thing you need is a pool subcontractor suggesting to your client that you are unnecessary. Ask about the warranties they give on their pool installations, and ask to see their written contract. Unlike other designers I know, I never sign pool contracts for my clients. When we have finally determined the entire scope of the pool installation, I have the clients sign directly with the pool builder. A pool is too large an investment to have me in the middle of this long-term warranty. This also means that the clients will be paying the pool people

An artistically landscaped pool seamlessly integrates into the setting.

directly, so you will not receive margin on the pool itself. This would be a situation where you are paid strictly for your time, but assuming you design and build the areas around the pool, you'll have ample opportunity to make margin.

Do ask the pool builders about average pricing and their terms of payment. If their initial payments seem inordinately high (for example, if they are requesting more than half of the contracted amount before work is started), question them about it.

Ask the pool builder what they feel are the most important considerations for a well-built pool. The most important parts of a pool are the parts you don't see: the structure and hydraulics. They should be able to discuss this intelligently and not just talk about materials for coping and tile colors. Ask about recommended safety precautions, including fencing and prevention of suction entrapment. Request a list of references, and ask to see a couple of finished installations. You will want to call the reference list and ask how the design and build processes went. If the project came in on time and on budget, how did the final installation compare to the initial design? Would they use this contractor again or recommend him or her to a good friend? These are all salient pieces of information.

The Association of Pool and Spa Professionals (APSP) has developed a professional training and certification program. Designations of Certified Building Professional (CBP), Certified Service Professional (CSP), and Professional Pool and Spa Operator (PPSO) are awarded to people who have attended hours of continuing education and passed rigorous examinations to become true professionals in the pool industry. When you choose to work with certified professionals who are committed to excellence in the pool industry, you and your clients will end up with a superior product. Ask pool builders who in their company holds industry certifications. They should be readily prepared to share this information with you.

Finally, trust your gut. When you've winnowed it down to two or three possible pool partners, ask yourself which one you would most enjoy working with. Oftentimes this is the best way to make the final decision. I know, sounds like a chick thing, but when the chemistry feels right, it usually works out well.

TYPES OF POOLS AND SPAS

There are two basic types of pools: inground and aboveground. You will spend most of your pool design time on inground pools and spas, but it's worth knowing about aboveground pools too. Please note that all inground pools require a building permit and usually a board of health inspection. Have the pool company work this piece. It's what they do, and they are really good at it.

Inground pools are generally concrete, fiberglass, or vinyl. Each type offers a wide range of price points and additional options that include the finish, water features (like water spouts, fountains, and falls), and heated spas. Generally you and your pool builder partner will decide what type of pool is best for the climate and application, and you'll work out what add-ons to recommend to the client.

Concrete pools are often referred to as gunite or shotcrete. These are both holes in the ground with steel framing, around which the concrete is blasted on with a concrete pumping hose. These pools can be finished with plaster, pebble aggregate, tinted or colored plaster, glass beads, tile, or natural stone. I nearly always build this kind of pool, which takes anywhere from four to ten weeks to install, with additional time needed to finish the surrounding landscape.

Vinyl liner pools are usually made of reinforced steel in the pool hole, with prefabricated walls snapped into place, after which the liner is applied. Care needs to be taken to keep the liner from getting punctured. These are the inground pools I grew up with here in New England. They generally take less time to install than concrete pools.

Fiberglass pools are usually one big shell (like an oversized plastic pond liner) that is shipped to the site. The hole is excavated, and the pool is set in and leveled. Sounds simple, but there are some helpful tips to remember. If you and your pool builder are going to install a fiberglass pool, don't choose exposed coping. Instead, go with stone, pavers, or decking. Don't let the tile be installed at the factory because it will almost never be straight. Instead, specify that the tile be installed on-site. Make sure the pool does not have a single main drain, because they can pose an entrapment hazard. Also know that lighter colors in fiberglass will last longer than darker colors, and fiberglass cannot be resurfaced in the field. The primary benefit to fiberglass is that installation is usually fairly fast.

Your clients can go from having nothing to happily swimming, often in less than two weeks.

Some clients opt for an aboveground pool for their economical price, or because they only want a pool until their children are grown. A less expensive pool that can be removed fairly easily is also a good option in areas where a pool may be a detriment to resale. And an aboveground pool is sometimes the best option for a sloped site. Whatever the reason, aboveground pools are often easily installed and won't break the bank. For very high-end properties, however, usually only an inground pool will do.

Swimming pool designs are incredibly varied, but no matter what the shape or layout, pools basically operate the same way and rely on fundamental plumbing and filtering. To keep the water clean, a pool needs

QUICK GLOSSARY OF POOL MECHANICS

Chemical feeder. Device that keeps the pool sanitized by maintaining a consistent feed of sanitizing agent into the pool water to kill bacteria and algae.

Drains. System of skimmers (at the top of the pool) and drains (at the bottom), which permit water outflow to the pool's support equipment. Multiple drains keep the water circulating if one drain becomes blocked. It is also safer to have multiple drains to help prevent suction entrapment.

Filter. Mechanism that removes small debris and contaminants from the water, including oils, grease, and dirt. Usually one of three types: sand, diatomaceous earth, or cartridge. Requires periodic cleaning and replacement.

Heater. Gas, electric, or solar device used to heat the water. Can extend the swimming season for months or allow it to be used year-round. Available in various sizes.

Pump. Motor-powered device that circulates pool water through the filter, sanitizing system, and heater, then back into the pool. The goal is to circulate all the water at least once a day. Your professional pool partner will know how to size the pump and motor to best suit your client's requirements.

Returns. Ports or inlet valves around the sides of the pool that move filtered water from the support equipment back into the pool.

Skimmer. Mechanism that removes large, floating debris from the water. We frequently find frogs in skimmers, so I caution clients to check them daily and release any frogs back into the garden.

circulation, filtration, and sanitation. Essentially, water is pumped in a continual cycle from the pool through filters, to a chemical treatment system, then back to the pool. This keeps the water free of debris and bacteria.

You and your clients will need to make a number of important decisions relative to the pool mechanics. Do this with the help of your professional pool builder. Let your pool partner be the one to explain various options and to make the recommendations he or she feels is optimal for your client's new pool.

ANATOMY OF A LANDSCAPED POOL

Together, you and your clients will decide on the siting and layout of the pool, pool construction type and materials, pool interior design and materials, and both coping and apron designs. You might also recommend options like spas, diving rocks, slides, beaches, lighting, landscaping, and furnishings, as well as safety features such as fencing, alarms, and covers.

When you start to site the pool, keep several things in mind. The pool's location will greatly affect how the family uses it. If placed in a convenient spot, it will be used more frequently. Your clients might want to walk out of their family room and right onto the poolside apron, then right into the pool. Or they might want the pool as segregated as possible from the rest of the yard to keep it private, or to keep the noise of frolicking kids away from the house, or so that it can be securely fenced off from the house and other recreational areas. Do the clients want to be able to glance outside and count every kid to make sure everyone is safe? If so, position the pool in an area that is easily viewed from the kitchen and family room. As nice as it is to have a shady area near a pool, large deciduous trees can be messy, forever dropping seed clusters or leaves into the water, clogging the filters, and adding to the sanitation burden. For this reason I try to avoid placing pools under or next to large trees.

Pool layouts or shapes can be formal and symmetrical or wildly curving and swooping. Some even have a side "river" for children to float through on a tube, or a spot for adults to do a little resistance swimming. Match the pool style to the architecture of the home, taking into consideration the site's attributes and your client's layout preferences. Other add-ons that you recommend should fill a client need. Do they want a diving spot at the deep end? Include a lovely diving boulder. Could they use a wading area for small children or older adults? Design a beach that transitions smoothly to the pool apron. Would they like a spa? This doesn't cost a whole lot more money and can greatly increase your clients' enjoyment of their new poolscape.

SPAAAHS

A spa is a lovely addition to a pool but is also a delicious stand-alone feature. Clients love being able to come home after a long day at work and slip into their lovely, bubbly spa. A spa can provide instant relaxation and can even help people sleep better. Categorically, a spa differs from a hot tub only in materials used and, usually, whirlpool action. Most hot tubs are made of wood and use heated water; they may or may not have jets or water aeration. Spas are by definition jetted, heated, water-filled tubs. Stand-alone units are usually made of fiberglass or acrylic, but custom spas can be made of a wide range of materials, including concrete, tile, and natural stone.

Contrary to what most people think, a spa is not a little swimming pool. Spas are designed for a much higher ratio of bodies to water volume and hold the water at a much higher temperature than a swimming pool. Because of this, the pollution density is much greater in a spa than in a pool, so it is critical the water is circulated and treated property to maintain safe bathing conditions. The mechanics of keeping a spa clean are similar to those for pools, but optimal water turnover is about once a day for a pool, and every seven to twelve minutes for a spa. A spa should have its own self-contained filter, pump, chemical feed, heater, and fresh water supply. Most spas are a prefabricated design that incorporates seating areas and water jets. The synthetic materials are able to cope with the sanitizing chemicals, heat, and water velocity in the spa.

Safety should always be a first priority when we're talking about water features. Hair entanglement in spa suction drains has tragically caused several dozen deaths. Make sure that any spa your clients consider can be installed with multiple drains with new drain cover standards to help reduce the risk of entrapment. Hot tub temperatures are also an area where caution must prevail. High water temperatures can cause drowsiness, which can lead to unconsciousness, resulting in drowning. High temperatures can also lead to heatstroke and death. Most modern temperature controls do not allow spa water temperatures to exceed 104°F. As an added precaution against drowning, alcohol should never be consumed while in a hot tub or spa, and neither pregnant women nor small children should use a spa before consulting their physician.

The U.S. Consumer Product Safety Commission (CPSC) recommends several other safety precautions. For starters, always use a locked safety cover when a spa is not in use, and only allow children near spas if there is constant adult supervision. Check the drain covers throughout the year. If a drain cover is missing or broken, do not use the spa until it has been replaced. Have the spa regularly checked by a professional to ensure it is in safe working condition. And finally, make sure your clients can locate the cut-off switch for the pump and know how to turn it off in an emergency.

Designing the addition of a spa is an area where I rely heavily on the pool builder or spa professional for appropriate sizing of pumps, sanitizing agents, and heaters, as well as professional installation and adhering to all safety standards and drowning prevention guidelines.

FENCING, ALARMS, AND COVERS

Most municipalities require safety fencing around any swimming pool. It is a very good practice to fence any water feature where accidental drowning is a possibility. Here in Massachusetts, fencing is required around all swimming pools, and in my town, there are additional requirements for fencing height, gate latching, and alarm systems, all for increased safety against drowning accidents.

Drowning is the leading cause of accidental death of children under age five in the Sunbelt states, which have the highest number of pools per capita. Proper supervision is the key to preventing drowning, but the CPSC suggests that all pools have layers of protection to prevent drowning accidents. Here are their safety recommendations:

- Fences and walls should surround the entire pool and be at least 4 feet high. There should be no footholds or handholds on the barrier. Make sure fence gates are self closing and self-latching, and that latches are out of reach for small children.

- If the house forms one side of the barrier to the pool, protect doors leading from the house to the pool with alarms that ring out when the door is opened.
- Use a power safety cover (a motor-powered barrier that can be placed over the entire water surface) when the pool is not in use.
- For aboveground pools, secure and lock steps and ladders, or remove them when the pool is not in use.
- Make sure all pools and spas have multiple drains with drain covers required by current safety standards. This helps prevent suction entrapment.
- As an added precaution, use pool alarms. Underwater pool alarms generally perform better and can be used in conjunction with pool covers. CPSC advises consumers to use remote alarm receivers so that the alarm can be heard inside the house or in other places away from the pool area.

Safety pool covers are designed to protect someone from entering the pool by falling, but they also protect against sliding into the pool underneath the cover. These covers are only as strong as their anchoring system, so choosing your cover early in the design process is important. It is imperative that you design the areas and the apron around the pool so that the cover can be anchored optimally. Safety covers can be solid, but most are made out of a strong mesh fabric. The fabric is sturdy and durable and comes in a variety of colors.

A variety of alarm systems are available, including pool alarms, which sound when the pool water is disturbed, and gate alarms, which sound when the pool gate is opened. The Good Housekeeping Research Institute recommends using both pool and gate alarms. The more layers of protection, the better.

WATER AND ELECTRICITY

Ground-fault circuit interrupter (GFCI) outlets are the only electrical outlets that should be outdoors, and certainly the only type of outlet that should be in use anywhere near a swimming pool or spa. This is code in most states, but should just be the standard for any electrical outlet installed outside or where there is water, like in a kitchen, bath, or laundry room. GFCIs offer protection against electrical shock hazards. They constantly monitor current flowing in a circuit to sense any drop in current. If the current flowing through two conductors differs by even a small amount, the GFCI instantly interrupts the current flow to prevent a lethal amount of electricity from reaching the consumer. The consumer may feel a shock, but they will not be electrocuted.

As a designer, you are in a position to inform and educate your clients. Assure that their pools and spas comply with all local and national safety regulations, and insist that safety be the first priority when designing any poolscaping.

LANDSCAPING THE POOL

When you are designing a pool, you are designing a place where your clients will spend a great deal of time. Using it will be like having a vacation in their backyard. Once the location and layout of the pool have been determined, your thoughts will turn to landscaping, which should incorporate privacy, safety, beauty, and functionality.

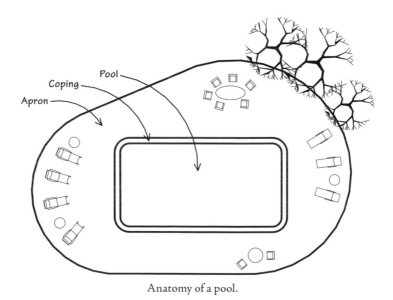

Anatomy of a pool.

To enhance the feeling that the pool area is secluded and private, make sure there is adequate screening from the street and from neighboring homes. Additional screening can be incorporated by fencing, plantings, and privacy-enhancing structures like vine-covered pergolas, trellises, or shade sails. Adding a combination of these elements can make a pool area, even one that is located in the midst of tight housing, feel well concealed.

Plantings integrate the pool with the surrounding landscape. I cannot imagine dropping a pool into any backyard and then plopping a fence around it and concreting over the rest of the yard. I've seen this, and it ain't pretty. Plants bring color, texture, and movement to the poolscape, soften the harsh lines of swimming pool equipment and pool hardscape, and make the pool feel nestled into the greater environment. Some plants are a better choice than others in a poolside planting. We've talked about matching plants to place, and this practice is critical here. Keep the following in mind as you make plant selections for a client's pool area:

- Use low-maintenance plants to keep the water and poolside areas cleaner.
- Avoid planting deciduous trees within 20 feet of pools, since they shed leaves, seeds, and fruits. Also, squished or rotting fruits from fruiting trees are not only messy but can also attract bees and wasps.
- The leaves and petals of shorter plants are less likely to be caught by the wind and blown into the pool.
- Plants that flower heavily are gorgeous but can send petals into the pool with every breeze. Use flowering plants with heavier spent blossoms that won't drop petals on the wind.
- Guard against using plants with invasive root systems, which can run along masonry seams or even damage a swimming pool structure.
- For the perimeter and privacy plantings, choose trees and shrubs that are evergreen or that drop their leaves in a short time period, easing the cleanup.
- Avoid plants with stickers or thorns. Pieces of these plants will invariably get scattered on the pool apron and will be sat on and walked on.

- Consider augmenting with container plantings. They are easy to maintain and rearrange, and when planted appropriately can bring bright color and drama to the poolscape without adding a lot of mess.

HARDSCAPE

The coping and apron around a swimming pool are critical parts of the aesthetics and functionality of the pool. As you develop plans for the pool and surrounding space, you will give a lot of thought to the materials used for the hardscape.

The coping is usually made of stone, concrete, metal, or some type of decorative paver. The apron is the patio or "firm surface" around the pool. I think of the coping as the decorative and functional edging that transitions the swimmer from the pool to the apron. Swimmers will hike themselves out of the pool, brushing their bodies up against the edge of the coping. For that reason, I like coping that is smooth, contiguous, and unlikely to scrape stomachs or knees. There are four basic types of coping. *Rough-cut coping* is made from stone and has a rough or textured edge. It is gorgeous and gives a pool a beautiful, natural look, but I am personally not a fan of the rough edges. *Bullnose coping* can be made from natural or manmade stone, brick, or metal. This coping has a smooth, rounded edge—no scraped tummies—and is the standard in most pools. *Cantilever coping* gives a pool a modern look. It makes the decking or apron material look larger and more pronounced, and can be used with almost any material. Last is *rolled-edge coping*, which can also be made from stone, cast stone, or brick. This style has a gently upturned edge that can provide a nice grip for hauling oneself out of the pool.

Choosing coping materials is like choosing a countertop for a kitchen. There are many materials and styles to choose from. I like a coping that subtly complements the materials used on the pool apron, rather than acting as a contrasting frame to make the pool "pop" against the apron.

The pool apron serves as the "patio" around the pool. All my clients have aprons around their pools. These are not only beautiful but also provide a firm, slip-resistant surface for walking and to support the placement of furniture. Aprons also serve as a solid, clean transition between any expanses of lawn and the pool, helping to keep grass clippings and other detritus from being tracked into the water. The options for materials can be overwhelming: natural stone, manmade stone, brick or concrete pavers, poured concrete, wood decking, composite or plastic decking, peastone, grass, even indoor-outdoor carpeting. When I'm looking for materials for a pool apron, what I want is something with minimal cracks or places for detritus to lodge, something without "stuff" to track into the pool, and something that is friendly to furnishings, easy to maintain, and cool on bare feet in hot weather. I prefer natural, flat paving stone above all, but I'll walk you through the pros and cons of each.

Natural stone. You must know by now my preferred hardscape choice is almost always stone. I love the colors, variety, beauty, and durability that natural stone offers. For pool coping, you can use both irregular flagging and cut pavers. The irregular flagging is stunning but will need something between the flagging pieces to cover the joints. If this is peastone or rice stone, it is not barefoot friendly and will be tracked into the pool, potentially fowling the pump or filter. Concrete in the joints works in many climates but not so well here in New England. The joints are bound to crack at some point, and mortar will chip and become a hazard. I prefer regular cut pavers that can be set—dry or mortared—tightly together, and butted up closely to the coping. This gives a smooth surface that is solid and comfortable.

Brick or concrete pavers. For all of the same reasons that natural stone pavers are my preferred choice, brick or concrete pavers make an equally good choice for a pool apron. Brick can heat up on sunny days, so between these two product categories, I would lean towards concrete pavers in lighter colors.

Manmade stone. Although cultured stone is mimicking natural stone quite well these days, it does look fake to me. That said, the regular concrete pavers that are designed to look like bluestone or brownstone are quite beautiful, durable, easy on the feet, and don't seem to overheat under a scorching sun.

Poured concrete. The apron of choice throughout the Sunbelt. Relatively inexpensive, durable in most climates, can be colored, tinted, or stamped into shapes, has a good tooth for a nonslip surface, and lighter colors resist frying bare feet.

Wood decking. Stunning, but will check and split over time and can pose a splintering problem. I don't have a problem with splintering on a deck where people are usually clothed, but around a pool? No. Natural wood decking is just not the wisest choice for a pool apron.

Composite wood decking or plastic decking. A definite option for a pool apron. For all of the reasons wood is gorgeous, you could consider using a composite decking product. Composite decking isn't quite as beautiful, but there is no splintering or warping, most colors are cool underfoot, and they last fifteen years or more.

Peastone or rice stone. Lovely to look at but impossible to step on with bare feet. I have seen this done around a pool, but it invites disaster. Tiny stones are tracked into the pool, get caught in the filtration system, and make their way into the house, where they scratch the floors.

Grass. I have also seen this done, although it was against my recommendation. It's beautiful: deep green lawn against soft gray coping framing luxurious blue-gray pool. But it's a pain in the arse for lawn maintenance crews, who need to haul their machines over the perimeter fencing. Even though the grass clippings are hauled away, tiny pieces remain and invariably get tracked into the pool and house. Lawn furniture legs make holes in soft soil. Towels thrown on the ground pick up grass clippings and don't dry. This particular application for grass is not my favorite.

Indoor-outdoor carpeting. Sounds tacky, right? Okay, hold onto your seats: in my opinion it's gorgeous. Indoor-outdoor carpeting used as a pool apron is functional, soft and cool on the feet, firm under furniture, easy to clean with a blower, inexpensive to install, and inexpensive to reinstall after ten years or so of use. This is actually quite a good choice.

As you design a pool area, you might also consider how to enclose or screen the pool equipment. Nothing is more unsightly than a bunch of pool plumbing, motors, and propane tanks staring you in the face. The equipment can also be noisy (although the newer equipment is quieter). If you cannot position this stuff away from the main pool area, screen it with a trellis or solid fence panel. Pop a little shed around it. We all know that pools are not a natural feature, but your clients don't need to see all of the hardware that goes into keeping their pool beautiful and clean.

Give some thought to adding a changing area, another nice-to-have feature. An outdoor shower can be a great way to clean off before people enter the pool, and a lovely way to rid themselves of treated water residue before coming inside. At the very least, consider having a foot-washing station next to the main entry from the pool to the house. This way, neither kids nor adults will track leaves or grass clippings into the house with their pool-wet feet.

I always try to connect the pool apron with a contiguous walkway that links to the rear house entry. This way, people keep their feet clean on the way to and from the pool area, helping to minimize the mess inside both the pool and the house.

Working a pool installation takes quite a bit of time, and at first it will take some courage. But it is wonderful to see these creations come to life!

CHAPTER NINE

Irrigation, Drainage, and Lighting

I N ANY LANDSCAPE, water plays a pivotal role. We add water in the form of irrigation to establish and maintain plantings, and to keep water features functioning optimally. Designers also need to focus on keeping water away from where it is not wanted, and must always consider drainage when planning grading, hardscape, and garden areas.

Light, too, is a critical element we use to great advantage. Well-designed landscape lighting creates sparkle and drama, increases safety, and can serve as the crowning jewel in any landscape.

A working knowledge of all three of these areas will assure the success of your designs as well as your business.

IRRIGATION

It's a fact of life: plants need water. Even gardens built in concert with the principles of Xeriscaping, designed to need no additional water once they mature, need water as they are becoming established. As you design gardens, how the gardens get watered has to be an essential part of your thinking. Delivering water to a plant is irrigation, and as a garden designer this will be a top priority.

Mother Nature provides the best irrigation. Rain is free, contains fewer chemicals and additives than traditional municipal water sources, and provides a light dose of nitrates, acting like a little burst of plant food. But Mother Nature is a fickle entity, and the rainfall many of us get comes in the form of periodic deluges, broken up by periods of drought. You will need to rely on human-provided irrigation to satisfy the needs of the gardens you design.

Good horticultural practices (matching plants to site, grouping plants with like needs, and so forth) will go a long way to reduce watering needs, but the trees, shrubs, borders, and lawn areas you design will still need regular supplemental water, particularly when first installed. Most of our clients want watering to be turnkey. They don't want to think about it, worry about it, tamper with it, or even really know it exists. Adequate water is critical to all of the softscape. Contrary to popular belief, a well-planned, well-managed irrigation system can provide that turnkey solution and be one of your best defenses against water waste.

You do not need to be able to design and install an entire irrigation system, but you do need to understand enough of the principles of irrigation to have an intelligent discussion with your irrigation subcontractors. They are your partners and will help make sure your installed plantings—and you!—are a success.

Four basic types of irrigation are used around the United States, and you need to understand how they differ so that you can identify the right option for your clients. They include automatic sprinkler or overhead irrigation, drip irrigation, hoses and sprinklers, and hand-watering with a hose, bucket, or watering can.

In sprinkler or overhead irrigation systems, water is piped underground to various watering zones. Each zone is comprised of a defined area usually determined based on a particular watering need. For example, a zone for lawn would require much more water than a zone that was irrigating a mixed planting of ornamental grasses. The water is delivered by overhead, pressurized sprinklers or guns, designed to bring a specific amount of water to each zone (the duration of the watering event), with a predetermined timing (the frequency of the watering events).

Drip irrigation, also known as trickle irrigation, uses slender, low-pressure, subsurface tubing to bring water directly to the root zone of each plant in a planting. This system has gained a great deal of popularity as it can provide the most water-wise irrigation. A properly designed drip system results in minimal evaporation and runoff, but the plants thrive. This is an exceptional solution for automatically irrigating planted pots, or automatically adding water to birdbaths and water features, and it is often the only solution for automated irrigation where the client has insufficient water pressure for overhead sprinkler irrigation. An exciting development is that drip is coming out of the experimental stage for lawn irrigation.

Drip irrigation is a little more expensive to install than traditional overhead irrigation because the process is more labor intensive, but given that it uses considerably less water, it is less expensive to run. It is also a feel-good system, because you know you are minimizing irrigation waste and getting the most out of every drop of water.

In any installed irrigation system, water waste will be minimized when we ensure the following:

- Sprinkler heads are aimed correctly to avoid spraying water onto driveways, streets, or other hardscape, or against houses or other buildings.
- The master clock has each zone timed to deliver enough water to irrigate the roots of the plants, but not so much water that there is runoff.

They can look like a war zone, but irrigation installations go quickly.

- Overhead watering is always done in the morning or early evening to minimize loss of water to evaporation.
- The frequency of irrigation events is scheduled properly so that the plantings do not receive too much water in a given period, nor too little.
- The system uses a dependable rain sensor or a computerized master controller, so there is automatically no irrigation if Mother Nature has provided. There is nothing more wasteful than irrigating the day after receiving a ton of rain—or worse yet, during the rain! I see this frequently and it irks me.

Usually the most cost- and water-efficient automated systems are a combination of spray and drip, designed in multiple zones based on water requirements. Remember that timing for the various zones should be fine-tuned several times during the active watering season, since needs will shift dramatically during the year.

We can certainly also irrigate with hoses and sprinklers or by hand. I do have clients who for reasons of cost do not have automated irrigation

Irrigation allows this lush courtyard to flourish in the dry heat of St. John, in the U.S. Virgin Islands.

systems. I even have one client with a roof terrace garden who hand-waters everything, keeping the garden meticulous in the bargain. She's a rare exception. But for clients whose property is small enough to cover in a short morning of watering events, and who have the motivation to stick with it, we can use a clever combination of hoses, sprinklers, and automatic timers to keep the plants adequately watered and the costs way down.

RESIDENTIAL IRRIGATION SYSTEM COMPONENTS

The basic components of a residential irrigation system are controllers, valves, sprinklers, and sensors, as well as tubing for drip irrigation systems.

Controllers are the brains of the system. They are usually set by turning dials or pushing buttons, allowing the irrigation contractor or homeowner to select when the watering will start, how long each zone will water, and what days the watering will take place. One on-off cycle is called an "irrigation event."

Controllers are electronically (or radio-frequency) connected to a control box, which contains valves that open and close. The valves open to allow the pressure-fed water into the subsurface piping that serves each zone. The water pressure forces the water out of the sprinkler heads, irrigating the planting in that zone until the end of the programmed duration, at which time the valve closes and another valve opens to irrigate the next zone.

We break up a property into zones because few water services or private wells can provide enough water pressure to water an entire property at once. Your irrigation contractor will recommend the zone layout after walking the property with you. The zones are based on what is being watered, the watering needs of this area, the type of watering delivery for this area (for example, spray heads versus drip), and how much water pressure is available in the system.

Nearly all residential systems use automatic valves operated by a controller. I have only encountered manual valves once, when I was the garden designer for a large country club and golf course. Their water pressure was so amazing that we had to be careful where we planted trees, since the water from the rotary heads could actually work the bark off the tree trunks.

Sprinklers are the heads used in modern sprinkler systems. There are two basic kinds, spray heads and rotary heads. We do not mix the two types of heads within the same zone, but we certainly mix them in the same irrigation system. Which head is used in each zone depends on the size of the area being watered, the water pressure available to the system, and what is in the path of the sprinkler.

Spray sprinkler heads and bodies are the most common type of sprinkler in residential irrigation systems. The heads are usually somewhat adjustable for type of spray and width or pattern of coverage. Spray heads are coupled with spray sprinkler bodies, which are available in several sizes, chosen for best use for the area they are irrigating. These types of assemblies are generally designed to sit just a bit above the soil surface when not in use. They pop up during watering and retract afterward, conveniently keeping themselves out of the way of mowing and normal property use.

Rotary sprinklers, which are larger, are used in open spaces and are designed to disperse water 25 to 30 feet or more. These heads can also be designed to pop up and retract, and they are also available in fixed models that can be set on risers for large planted areas.

Sensors are an essential part of any automated irrigation system. They are optional, but frankly I think rain and flow sensors should be required additions.

Rain sensors are installed in locations that are exposed to normal rainfall but that are outside the irrigated area on the property. Natural rain will trigger the device and cause the automated system to stay off if the rain sensor has measured sufficient precipitation.

Freeze sensors interrupt the signal to the control valves when temperatures fall below freezing. This ensures the irrigation system won't add a slick layer of ice to walkways and driveways just before dawn on any given day. It also helps prevent freeze damage to the automated system. Of course, by the time freezing weather settles in, most of your clients' automated irrigation systems will have been blown out and shut down for the winter.

Flow sensors can identify a break in the system before major damage occurs. A broken head or ruptured pipe can flood the ground, cause erosion, even undercut sidewalks and driveways. A flow sensor will go off at a certain level of flow and automatically shut off the valve to that zone.

Drip irrigation tubing is installed by switchbacking through the planting beds. There are several types, but they all function similarly. Some versions have small holes perforated through the entire length of the tubing, others allow water to permeate through the entire tubing, and still others require smaller tubing to be connected to the main feeder tube, with the small tubing terminating in the drip end at the root zone of each plant in the planting.

Drip irrigation zones can be mixed with sprinkler zones, but the water pressure is controlled differently. Your irrigation subcontractor will know how to step down water pressure so that drip irrigation can be used where it makes sense.

I ROBOT

For maximum irrigation control, perhaps the best systems available today are smart controller systems. Regulated by a small computer that combines local data from the site with information from online weather-monitoring services, these smart systems adjust the irrigation delivery every day, and allow your irrigation subcontractors to remotely see what is going on at your client's site. If there is a line blowout or a broken head, the system will sense the problem and immediately notify your irrigation professional. These high-efficiency control systems can reduce water usage 30% to 40% (sometimes up to 50%) over conventional on-off controllers.

The smart controllers calculate how much water is necessary based on a wide variety of factors, including rainfall, wind speed, temperatures, plant types, soil type, and sun exposure. They keep a constant eye on the watering needs of the site and can play a critical role in long-term water management strategies.

NO WATERING

So that's watering in a nutshell. Now let's talk about no watering. In the late summer of 2007 we had to cancel plantings because of drought. You cannot plant if there is a total ban on watering, or even if a water ban threatens. It's just not worth the risk. As you mature as a designer and get more and more installations under your belt, you'll know to watch the weather. You'll study today's weather, tomorrow's weather, what the meteorologists think is in store for the next week or month, what weather pundits are saying about this season. You will especially tune in if you have a large planting on the near horizon. If there is any chance that precipitation in your locale has been so low that the area might face water restrictions—or worse yet, a complete moratorium on all outside watering—you need to weigh whether you want to plant now or wait. I had $30,000 worth of plant stock that I wanted in the ground, that the clients wanted in the ground, and that the nursery wanted to move. But had I thrown caution to the wind and installed the plants it would have been a financial disaster for me. Two weeks later a complete moratorium went into effect, and I likely would have lost not only the cost of the plants but also the cost of the several days of labor required to install it, and the bulk materials used to mulch it. It would have been a very expensive mistake.

Fortunately, caution prevailed. When the planting finally did go in the following spring, we had a lovely year with good rain. The plants have thrived, and the clients are happy. All's well that ends well.

DRAINAGE

Drainage is one of the least glorious aspects of what we design but is critical nonetheless. Inappropriate drainage can lead to major damage to the house, erosion and destruction in the landscape, and very unhappy clients.

When relandscaping part or all of a piece of property, we have a major opportunity to look at the current drainage situation and improve it if necessary. The goals for good drainage are getting water away from the foundation, keeping drainage directed so that it does not undermine anything in the path of the moving water, and avoiding water runoff on a neighboring property. Look at the house and around the foundation. Where do the gutters tie in? Where do the downspouts direct rainwater? Is there damage or rot on any siding near the downspout tie-ins? Where is there puddling or erosion on the property? Do the clients have a problem with a wet basement after rainstorms? We cannot solve every drainage issue (high water table, for example), but we can help relieve many of them.

Most municipalities do not allow you to tie residential drainage into the local storm drain system. A local storm drain may look like a tempting solution, but don't do it if local code does not permit this.

Much of what I do when I rework drainage is keep water out of basements and off of walkways and driveways by capturing downspout water and carrying it away. We frequently accomplish this with the installation of simple subsurface plastic drain lines. It is an inexpensive solution that often completely takes care of any water problem. When the problem is larger, we can carry the water further away from the house, and empty it into a dry well. Why keep water off of walks and drives? In cold climates, drainage water running over hardscape can flash freeze, creating a dangerous icy situation. We don't want people slipping and falling (or any resulting lawsuits). In all climates, drainage water running over hardscape can undermine masonry, wash out base materials, and eventually make the hardscape unstable, requiring repair or replacement. So getting drainage water away from any surfaces where people walk or drive is a good thing.

If your client's property is receiving a great deal of runoff from a neighbor's property, you can try to capture the water as it enters your

The large drainage basins required for most development projects are usually unimaginative and unsightly. These could be redesigned to create native habitat that is functional, filters toxins out of the runoff, supports wildlife, and looks beautiful in four seasons.

client's property with some local regrading, then direct the runoff to a dry well or rain garden swale, depending on the topography. Make sure that whatever solution you devise does not put additional water onto any other neighboring property. This is the stuff that messy and expensive lawsuits are made of, and if you did the work, you could be hit with the lawsuit along with the property owner. Ick.

We worked a site where three roofs converged to pour a veritable cascade of water whenever it rained. The water ran to a small, hard-packed clay side yard area that was surrounded by hardscape, fencing, and driveways. In driving rains this area could not drain fast enough, and the water would come over the sills of the doors into the garage storage room and the sunroom. Not good. So we tied in drainpipes to the two downspouts and redirected the gutter water to an area in the backyard that sloped down to the woods. The next rainstorm showed us that this solution didn't completely take care of the problem, so we knew we needed to put in a dry well. A dry well is an underground chamber into which water can drain quickly and then be absorbed underground. First we called our local dig hotline (see chapter 10, and find your own hotline at call811.com). Three days later we excavated the entire side yard area out to a depth of 7 feet. We lined the pit with landscape fabric to keep the side soil from

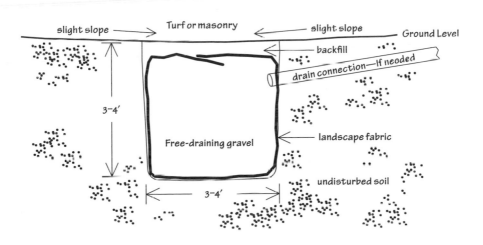

Cross section of a dry well.

migrating into the well, then added in 5 feet of 1½-inch gravel. We topped this with smaller gravel, tamped, then added more landscape fabric. Over this went our hardscape of dry-laid brick patio, with a cast-iron drain in the center. The entire patio was gently pitched to the middle so that any driving rain would immediately sluice down into the dry well. Eureka! The next rainstorm didn't cause a teaspoon of water invasion into either the garage or the sunroom. This was a fairly draconian solution, but the drainage problem was huge and we solved it.

You will be your client's hero if you can help solve a drainage problem. A drier basement, no puddling or erosion, fewer streams running through the landscape—they'll be delighted.

LIGHTING

Nothing can enhance and transform a landscape like well-designed landscape lighting. Good lighting can accent the house and gardens, provide direction, highlight special features, and enhance safety. That said, this is definitely an area where "more" does not mean "more." The most beautiful, elegant, and functional landscape lighting installations are also among the most subtle.

Well-designed landscape lighting should show family members and guests how to get from their vehicles to the house entries. It should gently illuminate areas so that people can safely find their way. It can softly highlight special trees or features in the landscape, and it can emphasize key architectural features of the house. What it should not do is blast you in the face, make jarring polka dots of light marching up a driveway or walk, or create black holes in the landscape.

Poorly done lighting is, to me, worse than no landscape lighting, and not just in terms of aesthetics. Too much or badly executed lighting is light pollution, a serious problem I discussed in chapter 4. This is not to say that we have to turn out all the lights. We just need to design appropriate outdoor lighting that is not only beautiful and appropriate but also energy-efficient and safe.

Lamp choices matter. They matter for lighting quality and they matter for energy consumption. For the greatest energy efficiency, stop using incandescent lamps and use LED technology. LED fixtures are usually low voltage, which provides an immediate energy savings over in-line voltage fixtures. They are also safer in the landscape (there's really no chance to get electrocuted). LED lamps use a tiny fraction of the energy that a similar incandescent light output would use, and the individual lamps can last ten times longer. LEDs are ecofriendly from cradle to grave. Despite all the recent hype, please do not use CFLs. Touted as the savior of lighting and energy use today, compact fluorescents will be the problem of tomorrow since every one of them contains a hazardous waste: mercury.

Fixtures also matter. Use shielded lighting fixtures that control the light output, putting it only where it is needed, and avoid fixtures that point the light up. No bulb should be visible, and no light should emanate above 90 degrees. I detest pole lamps—there, I've said it—which shut down the pupils in our eyes to pinpoints, actually making it more difficult to see and drive in the dark. Better would be soft lights that wash down a few tree trunks, gently indicating the way, or low lights that splash over the face of a stone wall along the drive. Even small pathlights that wash across a path or driveway. Subtle, efficient, lovely.

A fundamental method of controlling light pollution is using a simple curfew: turn off lights at appropriate times. No home or property needs to be lit up all night. Additionally, timers, motion or occupancy sensors, and dimmers should be a part of every lighting design. I have dimmers on nearly every light inside and outside of my home. By dimming lights, not only am I able to reduce the electricity each fixture uses, but the experience of the lighting is considerably more pleasant and easy on the eyes.

WHAT CONSTITUTES GOOD LIGHTING?

- Avoid glare, which decreases visibility.
- Use the right amount of light, not too much nor too little.
- Use fairly uniform lighting so that our eyes can adjust easily.
- Avoid deep shadows. We need smooth, gentle transitions from light to dark.
- Avoid light trespass, shining light only where it is needed and wanted.
- Eliminate uplights. We don't live up in the sky!
- Avoid the clutter and trashy look of areas with poor-quality lighting.
- Save energy.

Motion sensors outdoors are good for safety and security. Frankly, I think motion sensors are the only reason to have flood lights. Why have flood lights? They are blinding if you are heading towards them, so they are no good for lighting guest arrival or recreational areas. And they don't increase security or decrease acts of vandalism or burglary. (That's right, they do not help, and this is because they leave a dark edge, making the dark areas darker and leaving more area for ne'er-do-wells to hide in.)

How do you evaluate the lighting in your client's garden? Ask these questions and identify where there is room for improvement or light reduction:

- Does the area actually need to be lit?
- If yes, for what purpose? (Safety, path lighting, ambiance, and so forth.)
- What level of lighting is necessary?
- Do any light fixtures emit light above 90 degrees?
- Is there any light trespass?
- Is glare, or perceived glare, an issue?

Depending on the answers, following are some recommendations. Either don't light the area, or turn off lights when they aren't needed. Direct light only where it is wanted. Eliminate all light emissions above 90 degrees. Minimize light output at high angles (70 to 90 degrees from the vertical). Conceal the lamp source and bright reflector sections from direct view. And finally, use energy-efficient lighting sources and bulbs.

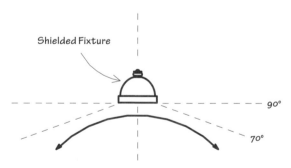

When designing exterior lighting, eliminate light emissions above 90 degrees and minimize high-angle light (70 to 90 degrees from the vertical).

CHAPTER 10

Occupational Hazards:
Lions and Tigers and Bears, Oh My!

WHEN TALKING ABOUT our profession, I've been known to say, "It isn't the job that'll kill you, it's the schlepping." But as much as the schlepping is a killer, that statement is not entirely true. Real dangers lurk in the urban jungle. If you aren't careful, frankly, the job *can* kill you.

Snake bites, mosquito- and tick-born diseases, dermatitis, phytophototoxicity, back injury, sunburn, heatstroke, sight damage, stings, hearing loss, rabies—some are annoyances, others potentially fatal. The potential for injury in this profession is high, even in our rather benign part of the world. But if you are aware of the dangers and take some precautions, you can tiptoe through the tulips without fear. Most of my contemporaries have suffered few job-related injuries. Lots of what we do to protect ourselves involves common sense and keeping safety in the forefront of our thinking.

BODILY INJURY

Sometimes the enemy is us. No, not dangers from other members of the human race. I'm talking about being a danger to ourselves. Back pain, snapped ankle, blown-out knee, carpal tunnel syndrome. For the most part we can avoid these problems if we just take a minute to look after number one.

The threat of bodily injury is a constant worry. I can work with carpal tunnel. I know it, because I have done it, but I cannot work with a broken ankle or knee. Back pain can be a nuisance, or it can lay you out for weeks. Taking proper precaution against bodily damage, knowing when to take a break or call it quits, and watching out for the health of your coworkers, all go a long way to reduce injuries.

Proper footwear is critical. You can work in sneakers or other types of work shoe, but you are better off wearing boots that lace up over your ankles. These may be hotter than sandals in the summer, but they will protect your ankles against glancing blows from shovels and hand tools, as well as provide support against a sprain or a break. In 2007 I was at a job site, and since I knew I'd only be having a chat that morning (I knew I wasn't going to be slogging plants or masonry supplies) I wore sandals. While talking to my carpentry contractor, I stepped backwards right into a small hole in the client's driveway. As I fell, my foot and ankle registered instant pain. Fortunately the ankle was sprained, not broken. But three weeks later it was hurting worse than when I first injured it, so I finally had it x-rayed and found that I had fractured three small bones in my foot. There was nothing the docs could do but tell me to keep wearing the over-the-counter support brace I'd purchased, and to stay off the foot. Yeah, right. The damage occurred in early June and the season had barely started, with several large projects just getting underway. Because I did not stay off the foot, more than a year later a lump remained over the break location, and the injury was still bothering me periodically. Proper footwear probably would have prevented this injury.

Most people do not even think about types of injuries until they happen. Like stepping on a nail. Whether or not your jobs involve any house construction, you will be amazed by the amount of junk you uncover as you build gardens and install plantings. The stuff you find buried will be amazing, horrifying, and everything in between. Unfortunately, some of it will be very sharp, and if you step on it in just the right way it could easily penetrate your sneaker—and foot.

Crushed toes. Just the thought makes me cringe. Picture yourself helping schlep a 200-pound granite step that slips and lands on your foot. If you were wearing a pair of sneakers, this could not only crush your foot or toes, it could sever them. Again, good work boots go a long way to prevent these types of injuries, particularly those with substantive soles and steel toes. Your footwear should provide good protection from the bottom, top, and sides, and it should be comfortable. If you don't already have a favorite brand, get fitted at a good retailer and try on several pairs. You'll be amazed to find how differently each type of boot can feel.

Lifting injuries are rampant in our industry. Grabbing heavy plant materials and stone supplies and lifting with our backs instead of our leg muscles is just plain bad. I have to admit I do the worst damage to my back either repetitively picking up things that are too heavy or awkward, or twisting as I pick up. I try to avoid this, but when it's the end of the day and I'm tired and rushing to finish up—irk! Pain. Using proper lifting techniques is an important way to avoid back injuries.

The stagehand's axiom applies well to our profession: "Never lift what you can drag, never drag what you can roll, never roll what you can leave." The best way to accomplish something is often also the easiest.

Here's how to lift and save your back. First, bend your knees while keeping your back straight. Firmly take hold of the item you are lifting

These guys are pros. They work as a team and use the right machinery to safely lift a heavy awning frame.

177

wherever it is comfortable to grab. Finally, slowly stand upright while keeping both your back and your body straight. Use the strong muscles of your legs to do the work. Avoid twisting—use your feet to make a turn, rather than torquing your body.

Another way to save your back? Ask for help. That's what a crew is for: lending a hand, working as a team, sharing the load. This helps avoid injury and also makes the whole job much more pleasant.

EARS AND EYES

A lot of what we do is noisy, and most people don't realize that frequent exposure to noise will damage your hearing. Make sure your crew members wear ear protection when using power equipment, and if you are around the machinery much, you too should wear ear protection or ear plugs.

Now we come to another critical sense: sight. I am so horrified when I see guys using blowers, chainsaws, nail guns, even stone hammers, without eye protection. My mother, who spent her life as a designer and dressmaker, lost her sight to macular degeneration in the 1990s. Losing your sight is a horrible thing, so I entreat you to never, ever take your eyes for granted. Something as simple as a branch whipping back can take out your eye. A chip of stone, a metal shard off a nail, a flying splinter of wood—any could permanently damage the sight in an eye. Safety goggles are cheap. Have several pairs around, give them to crew members, and insist that they wear them when they are doing anything that can throw detritus or chips into the air.

Eyes also need UV protection. My mother's retinologist, one of America's top ophthalmologists, insists that UV exposure contributes to the rising incidence of macular degeneration, the leading cause of legal blindness in the country. To safeguard your eyesight over your lifetime, use eyewear with adequate UV protection, ideally full-wrap sunglasses that protect against UVA and UVB light wavelengths.

TETANUS

Tetanus is an infection caused by the bacterium *Clostridium tetani*. The spores of tetanus are commonly found in dust, soil, and manure—you know, the stuff we garden designers are working in and around incessantly.

We are taught from childhood that deep puncture wounds are the type of injury that can give us tetanus, and it's true that large wounds are more susceptible since there is more surface area for the bacteria to gain entry. But tetanus is dangerous if it enters any open cut; even tiny injuries like a small scratch or pinprick can provide access.

Once the tetanus bacteria enter the body, they multiply, forming large colonies and releasing a toxin that affects the body's nervous system. Symptoms can include irritability, neck stiffness, trouble swallowing, rigid abdominal muscles, muscle spasms, and severe convulsions. Perhaps the most well-know symptom of tetanus is its alias, lockjaw, which occurs when muscle spasms and stiffness become severe enough to make it impossible to move the jaw muscles. Despite modern treatments, about a third of people who contract tetanus die.

The best way to protect yourself? Get vaccinated. Tetanus bacteria truly do exist just about everywhere, and the vaccination has few side effects and is effective against the disease. Now that you have chosen to adopt a garden designer's life, make sure to keep your tetanus vaccination up to date. And if you receive a major skin injury, take care to wash the wound well and apply an antiseptic or topical antibiotic, and see your doctor to get a booster if it has been more than five years since your last tetanus shot.

SUNBURN

The life of a garden designer can be much healthier than that of, say, a basement-dwelling programmer. One reason? Exposure to the sun. Our bodies need sunlight to manufacture vitamin D ("the sunshine vitamin"), which in turn allows us to effectively absorb and utilize calcium. A double benefit is that concussive exercise (read: digging) is the second best way to maintain bone strength and guard against osteoporosis (the best way is weightlifting). So older folks, take note!

Feeling the sun on your face is wonderful, life-giving, and life-affirming. My idea of nirvana is a beach, the sun, and a good book. But like so much in life, too much of a good thing is bad. Garden and landscape designers work outdoors much of the year and are constantly exposed to the sun. Sunburns will be frequent unless you take precautions, and frequent sunburns can lead to early aging and skin cancer. Lots of designers I know wear hats and long-sleeved shirts, and slather with sunscreen. Considering, however, that many sunscreens contain substances even more carcinogenic than sunlight, you might opt for an all-natural product.

DEHYDRATION

Dehydration is a medical condition in which the body experiences an excessive loss of water. It is frequently seen in people who perform physical labor in harsh conditions. Sounds like the definition of a landscape crew, doesn't it? Symptoms generally become noticeable after 2% of normal water volume has been lost, and include fatigue, discomfort, and thirst. It's important to note that thirst is actually a late sign. A useful rule of thumb for avoiding dehydration involves monitoring the frequency and character of urination. If you develop a full bladder about every three to five hours, and the urine is lightly colored or colorless, chances are that dehydration is not occurring. If urine is deeply colored or scant, water intake may not be adequate.

In landscape professionals, dehydration is often caused by prolonged physical activity without consuming adequate water, especially in a hot or humid environment, or during prolonged exposure to dry air. Note

The ever-present water bottle on the job site. The day we installed this fountain it was 97°F and humid on this south-facing patio. We went through lots of water.

that caffeinated beverages are not as beneficial as water, since the action of caffeine can contribute to dehydration. An average body in a temperate climate can lose approximately 2½ quarts of water in one day. Body fluids are lost through the skin as sweat, through the lungs as water vapor, through the kidneys as urine, and through the bowels. In warm or humid weather or during heavy exertion, water loss through perspiration can increase by an order of magnitude over the same body at rest. Avoid dehydration: drink plenty of water.

HEAT EXHAUSTION

Heat exhaustion can range in severity from mild heat cramps to life-threatening heatstroke. Symptoms, which often begin suddenly, sometimes after excessive exertion and inadequate fluid intake, can resemble shock and may include dizziness or faintness, nausea, heavy sweating, rapid heartbeat, low blood pressure, pale skin that is cool to the touch, low-grade fever, heat cramps, headache, fatigue, and dark-colored urine. Those most prone to heat exhaustion include the elderly, people with high blood pressure, and people working or exercising in a hot environment.

If you suspect that one of your crew members is suffering from heat exhaustion, get them out of the sun and into the shade or an air-conditioned area. Lay the person down, elevate their legs and feet slightly, loosen their clothing, and encourage them to drink cool water. Spray or sponge them with cool water and fan them to accelerate evaporation. Watch the person closely, as heat exhaustion can quickly become heatstroke. Encourage them to drink water or a sports drink (to replace lost salts), and to eat a salty snack if they'll tolerate it. If the person experiences a body temperature greater than 102°F, fainting, confusion, or seizures, call 911.

HEATSTROKE

Heatstroke, also known as sunstroke, is an advanced state of hyperthermia, an acute condition that happens when the body produces or absorbs more heat than it can dissipate. Hyperthermia is usually caused by prolonged exposure to heat, and the body loses its ability to regulate temperature. One of the body's most important temperature regulation methods is perspiration. The act of perspiring draws heat from inside the body, allows it to be carried off by radiation, and then further cools the body as the sweat evaporates. If the body becomes sufficiently dehydrated and production of sweat ceases, this heat regulation system shuts down, and the body loses its ability to regulate temperature. Once this happens, core temperature rises quickly.

Victims may become confused or hostile, often experience a headache, and may appear drunk. The skin becomes red as the blood vessels dilate to try to dissipate body heat, but as the heatstroke progresses the resultant decreases in blood pressure cause the blood vessels to contract, ultimately resulting in a pale or bluish skin coloration. As body organs begin to fail, unconsciousness and coma result.

Heatstroke is a medical emergency requiring hospitalization. Call 911 if you even suspect one of your crew members might be suffering from heatstroke. As you wait for emergency teams to arrive, immediately move the victim to a cooler area, keep trying to bring the body temperature down by sponge bathing him or her in cool (not cold) water, and put cool compresses on their torso, head, neck, and groin. Do *not* use alcohol rubs, which can cause further dehydration. Encourage the person to sip cool water to try to rehydrate only if they are conscious and tolerant. Heatstroke victims are usually hospitalized for further tests and observation.

To prevent heatstroke, wear light, loose-fitting clothing and hats that provide shade and that are vented to allow for cooling perspiration. People who must be outside, like landscape workers, should be aware that humidity and direct sunlight can cause the heat index to be 18 degrees hotter than the temperature indicated by a thermometer. When exerting in hot weather, drink plenty of liquids to replace fluids lost from sweating. Water, not sports drinks, is the most effective liquid to replace lost fluids. However, drinking only water without ingesting any salts can lead to a condition known as hyponatremia, which can cause sudden death from cardiac failure. We lose electrolytes through sweat and urine, and these need to be replaced.

ADVERSE WEATHER

"Oh, you work outdoors. How lucky!" Well, sure I am, and you will be too. But just because we work outdoors doesn't mean it's all roses. In my climate, about ten days each season are perfect days to be outside. The others—well, not so much.

Acting as a benevolent friend or an evil foe, the weather drives nearly everything we do. It can mean work or no work, plant death or plant life, pleasant work conditions or dreadfully nasty conditions. Weather can derail a job for several days after the actual weather system has departed. You can't grade muck after 3 inches of rain; you have to wait until the area has drained enough to work the soil. If you seed a lawn one day and get heavy rain the next, the seed can easily end up downhill, making a glorious carpet in the neighbor's backyard.

Whatever it is dishing out, the weather will become your constant companion as it has never been before. I check the weather before saying good morning to my family, and it's the last thing I check before retiring at night. I keep an active weather alert system on my computer. I watch forecasts for the day and for a week out. I take a look at the radar tracking at least twice a day, more if I'm at a job close to home and indicators are looking iffy. If you really get into it, you can have weather updates sent automatically to your cell phone.

We often plan our construction activities based on sun exposure. If it's a hot day, we'll try to start in the shade on the west side of the house and end the day in the shade on the east side. Conversely, if it's a cold day, we'll start in the sunniest spot and work our way around, following the warmth. And at windy sites we try to work early before the winds come up, or plan to work later after the winds die down.

Sometimes, though, we have no control over where we work. I have several regular spring jobs installing colorful tropicals on roof terraces. These locations face due south and are up against six stories of brick walls. Even in the relative chill of May, when conditions are still and sunny it can reach 95°F or more. I try to schedule these installs when the weather is cooler or the skies a little overcast, but this isn't always possible. Once plant and machinery deliveries and crew availability have been coordinated, putting things on hold isn't feasible. We have to get in there and just do it.

Big weather often results in a go–no go decision on the work, but we also plan activities based on "little weather." We can plant in light rain (actually, this is perfect weather for planting), but we cannot grade soil.

We can unload a truckload of plant materials in a virtual monsoon, but heavy rains make almost everything else impossible. Sleet and light snow are no problem, but we make sure to get the heck outta Dodge when thunderstorms and lightning head our way.

Lightning is one of the leading causes of weather-related deaths in the United States. If you see lightning or hear distant thunder, employ the thirty-thirty rule. As soon as the lightning flashes, start counting, "One one-thousand, two one-thousand, three one-thousand." The sound of thunder travels 1 mile in five seconds. If you can count to thirty after you see lightning, the storm is 5 to 6 miles away and you can continue working. If you can't make it to thirty, immediately collect your crew and seek cover in a plumbed, electrified, closed building, or in your cars and trucks with the windows up. Do not stand under trees, and do not seek refuge in a shed, carport, or tented structure. Do not run towards where you just saw lightning strike, because lightning can and will strike the same place more than once.

According to the National Weather Service, when there is lightning you should avoid water (no showers, no hand washing, no laying in a water-filled ditch), high ground (lightning usually strikes the highest points), open spaces (lightning usually strikes objects that project up in open space, and you don't want that to be you), metal objects (fences, machinery, power tools, motors, bikes, backpack frames), phones (land or cell), and appliances.

If you are caught outside in a thunderstorm, find shelter in an enclosed building with plumbing and electricity (the metal in the electrical and plumbing lines acts like a Faraday cage to disperse the electric shock). Alternatively, get inside a truck, car, or van, roll up all windows, and do not touch anything metal inside the vehicle. (Note that fiberglass-bodied vehicles do not provide safety.) If a car or building is not an option, crouch down with your feet touching to minimize current flow, and cover your ears to protect your hearing from the thunder. Ideally you should get into a ditch or other place that is lower ground, but remain on a dry surface. Do not lay on the ground, which makes you more vulnerable to lightning strike, and stay at least 15 feet away from any metal object or any other person, to avoid transfer of electric shock.

Thunderstorms aside, bantering with the weather is one of the delights of our work. Some days you win, others you don't, but it is never dull. I keep rain parkas in my vehicle, but trash bags can be customized in a pinch. I try to keep a change of shoes and socks with me at all times. I pass out sunscreen and insect repellant when required. I bring cold water and sodas to the crew in the heat, coffee and hot chocolate in the cold. It's a challenge, but I love it. Being one with the weather, particularly in the capricious climate of New England, means being part of an ever-unfolding drama.

ACCIDENTS

A few years ago I was at a local garden center checking out a granite lantern sitting on a high shelf. When I reached up and gently leaned the lantern towards me, the top of it—a 20-pound piece—slid off and landed on my face just to the right of my nose. The pain exploded in my face, and I started bleeding profusely. Figuring I had probably smashed three teeth, I ran out of the building to my car (big mistake) and raced home. When I finally looked in the mirror, I saw that there was a ton of soft tissue damage but no loose teeth, so I figured I was basically okay. A month later, however, long after the wounds had healed, a dental hygienist cleaning my teeth told me I was suffering from resorption, a condition in which a tooth starts to attack itself and eat away at both its own root and the surrounding jaw bone. The condition is usually caused by a blow or other sharp trauma, and I guess you could say 20 pounds of rough-cut granite falling on the face qualifies. The only recourse is immediate removal of the tooth, grafting bone at the site, and putting in an implant. In the end it cost me $9000 and a lot of lost work. I know now that had I immediately let the garden center know the lantern had fallen on me, their insurance would have covered my medical expenses. Still, despite everything, I'm grateful that the stone fell on me and not on some little child, who could have been killed. And losing a tooth isn't the end of the world—I could have lost an eye! The point is that accidents happen, even in the most innocuous places.

Working as part of a team is terrific, but since we use machinery, chain saws, power saws, drills, nail guns, and other instruments of destruction, you have to maintain awareness at all times and watch what both you and your teammates are doing. Stay out of the path of all machinery, keep a broad safety circle around anyone using cutting machines, watch where you put your feet because the nature of what we do means there are all kinds of holes and trenches as we work, and always keep a cell phone handy in case of an emergency.

DIGGING

Digging can be dangerous, even deadly, if the excavator unknowingly pulls up utility lines, breaks a water main, or rips open a gas line. For this reason, state laws require you to notify utility companies before digging. Dig hotlines (see call811.com for a list of numbers) operate throughout the United States and Canada to assist excavators, contractors, and property owners with this process. You simply call the hotline, they notify the appropriate member utilities on your behalf, and the utilities come to the area and locate any underground facilities. It's fast, it's free, and it's the law.

I can't stress the importance of this enough. As soon as you get the go on any project, before you ever stick a trowel in the ground, call your local dig hotline—even if you feel certain you will not be digging in any area with underground utilities.

When you call the hotline, they will ask if you are a member contractor or have a member number. Unless you're working for large company, the answer will be no. They'll need information about you (phone number, company address, and so forth) and the excavator doing the work (your subcontractor). Be prepared to provide the address of the excavation site, nearest cross street, type and location of the work you're doing, and proposed depth of digging (to the foot, as in "not more than 2 feet" or "up to 4 feet"). They'll need to know where they should mark, and they'll ask whether you have premarked the site (this is required in some places). Then they'll give you a permit number, a list of utilities they are notifying (write these down), and they'll say something like, "You are safe to dig as of 11:23 a.m. on Thursday, June 7." This means that by that time on that day, the member utilities will have come to the site and marked their utility line locations with spray paint. Keep your permit number in a safe place, and share it with your digging contractor. I keep a copy in my glove compartment for the life of the project. If there is a problem, you can call your dig hotline or a member utility and refer to that permit number.

If there is nothing underground, the member utilities will use spray paint and mark, usually on the street, something like "no cable," meaning there is no underground cable line, or "no gas" for no underground gas line. If there is an underground utility, they will mark the location where the utility exits the street and enters the property. They will spray-paint a slash that parallels the lines, and mark "elec" for electric, or put a symbol for water, and so forth. This ultimately makes the property look like a graffiti artist has visited, but it gives you confirmation that each utility has been there.

Uniform color codes are supposed to be used to identify the type of utility. Unfortunately, the only two utilities that have been consistent at my sites were the local gas company and local water provider; most of the others mark in white paint. Nevertheless, color codes for markings are as follows:

Red = Electric
Yellow = Gas, oil, steam
Orange = Communications
Blue = Potable water
Purple = Reclaimed water
Green = Sewer, drainage
Pink = Survey marks
White = Proposed excavation

Note that the last item is "proposed excavation." That's your job. Before calling the dig hotline, you need to premark the site. This lets the member utilities know where the proposed work is, and they want it premarked in white. (Use "upside-down" landscape spray paint, not the kind designed to be used in a rolling spray assembly. This type of paint is available from any local hardware or big-box store, usually in day-glow orange and white.) Notations in white paint are instantly readable as your instructions to the member utilities. I usually put in stakes across the front of the property, next to the street, and mark the extents of the proposed excavation with a dotted line, adding "Dig Safe," the name of my dig hotline, in the middle. Then there's no mistake.

Though utilities mark the location where underground lines exit the street to connect to the property, most do not follow the lines all the way to the house. Gas companies are the exception, which is a good thing, because digging up a gas line pushes the potential digging danger way into the red zone. But aside from gas, you are responsible for finding out where the utility lines connect to the house; you can usually see this from meters on the outside of the house, or, assuming there is a basement, by looking to see where the lines come in. You as the contractor are responsible for maintaining the markings until the excavation project is over. I often have flags or painted marks positioned for months as we complete a project.

The member utilities will sometimes call to tell you they have marked the site. Sometimes you'll receive a confirmation fax or e-mail. The faxes can come in at odd hours, like 3:00 a.m., but I rarely get more than one or two calls or faxes for each project. If it's a call and it's a live person, just jot down the info ("Verizon—no underground utilities") and say thank you.

Dig Safe allows for a margin of error for their member utilities, and for the bucket on a machine. The general rule is that you are allowed to dig mechanically (with a machine) up to 2 feet on either side of any utility marking, and then you switch to manual digging until you locate the utility lines. This is an excellent safety rule. It is safer for you, your workers, and the property.

I have only had to call back Dig Safe on one occasion. It was about a week after our allowed time to dig, and we were there in force: men, machines, and me, all ready to start the job. The gas lines had not been marked, and I knew there was underground gas. Not good. I had my trusty permit number, called Dig Safe, and told them that the gas lines had apparently not yet been marked. They called the gas company, and a representative arrived within fifteen minutes to mark the gas lines. I was incredibly impressed. This is another reason to keep the dig permit number for every job with you and in a safe place. You can even put the number on a Post-it note in your wallet! Just make sure you are able to get to it quickly at all times.

If you do hit a utility line of any kind, immediately call 911 and explain what type of lines you hit and where you are. If you dig up cable lines, it is inconvenient but rarely fatal. Water is messy and annoying but also rarely dangerous. If you hit electric lines or gas lines, make sure the gas line is venting up freely and no one is smoking, turn off all machinery and cell phones, and get everyone out of the residence and to a neighbor's house. Stand a safe distance away and wait to guide the emergency repair crews as they arrive.

If something like this happens and you have already called your dig hotline and maintained the line markings, you will not generally be liable for the cost of repairs. When one of my contractors pulled up gas lines at a job, it took the gas company nearly two days to complete the repair. Ultimately Dig Safe felt that we had not adequately maintained the markings, but still they only charged us $700 for the repair work. I'm sure it took closer to $5000 to fix the line. Dig Safe truly came to our rescue.

You will need to remember to mark areas you want your demolition contractors to avoid. This is no time for subtlety. Make your markings scream, and bring them to the attention of the crew when you walk them through the job.

From this point on, the safety marking is your responsibility. Whenever you have a hole in a yard and are leaving for the day, stake around it, and run caution tape around the entire perimeter of the area. Even if the hole isn't big enough to fall into, if it can be a tripping hazard, mark it. Always think safety: for yourself, your crews, your clients, and the neighborhood. If you have excavated a hole that is deep enough to be a danger to neighborhood children or pets, stake plastic snow fencing (yeah, that hideous orange plastic stuff) around the entire perimeter and secure the bottom. Stakes and caution tape are available at most hardware stores, and the big-box stores always have these supplies. Use them.

THE POISON THREE

Some plants are just plain mean (I like to call it horti-torture). Sure, except for most cacti, and maybe *Pyracantha*, most plants look innocent enough, but you have to watch out for the sneaky ones.

At the top of the list are the overt three: poison ivy, poison oak, and poison sumac. These three species of *Rhus* are the most common cause of allergic contact dermatitis in the United States, and the particularly nasty reaction they cause is named rhus dermatitis. They are truly an occupational hazard for garden designers, and you will need to be able to identify each of them. According to the American Academy of Dermatology, about 85% of the population will develop an allergic reaction if exposed to one of the poison three. Usually people develop sensitivity to these plants only after several exposure incidents, but a rare few show sensitivity after only one exposure.

The active ingredient that causes the rash, blistering skin, and maddening itch is urushiol, a chemical in the sap of these plants that binds with the protein molecules in your skin. That is why it is nearly impossible to wash off a run-in with any of the poison three. Common reactions include not only the familiar skin rash but also potentially serious lung irritation.

Treatment and preventive measures are the same for all three plants. Avoiding direct contact with the plants helps, but urushiol can stick to pets, garden tools, clothing, and just about everything else. And if it isn't washed off, urushiol can remain active for years. Imagine digging out an old favorite pair of gardening gloves and then remembering two days later that they were previously used to weed out poison oak. Yikes! Only humans and a few other higher primates are sensitive to urushiol, so this is why you can get poison ivy from your dog without the dog getting it.

Poison ivy, poison oak, and poison sumac plant material that has been removed should never be composted (bag it and throw it away with your trash), nor should it ever be burned. You can be exposed to the chemical any time of year, from any part of the plant, even years after the plant has died. The first time I had a reaction to poison ivy, it was late November in New England. I had never responded to poison ivy, despite having basically played in it throughout my growing up. So here we were, late fall, and all of the leaves had dropped. My husband, Bruce, and I were (carefully) pulling up thready roots of poison ivy to prep a new garden area. We (carefully) bagged the roots, and got them ready for disposal. After our day in the garden, I (carefully) removed my clothing and put everything in the laundry. Then I (carefully) showered. Ha! So much for being careful. Three days later I was covered with blisters and itching insanely. My face, neck, arms, legs, ankles, torso: a mess of rash, blisters, oozing. The blisters ripped open as I scratched in my sleep, leaving bloody smears all over me, the sheets, everything. It was ugly, and this exposure left me violently allergic to poison ivy. I was thirty-three years old at the time, so it took decades to develop the allergic reaction, but once I did, yowza! I swear I am so ultrasensitive to poison ivy now that I can get it by just standing downwind of it. Not fun.

Because urushiol can penetrate the skin within minutes, you need to cleanse your skin immediately. We're talking minutes. If you have been exposed to one of the poison three, the U.S. Food and Drug Administration recommends the following. First, clean the exposed skin with generous amounts of isopropyl (rubbing) alcohol. The alcohol will remove your skin's protective coating, making you that much more vulnerable to further contact, so don't return to your task that day. Next wash the affected area with copious amounts of water—warm or cold, doesn't matter. Do not use soap, which at this point will just move the urushiol around. Remove your clothing and put it in the wash with detergent and warm water. Shower with soap and warm water, making sure to clean thoroughly under your fingernails. (Under-fingernail exposure to urushiol is often the culprit when people say their reaction is "spreading." It's not spreading, it's just delayed exposure.) And finally, hope for the best!

If you do get the rash, it will appear within twelve to forty-eight hours, inevitably followed by blisters and itching. The oozing blisters are not contagious, nor can they cause further spread of the reaction, because they do not contain urushiol. Try not to scratch, though, because compromising the blisters can open them up to possible infection.

The blistering and itch normally disappear in two to three weeks without any treatment. Oatmeal baths can help with itching, as can applying a paste of baking soda and water, though both are messy. Cooling compresses are a welcome relief, the old standby calamine lotion is wonderful (there are even nonpink versions now), and many over-the-counter products can also help.

In the case of a severe reaction, seek medical help. You might need prescription oral corticosteroids for about three weeks to help with the itching and to prevent infection of the blisters.

"Leaves of three, let them be" is a useful adage, except that not all of the poison three play by the rules. Some will grow with leaves in clusters of five or nine, for example. To avoid these plants, know what to look for.

POISON IVY

In the United States, poison ivy can be found almost everywhere in the Midwest and the East. It can be woody, a ropelike vine, a groundcover, or a freestanding shrub. Normally three leaflets come off of the main stem. New leaves are shiny and beautiful with a burgundy cast around the edges. The leaves are bright green in summer and brilliant red—truly gorgeous!—in the fall. The tiny flowers are yellowish or green, and the white berries that appear by late summer persist into fall. Birds love them.

Poison ivy happens to be a successful New England native, so we can find it just about anywhere, from sunny, sandy coastal areas to the densest forests. In my area it takes on many forms, from groundcover to tree-like shrub. I once counted fifty-seven growth rings at the base of a stalk of poison ivy we were removing from an old apple tree. The stalk was as big around as my wrist.

POISON OAK

Poison oak grows as a low shrub along the East Coast from New Jersey to Texas, and in the West along the Pacific Coast as 6-foot-tall clumps or vines up to 30 feet long. It is a beautiful plant with oaklike leaves, usually growing in clusters of three, and has bunches of yellow berries late in the season. The fall foliage is scarlet and burgundy.

POISON SUMAC

This Southeast native grows in boggy areas as a rangy shrub, reaching up to 15 feet tall. A pretty plant, poison sumac has seven to thirteen leaflets and glossy, pale yellow or cream-colored berries. Like its poison sisters, it has gorgeous scarlet foliage in the fall.

I have had many mini-arguments about this, but I know definitely that poison sumac is different from staghorn sumac, which is not poisonous. Poison sumac is fairly rare, growing only in wetlands. It has smooth leaf edges, a smooth stem, and small white flowers, and there are seven to nine leaves per stem. Staghorn sumac forms colonies in just about any area where there is enough light. The leaf edges are jagged, not smooth, it has blood red berry clusters, and the stalk and stems are hairy to the point of looking flocked.

REMOVAL

It's important to know how to remove these poisonous plants from a client's property. I don't use chemicals, and those that could be used—like glyphosate, the active ingredient found in many weed killers—are non-selective, so anything around the poisonous plants could be killed as well. I believe in hand-pulling.

How we do this is we first empty our bladders. ('Twould be very inconvenient to have to use the potty during this operation.) Then we secure our hair, glasses, and so forth. We don old clothing, and we triple glove. Triple glove means putting on cloth gloves (to absorb sweat) followed by rubber or latex gloves, and then bagging our hands and arms in plastic trash bags up to our shoulders. This is all taped fairly securely, so we can still work and grip. (Yes, we look like bizarre surgeons.) Then we hand-pull the poisonous plant, carefully bagging it as we go. We do not scratch our noses, nor do we brush mosquitoes from our faces since our hands are now polluted. When we're done pulling, we carefully untape and peel off the plastic bags and bag them for throwing away, along with the latex or rubber gloves. Finally we remove our clothing, bag it for laundry, and change into clean clothing.

After the initial eradication attempt, more poison ivy, poison oak, or poison sumac will sprout, but if you keep weeding every month or so, the plant's reserves will finally be exhausted and you will have gotten it all.

GRASS CUTS AND OTHER STORIES

Ornamental grasses are glorious but can be punishing too. Carry a couple of armloads of grasses from the delivery truck to the installation location, and you'll be amazed at the end of the day to find a zillion little slices on your arms and face. When the scratches start to burn and itch that night, it'll bring to mind the axiom, "Death by a thousand cuts." A soothing lotion, like aloe gel, goes a long way to quiet the irritation, which will disappear within about two days.

Junipers and spruces can cause a similar outcome. Those needles may feel nice when you palm them, but carry around and plant a bunch of these suckers and the punishment begins. The needles make a jillion little punctures as you work with the plant. Again, you generally won't notice it all that much during the day, but when you're driving home, or when you get into the shower that evening—eek! Stinging and burning. It may look like you're covered with a tiny rash, but it will actually be little individual puncture wounds given to you by the needles of the plant. I like to relieve the histamines from the irrigation, so when I'm showering I take a little surgical brush and scrub the irritation quite vigorously under the hot water. Burns like crazy, but when I get out of the shower and towel off, I apply aloe or a clear calamine, and the irritation is less severe that night. Whatever you do, it will generally heal in a couple of days.

Be aware of working around plants that can cause phytophototoxicity, a type of photocontact dermatitis. Plants in the carrot family (Apiaceae) are particularly known to be phytophototoxic, including parsnip (*Pastinaca sativa*), celery (*Apium graveolens*), parsley (*Petroselinum crispum*), and hogweed (*Heracleum*). Some members of the rue family (Rutaceae), fig family (Moraceae), and legume family (Fabaceae) can also cause photocontact dermatitis.

Gas plant (*Dictamnus*) is a member of Rutaceae and gives off a gas that can cause incredible photocontact dermatitis. If you include this plant in a planting plan, or if there is an existing one at a site where you

The blades of ornamental grasses can make hundreds of tiny cuts on unprotected skin.

are working, handle it carefully and wash your arms and hands with soap and water after you are finished, then apply sunscreen to the affected areas. Warn your crew members, too. Other plants, including common rue (*Ruta graveolens*), can cause the same reaction. The phototoxic inflammatory eruption will usually appear within twenty-four hours after exposure, and will peak within two to three days. Note, too, that phytophototoxicity seems to be amplified by humidity and perspiration, the conditions we often find when working on a landscape.

INSECTS

If you discount the possibility of a car accident, my guess is that the most danger that threatens a garden designer working in my part of the United States comes from insects. Bees, mosquitoes, ticks, and spiders are the major insect pests we have to watch out for, although in parts of the United States there is also risk from scorpions, fire ants, and other stinging and biting critters.

BEES AND WASPS

If you are not allergic, bee and wasp stings are a bit painful and annoying but not life threatening. Always on the lookout, my crew and I usually spot wasp or bee nests before stumbling upon them, so we are able to give them wide berth. We do, however, get surprised by ground-dwelling bees. We might be clearing an area of brush or starting to grade some space that hasn't been worked for a while, and suddenly hit ground wasps, which swarm out by the hundreds, completely pissed and looking to punish anyone they encounter. Most of the wasps or yellow-jacket type of hornets (not true hornets) can sting multiple times, and when they are angry it's what they are designed to do in order to protect their hive. Usually our best defense is to drop everything and run for the cover of our trucks. I don't like killing anything, and I'm particularly fond of any pollinator, but in this case we do have to use wasp or hornet killer spray, and then wait about an hour to make sure the hive occupants have died or dispersed.

One of my workers is allergic to honeybees, but honeybees are so docile that he just works carefully around them, and he hasn't been stung in many years. If you or any of your workers are allergic, carry an epinephrine kit in your car or on your person, and make sure that several people know where it is and how to use it.

People living in the southern tier of the United States do have to worry about Africanized honeybee (AHB, also known as killer bee) infestations. A hybrid of the African honeybee and various European honeybees, the Africanized honeybee became the preferred type of bee for beekeeping in Central and South America because of its increased vigor and productivity. Unfortunately, the hybrid retains the aggressive behavioral traits of its African ancestor. As compared to the relatively gentle European honeybee, Africanized honeybees exhibit greater defensiveness, swarm more frequently, and guard the hive more aggressively, deploying in greater numbers and pursuing perceived threats over much longer distances from the hive. They tend to live in ground cavities more often than European honeybees. Africanized honeybees are widely feared by the public, and it certainly doesn't help that the media has latched on to the epithet "killer bees" and sensationalized their spread in warmer parts of the United States. In reality the venom of an Africanized honeybee is no more potent than that of a normal honeybee, though they do tend to sting in greater numbers. They also cause far fewer deaths than venomous snakes, though it's true that they cause one to two deaths per year. There is some good news. As Africanized honeybees move into new areas and breed with existing colonies of European honeybees, the offspring become less aggressive.

MOSQUITOES

Mosquitoes are phenomenally irritating, and their bites can just about drive you crazy, but these pests can be more than an annoyance. They can harbor a number of diseases, notably equine encephalitis and the West Nile virus.

Two strains of equine encephalitis exist in the United States: eastern equine encephalitis and western equine encephalitis. Both are spread by blood-sucking insects like mosquitoes, and the symptoms are nearly identical. Infection can be mild and cause flulike symptoms such as fever, headache, and sore throat, but for people with infection of the central nervous system, sudden fever and severe headache can be quickly followed by seizures and coma. About half of patients experiencing central nervous system infection die. There is no specific treatment. Prevention centers on controlling mosquitoes and avoiding bites.

West Nile virus, also mosquito borne, mainly infects birds but is known to infect humans and other mammals. It affects humans as an asymptomatic infection, a mild infection with fever, or a neuroinvasive disease. Most symptoms resolve within seven to ten days, but can last up to two months if the disease invades the nervous system. Listen for news from your local health department about West Nile virus activity in your area, and take precautions to avoid mosquito bites.

These viruses sound dramatic, and the media makes them out like they are carried by every mosquito lurking under every leaf, but the reality is that very few people each year contract these viruses. Don't be afraid of going outdoors! Avoiding mosquito bites is the easiest way to avoid infection. Remain indoors at dawn and dusk when mosquitoes are their most active, use mosquito repellent, eliminate standing water where mosquitoes can lay eggs, and install and maintain screens in all door and window openings.

TICKS

When I was a kid, we picked up lots of dog ticks in the course of playing in the fields and wandering through the brushy areas around our neighborhood. We'd de-tick ourselves and the dogs every night.

Ticks are no longer the little annoyances they were when I was a child. Maybe we were blissfully ignorant, but we just never gave a tick a second thought. Times have changed.

The incidence of tick-borne diseases is increasing, and their geographic areas are expanding. Tick-borne illnesses are caused by a variety of pathogens, including bacteria, viruses, and protozoa, and ticks can harbor more than one disease-causing agent, so people can be infected with more than one pathogen at a time. The diseases you should be most concerned about are the two that are the most prevalent and widespread: Lyme disease and Rocky Mountain spotted fever.

Lyme disease is by far the most often reported tick-born disease in humans in the United States, and it is quickly becoming the nation's fastest-growing infectious disease. It is particularly prevalent in the

Northeast; after all, the first outbreak occurred in 1975 in Lyme, Connecticut. Lyme disease is caused by the bacterium *Borrelia burgdorferi* and is transmitted to humans by the bite of infected deer ticks, also called blacklegged ticks. Early symptoms can include soreness at the bite location, a characteristic red, circular "bull's-eye" rash, fever, headache, swollen lymph nodes, fatigue, and depression. Most infections can be treated successfully with a few weeks of antibiotics. Left untreated, Lyme disease can involve the joints, heart, and nervous system. In 2005 my husband contracted a severe case and was extremely ill with debilitating fevers and bed-soaking sweats. After finally receiving a diagnosis and starting treatment with a long period of antibiotics, he was still left with some neurological deficit in his hands. All this from a little side trip to pick blueberries on vacation.

Deer ticks are tiny, often no larger than the head of a pin, so are particularly difficult to see and find. They also tend not to go to the spots we think of when we think of ticks, instead attaching themselves to places like the outside of the arm, the stomach, the back of the knee, the front of the thigh, even the middle of the back. This past summer one attached itself to the outside of my earlobe. Weird.

Lyme disease prevention is the same as tick prevention. Use insect repellent, wear light-colored clothing, tuck your pant legs into your socks, check yourself for ticks after walking in the woods or through long grass, and remove ticks promptly. If you exhibit any early symptoms, see a physician.

Rocky Mountain spotted fever (RMSF) is the next most prevalent disease from ticks, and the most severe tick-borne illness in the United States. It is caused by infection from the bacterial organism *Rickettsia rickettsii*, and the disease can be fatal. Unlike Lyme disease, the primary arthropods that transmit Rocky Mountain spotted fever bacteria in the United States are the American dog tick and the Rocky Mountain wood tick.

Symptoms of Rocky Mountain spotted fever may resemble those of many other diseases, including fever, rash, nausea, vomiting, muscle pain, lack of appetite, and severe headache. Later signs may also include abdominal pain, joint pain, and diarrhea. Most infected people are hospitalized.

Rocky Mountain spotted fever is a seasonal disease and occurs throughout the United States from April to September. The Centers for

Disease Control and Prevention reports that over half of the cases occur in the South Atlantic region, with the highest incidences found in North Carolina and Oklahoma. Although the disease was first recognized in the Rocky Mountain area, relatively few cases are currently reported there. Prevention is the same as for Lyme disease.

If you discover a tick, don't panic. Most ticks do not harbor these dangerous diseases. The Turn the Corner Foundation, dedicated to supporting research, education, awareness, and treatments for Lyme disease and other tick-borne diseases, recommends removing the tick as soon as you notice it by grasping it at the place of attachment, as close to the skin as possible, using a fine-point tweezer, and then gently pulling it out. Avoid squeezing the body of the tick. Afterward wash your hands and disinfect the tweezer and affected skin with alcohol. Save the tick in a jar or pill vial, plastic bag, or sandwiched in a piece of clear tape. Stick it in your calendar, label who it was taken off of, and then watch for symptoms. If symptoms manifest, you'll be able to take the tick specimen to the doctor.

The Centers for Disease Control and Prevention offers additional tick removal information. In the absence of a fine-point tweezer, your moderately long fingernails can be used to effectively remove a tick, but avoid squeezing the tick's body. Do not use petroleum jelly, a hot match, nail polish, or other products to remove a tick.

My deer tick bites have always gotten infected, so after removing a tick I dab the bite site with antibiotic ointment and cover it with an adhesive bandage. I replace the ointment and bandage daily for two to three days. I asked my doctor about doing this and her response was, "Can't hurt."

SPIDERS

Spiders love me, and I don't know why. I don't particularly love them. Well, okay, I think they are fascinating, some are actually beautiful, and I know they are an incredible benefit in the garden and for the planet. I just don't want them on me. If I find one in my home, I try not to harm it as I carefully move it outdoors. They are often in my car, but that couldn't be because I'm always moving plants in my car, could it?

For whatever reason, I get frequent spider bites when no one else seems to suffer from them. You can tell a spider bite from a mosquito bite by the double "fang" marks at the site of the bite. Sometimes there is a little trail of bites along several inches of skin, created as the annoyed spider is walking along (walk, bite, walk, bite). Fortunately the various spider species that come in on my fireplace wood, plant materials, and other formerly-in-the-yard items are not poisonous, but their bites are still itchy and take a while to heal.

Nonvenomous spider bites can cause local pain, usually mild. Sometimes the bite location has some swelling, and it often itches. It may also turn red or look somewhat bruised, and can be warm to the touch. Calamine lotion usually takes care of the discomfort. The itching generally ceases after a few days, and there may be a little peeling of the skin (like a mild sunburn) around the fevered bite site.

Fortunately I have never been bitten by a black widow or brown recluse spider. Three species of black widow live in North America, and they are considered the most venomous spider on the continent. The good news is that these spiders are not particularly large, so even if you're bitten you usually won't receive enough venom for the bite to be life threatening. A mature female, about ½ to 1 inch long, is able to inject venom deep enough to make it potentially harmful, but males are smaller and inject far less. In the body of a mature, healthy human, a widow bite is usually not fatal.

The territory of black widows extends from Massachusetts to Florida, and west to Texas and California, although they can be found in nearly every state and parts of Canada. Their preferred habitat is the underside of ledges and rocks, or the space beneath plants and debris, and they usually build their webs near the ground. They are often found around woodpiles, in low-lying areas of garages, beneath unused construction materials, in meter boxes, or other places that have not been disturbed for a while. Unless cornered, black widows are much more likely to run away than to stand their ground and bite.

If bitten by a black widow, you'll notice one or two small fang marks and minimal to sharp pain followed by swelling and redness at the bite site. If symptoms are more severe, they will develop within thirty to sixty minutes and may include muscle cramps and spasms; chills; fever; nausea; vomiting; sweating; severe abdominal, back, or chest pain; headache; stupor, restlessness, or shock; and severe high blood pressure. If you think you or a crew member has been bitten by a black widow, remain calm, apply ice to the bite area, and get medical help immediately. An antivenin is commonly available at hospitals throughout North America.

Replacing outdoor privies with flush toilets has greatly reduced the number of bites and fatalities. Just be aware and use some caution. Don't stick your bare hand under pieces of wood, around building foundations, or in odd holes in storage areas or in the woods.

The brown recluse spider prefers seclusion, hence its name. It is native to the United States and is found mainly in the central Midwestern states and south towards the Gulf, but there are isolated reports of the spider being transported north. The brown recluse is not aggressive and only bites when handled, displaced, or crushed. Bites can occur when cleaning storage areas, or when putting on clothing or shoes inhabited by a brown recluse. The physical reaction to a bite depends on the amount of venom and the individual's sensitivity. Some people are unaffected by the bite, while others experience immediate or delayed effects. The venom can cause almost no reaction, or it can cause severe necrosis (tissue death) at the bite site. Some people may not feel the bite or may not notice it for several hours. Still others feel immediate intense pain. If you are bitten, remain calm, put an ice pack on the bite area, and seek immediate medical attention. As with any insect bite, if you can collect the specimen, put it in a plastic bag or jar and bring it with you to your medical professional for identification.

To prevent spider bites, shake out clothing and shoes before getting dressed. My mother grew up with centipedes and scorpions, so I have always done this as a matter of course. Give bedding and towels a shake before use. Wear gloves to handle firewood, lumber, and rocks (check inside the gloves for spiders before putting them on).

REPTILES

About twenty species of venomous snakes, sixteen of which are rattlesnakes, reside in the United States, and venomous snakes occur in every state except Alaska and Hawaii. That said, snakes are not a huge threat. Rattlers, water moccasins, and copperheads are a reality, but you're more likely to drown in your bathtub than be killed by a snake. About eight thousand people a year receive venomous snake bites in the United States, and for about ten unlucky people a year, the bite is fatal. The vast majority of snake bites occur in warm-weather states like Texas and Florida. And it is interesting to note that most people are bitten when attempting to catch or handle the snake. So, don't do that.

Of course, you can surprise a venomous snake and be taken unawares. Know what types of snakes—both poisonous and nonpoisonous—live in your area and learn how to identify them. We have such innocuous snakes where I live that when I come across one I'm actually delighted. Overall I think snakes are gorgeous, and they help to keep rodent populations in check.

Aside from snakes, the other reptile that poses a potential threat to garden designers in the United States is the alligator. Found in the Southeast from the Carolinas to Texas, alligators inhabit freshwater ponds, marshes, rivers, lakes, and swamps. Even though the risk of being injured or killed by an alligator is low, it does exist. If you'll be living or working in an area where alligators might be present, familiarize yourself with them before entering their habitat.

MAMMALS AND RABIES

Rabies is a viral neuroinvasive disease that causes acute encephalitis in mammals. If left untreated, it is invariably fatal. You can only contract it from mammals; you cannot get rabies from insects, birds, reptiles, or any other species.

In the United States, rabies is primarily a disease of wild animals, with fewer than 10% of reported cases from exposure to domestic pets or livestock. Though most commonly caused by a bite from an infected animal, rabies can also be contracted by aerosol transmission. The virus is not especially persistent in the environment; at room temperature it is destroyed rapidly, usually within a few hours.

Rabies was once rare in the United States outside of the South, but raccoons in the mid-Atlantic and Northeast have been suffering from a rabies epidemic since the 1970s. In the Midwest, skunks are the primary carriers of rabies. Coyotes, dogs, and cats can also be vectors of the disease. Rodents are rarely infected. The most widely distributed vectors of rabies in the United States, and the sources of most human cases, are infected bats.

Prevention is the best way to avoid contracting rabies. Bats are incredibly beneficial to our environment, but avoid direct exposure to them. If you see a bat that is active in broad daylight, avoid it and warn others nearby. Be very careful around stray dogs and cats. And if you do receive a bite or scratch from an animal that no one can vouch for, immediately wash the wound with soap and water for approximately five minutes, which will effectively reduce any viral particles. Then seek medical attention. Treatment after exposure, known as postexposure prophylaxis (PEP), is highly successful in preventing the disease.

MICE AND HANTAVIRUS

Although they make some people squeamish, mice are a danger to humans only because they are potential vectors of hantavirus, a deadly disease transmitted by infected rodents through excreta or saliva. Humans can contract the disease if they inhale aerosolized virus from mouse urine, feces, or nesting materials, or are bitten by an infected mouse.

One form of hantavirus can manifest as hemorrhagic fever with renal syndrome (HFRS). In HFRS the most dramatic damage is seen in the kidneys (hence, renal syndrome), and victims usually requires hospitalization. In 1993 a newly recognized form of hantavirus was found to cause hantavirus cardiopulmonary syndrome (HCPS, also called HPS). In HCPS the lungs and spleen are most affected, and the virus can be deadly.

Rodent control remains the best way to prevent hantavirus infection. As a garden and landscape designer you might find yourself helping to clean out areas where mice have been living, such as sheds, garages, basements, storage areas, woodpiles, even dense brushy areas. Take the following precautions. Wear a surgical mask and latex or rubber gloves. Avoid stirring up dust by sweeping or vacuuming droppings or nesting materials. Instead, thoroughly wet contaminated areas with detergent or a hypochlorite solution prepared by mixing 1½ cups of household liquid bleach in 1 gallon of water. The hantavirus is surrounded by a lipid envelope, and this envelope can be destroyed and the virus killed by fat solvents like alcohol, ordinary disinfectants, and household bleach.

Once everything is saturated, remove and bag the contaminated materials, and thoroughly clean the area with disinfectant. Double-bag, and throw materials in an appropriate waste disposal system. Disinfect gloves before removing them by washing thoroughly with a disinfecting soap and water, and then carefully wash your hands with disinfectant soap. As an added precaution, immediately launder your clothing and take a shower.

HOMO SAPIENS

That's right, dangers posed by humans are the final threat from mammals on my list. We garden designers frequently find ourselves working alone at remote sites. I feel particularly vulnerable when the site is just being developed and there seems to be no one around. I worked these types of sites for years and never really gave it a second thought until I was at a fairly isolated coastal location doing my thing, measuring away, when a man startled me from behind. For some crazy reason, my internal caution flags instantly went up. He started asking me all kinds of odd questions about what I was doing. I indicated that my partner and I (yes, I lied) were photographing and measuring the site to do landscape planning for the new homeowners. Shortly after, the man abruptly turned and went back over the ridge and down to the beach. That night, when I relayed the story to my husband, he was concerned (read: freaked) and insisted I no longer work remote sites alone. That's a pretty good suggestion. From an operational standpoint, it's always better to have help when taking measurements anyway. But if you cannot find someone to accompany you to work an isolated site, consider getting licensed to carry pepper spray. The age-old adage, "Better safe than sorry," strongly applies here. Male or female, you could be robbed or accosted. Don't take chances.

CHEMICALS

An unfortunate number of dangerous chemicals are used in this business, and the many professionals that use them are essentially poisoning themselves, their crews, their clients, and the wildlife around them. I believe we owe it to our loved ones to limit our exposure to substances that can cause cancer, Parkinson's disease, asthma, depression, and anxiety, to name a few maladies. Relieving ourselves of the burden of working with toxic chemicals leaves us with greater peace of mind. Go green.

CHAPTER ELEVEN

Defining Your Business and Getting Your Name Out There

YOU FEEL YOU'RE READY for the next step. You've been learning how to gain knowledge in horticulture and getting exposure to the various pieces that make up the industry. Now it's time to articulate and package what you are going to offer to the marketplace. What will you do for people? What is it you will be selling? You need to define your offer, develop a business name, design a visual identity, outline a business plan, and create marketing materials. These are critical initial steps to making your fledgling business real and to having something concrete and credible to present to potential clients.

DESIGN VERSUS DESIGN-BUILD

Based on your interests and capabilities, you need to decide what to offer and whether to design or design and build. I know several people who just design gardens and landscapes. Then they turn it over to their clients to implement in whatever way they choose, whether that means the clients hire a landscape general contractor, subcontract the job in pieces and act as their own project manager, or do the work entirely themselves. The designer creates the design and provides the information and instructions necessary to construct the design, then steps out of the implementation entirely.

You can make a living doing this, and I'm pretty sure you'll be able to avoid wrenching your back, breaking an ankle, or getting a sunburn. But some of my greatest satisfaction comes from getting dirty and participating in the transformation. While pondering my aging body, I've thought about whether I'll eventually shift my focus and only offer design, but I'm not sure I'd want to design without also building. I love the construction process. *Viva la transformación!*

The other side of this is income. Most of us make the lion's share of our income during the build phase. Yes, design brings in some dough, but it is in implementation that we rack up profit. And this is also the phase where we rack up additional clients. Successful implementations always result in more client inquiries. It's a positive spiral.

YOUR BUSINESS MODEL

Like most other businesses, your garden design business will generally follow one of three models.

The first is a company that provides a plug-and-play type of product or service that is process driven, highly replicable, and competitively priced. An example would be a firm that installs instant water features. "In only one day, a small pond and waterfall can be yours!" These are not custom creations. You would offer perhaps three different styles, each at a specific price point, and your crew could install several of these per week, boom, boom, boom. You would make your money through volume and compete on price.

In the second model, you develop a signature style, so at a certain point anyone in the know could arrive at your client's residence and instantly recognize that Serina Martinica Design created the landscape. Clients would seek you out and hire you because yours is the exact look and feel they want for their home. You can earn a good living this way because you become the de facto expert and designer of the style, at least regionally or locally. Internationally revered landscape architects Wolfgang Oehme and James van Sweden, of Oehme, van Sweden and Associates in Washington, D.C., developed a signature approach coined the "New American Garden" style. The landscapes they create, though all site driven and magically different, have a dramatic and instantly identifiable treatment of space that evokes a particular ambiance.

The third model involves a customer-specific business and design approach. No assembly-line replicability, no signature style—each design is particular to each customer and site. This is how I operate. You would never be able to tell that I worked sites A, B, and C even if they sat side by side (and some actually do sit side by side). This is because the use of space, the plant selections, hardscape, and various treatments would all be as different as the clients and their homes. This requires a level of intimacy that the first business model does not. You become personally involved with your clients during the design and implementation of their new landscape. I cannot imagine working any other way, although when I am dealing with a more challenging client, I do enjoy dreaming of a plug-and-play offering—get in, get it done, get paid, get out. There is a lovely simplicity to that!

JUST SOUP? OR ALL THE WAY TO NUTS

Based on your knowledge and experience, you'll either want to make a vertical, niche offering or, if you're feeling particularly confident, offer everything.

I started out offering container gardens. Big, bodacious, dramatic statements were my signature in my own yard, and for several friends I'd helped over the years, and containers seemed the right start. I'm an inveterate junk collector, and I plant everything. Sinks, tubs, watering cans, teapots, troughs, urns, wooden boxes, breadboxes, chairs, birdcages, baskets, hay racks—you name it, I've planted it. (Except for a truck. I've always wanted to plant a cool, old pickup truck.) I thought containers were a good way to get my name out there while doing something I could handle alone, since I didn't yet have relationships with any crews. Before long, a new client asked me to plant a cutting garden. Then came a request to refurbish a foundation planting to add curb appeal to a home. Then a front yard. Then a patio. In no time I was designing walls, walks, pergolas, driveways, terraces, decks, pools, sheds, lighting, summerhouses. You never know where the road will take you. You just need to start somewhere.

NICHE-TYPE OFFERINGS

As you're starting out, niche offerings are a way to get out there and get your feet wet doing something you feel comfortable and confident about. They can also help you avoid getting in over your head. If this is the direction you want to go, think outside the box, and leverage your particular experience and interests. Follow your instincts on what you know you will enjoy doing, and consider what you think you could turn into a successful business operation. Test your market to see if it can handle your offering, and spend some time identifying your ideal customers and thinking of ways to target them in the marketplace. Here are a few examples of niche-type offerings that could get you started:

Bird and butterfly gardens. These popular theme gardens are requested more and more. If you have an interest in and knowledge of local wildlife, offering bird and butterfly gardens is a great way to get your gardening business off the ground. Note that these gardens are intentionally not incredibly tidy. Many tall, wild, gangly flowers are optimal for butterflies and bees; plants with arching, trumpet-shaped flowers attract hummingbirds; and we do not deadhead, since the seeds bring in birds. Many species plants offer more benefit to wildlife than hybrids, so learn your plants and choose with care. Clients with children are especially enamored of bird and butterfly gardens, since they attract wildlife, and this encourages the children to be more aware and appreciative of nature. Chemicals are an absolute no-no.

Conservation gardening. Offer to work with local conservation groups, wetlands specialists, and civil engineers who do remediation. If you network and develop a good reputation, conservation agents and commissions will point clients your way.

Container gardens. You're really into planting pots, using a wide variety of plants, and working with color, color, color! Sell yourself offering container plantings for entryways, patios, pools, window boxes, deck embellishments, hanging baskets, outdoor celebrations, sunrooms, and so forth. This is often the type of design-build you can do alone, which minimizes your out-of-pocket expense. Get to really know your tropicals, how long they bloom, what care they need. See how perennials and annuals can work together to give you a long season of beauty and interest. Offer pot maintenance—for a fee, of course—and stop by every couple of weeks to deadhead and trim, replacing any tired-looking plants with fresh ones. Learn to install simple drip irrigation for containers; you can work this off of an available hose connection. Irrigation is a huge added value and makes the addition of planted pots a complete no-brainer for the client. Investigate what container styles and materials are out there (the variety is mind-boggling), who is selling what, what's available on the Internet, what you can get wholesale, and what you can get locally. Armed with your business cards, ask local retailers if they'll give you a courtesy trade discount of 10% to 30% for purchasing from them. Call real estate companies and offer your services to add curb appeal to houses that are for sale. Take a staging course to see how your horticultural skills can complement the need for that "sense of beauty and welcome" that can speak volumes in a tight housing market. Recognize that there is seasonality to container gardening in most climates, and yet your container business can operate year-round. Even here in New England you can garden with containers all year long: pansies can be planted in frost-resistant containers as early as March, followed by the spring cool-season flowers; in summer, tropicals and heat-lovers; in fall, mums, asters, and pansies, with Thanksgiving gourd, pumpkin, and dried-flower-themed containers; and finally, holiday glitter and evergreens for winter. You can even offer to empty and store containers until spring. Yes, there's a year-round business, and virtually year-round income, in something as seemingly narrow as container gardening.

Garden maintenance. This underserved area should not be confused with lawn maintenance, a highly competitive field. Garden maintenance usually involves caring for mixed borders and containers. Every other week or so, you weed, deadhead, tidy up, and take out tired annuals to add fresh seasonal ones. It's also nice to check out things the client's lawn service should be doing: edging here, overseeding there. Then you position yourself as their go-to person. You'd be amazed how this can grow into full-service garden design, or even a profession in property management.

Green roofs. A high-knowledge specialty but an exploding field. Green roofs (also known as ecoroofs, living roofs, and vegetated roofs) are roofs partially or completely covered with soil and vegetation, and they are playing an important part in the overall strategy to reduce heat sinks in major cities. A growing trend for private residences, as people want to experiment with outbuildings, garages, and roofs of sunrooms and porches.

Handicap-accessible gardens. These feature raised beds, wide and solid-surface walkways, and fragrant, colorful, easy-maintenance plants. Due to the aging of the baby boomers, and tragically, because of the tens of thousands of wounded soldiers returning from the Middle East, there is a growing need in the marketplace for handicap-accessible gardens. Also a good offering for nursing homes, rehabilitation hospitals, and assisted-living facilities, or even primary schools and colleges.

Horticultural therapy. A high-knowledge specialty and a burgeoning field. The American Horticultural Therapy Association defines horticultural therapy (HT) as "a process utilizing plants and horticultural activities to improve social, educational, psychological, and physical adjustment of persons thus improving their body, mind, and spirit." If you like people as well as plants, working in horticultural therapy might be perfect for you. Paired with handicap-accessible gardens, this could be a wonderful, rewarding business. As for the effect of horticultural therapy, I honestly believe that if everyone—and I do mean everyone—had a

Perennial garden maintenance is truly an underserved niche in the market.

garden to nurture, even a tiny garden, there would be no time nor inclination for war.

Meadow gardening. Harder to do than it would seem, but can be very successful, particularly since municipalities are encouraging people to give up portions of their lawns to waterwise gardens or meadows in an effort to conserve water. When proposing a meadow, you'll need to overcome what I call the meadow-in-a-can prejudice—objections voiced by those who have attempted to grow a meadow using inexpensive wildflower seed mixes only to have ended up with a patch of sickly weeds. Personally, I think the best meadows (other than those created by nature) are planted, not seeded. Meadows do still require periodic maintenance, but they can be a wonderful, dramatic, low-water-use solution in the right areas.

Native plant gardening. I do quite a bit of this, particularly when working in a conservation zone or near a sensitive habitat area. Native plants are ideally suited for the climate conditions your particular area dishes out, can be long lived, often need no supplemental water or fertilizing after the first year, and are usually beneficial to local wildlife, with whom they have evolved. For example, the native eastern flowering dogwood, *Cornus florida*, supports 118 different forms of wildlife, whereas Korean dogwood, *C. kousa*, which is planted so frequently in my area (primarily because of dogwood anthracnose, which has killed many specimens of C. *florida*) supports one. Yes, one. Native plants really are beneficial.

Patio and deck gardens. These are variations on the container garden offering. Provide pots as well as plantings in the beds around the deck or patio. You can offer maintenance, too, as well as installation of drip irrigation with an automatic timer. You could couple this with providing pressure washing of decks in the spring, and offering to restain or waterseal as needed. Don't want to do that yourself? Farm it out, but make margin on it. Cast a critical eye over the entire patio or deck area and suggest improvements. Note that the client could use a cleaning between the patio pavers, or removal of moss from the bricks. Gutters full of leaves? Suggest a cleaning. Look at what needs doing and offer to do it, always for a price. It doesn't have to be you who does it all. This is where subcontractors come in—they do the work, they charge you, and you charge the client (after adding a markup percentage, plus a line item for your coordination and supervision time).

Rain gardens. As we watch our water resources become scarcer and more fragile, and see our wetlands faltering, this field is really taking off. Rain gardens are designed to capture water runoff, redirect it from streets and storm drains, and gently allow it to percolate into the soil, ultimately helping to recharge the groundwater supply. Besides offering this to your average homeowner, you could start a business offering rain garden design to municipalities, commercial sites, and conservation commissions. Many new housing developments are required to construct a large drainage basin for water runoff. These are usually fenced with chain-link and left to nature, and tend to be a hideous eyesore. Landscaping these as rain garden swales would make them not only more functional but also dramatically more beautiful, and they would become wildlife sanctuaries in their own right as they matured. This type of rain garden would be positive and welcoming at the entry to an area of new

Birds enjoy these crabapples in late winter, often not stripping the tree until the end of January.

homes. You could build a business starting as a rain garden expert, and ask for client referrals from watershed resource authorities, municipal water purveyors, water gardening companies, and irrigation companies. Here in Massachusetts we have a stringent private septic system code, which oftentimes results in a stripped and less-than-gorgeous landscape. Offering rain garden services through private septic contractors might work in your area, too, so check it out.

Seaside gardens. Requires special knowledge of salt- and wind-tolerant plants, coastal soil systems, and—usually—gardening on a slope. Knowing how to work with the plant varieties that can take the salt, wind, spray, sand, and sun that coastal areas deliver is a distinct skill set and is in demand. Since waterways and coastlines are often protected, presume that you'll need to learn how to work with local conservation commissions. Even if this isn't required, having a good relationship with your local conservation commission can result in great client referrals. This assumes, of course, that you live near a coast!

Shade gardens. I have a particular love and knowledge of shade gardening. Most people who bring me to a shady yard apologize for it. Little do they know how exciting I find a shade-filled property! Shade gardens can be lush, dramatic oases that are much easier to maintain than their sunny counterparts. They require less water, less weeding, less work. And they can be stunningly beautiful. Bone up on your shade gardening knowledge. This will serve you well, whatever your gardening specialty.

Vegetable gardens. Several people I know offer plug-and-play vegetable gardens. They've developed a series of sizes, and each has a price. For each price point, they site the new garden, set up the raised beds with cedar framing (no chemicals to leach out), add organic soil and amendments, plant it, fence it, trellis or provide supports where needed, and provide instructions to the homeowners on how to water, care for, and maintain their new veggie garden for the season. One dude is also available to consult during the growing season, and another person I know includes maintenance (weeding, mulching, advising on when to pick, replanting when a crop is exhausted, cleaning up and planting winter rye in the fall, storing the trellising, turning in the rye in spring, fluffing the soil and replanting the next season, and so forth). All for a fee, of course. This simple offering is fairly easy for one or two people to implement using easily found materials. Clients sometimes also want their gardens to include plants with edible blossoms. If you want to expand your offering to "edible plant gardening," you will need a very good working knowledge of what is edible and what is not, and you'll need to instruct clients to never eat any plant part unless they know beyond the shadow of a doubt that it is the plant they think it is, and that it is incontrovertibly edible.

Water gardens. If you've built and maintained your own water garden, pond, or waterfall, this burgeoning business may be your thing. Water and fire seem to be the big design elements in every magazine and on just about every landscape design show. You can exploit this market coverage. You'll need experience in water gardening, and you'll need some reliable brawn to help you with excavation, earth moving, and rock placement. Take classes offered by local retailers and wholesalers. Ideally, work in the business for someone else for a couple of years. That way you'll learn from people who are already experts, minimizing the mistakes you'll make on your own. You can also offer maintenance for water gardens, but you'll really need to know your stuff. Learn and experiment with design. Learn about fish, water plants, the horticulture of plants in the margin zones, pump and filter function, signs of a water feature in distress. You'll need to work with outdoor electricity, so pal up with a couple of good electricians. Water gardening is a high-knowledge specialty, and you'll find there is a steep learning curve to become even marginally proficient. This is an area of gardening and design where the more you learn, the more you'll see there is to learn.

Waterwise gardening. Other terms for this approach are drought-tolerant landscaping, water-conserving landscaping, and smartscaping. Of course, all of your gardens should be waterwise. Develop this knowledge and sell yourself this way. When you match each plant to a location and conditions that closely resemble its optimal cultural requirements, the plant is likely to get along after the first year with little or no additional water. With the recent stresses on our water supplies, stresses that will only get worse, it is critical to design with water conservation in mind.

Wildlife gardens. A variation on the bird and butterfly garden. Wildlife gardens are designed to provide a nurturing refuge for wildlife and to attract songbirds and hummingbirds, butterflies, bees, moths, frogs and toads, and lots of other wonderful creatures. These designs are based on sustainable gardening practices, including reducing lawn size, eliminating chemical fertilizers and pesticides, conserving water, adding native plants, and providing the four basic elements that all wildlife needs: food, water, cover, and places to raise their young. The National Wildlife Federation can walk you through what is required for a property to be designated a certified wildlife sanctuary. Offering wildlife gardening can certainly be a viable entrée into this industry. You could start by offering this service at public and private schools, nursery schools, public parks, and other high-visibility locations. Add your signage, of course.

Xeriscape. This does not mean "just rocks." A registered trademark of Denver Water, the water department of Denver, Colorado, Xeriscape is

Daphne ×*burkwoodii* 'Carol Mackie' is a phenom of fragrance every spring.

actually a combination of seven common-sense gardening principles that save water while creating a beautiful landscape, including proper planning and design, soil preparation, efficient irrigation, clustering plants with like needs, appropriate use of mulch, using alternatives to turf, and providing appropriate maintenance. Given recent droughts in the United States and elsewhere, plus the dire predictions about the reservoirs in the American Southwest, the quicker we adopt Xeriscaping practices, the better for us all.

Additional possibilities include alpine gardens (for mountainous or windswept areas with sun and good drainage), carnivorous plant gardening, cutting gardens (you'll need lots of space and lots of annuals to keep flowers coming on for most of the growing season), and fragrance gardens (locate plantings near a window, doorway, walkway, deck, or patio where their aroma can best be enjoyed).

You'll need to look at your interests and knowledge relative to how you'd position and sell your offering in the marketplace, as well as how much demand you think there might be out there for it. I'd be willing to bet, for example, that there is greater demand for bird and butterfly gardens than for carnivorous plantings.

GARDEN CONSULTATIONS ONLY

Your whole business could be simply garden consultations. You meet with a client, tour their gardens, discuss their likes and dislikes. Then do a formal write-up on what they could do to achieve their goals, plants they could use in this or that garden, functional elements to add (firm pathway linking shed to garage, for example), and construction they might consider (stone patio off of the kitchen). Charge a flat fee, or have a number of different prices based on the comprehensiveness of the consultation and size of the site. Bam! You have a business.

OFFERING IT ALL

Let's say you really want to stretch. You don't want to be labeled as one type of designer. You feel ready to offer all of it, from soup to nuts. Keep in mind that in each area of design that you take on, you'll need to be familiar with the types or styles available, varieties of materials, various uses, how they perform in your locale, suppliers, installation crews, and relative costs. As just one example of how many factors you can consider when approaching a new design, here is my own reminder task list:

Plants. Includes perennials, annuals, nursery stock. Note that "nursery stock" generally refers to woody stock, shrubs, and trees, while "perennials" usually refers to herbaceous perennials, even though most nursery stock is perennial. Confusing? Well, yeah, a bit. Annuals, greenhouse plants, plants best grown from seed, vegetable starts, large tropicals—you'll eventually learn where to find and how to use all of these.

Lawn. Know about turf types, seed mixes, sod types, availability, hydroseeding versus hand-seeding, seed start mulches, how to best coddle sod, watering, fertilizing, best maintenance practices.

Soil. Recognize types. Know how to work with sandy or clayey soils, get a soil test, amend soil and prepare it for planting or for seeding a lawn. Understand what plants and turf types work best in what soils.

Design. Know good principles and practices. Be a sponge and absorb the knowledge that is readily available from zillions of books, seminars, coursework, plus your own instincts.

Fencing. Use for privacy, accent, enclosure. Be familiar with the materials and styles available. Follow local codes for placement and height.

Lighting. Understand low voltage versus in-line. Use for security, task, ambiance, or specialty.

Irrigation. Understand drip versus broadcast, types of spray heads, frequency and duration, irrigation versus getting wet, lawns versus planting beds, design and management of irrigation zones and types.

Masonry. Be familiar with design and construction of walkways, walls, patios, steps, cobble edges and drive collars, built-in grills and fireplaces. Differentiate between rustic, dry-laid, and mortared, and between veneering versus whole stones. Know types of stone and stone finishes available; varieties in stone fabrication; brick types, applications, and patterns; and varieties, applications, and uses for concrete pavers and wall systems.

Pest control. Know why, what, and how, including information about dangers caused by pests and how to prevent them. Be aware of integrated pest management and biological control alternatives.

Ornamental water features. Know your way around ponds, rills, fountains, falls, pools, streams.

Recreational water features. Understand the fundamentals of pools, spas, outdoor showers.

Pergolas, arbors. Understand structure and use.

Awnings, shade sails. Know types of structures, functionality, materials available, performance characteristics, suppliers, installers.

Driveways. Be familiar with the large variety of materials available.

Outdoor kitchens or barbeques. Know what cooking and cooling appliances are available. Identify surfacing options, types of installations.

Sheds, outbuildings, pool houses. Be able to use these structures to complement activities in the landscape. Understand prefabricated versus custom.

Furnishings. Know how best to use exterior furniture, pots, accents, statuary, garden art, bird accoutrements (feeders, houses, baths), whimsical additions.

Maintenance. Gauge need for landscape maintenance (lawns, beds, borders, shrubs, trees) and exterior house maintenance (painting, roofing, power washing, window washing, gutter cleaning).

Business end of the business. Includes design, presentations, proposals, estimating, invoicing, ordering, communicating with subcontractors and suppliers, managing the project construction.

If you do decide to offer the whole banana, let me suggest that you still tread softly and start out small. Be careful with the jobs you go after, and be careful what you wish for. The last thing you need is to be hired for a large job and not know where to start, because this can bury you faster than a John Deere tractor. Make sure you partner with solid, proven professionals. Johnny's chainsaw doesn't make him an arborist, and Joe's hammer doesn't make him a carpenter. Running a business can be overwhelming, particularly when it is all new. Know where and when to ask for assistance.

MAKING IT REAL

Whether you're jumping in head first or taking it slow, you need to start selling yourself, and you need a means to provide a professional response. I like to have a firm foundation before I start installing the roof, so I say start by developing some "response mechanisms." This is a really fun, creative process. It's also a reality check, because as you formulate sales materials that will represent you and your business, you'll do a little healthy soul-searching about where you're headed with this endeavor. The results may inspire you to follow your dream. Having something concrete to hold in your hands not only communicates your credibility and professionalism to potential clients, it also helps to make this business real to you.

WHAT'S IN A NAME

You need a company name. It can be as simple as your name: Landscapes by Lanny, Marlenne Design. It can be a new fabrication: FoliAge East, Concepts in Green. Your company name can speak to your specialty: WaterWise Gardens, Vessels, Fountainia. For myself, I tried a number of cutesy titles attempting to play off my first name: Love Your Garden, Gardens to Love, and so forth. But I'm really not the cutesy type, and because I grew up around here and my name is unusual enough, I didn't want everyone locally to know it was me being cutesy. I like to operate a little under the radar. So I decided just to use my name, and opted not to use signage at my job sites. Love Albrecht Howard G A R D E N S, it is.

LICENSING

Most states allow you to operate as a garden or landscape designer without any particular certification or regulation, although you cannot, by law, call yourself a landscape architect without holding that particular certification. Contact your local Small Business Administration office or chamber of commerce to find out about regulations in your state. The Association of Professional Landscape Designers is also a wonderful resource.

BUSINESS LICENSE

Once you are happy with the name you have chosen, it's a good idea to get a business license. I have a business license from my town. It states, "Love Albrecht Howard doing business as Love Albrecht Howard G A R D E N S." This cost $30, took ten minutes to get, and requires renewal every three years. Pretty simple. But what will a license give you? First—and this sounds a little touchy-feely, but it's true—it makes your endeavor feel like it's really happening. Second, it enables you to set up a DBA (Doing Business As) checking account. Look for a local bank that offers DBA accounts with free checking. Put $100 in the account and order some personalized checks. Now you have a business account! Third, having a business license can help give you an entrée into the wholesale world. Wholesalers only want to talk to you if you have other wholesale accounts you can reference, which is tough when you're just beginning. When I needed to get around this, I used my business license and asked for referrals from a couple of their existing customers. This is where having a network in the industry can serve you really well. If a good customer of Wholesaler X gives you a reference, then that wholesaler will generally be quite happy to take you on as a cash-on-delivery customer.

WHAT STUFF DO I NEED?

Once the phone starts to ring, how are you going to respond? What do you have to give to prospective clients? Do you need a portfolio? Web site? Business cards?

You can launch your business without any of these things, but sales materials make the entire process easier. It's easier for you to advertise your services, easier to attract and sell clients, and with sales promotion pieces in hand you will feel like your credibility is on firmer ground. It's easier to converse with a prospect when you have a prop to help guide the conversation.

When you are just starting out, anything that can speak to your professionalism and credibility is crucial. These little things can make a lot of difference in how you sell yourself and how potential clients perceive you. There's something satisfying about presenting a beautifully assembled folder or sales brochure to a prospective client and being able to say, "Here's a little more about me, my business, and how I work."

LOGO

Once you have your company name, you need to develop a visual identity. This is something you develop knowing that you will replicate it everywhere, from your letterhead to your yard signage. The Nike swoosh is the perfect example of a successful logo, now so recognized that no one needs to see the name of the company to get the message. Your logo serves as an emblem that is synonymous with your business, and you reinforce the image by including it on every piece of communication, including the signoffs on your e-mail. Every time your business name comes up in front of a customer or prospective client, you want to reinforce "the look."

My logo is my business name, phone, and fax number, in a particular font, laid out in a block format. That's it. I had always intended to create an actual logo, perhaps a stylized leaf or blossom, maybe the silhouette of a tree. When I started out I figured the right image would eventually emerge from the ether. But somehow my business grew without it, so eventually I stopped worrying about it. I don't suggest doing what I did, however, and encourage you to think about a logo intentionally. It can be invigorating to get just the right design, just the right look that says *you*. This can help you feel prepared and ready to go.

If you design something special, think about protecting it. Project ahead and imagine that your company is doing well and you are expanding. You will have succeeded in creating an identity in the marketplace, and you will want to deter other people from stealing or using your work without your permission. If there is sufficient authorship, copyright protection may be available for your logo. In some circumstances, an artistic logo may also be protected as a trademark. If this seems like it might become important to you, first do some investigation on the Internet. If you google "copyright" plus "logo," you'll find a wealth of sites that can walk you through the process. After you have done your own due diligence, if you want to investigate still further, contact an attorney for assistance.

SLOGAN

A slogan is a short, memorable phrase used to advertise a product or identify a company or organization. One of the most successful slogans of our time is Nike's "Just do it!" This slogan is now so ingrained in our consciousness that one look at the swoosh causes us to think, "Just do it!" I do have a slogan, but I only include it as an automatic tag on my e-mail, and it is on the marketing materials I leave behind with prospective clients. I'm breaking my own rule by not including it on every piece of marketing communication, but I felt the addition of the slogan looked too cumbersome on letterhead, invoicing, envelopes, and so forth.

You'll need to look at your marketing materials as a whole to decide what to make as your signature. I implore you to do this with intention, because it can be difficult—and confusing in the marketplace—to shift gears and change your visual identity later on.

BUSINESS CARDS

It is appropriate to have something to leave behind when you meet with prospective clients. It is professional and gives you instant credibility. Minimally, you'll need business cards. You can make them on your computer and purchase stock that is preperforated so that you can just design them on a provided template, run them off in your printer, and rip them apart. Unfortunately, I have yet to find card stock that is designed for this use that feels substantive enough to me. Having a background in advertising and direct marketing, I know that paper stock is important and subliminally says a lot about you.

For my latest business cards, I took a rough design and preferred font sample down to a local copy and graphics shop. I picked out the card stock from a wide range of possibilities, they designed the face of the card (using the fonts I suggested, they basically provided a layout of my business name and phone number), faxed it to me for approval, and we were off. It cost about $75 for 250 cards. I chose a heavy-weight recycled card stock with intentional imperfections and had them printed in raised black ink. Back at home, I rubber-stamp leaves on them in soft autumn colors, usually in batches of twenty or so cards at a time. The cards are simple, quite lovely, and never fail to get a positive comment.

I highly recommend keeping your business card simple. I have seen cards that accordion out to accommodate reams of copy. (They are exhausting to even contemplate reading.) Cards with four-color glossy photographs—some work, some don't. Oval cards, pentagon-shaped cards, cards shaped like a leaf. Cards with so much type you almost cannot see the paper. Magnetic cards to pop on your fridge. Thin cards that feel cheap in the hand. Heavy, laminated cards that can take rain and mud. The variety out there is amazing.

Obviously your business card must include your business name, your name, and your business phone number. If you have developed a logo or slogan, certainly this is the place to use them. Make sure that the information you compose on your business card is valuable and easy to read. Having reached the age where I need reading glasses, I am incredibly irritated by tiny or light-colored type. You don't want prospective clients to have to reach for reading glasses every time they want your phone number. Make it easy for them to find you: make your business card eminently readable.

It's entirely up to you what you want to include besides name and contact information: copy that states what you do, photos, an illustration, a Web site or e-mail address. My former e-mail provider changed their name three times in three years. Annoying to say the least, and I was grateful I had not included my e-mail address on my business cards. I also do not include my business address, which happens to be my home address. For the same reason that I don't want prospective clients dropping by the homes of my existing clients, I don't want drop-ins at my own home. My time with my husband and son is precious to me, I don't always look presentable (to say the least), and my gardens are not always pristine (for sure). I live on a busy street that is easy to find, so I do not give out perennial invitations to potential garden gawkers. If someone asks where I live, I'm happy to tell them, but I don't advertise it on my cards.

You can find quite a few business card Web sites online. Some walk you through the design process with little effort, but others might require you to have CAD or graphic design experience to fully utilize their tools. Spend a couple of hours surfing the Web and you'll see zillions of examples.

A word of caution about overkill. One of my friends in the industry spent quite a bit of time on his business card while reworking his marketing materials. He showed it to me and asked what I thought. Let me give you a wee bit of background. His offering is high-end landscape design-build services, he touches almost nothing for less than $100,000 in implementation costs, and his design fees are anywhere from $8000 to more than $15,000. His card, however, screamed "used cars." Garish colors, way too much copy, the use of several different fonts, cheap, glossy, do-it-yourself stock. It was horrid. I suggested he remove almost all of the copy, get rid of the bright color blocks, and simplify the information, instead pointing people to his Web site, which is glorious. He hesitated to give up the "real estate" to just space, but ultimately came up with a beautiful card that spoke to the elegance of his offering.

BROCHURES AND SALES MATERIALS

In addition to business cards, it is really nice to have a brochure or other leave-behind material. In this larger format, you have real estate to expand what you say about yourself and your offering. Thanks to the flexibility of digital photography, word processing, and desktop publishing, as well as full-color printers and beautiful paper stock, it's easy and inexpensive to produce a business brochure. Photographs of your own gardens and pro bono work, descriptions of who you are, your work, and

My leave-behind business cards and some images I might share with prospective clients. Simple, easy to change, easy to print, low-key, effective.

224

what you can do, your contact information—all combine to make a simple but effective leave-behind. Beware of cheesy card and printing stock, don't put too much copy on your pieces, and when in doubt, keep it clean and classy. Minimize the number of printing fonts you choose. Readability is critical, so take it easy with bold, italicized, centered, and scriptlike fonts. Simplicity usually speaks for itself.

PORTFOLIO

Many designers bring a portfolio to show prospective clients. A portfolio is a key marketing ingredient, and it really works. I personally do not use one, but I have been rethinking this. Because the landscapes and gardens I design are entirely customized for the site, for the clients and their family, for the way they want to use their property and to complement the architecture of their home, what I have designed for one client has little to no bearing on the design I create for another. However, "before" and "after" photos do tell a compelling story that illustrates the power of the potential transformation, and showing images makes your work immediately real to prospective clients. Given that pictures truly are worth a thousand words, if you decide you want to work with a portfolio, certainly do it. Sometimes it is much easier to talk with prospective clients if you have something (a "prop") on which to focus your dialogue. A portfolio serves beautifully for this. Once you have a body of work you can refer to, assemble a visually arresting "story" that represents your work. Make sure the images are large, in focus, and gorgeous. Package them in your portfolio case or notebook clearly, and have them assembled for easy viewing. I suggest you avoid including captions, addresses, or even towns. First, this allows you to talk about each image without having the prospective client's attention fractured by trying to look at the picture, read, and listen to you all at the same time. Also, without towns or addresses, it's highly unlikely that they can hop in their car to go gawk at some of your finished work. I guard my existing clients' privacy and only rarely ask permission for someone to see their property.

WEB SITE

Having a presence on the Web is another way to reinforce your credibility, illustrate your work and creativity, and provide a flexible way to start a dialogue with prospective clients. A Web site used to back up your credibility, but now it is virtually a requirement. Without a Web presence it is almost as if you don't exist, particularly among people younger than fifty, which represents most of your potential client base.

Having a Web site designed can range in price from about $500 for an individual who works from home, or for a small Web design shop, to many thousands of dollars for design from larger Web agencies. One way of finding a Web designer is to search on local sites, and when you see something you like, contact the site owner and ask who designed their site. They'll be flattered that you like their offering, and you'll be letting them know that what they are showing on the Web really works. Usually, people are happy to tell you who designed their site.

Very briefly, things to consider when developing a Web site include your domain name, what type of site you need to represent your business, the level of technology you need to support your site, where your site will be hosted, and whether you will build the site yourself or find a Web designer to do it for you.

First you need to choose a domain name. This is a name that identifies an IP (Internet protocol) address. This should be simple, descriptive, and as short and easy to spell as possible. Google.com is a domain name. A URL (uniform resource locator) is the address that specifies the location of a document—your Web site—on the Internet. Google's URL is www.google.com. Play with your business name, and when you have several possible names you like, click on a domain registration site (to find these sites, search "domain registration") and it will take about thirty seconds to find out whether your domain names are available.

Keep in mind that you can register several domain names and have them all access the same Web site or homepage. My friend Mike Walsh (also lovingly known as Techno Boy) has been using the Internet to great advantage since the 1990s. His landscape design-build company is Horticultural Concepts, so he owns the URL www.HorticulturalConcepts.com. But since that's a lot of type, he also registered www.HortCon.com. How much simpler is that?

In addition to building his own Web site, Mike has created sites for clients, friends, and several nonprofits, so he is knowledgeable about what works. He suggests making sure your URL includes your company name (your "natural" URL). Otherwise, people who know your name might have trouble finding you. This is so critical, Mike says, that "if you plan on using an Internet marketing program and the URL is not available, seriously consider changing your business name to one that is available. Be inventive. Be flexible. But above all, be unique!"

Because your Web identity is so important, Mike also suggests using "upper- and lowercase letters to make the name string more readable" in your URL. "You can even skip the 'www' since it's not needed now—www.HorticulturalConcepts.com becomes HorticulturalConcepts.com or simply HortCon.com. Much more memorable and to the point." He also advises avoiding dashes and digits.

When you have determined a domain name that is really "you" and is available, consider registering several extensions besides .com. Other extensions available include .edu, .net, .org, .info, and so forth. Owning multiple extensions helps minimize Web confusion, and your clients and prospects will be much less likely to end up at some other site. When you are happy with the names, buy them. Seriously, registering a domain name can be as inexpensive as $20 a name for two years. Remember to reregister your name before it expires.

The type of site you build reflects the type of company you have. Brochure sites list products or services and contact information. Most landscape or garden design sites fall into this category. Catalog sites sell products directly to the consumer. Blogs offer commentary, articles, opinions, and educational materials, usually organized around a particular topic, and allow readers to leave comments in an interactive format. I'm not sure I'd really want a gardening blog, although many designers offer blogging on their sites. I enjoy having a dialogue as well as anyone else, but I'm tied to a computer enough as it is!

You'll need to choose a Web hosting service. Find one that offers low startup costs and inexpensive monthly fees. Remember, keep thinking and acting frugally to keep your overhead costs down. Purchase a small service package that contains only the options you need. If you are creating a fairly normal Web site, you will almost never run out of bandwidth even if you choose a low service level (levels of bandwidth are how the hosting services charge). You can always add more bandwidth and services later.

Is this feeling complicated? Don't freak. If you hire a Web designer, they'll be investigating much of this and making decisions for you.

Do you want a flash or static site? Flash sites allow you to do animation, music, and special effects like wipes and fades. It makes for a glorious viewing experience, but there are downsides to the format, beyond just the added cost. A static site is simpler. With a static site you cannot have animation, but you can easily link to another page and can include nice effects like "mouseovers."

For our industry, your site should be visually arresting and include stunning images of your best work. The content should be information rich but clear and succinct. People don't want to have to work to get the information they want, so if your site looks too dense or arduous, potential clients may quickly (often in fifteen seconds) go back and click on someone else's site. Do include key search words in your text so that browsers can find you when a prospect is doing a search. These include words describing what you do (landscape, garden, flowers, screening, pool, organic) and where you want to center your work (New York, Rochester, Syracuse, Finger Lakes).

Before you go live, test your site thoroughly. Make sure all links work, check to see that the layout, information, images, and captions are all correct, and look at the site on other people's PCs and Macs to make sure it comes up consistently.

To assure the appeal and success of your site, keep it fresh and update it periodically (quarterly would be a really good idea). Check out what a few other local designers are doing with their Web sites, and make sure your site continues to look good in comparison. You can use the Web to great advantage to drive growth and success for your garden design company.

HOW DO POTENTIAL CLIENTS REACH YOU?

Home phone, business phone, cell phone, fax, e-mail. You'll need all of these. But you need to decide up front where you want the calls coming in, because changing it later will be difficult. Since the beginning of my business, I've wanted to keep my overhead low, so I still use my home phone number as my "working" business number. It is also my fax number. This is the number I give to clients, and it is the number on my business card. I have a business phone line, which is an inexpensive line just for local calls. I never call out from this phone, using it for incoming prospect calls only, and it goes straight to an answering machine. In hindsight, setting up my client contact in this way was a huge mistake. Many evenings and weekends, I would prefer not to have any client contact (I return calls from clients who leave messages during the day, but I try to get through these by dinnertime). I need my down time, and so will you. It's annoying to have to screen calls after 7:00 p.m.—or all weekend—and have to decide whether I'm going to answer.

If I had it to do over again, I would start with a separate business line that has a separate answering machine, and I would have an entirely separate fax number. I would keep both in my office. And I would keep my home phone number private.

Cell phone. Many of my colleagues in the industry use their cell phone as their business line. I don't. I don't want precious minutes eaten up by chatty clients, and I do not like to be distracted from my on-site work at the Harpers if the Johnsons decide to call. I only use my cell phone for communicating with subcontractors and suppliers. Yes, I sometimes forget to block my calls when I'm phoning a client using my cell, and some of those people are smart enough to save the number. (Darn!) But as a general rule, my clients do not have my cell number and this works out just fine.

This might be the best overall solution. A couple of friends of mine who started with a cell phone for their business lines now carry two cell phones: one for work, one for family and friends. They can turn the work phone off on Saturday night and not be distracted by work calls until Monday at the crack of dawn. The cost of additional cell lines has become so economical that this makes more and more sense.

Of course, e-mail has made communication marvelously easy. I can return a client's "call" at midnight if I want to. Or at 5:30 a.m. It doesn't completely replace live chats—you wouldn't want it to, since part of what you're selling is you!— but it's a tremendous convenience. You can also take your time formulating exactly what you want to say. Always be clear. Use a consistent business format, appropriate grammar and punctuation, and check for typos. I am appalled by some of the business e-mail I receive. Always start with a salutation and end with a good closing. You want to be professional in all communications with your clients and subs, because these reflect directly on your abilities and professionalism.

You will absolutely, positively need a fax machine. The all-in-one printer-copier-fax-scanner machines are fabulous, and you can get a really good one for a few hundred dollars.

A digital camera is another critical piece of equipment. You will be taking "before" photos, and you'll refer back to these as you design your clients' gardens. Also take photos of work in process—it's always great to see images of how the work got done. For some of my larger projects I provide a project "book" to my clients at completion. They love seeing "before" and "after" photos but most enjoy shots of men and machines working to create their new landscape. A critical mass of digital images is essential if you are going to build a portfolio or create a Web site to support your business. You can shoot a hundred digital images, and it will cost you nothing but a little time. Photograph your own work at least every week, and go back to completed projects after a few months or even years to document how the landscape and gardens are maturing. These shots can illustrate a success story.

If you build a successful garden design business, invariably someone will ask you to lecture about something, somewhere. You'll need photos. If you've been taking photos all along you'll have a plethora of images to choose from. Yet another reason to take photos is that sometimes it's just fun for *you* to look back. And if you do end up creating a portfolio, some "before," "during," and "after" shots can be incredibly compelling and will give you great stories to tell a new prospect.

GETTING THE WORD OUT

This is the launching point. You've determined your focus and your offering to the marketplace. You have chosen your business name and prepared sales support materials, and you're raring to go. Now how do you make the phone ring? You can start low-key or do a full-fledged campaign. For starters, if you have even a single existing client—even a friend you've worked with or for, or people you've volunteered with—ask them to refer you to their friends. This is the best form of advertising, because your work is prequalified.

The "before" shot. Overgrown foundation plants were eating this lovely antique farmhouse.

The "during" shot. The trees come down and the face of the house becomes visible.

The "after" shot. New plantings are in, new trees provide a feeling of privacy, a new walkway connects to the new driveway layout, and the charming house seems reborn.

If you've done any pro bono or volunteer work, contact the people you met while doing the work and put the word out. Let them know what you're doing and ask for them to refer you. Offer them a few business cards to hand out.

Select from your marketing materials and make some posters or notices. Ask for permission to hang them in local churches, coffee shops, town hall, grocery stores, shipping stores, or post offices. Ask at local nurseries, assuming you won't be competing with them. Keep your poster easy to read, and make sure to use color. One or two stunning photos will work well for this application. Include your contact information—one phone number will be more than adequate. Tear-off pieces with your business name and phone number are a convenience for the prospective client; just remember to replace those posters regularly so they don't look shabby (and remove one of the tear-offs yourself before you post it—makes you look wanted!).

Remember that repetition drives the message home. Getting your name out there over and over again will bring you business.

You can purchase a line or small ad in the business pages of your local phone book. Ads in area phone books or the yellow pages for larger cities are quite costly, and most of the designers I know who have tried this have netted almost no business from the investment, so weigh this option carefully. You don't need to be out of pocket a great deal of money when you're starting out. Note that for printed phone books you will need a minimum of six months to a year of lead time.

Advertising needn't break the bank. Online advertisements are available through local news outlets in many communities, and you can also advertise your services on free sites like craigslist.org. You can advertise fairly inexpensively in the landscape section of your local weekly newspapers. Many daily newspapers offer a lower rate per ad if you purchase a block of advertising (say, twice a week for eight weeks). Make sure if you decide to do newspaper advertising that you commit to publishing your ad consistently. Single ads rarely work. People will scan the paper for several weeks (months, even years) and then finally be ready to pick up the phone. So if you are going to take the newspaper advertising route, make a commitment to advertise through the entire season; you can't risk missing a week when the client is finally ready to call and your number isn't there. Trust me, when a client is ready to make the call, they make the call—and if they aren't calling you, they will call the person who is consistently advertising. The more times a potential client has seen your name, the more likely they are to call you. This is called "developing mindshare" and is the foundation of awareness advertising. I have friends who advertise year-round for this very reason.

People who call after seeing an ad will be cold-calling you. They won't know you or your work. Strangely, many of them won't even know why they are calling, nor will they know what you do. You'll have quite a few tire kickers, calls from people that will go nowhere. But you know what? Still try to get a meeting and go see these people. Particularly as you are building your client-wooing talents, this is a great way to become comfortable talking with people about you, your skills, the vision you have to offer, and the beauty, functionality, and professional results you can deliver to their property. Practice makes perfect. So when you finally do get the right call from the right client, your spiel will be practiced and smooth.

If you are feeling particularly gutsy and want to launch a targeted campaign, select a few neighborhoods where you think your services would be valued. This would generally be the higher-end neighborhoods, yes, but midscale neighborhoods may also work. Target more than one town. Figure out how many houses you would like to directly approach, print up the quantity of fliers or brochures you will need, and hand-deliver them to each house. By law you cannot put nonmail items into a mail box, but you can slip your sales material into a screen door or onto a bench next to the door. Make sure you include color photos, quickly bullet what you are offering (should be a quick read to catch their attention), and include your name, business name, and phone number. Timing will be everything, so plan your marketing just ahead of the season. This would be a great way to pick up container gardening customers these prospects know the season is approaching, people are usually really anxious for a spring pick-me-up, and to think that "instant beauty and refreshment" is just a phone call away! Phase out your advertising by picking a street or neighborhood a week for three or four weeks or so. If you start getting deluged, you can stop the advertising. Don't spend a ton of money on this, because it might net you nothing. On the other hand, you might get a dozen or more phone calls.

A caveat. Until you really know what you are doing, do not canvass your perfect target town or neighborhood. You want to do your learning in a less key area. Wait until you have a year or two or three under your belt. Then you can concentrate on promoting your work to your ideal client.

Once you have a few clients, you'll be surprised how quickly the knowledge of your talents will spread. I had a client who had me install a cutting garden and "tart up" her patio with gorgeous pots. All of a sudden all of her friends had to have me. I enjoyed a six- or seven-year run of constant referrals from this group of (primarily) women. If you're lucky enough to get into a "Me, too!" crowd, run with it and enjoy it. The only caveat, if you say anything about any of them to another, make sure it is 100% complimentary, or it'll come back and bite you in the you-know-where. The only thing that grows faster than kudzu is gossip.

WHAT ABOUT COMPETITION?

Don't worry about what other people are doing. When I began talking to Timber Press about the possibilities for this book, one comment was, "Well, a downside is that you'll be telling people how to become your competition." No problem. There is plenty of work out there for all of us. I cannot imagine a time when there will be a glut of garden and landscape designers, even in a tough economic climate. Yes, recessions impact our business, as they do everyone's. But if you are good at your work, honest, diligent, and play well with others, you will always have work. Other designers are not my competition; I consider them my colleagues. Even when I lose a prospective client to another designer, that's fine. Clients need to choose the best fit from a "scope of work" standpoint, and interpersonal chemistry needs to work. Do quality work, conduct yourself professionally, take pleasure in the collaboration with your clients, and you'll always enjoy a great reputation and ample work.

CHAPTER TWELVE

Basics of Running a Small Business

RUNNING YOUR OWN BUSINESS is much like other work you have either done yourself or been a part of. The idea for the business starts the process. You create an entity and define your offering, followed by developing the product; selecting materials; identifying vendors, providers, and partners; promoting your offering; fostering customers and sales; estimating; implementing; and delivering. Many businesses, both large and small, follow this general structure, and for the most part, so will your garden and landscape design business. Being solely responsible for a business will allow you greater choices and a larger degree of flexibility than you have ever had working in other businesses, but it is also a tremendous responsibility to have the buck stop with you.

The motto of the Boy Scouts of America is "Be prepared." Preparation will certainly serve you well, so before you're off and running you need to consciously decide on a few things. I say consciously because you don't want to be in the middle of actually starting with a client and then have to stop—or work frenetically, which will assuredly add to your stress—to figure all of this out. Spend some time now figuring out where and what and who.

WHERE WILL YOU PLANT YOURSELF SO YOU CAN THRIVE?

For most of us, starting a garden design business means working from home. First, it keeps your overhead to a minimum and minimizes your risk. Always think frugal, frugal, frugal. When you have little to no income there's no need to pay $1000 a month to rent an office when a small spare room, or even a corner of a room, will suffice. And then there's the commute. Being able to walk out of your morning shower, pop on a pair of jeans, and sit down right in your own office is the ultimate luxury (and the ultimate in a great carbon footprint!).

Years ago my mother ran her business and our household using two things: the checkbook and her phone. She operated her entire design and dressmaking business on small slips of paper and in her head, her trusty personal phone book by her side. But life, including work life, is significantly more complicated now, and we need space to accommodate our stuff.

Having a dedicated workspace will keep you more organized and efficient than having your work spread out in pieces all over your home, or worse yet, having to take out and put away your work repeatedly because it is in the way. The latter scenario just sets you up to procrastinate, and that's the last thing you need.

When I started out, I set up a rough home office in the front foyer of our little bungalow. That was the only room that wasn't dedicated to other functions. I knew I needed a space where I could walk away and leave it, then return to the work in progress the next day. I thoroughly believe that the bedroom should be a refuge for sleeping and reenergizing, so that left the kitchen, living room, dining room, or foyer. Foyer it was.

My husband, Bruce, was supportive and wanted to help me find a workable solution. The foyer was truly tiny: 12 feet by 7 feet, with two doorways, two windows, a big ol' radiator, and a staircase leading off of it. It was tight but we made it work. We covered the one large available wall with ceiling-to-floor bookshelves. I added a large desk made out of an old door popped on top of two deep filing cabinets. I purchased an all-in-one printer-scanner-copier-fax machine, which went under the desk on a small rolling platform. We set up the keyboard and monitor, extra wiring and outlets to accommodate the tower, phone, answering machine, desk lamp, calculator, and eventually the cell phone charger. My chair just fit in the 3 feet between the desk in front of me and the wall of bookshelves behind me. It was marvelous. Enjoying the lovely east and south light, with houseplants and stained glass finds in the windows, along with my son and kitties at my feet—from that little space, my business grew.

In 2003 we renovated our home and gave ourselves a little more space. My son's former bedroom was enlarged and is now home to my office. It's about three times the size of the former foyer, but it holds about five times the stuff, so it's still relatively piled with books and files and images and magazines (you know, my life). I arranged the furniture, banks of files, and desk-workstation orientation, by light exposure and what's outside the windows. I now look out to a view I enjoy (a south-facing garden with frolicking birds) and that offers more inspiration than the east view, which faces the street. My computer screen is positioned so that it is out of direct sunlight all day, and I only get about an hour of sun midmorning that causes any glare. One of my cats feels she can never get close enough to me, so rather than have her under my arms against my chest the whole time I'm sitting at the computer—or constantly having to put her onto the floor—I keep a little pillow next to my workstation, and she happily sleeps there, inches from my elbow.

My office. As you can see, the cat really does sleep just inches from my elbow.

I humbly suggest you carve out a garden design work niche for your-self. Outfit it with the things you need for design, reference, communications, and production. Let everyone else in your household know that this area is now your work space (so don't touch!), and allow the space and your venture into this business to morph together, symbiotically. It happens.

Down the road as your business grows, you might have employees. You might have lots of landscaping equipment. You might still be on your own but wildly successful and wanting more of a physical definition between work and home. So then might be time to build, rent, or buy office space. If that time comes, write down every need and every wish for your new location, and use this list as the basis for searching out and designing your new workspace.

SUPPLIES

Get yourself what you need. I love, love, love office and drafting supplies. The larger national office supply chains now deliver to your home the very next day for free if you order $50 or more online. One printer cartridge costs almost that much, so I order frequently. (And yes, I have to guard against ordering more than I need.) You will need ample supplies to create and produce your design presentations. You'll need supplies for your client files, financial files, and product files (warrantees, software CDs, and so forth). You'll want things to hold business cards (yours and the ones you'll invariably collect), invoices, receipts, nursery and supply catalogs, notes to yourself. Lots of stuff equals lots of office supplies to manage the stuff. Joy!

KEEPING TRACK

I used to ring my computer screen with a zillion sticky notes, until I realized the notes were becoming their own distraction. I'm now down to about five notes with infrequently-called-but-important-to-be-able-to-quickly-access phone numbers, and a couple of notes about critical things—this keeps these items in my face and at the top of my mind. A bad mistake forced me to start doing this. I once entirely forgot about a client for six weeks. Really. It was during an especially busy spring, and when I came home from the initial meeting I managed to forget about these people until I came across the meeting notes I'd buried. Yowza! Really embarrassing and unprofessional.

A good calendar will prevent this from happening. Notes to yourself, not only regarding where you need to be and when, but also about when things are due or should be attended to, will help keep you organized and on top of your life. Computerized calendar systems are great for this kind of thing, although I still use a book-style calendar. It's comforting to me that the calendar is physically there at all times. (I do not carry it with me. I do not take it anywhere. It resides in the same spot next to my workstation, year in and year out.) Basically, my whole work and personal life is in it, as well as pertinent notations about my husband's schedule and travels, my son's agenda and project due dates, and so forth. All of this information in one place. Works for me.

But I do have to admit that computer-based calendar systems are fabulous. Friends of mine use the calendar system that comes with their suite of professional software, and they live by it. You can set alarms and reminders, have the computer search for convenient meeting times between two calendars, and add long notes to a highlighted block of time ("Thursday, 2:00 to 5:00: Design Jones patio. Note: Want bluestone multi, like curves, need shade, have toddler and dogs. Pay attention to proximity of large oak").

BALANCING WORK AND HOME

Some people find it difficult to work from home because there is a constant stream of distractions. Housework can call to you. "Oh, the laundry is done, let's just grab that, take a little break, and get it folded and put away." Then make the beds, then do the dishes, then think about dinner. Three hours later you sit back in your office and see that you've lost half a day. Even business-related work can distract you: the utterly compelling chime of a new e-mail, deciding you *must* eat that last half bag of M&M's while pondering the Sullivans' planting plan, and yes, let's weed the walkway on the way to get the mail.

In 2005 my husband became a consultant and started working a lot from home. This after nearly thirty years of working Monday through

Friday in an office environment. Several months into this new working paradigm he confided that it was incredibly hard to concentrate, because "everything" called to him, from the refrigerator to the lawn. Even having me in the next room was a distraction, since he wanted to share everything "real time" as we do in our nonwork hours.

How do you turn off the distractions? For me it comes down to overt self-discipline. When I recognize that I'm staring out the window, doing the laundry thing, or choosing to answer a friend's joke e-mail because that's more fun than the work I have ahead of me, I sometimes snap myself out of it by saying, out loud, "Okay. Now stop it." Then I force myself, sometimes inwardly groaning as I do so, to turn to the task at hand. This is particularly useful when I'm working under a deadline. And, frankly, I work under deadlines most of the time.

This works. I force myself to ignore distractions. I get myself into the work that is required, and in this way I invariably get done what needs to get done.

This brings up another potential problem: how do you turn off the work? When you work from home, the work is always there, in your face, all the time. It can be easy to let work completely usurp your personal and family time, particularly if you like working and being in "the zone." I love being in the zone, where inspiration is lightning in your brain, work flies from your fingers, and you're really accomplishing things. The torturous part is when you try to balance this with your personal life. For me, again, it requires overt self-discipline. There is a time to stop. Period. There is a time to be a mom, to be a partner, to chill out. And you have to grant yourself this, or your family (and deep down, even you) will begin to resent your business.

Thanks to modern technology, work follows us everywhere now. Do you check e-mail and voice mail on the way to bed? I say, no. Not if you want to sleep. If you get an annoying message or one that requires problem solving, it could keep you restless most of the night. Know that the message will be there in the morning, when you are refreshed, thinking more clearly, and able to do something if that's what is required. This advice is coming from a person who is not a natural morning person, and who is—yes, I admit it—completely addicted to e-mail. You need to set boundaries for yourself, and allow yourself permission to respect those boundaries. You don't have to be a nazi about it. There are times that the work will justify staying up until 2:00 a.m. But you need to give yourself an overall umbrella of structure, so that your work life and personal life can both thrive.

WHERE IS THAT STUFF? KEEPING ORGANIZED FILES

The Information Age was supposed to end up being almost paperless. Instead we are bombarded with more information—and paper!—than ever. Keeping the information organized and accessible is critical to feeling in control.

First and foremost are client files. You'll want to maintain quick and easy references for every client. I have one hard-copy folder for each client, where I keep a copy of every note and printed document in reverse chronological order. I also keep four electronic files on my computer: recommendations and design notes, a CAD folder of design layouts, a photo file, and e-mail and other communications.

I keep my hard-copy client files in colored, slick-covered folders that open with a pocket on each side. In the left pocket is a cover sheet with the client's contact information at the top (including names of their children and pets) and contact information for every subcontractor and supplier I have used on the project. Behind this master list I keep a copy of every invoice I have sent to the client, also in reverse chronological order. This has served me well, for example when I have had to respond to a question like, "In 2006 you did x for me, and this year it costs y. Why the change?" I can immediately reference the specific charge and respond intelligently. In the right pocket of the client folder, I keep everything else: notes, samples, pages ripped out of magazines, fabric swatches, paint chips, copies of all correspondence, proposals, design layouts, planting plans, estimates, printouts of pertinent images. This is the project folder, and I can pull any of these out on a former client and know exactly where we ordered the benches, what type of stone was chosen for the patio and where we purchased it, the paint color for the shutters, and what annuals were used for the pots in 2007. Everything.

For the most part the client folder never leaves my house. It contains notes and details I would not want to lose, as well as data I would prefer my clients not see (information on actual costs versus margin charged, stuff like that).

On a macro level, I have three filing categories for client folders: current clients, recent clients, and defunct clients. I keep my in-process folders in vertical file holders on top of my credenza. I reference these nearly every day during the project implementation, so they're front and center, handy to grab. Then I have an upright file containing folders for clients I've worked with in the last three years. Lastly, I store my defunct-client folders in the bottom drawer of a less-used file cabinet—a little tough to get to, but I know where they are if I need to look something up.

I do have friends in this business who keep virtually paperless offices. They scan and file everything electronically, do not collect reams of industry information as I do, do not save every inspiration reference, and aren't book hounds like I am, so this works well for them. None of them can understand why I would bother with my space-consuming, paper-filled system, but I'm happy and comfortable with it and am unlikely to change anytime soon. Be assured that you can make either system, or a hybrid of the two, work for you.

For each of my clients, I maintain an e-mail correspondence file as well as a Word file. The Word file contains all proposals, estimates, and snail mail. I also maintain electronic folders of client photos, images taken of their entire property that are categorized based on the stages of the project construction (for example, a folder labeled "Rodriguez images" may include subfolders tagged "before," "during," "after," and "best"). This helps me to quickly find exactly what I want to reference or print out. Last, I create a file of CAD layouts for each client.

I also keep a master Word file of invoices, and a master file of addresses in a format for printing envelopes. Each are simple to update and print.

Remember to back up your files regularly. Electronic files and images are just one thunderstorm away from being fried (or your workstation or laptop could be stolen, along with your files). Get into the habit of regularly copying your business files onto CD, or choose a simpler solution: get an automated backup service by searching online, or purchase an external storage device. For about $100 you can get a 250- to 500-gig portable hard drive that plugs into your USB port. These suggestions are all inexpensive and easy to use, and are a critical part of protecting your business files and photographs.

The final hard-copy files I keep are for invoices sent, and for all of my receipts of all kinds, both in reverse chronological order. I maintain new files for both the invoices and the receipts each year, because I store all of the previous year's information with my annual tax information. Just for the sake of organization during the season, I do maintain a "to be billed" throw-the-receipt-in-here file, into which goes every receipt or subcontractor invoice that I receive. I make notes on each receipt or invoice as soon as I have it in hand, even at a retailer. You don't want to be wondering two or three weeks out which cryptic receipt belongs to which client and who you need to bill for what. Trust me, you'll go nuts. It's much easier to write "Connors" on the corner of the invoice and toss it in the "to be billed" file.

Staying organized will help you streamline your client communications, simplify billing, maximize your efficiency, and keep you feeling in control.

STREAMLINING SYSTEMS

Try to seize any opportunity you have to simplify your work and save yourself time. Saving time really does translate into saving money, and overall it will also save you frustration. An easy and effective way to help streamline your work is to use software to best advantage and set up templates for many of your systems and documents. This is called boilerplate. Doing things with boilerplate can save you a ton of time and can even spare you mistakes. For example, when preparing an estimate, you don't need to reinvent the formatting; if you have a template stored, just bring it up, immediately "Save As" a new document under the client's name, and fill it out like a form. This is much easier than reinventing the wheel and setting up a new format every time. It also helps you remember every piece to include in the estimate. Before I created an estimate template, I pulled together estimates from my notes. Imagine my embarrassment when I went to present a final estimate to a client and found that I had forgotten to include something like soil and mulch. The client would invariably think, "If she can forget something like this on an estimate, what will she forget to do during the course of building my landscape?"

A small mistake can undermine your clients' trust, or end up costing you money. Not good.

I use a template for my design narrative (a leave-behind document that I prepare as my talking points for the design presentation), template drawings for my CAD designs and layouts, templates for photograph printout labels, and templates for just about everything else, including my master client contact form, estimates, and plant orders. My master CAD prototype drawing saves me at least an hour or two on every design. It includes all of my plant symbols, text headings, hatch and boundary creations, clip art for stones, people, and automobiles, my logo, scale information, printing frames—everything. All of the electronic data I need to complete my design is right there already compiled for me.

For me this works better than opening another finished drawing or document and hitting "Save As" because it helps prevent any major "I cannot believe I was stupid enough to do that!" moments. In the past, when I used this method, I would start by stripping the drawing of the former client's site and design information and then work in the new client's home and garden layouts. Unfortunately, a couple of times I was so in the zone that I made the huge mistake of clicking "Save" and inadvertently overwriting the previously stored information. Yikes! Hours and hours of work lost forever. This actually happened to me twice, and twice was two times too many, so I finally bit the bullet and took the time to set up templates for every computer-generated function.

If you make the same mistake of hitting "Save" while entering new data onto your prototype template, it's annoying but far from fatal. You can always "Save As" like you should have done as soon as you opened the template, but you can return to the proto document or drawing later and spend a few minutes stripping it back down to its naked, boilerplate self again. No major work lost.

Automating your accounting is another great time and expense saver, and accounting software has become so user-friendly that it is ridiculous to operate without it. Using software to keep track of your financials not only saves your brain for other tasks, it also makes you feel more secure. When you know your numbers are in order and you aren't missing critical billing items, which could result in lost revenue, energy-wasting anxiety is greatly reduced. Accounting software is inexpensive, easy to use, and contributes to the bottom line in more than just dollars saved.

PROFESSIONAL FEES

What services will you charge for, how much will you charge, and how will you ask clients for money? Handling fees is one of the hardest parts of starting out. Designers receive payment for a variety of services, including site consultation, garden and landscape design, construction management, and maintenance.

INITIAL CONSULTATION FEES

Some designers charge for the first visit to a client, which they consider an initial consultation. They are paid anywhere from $100 to $1000, whether or not the potential clients move ahead with design. This is a good practice to adopt for a number of reasons. First, it weeds out the tire kickers, people who want to pick your brain but aren't really interested in design services. Second, it pays you for the time you are investing, which is valid. Third, people value what they pay for. Prospective clients are more likely to move forward and spend additional money in a design phase if they have already invested a couple of hundred dollars.

DESIGN FEES

Some professionals charge nothing for designing a garden or landscape, assuming they will get paid during the installation. Not only does this not pay them for the time they have spent and the work they have invested, but they might end up with nothing. The client could decide against having that designer perform the installation and either do it themselves or hire another person. Or the client just might not take the designer seriously. If your work is good, it is worth getting paid for, whether or not the design is actually built.

I know designers who are paid just a few hundred dollars for their design work, and I know designers who are paid many thousands of dollars, including fees that can go well into five figures. Designers on the low end of that spectrum are usually new to the business and feeling tentative and insecure about charging for design. Or they live in an area that cannot support higher fees. Or they are uncomfortable charging for their intellectual work, assuming that if you don't actually have a product (but you do!), it isn't worth much.

You need to decide for yourself what hourly rate will feed you as you get started in this business. Obviously, out of the starting block you're not going to be charging as much as a seasoned professional, but don't sell yourself short. Average hourly rates of designers that I know generally range from $25 to $300 or more. And yes, if you're charging upwards of $300 an hour for design, you should be very, very good.

Most of us quote a flat fee for a design, taking into consideration our hourly rate and how much time we think it will take. So if I am working Design X for the Cataldos, I list the areas we will address for the property, and quote the total fee. Here's an example of a design fee receipt:

CATALDO PROPERTY
Spring 2010

Design Fee for 238 Warren Street, Bristol, MA

$5000.00

Fee includes
- Initial on-site meeting
- Assessment of site conditions
- Site data collection and photographs
- Preparation of base map and schematic
- Interim discussions with clients and subcontractors, as needed
- Development of landscape treatment options, including
  pool and apron, pondside deck, new walkways and
  driveway, plantings
- Materials and plant selection options
- Design presentation meeting—date TBD

March 21—50% deposit request ($2500.00)

Received 6/29/09, Check 422—Thank you.

Balance of $2500.00 is payable at the design meeting
(date to be determined)

My intention is to receive the 50% deposit at the end of our initial on-site meeting. I include the information above on their receipt for the deposit, and state that I expect final payment in full at the design presentation meeting. These are pretty standard payment terms in our industry.

Some designers do charge for design by the hour. If you want to work this way, give your clients an idea of how much the final design will cost. "I charge $50 per hour for design, and I estimate that your landscape design will require approximately twenty hours, so the total will be in the vicinity of $1000."

I know several designers who charge to price a job. This is completely separate from the design fee and construction costs. Charging to price a job is valid, since you will spend many hours crunching numbers, perhaps meeting with other subcontractors and vendors, and getting additional quotes. It is indeed work, and tedious, exacting work at that. Most of us fold this into our construction fee for managing the job, but I have warmed to the idea of getting paid for compiling numbers and developing estimates. At the very least you'll pay more attention to the numbers, since you're getting paid for it, and seeing more areas of potential expense could result in justifying that you charge more for your installations. This is completely appropriate. But if the construction does not go through, for whatever reason, you have been compensated for your time. Always a good thing.

CONSTRUCTION FEES AND MARGIN, OR HOW WE MAKE OUR MONEY

Garden designers charge for two major categories of work: design and construction management. I used to charge clients differently based on what I was doing. Design: top dollar. Construction: a little less per hour. Maintenance: about half the hourly rate for design. One day I realized that my system was annoying for me and a little confusing for my clients. So now I just charge one rate. At my hourly rate I am paid well, but my business income did not become truly substantive until I wised up and started to charge margin.

When I was first starting out, I never charged margin. I charged for my time, added my out-of-pocket expenses (labor, materials, everything), and that was the price. I made a little money. I mean, I was paid, but my income was far from lucrative.

Most of us who provide landscape construction make a living by charging margin. Margin is an amount you charge above your costs. For example, if plants for a project cost you $8000, and you have set your margin on materials at 40%, then you would charge the client $8000 plus 40% of $8000 ($3200), a total of $11,200. If this makes you uncomfortable, not to worry. First, you're going to be purchasing nearly all of your materials wholesale, and most markup from wholesale to retail ranges anywhere from 25% to 200%. Second, trust me when I say that this is how you will make a lucrative income. People who live on an hourly rate alone rarely make a living wage. Third, everyone in the industry charges margin. It is not gouging, nor is it highway robbery. This is the market. I have friends who charge 300% markup on plants, stone, and furnishings but 20% on labor. We all devise what works for each of us. If you want to charge affluent people a higher amount, you can. If you want to work with someone but they have less means, you can charge less. I work this way. I have no hard or fast rule, and I work to my own comfort level.

Some contractors, landscape or otherwise, are up front about margin, telling their clients, "I charge 45% margin." I am not. If someone asks if I charge margin, I am honest and say, "Yes, I charge an industry-standard margin." But I do not divulge how much. If people ask if they can purchase the plants or stone or whatever themselves (to save the margin), I let them know that I am a single-source supplier and that I need to have direct control over the suppliers and subcontractors to maintain my quality standards. After all, the person writing the check has the control. I also reiterate that I purchase at a wholesale level and consequently often save my clients 50% or better. No one has ever pushed me to the wall on this.

I learned quite a bit from the contractor who managed my house renovation. In his contract, he spelled out the hourly rate for his carpenters and himself, as well as what margin he charged on subs and materials (20%). Apparently it is common in the building industry to be completely transparent about hourly rates and margin charges.

Most people want you to be able to make a decent living, but no one wants to feel ripped off even if they have oodles of money. At the end of one design presentation, a client said to me, "Oh, I'm sure you'll charge me twice what you'd charge anyone else just because I live in Hingham." Hingham is an affluent town. I replied in a gently mocking tone,

"Actually, I would have been inclined to give you a bit of a break, since I live in Hingham as well, and that means I'd have no highway drive time to manage your project. But now that you mention it, well, yes, I just might charge you twice my going rate, because I always like to exceed my clients' expectations." Then I grinned. Of course, I didn't charge them twice my usual rate, and the project went smoothly. But it's funny how some clients expect contractors to rip them off.

I've noticed that some interior decorators publish their margin on their rate card ("Rate: $150 per hour, minimum $10,000 per room, furnishings at 200%"). Plainly, in some industries, discussion of margin is quite out in the open, while in other industries, there is a quieter knowledge of the financial mechanics. Ours is the quieter type.

PREPARING AND PRESENTING AN ESTIMATE

Whether or not you charge for your time to compile costs for a project, you will need to learn to develop pricing, also known as preparing an estimate. Where the heck do you start? Well, when you're new to this business it is difficult to guesstimate how many labor hours a project will take, as well as how much of any material the particular job will require. You can rely on input from some of your subcontractors (most are quick to share their knowledge). Soon you will get an instinctive feel for exactly how many laborers will be needed for how many days, how many plants it will take to cover a certain hillside, and so forth. Until then, just proceed cautiously.

Some people work entire jobs on "time and materials." This means that there is no formal agreement or total dollar figure that the designer or client are working off of. I don't recommend this, since you can be caught with your proverbial pants down if the job goes over what the client expects to pay. I feel the client should always have a really good feel, if not absolute knowledge, of what the job will cost. The best surprise is no surprise.

Having said that, at times working on time and materials is unavoidable. I met with a client and a general contractor about refurbishing the client's custom garage doors. Even detailed poking and prodding could not give the contractor full knowledge of what the crew would get into when they started taking the doors apart. We told the client that we'd put two guys on the job for two days, and that it would cost a certain amount, but added that since we didn't know all that would be involved, they might not be finished by the end of the second day. She understood and was fine with that. From the beginning I kept her apprised of what we found and how we were progressing. Had costs looked like they were going to run over, I would have given her the heads-up on that, too. So there are times that you will be required to work this way, but it should be the exception rather than the rule.

Some designers present estimates that are just one large number. No line items, no detailed explanation, just a total. Some of them figure that in a bid situation the client cannot compare apples to apples (except for the total), and that works for them. That's all well and good, but if I were the client I'd like to see a breakdown of that total number. So I provide a breakdown, including the following major line items:

- Nursery stock (all plant materials—woody, herbaceous, annuals, and so forth)
- Landscape labor and machinery
- Bulk items (loam, mulch, amendments, lawn seed)
- Masonry (materials and labor)
- Carpentry
- Painting
- Electric and lighting
- Irrigation
- Fencing
- Tree work
- Water features
- Driveway
- Furnishings (pots, furniture, garden art, bird feeders)
- Sales taxes and delivery charges on appropriate line items (or fold this into each line item)
- Disposal fees (excavating, grading, or clearing detritus, debris, construction waste, plastics from nursery stock—consider everything that must leave the site)
- Project management (my fee to manage the project implementation)

Obviously not every job has all of those categories, but that's my master list, and within each of those expense categories the line item includes both labor and materials, except where noted. When I give an estimate to a client, sometimes I provide a range for each pertinent line item, from the least expensive way we could accomplish the job to the sort of worst-case scenario. If I am providing a range, there's usually only a 10% to 20% spread from low to high, but at times it will be more. Why would I bother? Sometimes we don't know what the hard costs are for some items until we get into doing the actual work. For example, say I have a perennial garden design that will require some grading and planting bed prep, and the installation of 150 perennials in 1-gallon containers. If we're digging at Site A, which has surface duff over sand over clay with no rocks, I know that three guys can crank through it in one morning. However, if we start digging and encounter typical mega-rocky New England soil (every time you put a shovel into the ground, it goes in about an inch and—clink!—you hit a big rock), that same digging could take one or two days, plus we'll need to pile up, collect, and remove stones from the site (yet more labor, plus additional hauling and disposal fees). Ka-ching, ka-ching. Providing a range of expected costs gives the client a feel for where that line item will come in, but also warns them that costs can shift due to unforeseen circumstances.

On line items where I truly have less of a handle on what it might cost but don't want to go to the effort of meeting with the contractor and getting a firm estimate, I will provide an "allowance." This is a typical practice in home renovation but is applicable to landscaping, too. Let's take electrical work. Maybe I know that we're going to need the installation of four additional exterior outlets, three exterior lights, and a transformer for low-voltage landscape lighting. This will take the electrician about a day, plus materials. So I'll add this to the estimate: "Lighting, labor and materials—$2500 allowance." This means that the cost could be anywhere up to $2500, but if the cost goes over the allowance, it will result in extra charges to the client. I explain this to the client. I will not ask permission to finish if the costs are running over; we have an understanding that even if costs escalate we'll do what it takes to finish the job. Of course, as a courtesy, if the costs are running over I do let the client know.

I am very forthright, so in every case where I've worked an allowance this way the client has been completely understanding.

Your estimate should include the terms of payment, which will be determined based on your preferences coupled with whatever the client will agree to. Always get a significant portion of the estimated costs up front. Most homeowners are honest, but there is the odd person who seems wonderful to work with but screws you over at the end.

Likewise, clients may be a little nervous about giving you a hefty chunk of change, because every story you hear or read in the popular press is about some unscrupulous contractor who took the money and ran. One well-known builder in my area disappeared with several hundred thousand dollars he had taken in deposits from various clients. He even left his subs hanging out to dry. Many of these subcontractors hadn't been paid for work they had already completed, and the clients were out huge sums of money and not about to fork over more to the subs. Everyone was screwed over. So if a client seems skittish, be patient, and know that having a solid estimate with defined payment terms will go a long way to relieving their anxiety.

Here are several scenarios for payment terms:

No money up front. You do the job and bill the client for the grand total at the end. This involves a great deal of trust on your part. If the client doesn't pay, or chooses to pay less, you're hosed. That said, I do work this way with clients who I have worked with for many years, particularly if the job is going to be less than about $10,000. This is because we have established trust both ways. But unless you're doing follow-up work for really good clients, I highly recommend you not use these payment terms.

Payment terms of one-third, one-third, one-third. These are typical construction payment terms: one-third to schedule, one-third to start, one-third at completion of job. This is pretty much how I handle jobs up to about $25,000. Sometimes I just lump the start payment with the schedule payment, so on day one when we show up, I'd receive a check for two-thirds of the estimated cost. This will cover most of what is or will become my out-of-pocket expenses, plus most of the labor. I take my profit in the end, meaning I don't get paid until after my subs and suppliers are paid. If anyone takes a bath on the job, it is me and only me.

Another way to work one-third, one-third, one-third. These are the payment terms of another landscape designer friend of mine. He gets one-third to schedule (which can be six or eight months before the start), one-third to start (day one on-site), and one-third at the halfway point of construction. Personally I would never pay a contractor like this, because I would feel like I had surrendered all leverage, but most of this guy's clients have no problem with it. True that he is an honest gentleman and completes every job to his client's satisfaction. But as he tells me, "I take my profit up front." And he has never gotten hosed. He holds the money, he holds the cards, he has peace of mind. I cannot work this way, because I would feel awkward trying to sell payment terms that I myself would never agree to, but a part of me envies him.

Payment terms of 50/50. A slightly less typical scenario is 50% up front, 50% at completion. This does give you working funds and will cover a portion of your out-of-pocket expenses, but if you have a problem at the end of the job that you cannot resolve with the client, they can hold up 50% of the total cost, which is usually far greater than the amount you will owe for materials and labor. I feel this puts you in a vulnerable position.

Milestone payments. Milestone payment terms are typical in the construction trades, particularly for jobs that are $25,000 or more. These payments are performance based. As it relates to our business, the scenario could be something like this: 30% to schedule, 20% at beginning of driveway demolition, 20% at completion of deck, 20% when front lawn receives sod, and 10% at completion. Milestone payment terms are usually very favorable with the homeowner, because they only pay when certain progress points are reached, and it breaks up the payments into more manageable amounts. This gets you about a third of the estimated total up front and leaves you with only 10% hanging in the end. You have operating capital when you need it and little vulnerability at completion. I use these payment terms on all larger jobs.

Balance at the end. An acquaintance of mine is a custom homebuilder, and he told me that he adds 10% to every estimate he develops, and his payment terms are "remaining 10% due at completion." In construction this final 10% is also called the holdback. He insists that every client with whom he has ever worked has wanted to hold back money for one thing or another at the end. By adding 10% to his estimate at the beginning, he's already received his profit and can walk away from the holdback with no regret. He told me it's "easier for me to say, 'Okay, you keep the $43,000, and you change out the windows you don't like yourselves.'" The clients are happy, because they think they've gotten something for nothing, but the contractor knows he's already made his profit, and it gets the client off his back. All I can say is that this is a very negative way to go into a business relationship.

I don't recommend operating this way. I have always believed that if you do a good job and work from a position of trust, people will be fair. And for the most part they are. It is true, though, unfortunately, that you can never predict who will rip you off. A couple of years ago I took on clients who were neighbors and friends of other really good, long-term clients of mine. These people had a conservation project they needed to complete in order to get permits to build their dream home on the waterfront. After going through the design process with them, I figured that this first little phase of the job would be about $5000, so why split the payments? We were, presumably, going into a several-year relationship with phases of landscaping to be completed before and after the house construction. So I opted for payment terms of "no money down." As we prepared for the installation day, everything was hunky-dory. The one-day project went swimmingly, and the clients said they were delighted with the work. We even managed to complete some tree work that they needed done, which was a free little bonus for them (had they brought in tree guys to do the work, it would have easily cost them $1500 or more). In the review that followed the riverside planting, the local conservation commission loved what we did and how we did it, and approved all of the permits. To put icing on the cake, my invoice even came in below estimate. Everyone should have been happy, right?

I invoiced them. A month later I sent a "second request" invoice with a nice reminder, but having heard nothing from them, I was beginning to feel naggingly uncomfortable. As the weeks dragged into months, I called several times and sent several e-mail messages but received no response. When I finally received a check in the mail, I was shocked to see that it was not for the full invoiced amount. They had shorted me $1400, my cost for the crew that day. They included a note, saying they wanted clarification of this and that. They didn't feel my crew was worth the money; they thought they had just been "hanging around" all day. One thing my crew never does is "hang around," and I had been with them the entire time, so I could vouch for the fact that we were industrious workers the entire day. But do whatever it takes to get the check, right? I immediately provided the clarification they requested and asked for them to kindly remit the remainder of the payment. Weeks later, nothing. After several more calls and e-mail messages, I knew I'd done everything except meet with them face-to-face (because they would not respond at all). So, after about six months, I finally bit the bullet and let it drop. The bottom line? They cheated me. I felt hurt and betrayed (and still do). But I got smarter. I also know that I'm lucky it was $1400 and not $14,000 or $140,000. Another one of life's lessons learned. (Another lesson this process taught me was to get my clients to sign a copy of the approved estimate before we start.)

CHANGE ORDERS, OR THE "WHILE YOU'RE HERE" SYNDROME

When you are working on a project, particularly a large project that requires you to be on-site for a period of time, the client will often ask for additional services. "Hey, while you're all here planting the deck perimeter, could you fix the drainage problem over there?" I always say, "No problem," and take care of it. But these little extras always cost a little extra, since they require labor, materials, and time. This generates a change order. Verbal requests and verbal approvals for anything that is changed or added to midstream is a change order.

I used to always bill for these extras with the final invoice, well identified as a change order and always with an explanation of the work. I never had any problem with managing it in this way until one particular job. I was working with long-term clients of mine, but this was the first time I was working with the wife. I'd worked with the husband on their property for several years, always in perfect collaboration. So we were there to landscape the new pool and summerhouse, but as she zipped in and out of the property she'd stop, check progress, seem happy, and then ask for more work. "While you're here, could you take care of another thing? I'd really like the drive entry planting redone." "Oh, and can you add annuals to bring a punch of spring color to the entire front?" "Wouldn't a hydrangea border next to the house be stunning?" "The limestone patio garden could use a colorful replanting." "While you're at it, now's a good time to enhance the meadow garden."

Each day over the course of about two weeks, we had request on top of request, ostensibly because the owner of the local football team was coming to dinner on our "deadline date" and she wanted the place looking spectacular. Fortunately we had the time to turn around these requests, and we worked furiously to get everything done and perfect. We made the deadline and she was thrilled with the work. But I never gave her actual numbers for all of her little additions. When I finally billed her for the whole job, the invoice was about $8000 more than my original total, and she kind of hit the roof. She also had the original number that *she* had proposed lodged in her head. I had told her at the beginning that this was not a realistic number for landscaping the pool. She had wanted to spend $7000, but the pots she wanted for the pool area alone were nearly $6000. I had told her that we could install the proposed design for about $20,000, and she had agreed. Did I put this in writing and get a signature? No. "My bad," as my son would say. So the client still had $7000 in her head, and the total was about $28,000. She eventually paid in full, but I was never invited back. Recently a subcontractor friend of mine who works for this same couple periodically said that he mentioned to them that he'd seen me, and the wife quickly retorted, "Oh, well, she does beautiful work, but she's way too expensive." Had I produced change orders and kept her apprised of the costs for additional plants, materials, and labor, her reaction might have been more positive. Live and learn.

A few years ago I worked on a large job with a masonry and landscaping contractor who was hired directly by the clients. Working with him taught me a lot about not mincing words when talking with clients about where the money is going, how much extra time things are taking, and how much moolah changes cost. This particular client changed her mind about every two days. We'd put in a walk, then take out the walk, put in piping for the pool, then need to shift the pipes as the pool location changed. Greg would look at her and say, "Julia, we'll do whatever you want, but just remember, the meter's ticking. You change, we add on work, you pay." She got it. These were *her* changes that *she* was requesting. She never questioned his bills, and she paid right on time. I'll never forget that phrase: "The meter's ticking." I've used it myself since then, and clients get it without having their faces rubbed in it.

When I was going through a major house renovation, my (wonderful, fabulous) general contractor handled the change orders in one of the best ways imaginable. We had a contract for the renovation, and most payments were based on milestones. Good. When we had agreed that something—anything!—was going to happen that was outside of our original contract, he would come to me the very next morning with the change order in hand. His change orders were numbered (they eventually totaled seventeen), and on each he would list a description of the work, the dollar amounts for labor and materials (which included his markup—he was very up front about that), and the total due. He brought forms in triplicate: one copy for my files, one copy for his on-site project file, one copy for his home records. He signed, I signed, and—here's the most brilliant part—he wanted a check right then and there for the total change order amount. The first couple of change orders, I was a little taken aback that he wanted the money instantly. I mean, why not wait until the end? Some change orders seemed silly to bother with—$300 here, $700 there. One was not insignificant: $17,000. But as I thought about this more, I saw the brilliance. In having us sign and pay for each change order, it benefited both the contractor and the clients. First, the contractor's cash flow was not interrupted; as soon as he anticipated extra money going out for labor and materials, he had the money in hand. Second, his policy was in keeping with the idea that the best surprise is no surprise. As with my own clients, it was easy for Bruce and me to get lost in the excitement of renovation and add on elements while the workers were there—elements that we might or might not have been able to afford. Because we had to sign and pay for the change orders immediately, we were fully aware of how much we were depleting our funds, and there was no huge surprise at the end. The change orders eventually totaled nearly $40,000. We were happy with the additions and grateful that we had paid for them along the way. One last bit of genius in our contractor's method: since he already had the change order money in hand, if any problems had developed between our contractor and us, he wouldn't have to wait for a payment if we delayed at the end, or be left high and dry if we reneged.

So do I handle change orders like this? Well, um, no. On larger jobs I get verbal approvals, and if the amount looks like it's going to be a couple thousand dollars, I get a signature. I list the change orders and when the next milestone payment is due, I add on the amounts for the change orders to date and get the payment at that point. This works for my clients, and it works for me. Why don't I get the payment the next morning as my contractor did? Sometimes I don't know what the labor will cost, or I don't know all the materials we'll need until we are actually doing the job. So I give the client a rough number and wait until the work is completed before billing them for a definitive amount. As you mature in this business, you will eventually figure out what scenario works best for you.

KEEPING TRACK

It is important to keep track of how the job is running against estimate to make sure you don't run into any financial snags. If labor or materials are running over, discuss this with your client as soon as possible to work out a solution collaboratively. Most people are reasonable, particularly if you have been communicating frequently and well. The client might just tell you to go for it, but if they cannot financially handle the additional costs, it might be necessary to reprioritize ("Well, since the excavation was so difficult and the walkway is going to go over estimate, let's leave the drainage augmentation till later"). Either solution will require a change order so that you can all stay on the same page.

REESTIMATING

You might go through a couple of rounds of estimating if the homeowner decides, for example, they don't want the driveway resurfaced, but they do want that deck. Or if they tell you that $53,000 is about $10,000 too much this year, and ask what portion of the project can be dropped to reduce the overall cost. Work with your clients to reprioritize what they want completed this phase, and reestimate.

REACTION TO THE ESTIMATE

Do my clients often react strongly to the estimate? No. The estimate is a place to start. If they can afford it, and want to afford it, they do. If they cannot or will not, we pare down and prioritize the scope of work to a level that works for them. It all works rather seamlessly, and better than I think you could imagine as you ponder entering this business.

Here's one tip, though: never apologize for numbers. Numbers are what they are, and we can work them, but never be ashamed or afraid of numbers, even if the total is quite large. I took a negotiating course many years ago, and the one piece of fabulous information I took away from it was that in dealing with money you must divorce yourself emotionally. Money is just a number. Whether you are negotiating a pay raise with your boss, an estimate with a contractor or client, or a simple item at a yard sale, it is just a number. If you disconnect yourself from any emotion around a number, you are in control.

Since I first got into the business of doing garden design, I've only had one real objection to an estimate. A number of years ago, before I charged margin, one rather well known local television personality and his wife were *almost* my clients. Okay, they actually were my clients, since they had me do a full design for their lovely Victorian home, and of course they paid for my design work. When we entered phase one, a small initial stage that didn't even cost five figures, the client called me after receiving the estimate and said in a panicky, irate tone, "You make $80 an hour? Are you kidding me?" I said no, I certainly wasn't kidding. Dead silence. I explained that I was good at what I did and was compensated appropriately. Well, he was on the freak-out trail, so he ranted a bit before closing with, "Good luck to you, Darlin', but I will never pay that much for a designer." This for an estimate, and at the time I charged no margin and had anticipated my time would be six hours, or $480, for two half-days managing a crew. Go figure.

If a potential client goes to pieces over an estimate, don't panic. Suggest to them that if we need to reprioritize to bring the number down, *we* can do so. By saying this, you are putting the client in control. And by speaking in inclusive terms, you are letting them know you will act as their partner to help them achieve their landscaping goals at a level they can afford. Calmly remind them that you do quality work, using proven professionals and the best materials available. At that point the client will probably see the light and be able to discuss everything rationally.

THE FINAL ESTIMATE

Once you have a final estimate that represents the work you've agreed to do, make sure it includes the date, the scope of work, the numbers, and your payment terms, and include space for both you and the homeowner to sign. Now print two copies (one for you, one for them) and have each of you sign both. This becomes a binding contract and can cover your arse in the unlikely event of a dispute.

INVOICING

When you bill people, you will need an invoice model that you consistently use. Again, I urge you to use a template. Sure, you will refine the model as your business grows, but being consistent helps to keep your billing methodology streamlined. If you keep it simple, you'll make fewer mistakes in the long run, and you'll present a consistent and professional face to your clients.

My invoices state my business name and contact information in the upper left-hand corner, with client contact information on the upper right. I clearly indicate "invoice" in large, bold letters at the top. I am equally clear about whether I am sending a receipt, or a request for deposit, or a "second request" for payment. Don't make your clients guess. You should see some of the invoices I receive from subcontractors. Some are handwritten on scrap paper. I'm not kidding. I'm a firm believer in recycling, but you need to be more professional than that. Use full words for description of work completed, not acronyms or cryptic abbreviations. Put dates next to the work accomplished. Make sure everything is spelled correctly, particularly your client's name. And add your terms to the bottom. My terms are net 1, meaning I prefer the balance to be paid when my client receives the bill, so I state, "Kindly pay this invoice upon receipt, please. An envelope has been included for your convenience. Thank you." And I make sure the envelope is stamped and addressed. I learned long ago that the easier you make it for your prospects, the more likely they are to respond.

If you are not paid within a month of sending an invoice to a client, send another request. Reprint your invoice, but print "second request" at the top instead of "invoice." I usually also include an informal note asking nicely for payment. This almost always results in a quick payment from the client. Bills do get lost in piles of paperwork!

SENDING A BILL TO COLLECTION

If an invoice goes unpaid for a long time and it becomes apparent your client is just not going to pay, first be courteous and send them one last written communication. Tell them that you are still owed x dollars and do not want to send the invoice to collection, but that you completed the work in good faith, an inordinate amount of time has passed without receiving payment, and you feel your hand is being forced. Would they kindly remit payment? Sometimes just the word "collection" can inspire someone to finally pay you because they know it will impact their credit record. If you still hear nothing, you can farm out the unpaid invoice to a local collection agency, and they will start hounding. Here's the deal with collection agents. They can hound and hound and still get nothing from your clients. Or they can get partial payment, of which they will take a percentage, usually 30% to 50%. Or they can get the whole payment for you, less their percentage.

If you ever need to head in this direction, my condolences. This is not pleasant for anyone. One option is to let the bill go. I know that's hard on several levels, but sometimes the easiest solution is to cut your losses and move forward. Another option is to offer the client a payment plan. Clients who just do not have the money will usually keep talking with you: "I don't have the whole payment right now. Can I send you $1500 a month until I've paid the balance off?" You can work out some arrangement. You might even suggest adding simple interest, like 1% per month charged on the balance. If you do this, you should invoice them each month, note all payments to date, and enclose a self-addressed, stamped envelope.

My friend Chris did a gorgeous landscaping job around a convenience store on Cape Cod. The new landscape was beautiful, with ornamental grasses, succulents, undulating swaths of *Perovskia* and *Hemerocallis*. Very beachy, very right for the site. Chris had only taken one-third of his payment at the outset, so at the end of the project he was waiting for the remaining two-thirds. And waiting. And waiting. He had invoiced and called the company so many times that he finally lost his temper and told his client, "Since you have not paid for the work I did for you, this means I still own the plants. I am removing my property from your site within the next three days unless I receive payment in full!" I don't necessarily recommend employing his strategy, but he did receive a check for the entire amount the following day.

To try to minimize the possibility of this happening, remember to do the following. Structure payment terms in your favor so that you are not owed a large amount at the finish. Keep communications with your client open during the course of the project, so that you'll be able to tell immediately if the client thinks things are not going well. Stay on top of your costs so that they don't run over. And present your final invoice as soon as you finish so that you can capitalize on the gratitude and excitement clients feel at the completion of a job. At that grand finale moment, they are always happy to write a check.

JOB BIDDING

At times I ask my subcontractors for bids of sorts. This is usually only when the budget is tighter than usual, and I need to find the best work at the lowest price. For example, I might ask two equally qualified subcontractors to give me an estimate for the rear patio masonry. I prepare a written document identifying the scope of the job, the materials specified, the materials I will want them to supply, and the relative timing to completion. I ask them about their availability, assuming we'll need the job done by a certain date. Most of my subs want a walk-through of the site, so we meet for that. In a couple of days they get back to me with their estimates. By the time I present pricing to the clients, I have chosen the subs for their project, the subs are holding the availability for me, and I have selected and priced all materials, so the client estimate I ultimately present is for the entire project through to completion. That is the extent of the bidding I might require on my projects.

I generally will not work in a position where I am bidding on a project, but through sheer ignorance I got myself into two situations where I found out at the end of the design process that I would be required to prepare documents to send the proposed landscaping out to bid.

In the first case the design process was so painful I no longer wanted to supervise the installation. What I should have done was thank them but tell them I was not going to provide my own bid on the work. Instead I provided an estimate, but just really jacked up the cost on everything. In hindsight, that was the coward's way out. I should have saved us all time, acted like a grown-up, and just bowed out.

In the second situation I was working for people who owned a commercial site, and I did several designs for them. Only after we had a final plan and were about to move forward did I realize that bidding out everything (and I mean everything) was just their modus operandi. Unfortunately, simply hiring vendors or contractors based on who gives you the lowest price often results in lower-quality work. I had no say in who was hired, and for the most part the subcontractors were a nightmare. Again, I should have just said that I don't work that way, but in an effort to preserve the relationship, I decided I could run the job, no problem. Wrong. We were behind schedule almost as soon as we started. Subs had excuse after excuse. Nothing came in on time, expenses ran over, two lead subcontractors did not have the expertise they had claimed they did. What a mess.

What should have been a fairly simple two-week installation turned into an agonizing six-month process. And lucky me, I was being paid a paltry fixed fee for "supervising" the whole thing, if you could call it that. The suppliers and subs had no loyalty to me, nor were they getting paid by me, so I didn't have the control I usually do. The client was clueless, and so myopic about the bottom line that they could barely maintain sight of the goal. I ended up in the middle of countless fractioned communications. Ugh. I think that project aged me five years.

I will not allow myself to get into a situation like that again. If I can't work with my own crews, someone else can manage the project. Part of the reason I am paid not only for my design work but also for estimating and project management is because I bring reliable, qualified subcontractors on to work the project. I do not sell quantities of widgets for the lowest price. I have relationships with my subcontractors, I know their abilities and the quality they can deliver, and we work as a team.

This is how I feel, but you might feel differently. As your design business grows, you might actually want to bid on jobs particularly if you get interested in doing work for municipalities. Cities and towns and sometimes even corporations or commercial sites require bidding for jobs because this is what their purchasing protocol necessitates. Here are some words to the wise: don't underestimate just to get a job. You will be doing yourself a disservice because you won't be adequately paid, you'll have to work on a shoestring, and if that shoestring budget means that you end up doing a poor job, you will either lose money or your reputation could take a hit. Furthermore, underbidding does not help our industry. You need to bid with honesty and fairness for yourself, which is fair to your industry competitors as well. If one of the other bid participants way underbid to get the job, let them. You should always do the best job you can and be paid appropriately for it. Ultimately, bid or no bid, the quality of your projects will sell themselves.

SMALL JOBS, BIG JOBS

I've come to believe I can make more money on five $20,000 projects than I can from one $100,000 project. I haven't tested this completely, but I truly believe that would be the result if I did the math. First, the $20,000 projects are faster in and faster out. You can usually complete the job in a week or so. Additionally, you're not married to the project, you're not there for months, and you actually finish, which is refreshing. The clients are even different, because their expectations are different. When you run a $20,000 project, the clients know you're going to come in, do *x*, and then be off. The $100,000 client is looking for follow-up visits, more hand-holding during the process, more money-handling issues, more subcontractor management, more of *you*. In 2008 I completed a three-year project. Though I loved the clients dearly, I was extremely excited to have the punch list dwindle to nothing. I had been married to the job for so long, even through winters, worrying about plant survival, masonry health, how the decks were weathering, whether the drainage was holding up, and countless other concerns. I'm not sure the income was worth the degree of worry.

So, small jobs. You'll get them, particularly as you are starting out. Enjoy them! It's like a great first date: you meet, you decide you like each other, you have a delightful dinner, you have some laughs, you say goodnight. And they pay. It's wonderful. These small jobs often lead to other jobs down the road, for the same client or their referrals. But if you spend the rest of your career working jobs that are $1000 to $10,000, know that you can make a lovely living and really continue to grow your business, while thoroughly enjoying your work.

You'll eventually get big jobs, and each can seem a little daunting at first. Once you are in it, you realize that it's like managing a bunch of smaller jobs at once—you will be juggling subcontractors like a circus clown juggles fruit. As long as you don't schedule the driveway surfacing guys before the excavator has cleared the space, you'll do fine. Think it through and know that once you feel comfortable with the smaller installations, you can handle the larger jobs.

Most of my comrades feel they can make more money on larger jobs, because they can charge more for their time and include larger percentages of margin. I have worked jobs ranging from a few thousand dollars to nearly half a million, and I still feel that cranking through smaller jobs can really bring in the income while saving your brain.

AVOID GETTING INTO A HOLE

Don't overextend. Okay, easy words to say, not so easy to live by. Most every spring I take about $10,000 from my household account and transfer it to my business account. That is my working capital to get going on until I start collecting deposit money. By early summer I have transferred the $10,000 back to my household account and am operating in the black.

I use a credit card a lot, but only because I am phenomenally responsible with it. Using a credit card can extend my payment for goods sometimes another five or six weeks, giving me time to bill the client and get the final payment from them before the credit card monies are due. I always pay my credit card in full every month. Always. If we don't eat, I pay the credit card bill. This really makes you go after those milestone payments and deposit requests!

The fastest way to get in the hole is to rack up credit card debt. Once you let a month slide, the next month is harder, the finance charges are crushing, and the following month can be insurmountable. If you tend to let your credit card bills slide, just say no, and don't use a card. Do not make an exception, do not say, "Just this once." Work as if you were running a strictly cash business and use business checks. I know several people who declared bankruptcy because credit card debt crushed their small businesses. If you don't use a card, it is much harder for this to happen to you. Operate a cash business and stay within your means.

Some of your suppliers will do a net 30 arrangement with you, meaning they'll allow you to pay within thirty days of the invoice date. I prefer cash on delivery (COD) or net 1. That way, I don't get a large, surprise invoice at the end of the month. I also know exactly which client each purchase is for, and I keep a mental tab of what monies are coming in and going out.

Some suppliers will give you a small discount for cash on delivery (which includes checks). Hey, a 2% discount on plants costing $15,000 is $300. Gas money!

To stay on top of things, make sure you get your deposits in from your clients, and get subsequent payments on time. Track your receipts. If you estimated the drainage materials were going to cost $150 and they cost $250, this requires a change order and a quick discussion with the client to clear the overage. This will keep you ahead of the game.

The U.S. Small Business Administration has great suggestions on how to run a business, and your local chamber of commerce can also be helpful. Banks can offer terrific advice, but recognize that they are looking to make you a business loan. This is how they make their money, so tread lightly when you are looking at startup costs. One of the beauties of starting up a garden design business is that you can do it with almost no money out of pocket. I feel strongly that if you can do this without borrowing money, you can operate in the black from the very beginning, feel successful much faster, and find enough peace of mind to justify staying away from bank loans and credit card debt.

HOW AND WHEN DO I GET PAID?

How do you pay yourself? This is a tougher question. I take my whole annual profit at the end of the year. In our New England climate, landscaping work for the most part ceases by about Thanksgiving. I do have projects that continue past that—we've even done some masonry in a warm January, and we've done interior construction and painting through the entire winter—but I close up most of my "year" by the end of the calendar year. I take my starting amount, zero, and once I've collected all of my billings, paid all of my subcontractors, suppliers, and credit cards, and paid my quarterly taxes, whatever is left is my business profit and salary—for the year.

Some of you will have to pay yourselves a monthly salary because, well, you need to eat! I encourage you to pay yourself modestly at first, just what you need to stay afloat. Pick a consistent amount and use that as your stipend. Don't fall into the trap of, "Well, just for now I'll take an extra thousand." Again, if you can stay afloat for a year or two with a minimal (or no!) income, your business will be on solid financial ground just that much faster.

Several of my designer friends have said they've gotten too busy to invoice their clients and let months slide by. I have done this too, and this is not good. Actually, this is really bad. When you are really running on empty, barely keeping your head above water managing jobs, it's hard to think about finding time to sit down and bill your clients. But you really have to do this. If you have to take a weekend day to sift through receipts and calmly work the invoicing, do it. Clients are much more likely to pay if you invoice them the balance due right after the job closes. If you wait weeks or months, they will often take at least that long to pay, because reimbursing you has now slid way down their priority list. So force yourself to bill regularly and on time. By doing so, you'll remember who owes you for what, you'll have good cash flow, you'll be able to pay your subs and suppliers on time, and you won't get behind financially. And trust me, you'll rest easier at night.

LIABILITY INSURANCE

I ran my business for several years before purchasing business liability insurance. I implore you, do not make the same mistake. When I look back at how naïve and vulnerable I was, well, my blood runs cold. Had something gone dreadfully wrong, resulting in a client successfully suing me, we could have lost our home.

Fortunately I was spared this potential fate because a client asked about my (nonexisting) insurance. I took a large job in an uber-affluent town, and the clients asked to see a copy of my liability insurance policy. I was flabbergasted but went into "search" mode. I called several friends who were in business for themselves. My friend who runs an acupressure business and whose husband is an independent master electrician told me about each of their business policies. I called their agent, and we walked through the terms of setting up a policy for my landscape design-build company. My type of insurance is called an artisan policy. It is only available through commercial insurance providers.

I got my insurance, received my documentation, and quickly gave a copy to my clients. That was in 2000, and now I cannot imagine being without this insurance coverage. I also learned a valuable lesson. I now know to ask all of the subcontractors I hire for copies of their insurance policies. This gives me the assurance that they are covered if one of their crew gets injured, or if they make some wild mistake and flatten the client's garage or something. I also now ask all of the people doing any kind of work in my own home for insurance policy documentation. This information is good to have, and it brings tremendous peace of mind.

PERSONAL INCOME TAX

Being self-employed means you are solely responsible for paying your state and federal income taxes. These quarterly payments to the Internal Revenue Service and your state's department of revenue are due April 15, June 15, September 15, and January 15. Your tax accountant will have simple worksheets for you to use to calculate your quarterlies. If you do not have a tax accountant, you can easily download worksheets from the Internet. Being self-employed also means that your Social Security contributions come out of your federal income taxes, so by paying your taxes you continue to pay in to Social Security. In addition to this I recommend you seriously consider contributing to a self-employment retirement fund. Called a simplified employee pension (SEP), this retirement plan is designed for self-employed individuals and small businesses. Contributions are tax-deductible and the earnings are tax-deferred. Of course, before you make any changes to your retirement savings plan, discuss your options with a tax accountant or financial advisor.

THAT'S THE BUSINESS SIDE OF THE BUSINESS

Can you now see how running a garden design business is not all that different from any other business? You need to select and equip a physical space to outfit as your home office, a place that is convenient and comfortable, with minimal distraction. You need to source the best suppliers and subcontractors so that you know where to turn for materials, talent, and labor, and know who you can count on to get the job done. It is critical to stay on top of your revenue stream. You must consciously manage your costs and work hard to maintain a healthy cash flow, not just at the beginning of your business but on each project every single year. You need to manage your business with professionalism and clearly communicate with all of your vendors and subcontractors. And you need to invest face time on every project; if your clients see that you are frequently there, checking in and supervising the work, they will trust that the work is getting done right and in a timely manner. Remember that every facet of your business that the client sees should be produced with thought, and all of it, from e-mail to invoices, should be professional and accurate. Above all, you need to stay tightly focused on your clients and maintain communication through all phases of the project.

It should be pretty clear at this point that this is not a profession where we primarily play with plants. This business is about dealing with people, and it is most definitely a service industry. Service the heck out of your clients. Your reputation will be golden, and your business will continue to grow.

CHAPTER THIRTEEN

Working with Nurseries and Other Suppliers

THE NURSERIES, BULK MATERIALS PROVIDERS, stone purveyors, and lumberyards you decide to work with will be partners in your business, since without them you could accomplish very little. It will require some research in the beginning to find the best companies to work with, but it will be time well spent. You'll also need to learn what to look for when selecting plants and other merchandise, and what to expect when placing orders.

WHOLESALE NURSERIES

Since you're a professional now, you can stop buying retail (well, almost). But how do you find the wholesalers in your area? A quick Internet search will bring up more suppliers than you can imagine. Google "wholesale nursery" plus the name of your state and you'll get a huge list of both wholesalers and local nursery associations that can point you towards the wholesalers you'll need. Some will sell only trees, some just shrubs, and others only annuals, and you'll uncover specialty nurseries as well. One time I found a grower in an obscure location who only grew hostas, but he had acres of stunning, mature specimens, some 4 to 5 feet across, and all available in the pot! They weren't cheap (nor should they have been), but they sure helped my clients' gardens look instantly lush and established.

Step two is to go knocking on doors. Okay, not literally, but you do need to contact the top ten or fifteen nurseries you think might be your key suppliers. Here are some criteria to select your first tier. You will need suppliers for woody stock (trees and shrubs, which professionals categorize as "nursery stock"), herbaceous hardy plants ("perennials"), and annuals ("tropicals"). I have three favorite nurseries for trees, shrubs, and herbaceous perennials, and two favorites for annuals. I augment this with smaller-quantity purchases from a handful of other suppliers.

When you visit the nurseries, you'll see almost immediately whether they can fill your needs. If you've never been to a wholesale nursery or grower before, be prepared for a treat—acres and acres of fabulous plants, all for the taking.

As for choosing several to work with, first figure out how far you're willing to travel on a fairly regular basis. This might frustrate you at first, but know that you won't always have the time to hand-pick the plants you want. I make a point of hand-tagging specimen trees and larger stock that will be prominently displayed in the landscape. When I have the luxury of time, I also hand-pick the herbaceous perennials and even the annuals I use. In the heat of the season, however, time is precious, so target three or four wholesalers that you'll be willing to travel to every couple of weeks, and make this your short list.

One of my wholesalers is 70 miles from my home, but I only go there a couple of times per year. I do this because I love the drive, I love being there, and I love choosing from their plant stock. That said, the whole trip takes an entire day, so I make the time count. I bring along lists of all the plant stock I'll need for the next several weeks, categorized by client, as well as a master list to maximize my time with the salesperson. I check in with the main office, and they assign me a salesperson. I show them my list so they can figure out the best route to take in the 80-acre nursery. We get in a cart, zip around, look at stock. I'll need something like *Quercus rubra*, and I'll have a feel for the size I need, so we head in that direction. When we get to the right spot, we get out and look at the selection they have on location. The trees are usually grouped by size. I look through the stand and choose the ones I want, and the salesperson tags them for me.

271

Once you feel you have found a good fit, go to the wholesaler in person and tell them you're a garden designer and would like to open an account. They will give you an application and ask for names of other wholesale accounts as references. This is a perfect Catch-22 situation where you need a wholesale account to get a wholesale account. When I was starting out, I had a friend in the industry make a call and vouch for me. I was applying for a cash account, so the nursery really had nothing to lose. My friend's call made all the difference, though, and from that first account I was able to get all of my other commercial accounts.

PAYING

Most wholesalers offer either cash accounts or credit accounts. Cash accounts are just that: you pay with a check or credit card at the time of pickup or delivery. Some nurseries offer a small discount if you do not use a credit card, and this is a nice way to make a few points of margin on each sale. Two percent on $10,000 is only $200. But $200 is $200.

A delicious sight for the hort-head: acres of lush nursery plants.
Photo courtesy of Sylvan Nursery, Westport, Massachusetts.

Multiply that by fifty orders, and there's $10,000. If you can manage the cash flow, it's a good policy to pay up front.

With credit accounts, materials are picked up or delivered during the month, and the bill arrives at the end of that month. Most companies are net 1, net 10, or net 30, which means they want the balance paid in full when you receive the bill (net 1), within ten days of the invoice date (net 10), or within thirty days of the invoice date (net 30). Making a payment after that grace period means the wholesaler can charge you interest or a rebilling fee.

If you work your business with credit accounts, make sure to pay your bills on time. Your suppliers are your lifeline to the industry, and they deserve to be paid. You would not believe the number of times a supplier has rallied to find something for me, or to deliver in a short timeframe. Part of the reason they are so good to me is because I am good to them. I never make my suppliers wait for payment.

With the exception of one wholesaler I use, who only operates by billing after delivery, I pay cash for all of my plants, bulk materials, and stone. Check is my preferred method of payment, but I do use a credit card if cash flow is tight. And I pay off that credit card religiously. There have been months when my credit card bill has been over $40,000, but tempting as it may be to let some of it slide to the next month, I have never done so. (Knock on wood.) I plan my cash flow to assure that I can pay for my purchases at the time of delivery, or certainly by the time the credit card payment is due.

When I don't get my 2% discount for paying with a check, I still make my credit card work for me. I have two cards. One gives me airline miles, the other gives me hotel points. Once I've maxed out the yearly airline mile total on Card 1 (which is 100,000 award miles), I charge for the rest of the year on Card 2.

Many people in small businesses apply for a state tax ID number and a resale certificate. Then they do not pay sales tax when they purchase the goods, they pay when they resell the goods. Talk with your financial advisor about what makes sense for your business. I have always preferred to simplify both the thought process and the paperwork around my business, so I always pay my sales tax at the time that I purchase any goods.

MICK WAS RIGHT—YOU CAN'T ALWAYS GET WHAT YOU WANT

I purchase the lion's share of my stock from several wholesalers in the area. I do my planting plan, tally up the plants, and fax in the plant orders, looking for availability and pricing. I tell them what varieties I am looking for, size of plant, quantities of each, and sometimes characteristics—for example, "*Cornus kousa* 'Constellation', 10 to 12 feet, quantity 4, multistemmed clump." I send my list to several wholesalers because Nursery A may have some of what I need, Nursery B some more, and Nursery C the rest. The sales teams call or fax the information in a day or two, and from that I carve out my plant orders.

Ordering plants is not like ordering from L.L.Bean. Time of year shifts availability of many things, and some plants that you may be able to get from several suppliers in June might be completely gone—or look horrid in the pot—by August. So, when some things are not to be had, you make substitutions. This is where your knowledge of plants and the breadth of varieties available really pays off. There have been instances when half of what I'm looking for is unavailable for the next few months. Some plants are only dug at certain times of year, and if the supply is exhausted before the next window for digging, you won't be able to get any of the plants you need.

When I ask for availability information, my suppliers also know I want them to tell me what substitutions are in stock. For example, I might want *Buddleia* 'Black Knight' in a 5-gallon container, but they don't have it. They'll tell me they have 'Black Knight' in a 3-gallon pot or 7-gallon B&B, and they have 5-gallon buddleias but only 'Royal Red' and *B. davidii*. In those instances I will rework my design with the plants I know are available, and complete my plant orders that way. I am rarely disappointed.

Being flexible with your designs will allow you to move beyond this little frustration. Know, first, that this will be *your* frustration; it needn't be shared with your clients, who will only think that corners were cut. Always reinforce the positive: the plants are beautiful, the gardens are gorgeous, and it will all get even better over time. Your job is to complete the landscape and garden construction, and make the client happy.

Having purchased plants for yourself for years, you may find it frustrating to be unable to pick out exactly every plant that is going into an installation. I would like to say you'll get over this, but you might not entirely. I'm a bit of a control freak and am particular about plant materials for clients. So for the times when you cannot physically see and preapprove all of the plant stock you are going to order, you have to cut yourself a little slack and know that it will all work out fine in the end. When less-than-stellar plants come off the truck, you might have to look beyond the imperfections. I should add that sometimes I'm very pleasantly surprised, in which case I always thank my supplier. "Hey, gorgeous hostas on that order. Thank you!" Get to know, trust, and appreciate your suppliers. They want you to be successful. Your continued success is their continued success.

There is an honor system to nursery stock tagging that, to my knowledge, I have had violated only once in my fifteen years of doing this work. Say you find the perfect tree, and it gets tagged for you. Your projected delivery date is a couple of weeks or a month out. Delivery date comes, you're unloading the stock, and wham! You notice that the tree coming off the truck is most assuredly not the tree you tagged. This means one of two things. Either the nursery inadvertently damaged the tree and sent a substitute (my nurseries would always call before doing this), or some unscrupulous landscape professional wanted the tree you had chosen and removed your tag in order to replace it with their own. Yes, this happens. In many cases you wouldn't even notice that you ended up with a slightly different tree. But the one time it happened to me, I had selected three very special, very expensive Japanese maples for a high-end job site. I had made my selection based on specific attributes, and I had not only tagged the trees but also photographed them. So when one of the trees bore no resemblance to the tree I had selected for that particular spot (and was unsuitable for the spot to boot), I called the nursery, and they suspected a tag switch.

This is one good reason to avoid selecting stock too far out from your delivery date. Someone else might really want your tree, and not all landscape designers are supervised 100% of the time at all wholesalers. Also, plant stock can become shop-worn. Just as an item in a retail store will be worse for wear the longer it stays in the store, a plant can lose its freshness the longer it stays at the nursery. This isn't always true, of course, but overall plants are happier in the ground than in a pot. The fresher the stock, the less chance it has to have been stressed by the weather, the nicer it usually looks when you receive it on-site, and the better it will settle into its new home.

SELECTING TREES

When choosing trees, begin by selecting the variety and then the size of the trees you need for the particular job. Trees are sized by pot or ball size and height in smaller specimens, and by caliper and height in larger specimens. Size directly translates to price: the larger the tree, the larger the price. Note, however, that a 4-inch-caliper tree is not twice the price of a 2-inch-caliper tree. A 4-inch-caliper tree will be three or four times the cost of a 2-inch, if not considerably more. "Heavy" is an additional category that means the tree (or shrub) is particularly thick, nicely branched, and lush. Once you know the relative size you want and the price your design can justify, evaluate trees using the following criteria:

Overall health. Is the tree healthy looking, the right color, without insect damage or indicators of disease? Is the trunk clear of cuts, gouges, and stripping?

Branching. Is the tree growing the way it should? Do the branches come out at the proper angle for the species? No bad crotches? No major branches crossed or rubbing? (Sometimes there will be some crossing branches that you conclude will be easy to correct with a little pruning.)

Shape. Is there a flat side, or is the tree fairly symmetrical? Judge this by knowing where the tree is going to end up. If it will be a specimen tree in the front yard, it will be viewed from all angles and will need to be pretty much perfectly shaped. If it will be part of a screening planting against an unsightly view, it is fine for one side to be flat or misshapen, since that side will be placed away from the client's view.

Root ball. Is the root ball intact? The cage or bailing twine should be firmly in place, and the root ball should not be falling apart nor bone-dry. Of course, if the root ball is truly bone-dry, the tree will usually show signs of dehydration, like wilting, drooping, or yellowing.

What you ultimately want is a vigorous, healthy-looking tree that you feel is the right size and shape for the selected area. I say, "This one!" and the salesperson takes out colored landscape tape and writes my name and the date on it, then notes on the sales sheet that a tree has been tagged, adding details about the tree's location and the color of the tag. This makes it easy for the pickup crew to locate the tree and get it ready for delivery.

You will not always have the time, motivation, or even the need to hand-tag all of your trees. This is where your relationship with the wholesale nursery comes in. I might call and say I need three plants of *Cornus kousa*, 8 to 10 feet, multistemmed, heavy. When they get back to me, they'll say honestly, "We have two beautiful trees that you'll like, but not three. We do have one size smaller at 6 to 8 feet that would work." So I'll okay the substitution. Part of the job of the salespeople is to get out there and see what they have, know what condition things are in, and be honest with their customers. When I have discussed my order with the sales department at a nursery, I have rarely been disappointed by what comes off the delivery truck.

When choosing varieties of trees for your designs, select for mature size and habit, ornamental characteristics, and four-season qualities. Also keep in mind which species are susceptible to whatever pests and diseases are present or threatening in your locale. Your local tree warden, agricultural extension office, or arboretum should have current pest and disease information and should also be able to tell you which tree selections can withstand zone creep. As global warming brings more fickle weather and shifting of climate zones, garden and landscape designers need to be

Rows of Kwanzan cherry trees (*Prunus serrulata* 'Kwanzan'). Photo courtesy of Veronica Wordell, Sylvan Nursery, Westport, Massachusetts.

flexible enough to work with these phenomena. Appropriate tree selection can be the difference between a planting lasting ten years and one lasting a hundred years.

SELECTING SHRUBS

When I'm at the wholesalers I might ask for a quick tour of the shrub areas to check out how the hydrangeas are looking, or which viburnums are spectacular and which are looking a little tired. Helps me to flesh out the order. And if I have the time, or if the particular job demands it, I will hand-select shrubs as well. I'll have my list, which I will have shared with the salesperson. Usually, shrub selections are less onesie-twosie than trees, and more like, "I'll need five of these, nine of those, and maybe sixteen of that variety." The salesperson takes me to the variety I'm seeking, and I look over the collection and choose the shrubs I want. Then the salesperson groups them together, puts landscape tape around the group, and tags the whole lot for me.

Judging shrub health is much like judging tree health. Look for shrubs with a healthy appearance, good color, no drooping, no yellowed or brown leaf tips, no breakage, no signs of disease or pests, and an intact root ball.

Shrub sizes are based on container or ball size and height in the smaller specimens, and both container size and height in the larger specimens. Some varieties can also have the designation "heavy" if they are particularly lush. You pay a premium for this, which is often worth it. You'll have to let your gut and your budget guide you on that.

SELECTING PERENNIALS

Generally I do not hand-select perennials, but—depending on the order, size, timing, and so forth—I will ask to tour the perennial area just to see what's there and what looks particularly good. This also helps me avoid ordering anything that looks particularly sad. I make notes as we tour around, and when I get home I finalize the order for delivery with the rest of the plant materials I need. At this point I often include perennials I saw that looked great and that will work well in the design.

I was recently choosing trees and shrubs to finish a large installation, and knew I'd be completing the design with a host of perennials, one of which was golden Japanese forest grass, *Hakonechloa macra* 'Aureola'. I needed quite a lot of it—two hundred plants. When we toured the grasses area, I noted that the hakonechloa looked a little ratty and thin and were in rather large gallon containers that would make the installation difficult. Down the row, however, I saw a stretch of what looked like the same hakonechloa I needed, and they were gorgeous. Different pot, smaller pot, but otherwise almost identical. Come to find out this beautiful group of grasses was *H. macra* 'Beni-kaze'. They were a little more expensive than the other variety, but oh so beautiful and well worth the extra expense. Just proves that it often makes sense to look over the plants at the nursery before finalizing your order.

Just like trees and shrubs, herbaceous perennials come in many sizes, but they are categorized by pot size. The most common pot size at a wholesaler is usually 1 gallon, also known as "1 gal" or "#1." This is a good-sized plant, generally with healthy root growth and sizable top growth, and is still pretty easy to handle. If the containers aren't too wet, I can carry two or three in each hand (otherwise, I can manage one or two in each hand). Other common sizes include 1-quart; ½-gallon or 6-inch; 4-inch, 3-inch, or 2-inch plugs; 2- to 5-gallon patio pots; and 2-gallon, 3-gallon, 5-gallon, or 7-gallon.

Unlike retailers, wholesalers often sell all perennials at the same price ($5.65 for all 1-gallon perennials, say). However, some plant varieties, like roses, peonies, hostas, and some ornamental grasses, are priced at a premium over other herbaceous perennials in the same 1-gallon containers.

PLANT SELECTION AND TIME OF YEAR

You won't always be choosing plant materials in the peak of their bloom or at the optimal time of year for each particular variety. In fact, you will rarely be choosing plants at their exact moment of perfection. You'll need to learn to look beyond the moment and project ahead. The one time I have a hard time doing that is in early spring before the herbaceous perennials have broken ground. Many of my designer colleagues plant what effectively looks like dirt in a pot, and are happy doing so. The plants, too, are surely happy as they wake up in their new home—no foliage bruising or breakage from installation, no transplant shock. But I don't like it. I like to see some plant growth in the pots before I place them. That's my little prejudice. Other than that, I am happy to choose deciduous shrubs and trees before they break bud, and evergreens are a pretty sure bet. I'm also fairly happy to select and plant materials later in the year when they're in fall foliage and finishing up the year. I make sure they still look healthy for their particular variety, and I get them in the ground as soon as possible. Another key to success in planting is to keep them well watered until winter has really set in. Here in New England, autumn is often glorious but dry, and plants going into dormancy need adequate hydration.

If you have an installation and your delivery comes just after some things have finished blooming, they're going to look a little tattered and tired as the blossoms age and fall off. I encourage you to groom the plants before putting them in the ground, and inspect them afterwards. Sometimes all it takes to make a plant look beautiful is removing any yellow or broken foliage, pulling or pinching off the spent blossoms, and making sure the tags are removed from the plant or pot.

In 2008 I was completing a large planting, and among the plant materials I had ordered were several hundred daylilies. The bulk of the perennials had been ordered sight unseen. Per usual, most of the plants that came in looked wonderful, but then two varieties of daylilies—plants that were to be the backbone of the slope planting at this site—came off the truck. They were nice and heavy but looked like they had been grown with the pots spaced cheek by jowl in fairly shady conditions. They were much taller than usual, inordinately upright, with lots of yellowed foliage and quite a few slugs. I had the crew put all of them aside until the delivery was finished. Then we settled into grooming all 350 of these 1-gallon plants. It took five of us nearly two hours. When we were done we had a huge pile of icky foliage and broken flower scapes, but we now had 350 daylilies in containers that looked good. It is always worth spending a little time grooming to be able to put healthy-looking plants into the landscape.

RETAIL NURSERIES

I wish I could do one-stop shopping for plant materials, but I can't. To get the range of plants I want, as well as the quality I demand, I order from several wholesalers, and I even buy—gulp—retail. Yes, I do! I have relationships with several good retailers right in my area, and when I purchase in quantity, they give me a break on price. Often they charge me only pennies per plant above what my wholesalers would charge, and the beauty is that I can hand-pick my stock and only have to drive ten minutes from home. Beats a three- or four-hour round-trip.

I have also picked up some wonderful plants for very short money by making regular pilgrimages to several of my area big box stores. They usually bring in new plant stock Wednesdays or Thursdays to service the weekend crowds. If you get there in the afternoon on either of those days, there are wonderful plants to be found. I often purchase plants there even when I don't have an immediate need for them. I keep a small nursery area at my home where I keep plants "watered and waiting." This plan can backfire if I forget to water, or if the plants succumb to critters or otherwise die. Still, big-box stores also take plants back, so save those receipts!

Why would I bother to do this? Money. Making margin. Here's the scoop. Say Plant X usually retails for $20, and I can order it from my wholesaler for $12. So I do, and when I charge the client, I add a margin to my cost and charge them roughly what they would be charged retail ($20). In doing so, I make $8. Now, that same plant at a large home store might cost $9, which is $3 less than the wholesaler. This means I can

Very early spring and I'm already populating my little "hold" nursery.

either charge my client less for the plant, or I can still charge them the regular retail of $20, and make $11 margin. Which do you do? Look at how the project is running. If there are some small money drains somewhere on the project, you might want to keep the additional margin to offset the loss. But if the project is running smoothly and profitably, you can give your clients a break on the plant price. You will make no less money and they will be pleased with coming in on or under estimate.

GUARANTEES

As a general rule, wholesalers sell plants with no guarantee. Once the plants leave their grounds, all bets are off, and rightly so. How on earth would they know if new plant materials had been planted correctly, or even watered at all? That said, I have a good relationship with all of my suppliers. Recently I had several really expensive trees die. They were part of a screening grouping that I purchased and installed late in the year, which is usually a perfect time to plant trees. By midwinter I knew there was a problem. I called the nursery and gave them a heads-up. Early that spring I explained that although they had been planted and watered correctly, half of them had died. When I showed them photographs and brought in a cutting for the sales manager to see, she agreed that the trees had probably died through no fault of mine or the clients. Because of our longstanding relationship, the nursery replaced the tree stock at no cost to us.

Make sure when you take delivery that the plants coming off the truck are plants you would be proud to show your clients. My suppliers know that I want plants that look good, period. I have received deliveries in the past in which half of the stock looked like it had fallen off the truck and spent the day on the highway. If it doesn't look good, or if you think there is any chance the stock won't survive, do not accept the plant. You might have to scramble if it is a variety that is critical to your design. I have been known to run out to local nurseries to see what they have to augment materials for a planting. This might happen if some plants I ordered are out of stock and the nursery failed to tell me the day before, or if I sent some sad-looking suckers back to the nursery. But luckily this doesn't happen often, and when it does it usually doesn't impact the design much. We make it work.

YOU WILL GET SPOILED

After purchasing nearly everything at wholesale prices, I'm now a pretty tough customer. I ask for discounts just about everywhere. You'd be surprised—even the big-box stores will often give you a discount if you're offering to take a large quantity of plants off their hands, especially as the season is winding down. In colder climates, both local retailers and area wholesalers are often happy to sell you quantities of plants at a discount towards the end of the season. They would rather not invest their labor and take the risk of wintering over the stock. If it looks like you can sell the plants and get them in the ground at a client's property before the winter freezes set in, it's a good deal for you. Recognize, though, that this is a gamble as well. If the plants don't have time to settle in, they can die over the winter, in which case you will need to replace them in the spring. Err on the side of caution to protect yourself.

OTHER SUPPLIES: STONE, BULK MATERIALS, LIGHTING

Designing gardens will quickly lead to masonry projects, there's no denying it, and you will need to develop relationships with a few stone wholesalers. Finding stone wholesalers is just like finding nursery wholesalers. Google "landscape stone supply" plus your state's name, or "stone supplier" plus your town's name (or the nearest city), and you'll come up with plenty. Visit the sites, get brochures, walk the yard, and see what they offer. You'll need several stone suppliers for the range of stone products you will eventually incorporate into your designs.

Finding other suppliers is much the same. Hunt down the ones within about 50 miles from your home, visit them, and find out what products and materials they carry. Ask about delivery options, average lead time from order to delivery, payment terms, and what discount they offer industry professionals (only applicable if the supplier sells retail as well as wholesale). Check out the yard. Is it fairly tidy? Can you find your way around easily? Does it look like a professional operation? Would you be willing to bring a client there? Tidiness in the supply yard doesn't guarantee the organization is run professionally, but it can be an indicator. On the other hand, one of the messiest stone yards I've ever been to has consistently given me some of the best customer service I have ever encountered. They really know their stuff and are prompt and professional, all visual evidence to the contrary. So the best advice may be to just try out the suppliers you feel have the right supplies for your projects. That's the only way you'll really know how a supplier operates.

A few other thoughts. Stone usually takes one to two weeks lead time from order to delivery. Stone that requires fabrication (custom treatments) can require six weeks lead, depending on time of year. For bulk materials, loam, mulch, and gravel, you can often call and get the material delivered the same day if it isn't the height of the spring rush. Lighting of all kinds can take six to eight weeks, particularly if you order specialty fixtures from an electrical supply house. I am amazed at both ends of the spectrum of the lighting quality at the big-box stores. They have some of the cheesiest piece-of-crap lighting I have ever seen, as well as some really nice-looking fixtures for fairly short money. So don't rule out the big-box stores for exterior lighting and electrical supplies. Additional good news is that they are cash-and-carry, so buying your supplies there can be quick, and they'll take anything back without a hassle (again, save those receipts). Buy what you like when you see it, though, because you cannot count on the same stock being there next week or next month.

When the naturalized scilla blossoms at this charming cape, it stops traffic.

Meticulously maintained by the homeowner, this rooftop garden has
a mixture of formal, Asian, and cottage design influences.

A planted pot brings a spot of color to an otherwise quiet Japanese garden.

The stunning, lush, container-filled pergola in my friend Ellen Lathi's magnificent garden.

An unusual masonry installation, accented with clinker bricks.

One of my favorite front walks of all time, made of exquisitely installed New England Goshen stone, designed by Ellen Lathi, the homeowner.

A generous front walk is gracious and welcoming.

Stairs with a low rise and a deep tread make a comfortable step
that is elegant in the landscape.

A small bed separates the upper patio from the kitchen patio, along which is a bluestone-capped seating wall. This space is wonderful for entertaining large gatherings.

This mahogany deck is terraced and large enough for several seating and lounging areas, all of which take advantage of a delightful water view.

This hundred-year-old promontory was resurfaced to serve as a wedding pavilion for the homeowner's daughter. Bluestone treads lead down to a patio of tumbled bluestone pavers. We kept out the deer with layers of monofilament, one strand of which is visible running across the middle of the photo.

This streamlined outdoor kitchen includes a grand grill, a sink, a long mahogany serving area, and two cutouts in the counter for stainless steel sink inserts, perfect for holding ice to chill wine, beer, and soft drinks; they drain right into the garden.

Trickling rills link a number of ponds in this New England setting, one of the most beautiful gardens I have ever seen.

Artistic elements add personality and distinction to any garden.
Gate by Jill Nooney at the gardens of Ellen Lathi.

It can be a lot of fun finding just the right "jewelry" to complete an outdoor space.
Exotic fixtures, like these lanterns offered in an open-air bazaar in Cairo, can add
sparkle and drama to entertaining areas. Photo courtesy of Laura Nowosielski.

Some designers specialize in seaside gardens. Here, a pathway waltzes
through a naturalized planting of rugosa roses and down to the sea.

Shade gardens are another potential design specialty. Always entrancing, they often
convey a lush peacefulness that I love, as in this serene corner of Ellen Lathi's gardens.

This lush grotto was built on a former dumping site between three garages.
It now offers a cool respite from Boston's sultry summer weather.

A garden design business truly can be four season (or at least three and a half), even in cold winter climates. Here, a collection of pumpkins and frost-tolerant flowers gives a late-season perk to the entryway.

The patio and gardens at this property were designed by the homeowner. Stunning in their formality and intention--only white blossoms are allowed, accented with the occasional blue—the gardens are a testament to singularly focused design, an artist's attention to detail, and the integration of objects the homeowners find as they travel the globe.

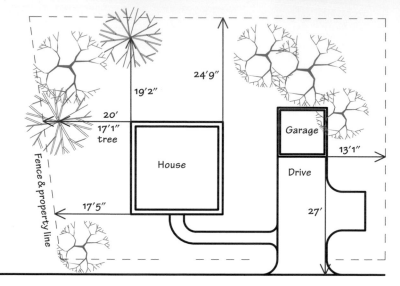

Ranges are clean, simple, and easy to plot. The front left corner of this house is 17 feet 5 inches from the fence and property line, and the rear right corner of the house is 24 feet 9 inches from the rear fence line. In some cases you can locate more than one object off of a range. For example, the left rear of the house is 20 feet from the side property line, but it is 17 feet 1 inch to the center of the tree that falls right on that range.

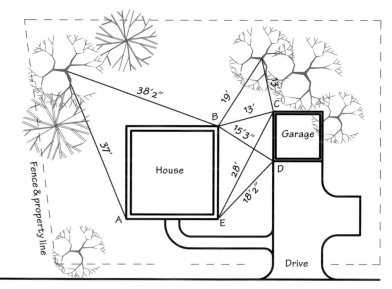

After measuring with ranges, you can take further measurements with swing ties. Say the tree in the upper left corner is an 18-inch-diameter pine. My encircled notation would be "pine 18 in.—A 37 ft., B 38 ft. 2 in." For an accurate measurement of where the detached garage is relative to the house, I need two points on the garage and a full measurement of the structure. I would note "gar. front left—B 15 ft. 3 in., E 18 ft. 2 in." Then I also need the back left location: "gar. rear left—B 13 ft., E 28 ft." When I have those two points plus the measurement of the garage structure, I know the garage is placed correctly relative to the house on my base map. You can accurately locate everything on a property using this method.

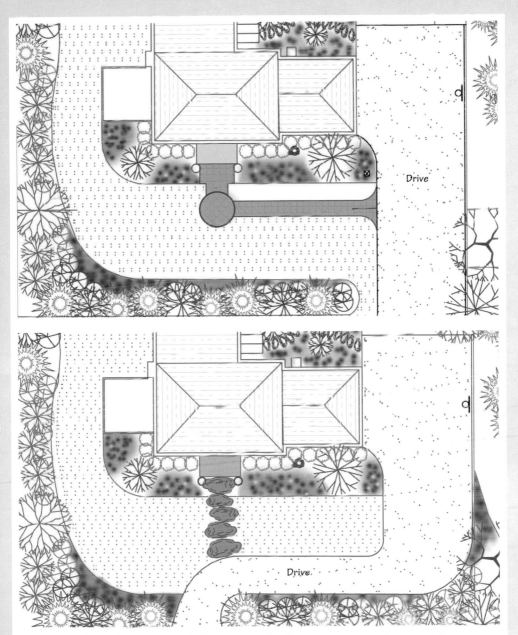

Offering design options for hardscape and softscape treatments takes very little additional time but makes a great impression on the client. Here we considered moving the driveway entrance to the center of the property to provide a dramatic "full face" view of the house upon arrival. This shows two drive options with different walkways.

A beautiful, custom-crafted pergola draws attention, encloses espaliers
and a knot garden, and reinforces the formal intent.

Formal topiaries and classic garden statuary grace
this elegant courtyard designed by the homeowner.

The planting and water feature at this professional building were not in keeping with the building's graceful façade, nor the elegant decor found within.

Reworking the fountain, adding a line of capped bluestone edging, and installing a new planting created the quiet elegance and low maintenance the clients were seeking.

The owners of this commercial site wanted more arrival appeal for their clients, and asked for oodles of color.

We defined the entryway with bluestone planters and added trees for a sense of enclosure from the street, then packed the planters with flowering annuals in a range of brilliant colors.

Beyond the lawn, this area was completely unusable due to a steep, bramble-covered slope and a weed-choked bottom. The clients suggested we just fence it off.

After some regrading, clearing, and planting, the area became a destination garden with a water feature and a unique shade structure, great for entertaining.

A crumbling front porch, rotted portico, and weed- and rubble-filled yard did not add any curb appeal to this home.

Since its transformation, the landscape now features a welcoming entry and color-filled front garden that brightens the entire street.

Nearly there! Some seasonal flowers create a little splash of
color to tide the clients over until their grass germinates, their
perennials are installed, and their furniture arrives.

CHAPTER FOURTEEN

Working with Subcontractors

S UBCONTRACTORS ARE A VITAL PART of any landscape and garden design business. After all, you can design gardens until the cowslips come home, but if the gardens never get built, what's the point? As your company grows, you'll need to partner with the talent to help your garden designs take shape.

So how do you find the best craftspeople to work with? Be relentlessly curious. You can let your proverbial fingers do the walking (in a phone book or on the keyboard), or join a local chapter of the Association of Professional Landscape Designers (which I highly recommend) and send this question to your local chapter members. You can also read the signage on trucks. Not the safest way to drive, but I have found great subcontractors this way.

If you're like me, you may find your very best subs when you stop to check out the work at a site that is under construction. Ask to talk to the crew chief. Ask for their card. Tell them you have a design-build business and are always on the lookout for good workers. They'll gladly tell you about themselves and what they can do, the geographic area they serve, how much they charge, and what types of work they might specialize in. Check out how they're working while you're there. Ask to see some of their other finished work. You may not know how to assess good work from not-so-good work when you are starting out, but you'll know what you like and what you do not. Trust that instinct. Talk to one or two of their clients about their work ethic, their price (actual versus estimate), their site cleanup, their finish. I found all of my best masons, landscape crews, painters, and carpenters by the side of the road (so to speak).

LANDSCAPE SUBCONTRACTORS

Once you move from work that involves dozens of plants to work that involves hundreds of plants, you will need assistance with the brawn. Garden installation subcontractors can be maintenance guys who have time on the side, or they can be dedicated install crews. In my design-build business, I do not have employees. I subcontract all of my labor, and I work with several preferred crews to do all of my landscape preparation and installations.

I will only try out new crews with a small, manageable project. I don't want to get involved in a huge project only to find out that an untried crew cannot cut it, despite the assurances that were made about their abilities. Disaster!

In a couple of instances I found out the hard way that new crews I had scheduled knew next to nothing about prepping a bed or planting a tree. When you're surrounded by thousands of dollars worth of stock and your client is peeking out from the living room window, it is a bad time to find out this particular piece of information. I now make sure I know what a crew is able to do by first observing their work. Reputable companies will not mind this; in fact they'll most likely be delighted to have the chance to show off a little.

Early in this business I made the mistake of bowing to a client's request that I use her landscape service to do an installation. She also wanted to participate in the planting and project management herself (an extremely unusual request). I met her and the crew at the site that morning, walked them around to confirm the prep we needed, and then met the truck to unload the plant stock. I laid out each plant and discussed with the crew chief what I was looking for in terms of planting. Compost for amending the soil was on-site, the plants had arrived, and the appropriate mulch for the finish was in the truck. Once I felt relatively comfortable, I left. (The client wanted to manage this project herself to save money. As I learned, this was a mistake, and I will never work this way again.) The job consisted of a relatively conservative shade planting, so it should have been an easy one-day gig for the four-man crew. I told them I'd check back about noon but would be available earlier if needed. When I showed up later, the guys had left the site for lunch, and I walked into the backyard where the planting was taking place. I was flabbergasted. They had put each plant, whether shrub or perennial, in the ground only halfway, and the plants now looked like top knots resting above zillions of termite mounts. (I honestly, I wish I'd taken photographs.) I looked at the client and said, "Um, why on earth are these planted like this?" A rather quiet thing, she blushed and replied, "Well, I asked them the same thing, but they said they'll mulch up around them."

Mulch up around them? Get a grip.

When the crew returned, I took the chief aside. He told me, "Oh, we always plant like that, and then we add lots of mulch so it will look flat." Once I could swallow my astonishment and find my voice again, I told him this was absolutely not okay. I described how a plant should be installed, told him that the planting bed is not supposed to be 5 inches higher than it already is, and asked him to have the crew rip everything out and do it properly. To make a long story short, he threatened to walk out, and I told him that if he did so I would instruct the client not to pay him. In the end the crew replanted everything correctly and the garden was glorious, but it took another three hours the next day to finish, the client's relationship with her service was ruined, and I'm sure the crew chief hates my guts to this day. Shame on me for hiring an untested source.

Your first experience with a new crew should be to assess their abilities and see what they can really do. Test them with small jobs first and slowly build up your reliance. You should eventually have several crews you can count on regularly. You don't want to get into a situation where you have only one crew you can work with, unless you have a formal agreement with the company owner about how many days you will use the crew each week. Otherwise you can be caught short when the owner needs the crew for other jobs.

When I start working with a new crew, I quietly discuss the ground rules with the crew chief or business owner. No swearing, shouting, or fighting on the site. The work area must be cleaned up daily, with trash removed and cigarette butts taken off the site. The crew must arrive promptly and keep moving while they're there (nothing irritates a client more than looking out the window at a group of guys just standing around—after all, the meter's ticking). Beyond that, if they do their work with a modicum of self-motivation and care, I am happy.

How you use your crews makes a difference. Some designers meet the crew, watch the trucks unload materials, walk the job with the crew chief, leave him a set of plans, and then go. In effect they rely on someone else to do their own project management. This is fine if the project manager is trustworthy. Know, however, that it's a rare soul who can take your vision and interpret every element as you would. As much as I'd like to sometimes, I cannot imagine turning over my design to another manager to implement. I have a streak of the control freak and need to assure myself that things are being done to my standards. So I stay on-site—not every minute on every job, but a good portion of the construction time—working in concert with my crews. I am around to guide the workers, answer their questions, and help them think through solutions to problems. I also place plants, dig holes, pick up and stack empty pots as the guys plant, remove trash, and basically help out the team.

Great crew members from Presidents Landscape and Design.

I always learn the names of everyone on the crew, not just the crew chief, and use their names when speaking with them. I shake hands when introduced, say "please" and "thank you," and express appreciation at the end of the day. Many designers make the mistake of treating their crews like, well, dirt. Or like they are invisible. We all need each other to turn out successful results. Everyone deserves to be treated fairly and with appreciation for a job well done.

If the crew really pushes to get something done by a deadline, or they really make an effort beyond the norm, I give them cash tips. The money comes out of my pocket and is my way of saying, "Thank you for a job extra well done." Sure the workers are paid by the hour, so a longer day means more income, but a little cash in hand is always appreciated.

Most of my crews bring their own break and lunch food to the site and eat in their trucks or on the lawn. On hot days I bring them extra gallons of cold water, on cold days hot coffee or tea. This costs me little in time and money but lets the crews know I appreciate their efforts.

I truly believe your partnership with your crews is paramount. Having a great relationship with your workers will bring you considerable job satisfaction and deliver terrific landscape results.

FOREIGN-BORN LABORERS

In my area, many of the employees of my subcontractors come from outside the United States. I work with people who are Brazilian, Cape Verdian, Colombian, Costa Rican, Dominican, Guatemalan, Haitian, Irish, Jamaican, Mexican, Portuguese, and Vietnamese. Frankly, I am angered by all of the hoopla around immigration. The United States was built on the hopes and dreams of people from all over the globe, and with the talent and sweat of immigrants. I think it is horrendous that we close our borders to willing workers and people chasing the American dream. I do feel it is the responsibility of the hiring subcontractors to assure that their workers are legally in this country and legally earning income, but I do not ask workers for citizenship information nor green card status.

Some of my crew members speak little to no English. To meet them halfway, I have taken several Spanish classes and have learned some phrases in Portuguese. It is only considerate to do this, and it is so appreciated. They often laugh with me at my attempts, and then explain how to say things properly. I'll tell you, those are the days I really love my job. I make an effort to work *with*, not over, my workers. As we walk through a new project, we prioritize things together. I look to them for suggestions on how to accomplish parts of the job. In turn, I learn so much from them. They make me a better manager and installation supervisor, and a better design professional. We all work incredibly hard, but we enjoy the work and find humor in the job. We are a team in the best sense of the word.

TAKING CARE OF BUSINESS—INSURANCE AND PAYMENT

Your subcontractors have a responsibility to you that includes having liability insurance, providing workers' compensation insurance to their workers, and hiring laborers legally. You have a responsibility to your subcontractors to treat them as your construction partners and pay them for their work in a timely manner.

Ask all subcontractors for a copy of their liability insurance policies. You'll actually need to do this yearly, since your own liability insurance provider will request this information from you. This assures you that in the event of an injury to a worker or damage to someone's property, your subs will be able to cover the liability. A couple of years ago my insurance agent called to tell me that liability insurance rates were going through the roof and that to save money I should reduce my liability insurance levels by half. When I told him the towns I work in (many high-end towns in the greater Boston area), he quickly said, "Oh, no! I was wrong! Don't reduce any of your coverage." I have never had a claim (knock on wood), but I gladly pay that annual premium purely for the peace of mind it gives me.

It is worth repeating how important it is to cover yourself by calling your local dig hotline whenever you dig (see call811.com). This "insurance" is free for the phone call, and it is the law in most states. They will need seventy-two hours to get the utilities to your site, but once they've marked you'll know where the underground lines run, and you'll be able to dig safely.

I try to pay my subcontractors the day they give me a deposit request or an invoice. Each of them represents a small business, too, and they have employees to pay, equipment to run, cash flow to maintain. Fast payment is courteous, responsible, and professional. Additionally, since my subs know they won't have to wait for payment, they are quick to sign on for my jobs. Money talks.

MASONRY SUBCONTRACTORS

Recently I was doing a landscape consultation as a favor for a friend and his wife. As we walked the property, the wife asked, "Do you know any masons who are good and cheap?" I stopped, looked her right in the eye, and said, "There is no such thing as good and cheap. There is good or there is cheap. Period." Anyone who does good work should be paid adequately for it. Anyone who is cheap, well, you get what you pay for.

I've found good masons the same way I've found good landscape contractors: by the side of the road. I have also received good referrals from my suppliers, so particularly when you are first starting out, don't hesitate to ask your stone supplier to refer you to a couple of good masons. Most stone yards also have a bulletin board where masons and other professionals post their business cards (psst! you can post your own business cards there, too). Pick ten masonry contractors located relatively close to your area, call them, let them know what type of work you need done (some specialize in walls versus flat work, or particularly like working with one specific type of stone product), and ask if you can visit three of their finished projects. In one or two days of driving around (remember to take photographs), you'll be able to see and assess a great deal of work. When you have narrowed it down to maybe five masons whose work you like, call them and ask if you can take a look at work currently in progress. Watch the site until they're finished. This will show you how clean they keep the site, how they manage stock, how they stage each phase of the project, how safe they are, and how the site looks when they are

A paver patio in progress.

finished. You'll also see how many guys they work with on a particular-sized project, and you can monitor how fast the job goes. All of these are indicators as to how they will work on one of your jobs.

When I was doing my first concrete paver driveway, I had no idea who to call for this type of installation. I phoned two of my suppliers, and one gave me the name of a guy who specialized in installing concrete pavers. I called him. Gary, a lovely, soft-spoken gentleman, agreed to visit the site with me and review the design plans. We talked over the design, his work, his availability, and he pointed me to several sites so I could check out his finished jobs. His work looked wonderful. Even though he and his crew would have to travel nearly 50 miles into the city to do the work, I knew I wanted them to do the installation, and Gary wanted the job, so we moved forward. These gentlemen did a gorgeous job on the driveway, but they also refurbished the entire front bluestone entry (no easy feat), repaired and repointed the formal rear raised patio, and installed drainage to stop a puddling problem. Ten years later, their work looks as exquisite as it did the day it was completed, proving that both the preparation and the installation were done perfectly.

You never really know when or where you will happen upon a great subcontractor. I found another supplier in a fast food restaurant. I was sharing a sandwich with my son, and at the next table was a group of burly men on lunch break. I saw that they were wearing BrickWorks T-shirts and remembered that I'd seen a BrickWorks truck in the parking lot, so I walked over and introduced myself. The boss, who was among the group, gave me his card, and we agreed to meet where they were currently working so that I could see their work. Their masonry was superb. Over the years they've installed quiet a bit of brick hardscape for me.

When it comes to deciding whether you want to work with a particular mason, you need to know what you like and don't like. Do they only work with mortar or will they do dry-laid projects? What do they do best? Some of my masonry teams only do flat work (pavers, bricks, and so forth), others only walls. Having known some of these guys for years, I know who is perfect for what project, so I just hold my breath until I can schedule them. Masons in my area are in great demand, and no kidding, good ones are often booked two years out.

As always, before working with any new contractor, ask for copies of their business license and insurance documentation.

ELECTRICIANS AND PLUMBERS

As your designing branches out beyond planting plans, you will eventually need to hire electricians and plumbers to work installations at your clients' properties. Setting up landscape lighting, running electricity to an outbuilding, putting in a fountain, adding a hose bib or irrigation station—all require licensed tradespeople. If my client has an existing relationship with an electrician or plumber, I like to use their person for the work, since the contractor will likely be familiar with the client's systems and be able to hit the ground running, saving time and money.

If your client doesn't have a regular plumbing or electrical contractor, bring in subs you've worked with before, or hit the phone book. There is probably nothing you'll need done that a master electrician or licensed plumbing contractor cannot do. If the job involves pool equipment installation, your pool contractor will generally have people they know and trust to take care of their part of the job.

Again, don't hesitate to ask anyone you see working for their contact information. They might prove to be the perfect professional for an upcoming project.

IRRIGATION COMPANIES

Irrigation is an area where I do not hit the phone book. I will only use a client's existing service or bring in companies I've already worked with successfully. Most irrigation companies service a fairly wide geographic territory, so I have never been left high and dry. All of my irrigation subcontractors are proficient with regular overhead sprinkler irrigation and are skilled at installing drip in planting beds, automatically irrigating pots and planters, and maintaining water levels in water features. They can all install smart controller systems, and they always use automatic rain sensors.

When you are looking for irrigation subcontractors, you can rely on some industry certifications. The Irrigation Association introduced a series of certification programs in 1983 to standardize the level of knowledge and proficiency among irrigation professionals. Designations include Certified Irrigation Contractor, Certified Irrigation Designer, Certified Landscape Irrigation Auditor, Certified Golf Irrigation Auditor, Certified Agricultural Irrigation Specialist, and Certified Water Conservation Manager—Landscape.

When you are meeting a potential subcontractor, ask what irrigation certifications are held by the employees in their company. This is no guarantee of expertise, but a company that encourages continuing education and values certification will generally be competent, and this is a good indicator that they will be a proficient company to partner with.

MAINTENANCE PROVIDERS

Some of your clients will want to maintain their gardens and lawns themselves, but others will look to you to recommend maintenance providers. Know who is working in their area, who is competent, and who they should stay away from. Know which services take care of both lawns and gardens. If you're in a climate with winter snow, find out who does snow removal and will clear walks as well as drives. Some clients will want one-stop shopping for all of their property maintenance, while others won't mind having lawn dudes, a plow guy, and a team that maintains their perennial gardens.

You will also need to learn who provides organic or sustainable landscape and lawn care. Meet with maintenance providers, question them about their practices, ask what they provide during a typical year of maintenance. If they use treatments, what do they use and what is the timing? What comprises a typical weekly spring visit, and how does that differ from a weekly summer visit?

PAINTERS

At some point you'll need to pull in some painters. Again, if the clients have a painter they know and love, by all means call them first. Otherwise you should be ready to bring in painters you know.

The first time I needed a painter for a project, I could not get one in the timeframe required. I had just started a big job, by far my largest job up to that point, which involved rebuilding a huge driveway and front yard. The mason was to be the first subcontractor working at the site, except that the entire front foundation planting needed to be demolished. I was planning to bring in my regular landscape crew to do the demo, but the masonry contractor said, "Why do that? We're going to be there with machines and everything. Just let us get all of the overgrown shrubs out of there. It'll be easy." I agreed, and it turned out to be a bad decision. (Note to self: use people for their core competence and expertise. Avoid pushing them much beyond that.)

Of course, the masonry contractor started the demolition while I was away, and he decided to remove some very large, overgrown yews and junipers by putting chains around them and pulling them out parallel to (as opposed to straight out from) the garage. Sigh. This resulted in several branches raking across the siding, gouging it and streaking it with green chlorophyll that could not be washed or bleached off. The mason apologized profusely, but the damage was done. Several pieces of siding needed to be replaced and painted. I knew almost no other subs in the area, so what the heck was I going to do? I made some phone calls, but the local carpenters and painters I found in the phone book didn't know me, so we had no history, and they were busy with their own commitments.

I bit the bullet and did all the repairs myself. I found the lumber I needed at a local supplier and replaced the gouged boards (I'm no carpenter, but I can cut a board and install it), then primed and painted the entire south side of the garage. Was this a good use of my time? Well, no. But it had been *our* mistake (the buck stops with the project manager, remember?), so I had to fix the damage as soon as possible and at my own expense. In the end it only took about two days of my time, but if I had been able to bring in professionals I knew and trusted (and who could have worked in a quick favor for me), it could have been done in a single morning.

CARPENTERS

When you design a pergola, arbor, or deck, having some skilled carpenters among your growing team of subcontractors comes into play. Note that when you need a building permit, you either need to hire someone with a general contractor's or builder's license, or you need to have the homeowner apply for the permit. If you do the latter, be prepared to submit framing plans for any construction work, and know that inspections will be required at several points. Pay attention to these and call for inspections at the appropriate times to keep the project moving forward.

As your design business grows and your clients learn how competent you are, you might get into a lot of building. In addition to deck work, this may include things like replacing doors and windows, building a sunroom or three-season porch, installing an outdoor shower, or adding a shed, summerhouse, pool cabana, garage, or barn. I rely on several general contractors to work with me to accomplish my clients' goals.

In 2007 my team actually gutted, redesigned, and completely renovated an entire home, from the framing to the kitchen appliances and paint colors inside and out. It was great! About ten years ago I had a client say to me, "Love, you and your crew are incredible. I have never had a project done so smoothly for my home. I just wish you did kitchens!" Now I can say that we *do* do kitchens.

ALL THE OTHERS

Driveway professionals, pool designers and builders, water shapers and fountain installers, arborists and tree care professionals, lighting specialists, gas fitters, roofers, gutter pros—you name the professional, at some point you'll need to find them. Sometimes the best place to find the right person is from your group of existing subcontractors. They know other people in the trades and have usually seen their work. Use your developing network and you will never have a problem finding the talent to do a job. When your client asks if you can do something beyond your usual scope, assuming that you want the work, your answer can always be, "You bet."

CHAPTER FIFTEEN

Now You Have a Client!
The Design Process

You're ready, and you're anxious for that phone to ring, all the time you're getting your name around, volunteering for a gardening cause or two or ten, and asking everyone you know to refer your name to their families and friends. It's time.

Then the phone rings. "Hello, this is Marta Ravins, and I was referred to you by George Stanwyck. I'd like to talk with you about my gardens. Can you come to see me?" Of course, you tell her that you are delighted she called and would love to meet with her. Now it is your turn to solicit some prequalifying information. Ask her at least eight or ten open-ended, conversational questions that will give you some idea of why she is calling: what is she looking for, what type of yard or garden does she have now, what is her family situation (partner, children or grandchildren [and if so, what ages], pets), what did George tell her about you, what is motivating her to call, and so forth. Take notes. If it would be more comfortable, draft a list of questions and have the list handy when someone calls. Then you'll know you asked for all of the pertinent information, including the prospective client's address and phone number. (Believe it or not, a friend of mine used to always forget to ask for a phone number. Thank goodness for caller ID.)

Asking these questions can get a great conversation going, provide useful insight into what the client is looking for, and give you both a feeling of familiarity that will make your first meeting much more comfortable.

Before you finish the call, make sure to confirm the appointment day and time, and let them know that you look forward to meeting them. If you are going to charge for your initial consultation, make sure to tell your prospective client up front: "Our initial visit is a working session. This will take between one and two hours, and the fee will be $100." As soon as you hang up, jot down any more quick thoughts that come to mind. It is amazing how valuable those last little notes can be a week or so down the road, or when you finally meet.

Now immediately send an e-mail or, better yet, hand-written note to George thanking him for the referral. This is important and is something you should continue to do as your business grows and matures.

Once you have your first phone call under your belt, you'll need a course of action. You will eventually develop your own way of working, from initial meeting to concept presentation and construction. As just one example, here's my general design process:

Initial meeting. Meet and greet, see the site, get a feel for the work. If the project is a go, collect half the design fee.

Field survey. Also called the site survey. Gather site data, usually including measurements, photographs, topography, and location of major elements in the landscape (home, garage, other buildings, large trees, septic, water and gas lines, patios, walks, fencing).

Design development. Prepare base map, elaborate options for new design possibilities, develop broad materials suggestions, consolidate all pieces of design for presentation.

In-process meetings. If required, meet to get clarification or collect more data.

Design presentation. Usually takes place several weeks to several months after the initial meeting. Meet with clients to present design ideas. Collect balance of design fee.

Further design presentations. If needed, meet to review refined design direction based on client feedback, target final materials selections, and so forth.

Estimating. Assign costs to implementation of defined project goals. Get client approval.

Construction. Build the design.

Maintenance. Provide care guidelines and follow-up for the new
landscape for the first year.

INITIAL MEETING

How you proceed at the first meeting is based a lot on your offering.
If you are building a niche business—say, container gardens—compile
any leave-behind brochures or sales information you have developed and
bring them with you. If you are working on your portfolio, make sure it
is ready to share. It doesn't matter if the photos are of containers that you
did for yourself, or your mother-in-law, or to grace the entry of a charity
auction. These are installations you custom created for a client, even if
you were the client. Sell them that way.

If you are offering a broad garden design service, you should also compile your sales support information and bring along something that visually represents your work. A portfolio is always nice, but you could even
bring a laptop containing photographs of your work and do something
as simple as pan through a file of preselected images as you describe each
one. If you have any ugly "before" shots, these make "after" shots much
more compelling. Feel free to bring photographs of gardens you have
worked on with other people, too, from community efforts to garden club
plantings. Just be honest and share the credit.

Once you have compiled your sales support materials and feel good
about what you're going to use at this first meeting, carry out a mock discussion. Out loud. Several times. Believe it or not, this can really relax
you and make you much more conversant in speaking with a prospective
client. Practice makes perfect, and it's all about exuding confidence in
yourself and conveying pride in your work.

No matter what you call this first meeting (planning session, site consultation, garden conference), keep in mind that first impressions are
truly lasting. Always arrive on time. It speaks to your professionalism
and says that you value the client's time as much as you value your own.
I had a prospect once say to me, "Oh, you're on time. How refreshing!"
Show consideration and park in a place that doesn't block the rest of the
driveway. Make sure you don't have bad breath, and check your teeth for
broccoli. I don't mean to sound patronizing, but most people don't pay
enough attention to these things, and they do make a difference.

2D rendering. Two-dimensional plan view of the property.

3D rendering. Three-dimensional perspective drawing used to convey completed results.

Balance. Relationship between elements in the landscape. Can be formal (generally symmetrical) or informal (based on scale and mass).

Base map. Drawing of the landscape showing all existing conditions, based on field survey data.

Bubble diagram. Rough illustration using rounded shapes to show placement of plants or to define areas on a landscape layout.

CAD rendering. Digital files or hard copy of a landscape design created on a computer.

Concept lines. Lines that define spaces or divide areas in the landscape.

Concept plan. Initial drawing of how the spaces in the landscape will appear. Evolves from thumbnail sketches or bubble diagrams.

Design elements. Plant materials and hardscape used to achieve design objectives.

Design objectives. The ultimate goals for the landscape, which drive the design process.

Design process. Collaboration between designers and clients to identify design goals and create a landscape design.

Elevation. Two-dimensional representation of a landscape plan viewed as though you were standing in the space.

Emphasis. Importance in the landscape of major versus minor elements, created through use of large swaths of plants, unique focal points, framing, symmetry, and so forth.

Focal point. Design element, such as a special plant, furnishings, or water feature, used to draw the eye.

Form. Outline created by a plant or hardscape element.

Functionality. Use of the landscape.

Furnishings. Furniture, planted containers, garden art, and other accessories used as accents in the landscape.

Hardscape. Features in the landscape other than plant materials, such as walks, walls, patios, driveways, fences, arbors, and water features.

Landscape. Defined outdoor area using hardscape, turf, and plants to create a space that is functional and beautiful.

Layout. Drawing showing placement of all the elements in a designed area.

Lighting plan. Plan of exterior lighting, specifying voltage and fixtures.

Master plan. Rendering of the completed design, including hardscape and softscape.

Needs assessment. Designer's initial evaluation to identify the client's needs, wants, and goals for the project.

Oblique drawing. An elevation, generally shown from an angle and including perspective.

Perspective drawing. A three-dimensional representation, with vanishing points.

Plan view, bird's-eye view. Overhead view of a design area. Completed landscape designs are usually done in plan view.

Plant grouping. Representation of the types of plants to be used in a certain area.

Planting plan. Layout showing the location of all proposed plants within each planted area.

Principles of design. Standards that define design and create cohesion, including simplicity, balance, scale, variety.

Scale. Size of an object in relation to its surroundings.

Schematic. Plan showing the finished design, including all information necessary to construct the landscape.

Screening planting. Plant materials selected and installed to provide privacy, block a poor view, or define a boundary.

Sequence. Transition from one area within a landscape to another.

Service area. Nicer phrase for "utility area."

Simplicity. Intent to keep the landscape design uncluttered.

Site analysis. Studying field survey data to determine its effect on landscape design.

Softscape. All plant materials in a landscape design.

Space. Area defined to serve a specific purpose in the landscape, for example, "lower lawn" as a recreational space or "trash storage area" as a functional space.

Thumbnail sketch. Quick concept sketch to convey or test a design idea.

Unity. How the landscape design works as a whole.

Variety. Form, colors, and textures combined in a landscape.

View line. Major line of sight from a principal vantage point (inside or out) leading to a focal point or distant view.

So you're at the door, sales support stuff in hand. The door opens. Look your prospective client right in the eye, smile, use their name, and then introduce yourself and tell them you're glad to meet them. Shake their hand. Make sure you have a good handshake, firm and real. (I am so disappointed by so many handshakes! If you don't know whether you have a decent handshake, ask someone you trust for an honest assessment, and if they think there's room for improvement, ask them to walk you through it. You can learn this skill in about three minutes.)

Meeting with a potential client for full property garden design usually takes one and a half to two hours at the site. If there are two homeowners, ideally both should be present at the meeting; otherwise, there is a good chance that the decision to hire or not hire won't be made and you'll have to wait for an invitation to return (waste of time). So request that both partners be present, but don't balk at an exception. In a couple of instances I have worked projects for years with just half of the couple. As long as you are working with a person who can make a decision, it won't hinder the process.

A side note about fees. I do not charge for my initial meeting, but friends of mine do. One designer I know calls the first meeting a "comprehensive landscape assessment," another says he's developing "the project master list," and a third calls it a "garden consultation." This works great for them, because if they don't get the job, they've still been compensated for their time. The reason I have always been reluctant to charge is that I like meeting with prospective clients without the specter of money hanging over my head. I also personally would hesitate to meet with a contractor who wanted me to pay for our initial consultation. Offering this meeting at no charge gives me more freedom to express myself, more liberty in the amount of time I want to take, and is just a more comfortable way for me to operate.

Gary Koller, president of Koller Associates, a landscape design firm in the Boston area, is an exquisite designer I first met many years ago when he worked with my father-in-law at the Arnold Arboretum. Gary says that he does not charge for his first meeting with a client because then he is not obligated. If the client wants to walk away, that's fine, and if Gary wants to walk away, he feels comfortable doing so because he has not accepted any payment. Good for him. Like Gary, you will eventually work out what makes sense for you.

Please note the semantics here. "Offering an initial consultation at no charge" says the exact the same thing, and yet is completely different from, "First meeting is free." Words are powerful. Craft them accordingly.

The designer takes the lead in the meeting. During this first face-to-face, my potential clients and I chat and feel each other out on several levels. We talk about their family and lifestyle, what they like to do, how they like to spend their time. We discuss the potential scope of work. I ask what they are looking to do, why they want to do it now, and what problems they have with their yard. I take note of their needs, while keeping in mind the wants we've uncovered. People often don't know what they need or want, and it's my job to point out possibilities. We walk around the property discussing how they currently use it and how they'd like to use it. We talk about types of gardens and plants that speak to them. (Often people cannot articulate this, but this is fine because I'll bring recommendations and photographs that illustrate my intention, my vision for *them*, to the design presentation, assuming we get that far.) I let them tell me what works and doesn't work. I also point out areas that I know are problems, even if they don't, making sure to do so in a roundabout way ("These steps are rather steep and narrow. Are you ever concerned about safety when you have people over?"). I give them my standard packet "about me" and walk them through what's in it. I encourage them to read through the information at some point in the next day or two.

As you talk with potential clients, you're not just discussing the potential work, you're also testing whether the chemistry works. Will your styles be complementary? Can you work with them? Can they work with you?

If you are meeting with a couple, no matter who seems to be the primary decision maker, make sure to direct your questions and answers to both clients. This is common courtesy, and you will be developing a relationship with both people, so it's important to start off right. When I'm on the receiving end, nothing annoys me more than being ignored by someone who decides to give their sales pitch entirely to my husband, concluding that since he is the man he must make the decisions. Big mistake. You can assume I am a lot of things, but treat me like a "dumb chick" and there will be no sale. When you meet with potential clients, treat them equally. It will net you considerably more clients.

Several designers I know take paper to the first meeting, sketch out a rough plan of the house and yard, and as they walk around with the clients, take notes about what they might do in each area. Effectively they come up with a plan of action—and a rough design—for the entire landscape, formulating the lion's share of their ideas right there. This "instant design" approach is proactive and gets the clients excited. You walk the property, see the potential, and immediately articulate solutions. I wish I could work that way, because I think it might save time, but I can't. I like to ruminate.

As the clients and I wander through their yard and talk, I take notes. This lets them know that I am paying attention and that I value what they are saying, and the notes are quite useful later to help me remember key items. I even jot down the names of children and pets, if they have any—and what a difference it makes in the relationship if you remember those details! I was collaborating on a job with another designer, someone who isn't a detail guy and who takes few notes. When we were finally designing the property, I suggested several considerations for the small children. He looked at me and said, "Oh, they have kids?" Can you imagine walking in to give a design presentation, presenting plans for a backyard, and realizing you have no idea whether the client has children? Eek. Take notes, and remember the little things. When you walk back in to meet with someone, greet the children by name, and say, "Hello, Rufus," to the dog. Your clients will know you will bring this same level of personal interest and attention to detail to the design and management of their project. It makes a difference.

Sometimes I tell a prospective client about me, my experience, and how I got into this business, since small talk can give us both a natural feeling of intimacy. But I don't always tell my story, because I listen much more than I talk. I ask lots of open-ended questions about their family, their lives, how they want to use their property. Not only do I learn more about them this way, but they come away thinking about how interested I am in what they have to say (which may or may not be true).

Subjects forbidden at the dinner table, like religion and politics, should stay out of the conversation. Even if you feel you're both on the same wavelength, it's safer to keep the conversation clean until you really know each other. If you're asked a direct question, I suggest dodging it or giving an answer that's well qualified. For example, my dear friend Laura has an acupressure clinic, and during an election year one of her clients asked how she voted. She knew the client was very political and leaned to the far right. Laura had voted Democratic and didn't want to lie, so she took the potential sting out of the answer by saying, "Well, you know I'm a tree hugger, so I had to vote Democrat." Her client grunted but forgave her.

Another potentially uncomfortable subject is money. Of course, you're going to have to talk about money at some point, but I never ask about budget at the first meeting. Most people have no clue what things cost, so having them throw out a number has no basis in reality. I have had people look at me and say, "What could we do for $5000?" The answer is, "Well, not a whole lot." When a small crew costs $1000 for the day, your time costs x, and materials cost y, work can add up to $5000 in a heartbeat. I also refrain from asking about budget because I don't want to limit my thinking. Clients may hire you with the assumption that they're not going to spend more than $10,000, but by the time they have seen your design proposal and walked through the possibilities with you, they often want to do more and are willing to spend more. That said, budget constraints are a reality that need to be considered when the time comes to present an estimate.

So what do you say when a client asks at the first meeting, before you really even have a clue what the project is, "How much will this cost?" I usually tell them that when we've determined the scope of the work and selected materials, then we will get down to pulling together some substantive numbers. Until that point, coming up with an estimate would be a wild guess. Other designers may go ahead and throw out numbers at the first visit, and I encourage you to do whatever you are most comfortable with. I just know that if I throw out a number, the client's brain will get stuck on it, and I'll have a hard time justifying the actual estimate later on. So, not throwing out any numbers works best for me, and luckily people end up being okay with this. I have a friend who nearly always answers the cost question with, "More than twenty-five thousand and less than half a million. We'll narrow it down later." That's usually good for a chuckle, and redirects the subject.

Towards the end of the meeting, after the walk-through, I tell my prospective clients how my design planning and installation work, and walk them through my leave-behind material, which articulates the process. I then tell them my fee for designing their project, as we've been discussing it. I let them know my payment terms (my design fees are half payment as a retainer, balance due at the design presentation). I also let them know that if they make the decision by a certain date to retain my services, I can start designing on such and such day, and I tell them roughly when we can meet for the design presentation. And that's the offer. Usually I am retained on the spot, but sometimes the clients want to talk it over together. They might call that evening and tell me they would like to hire me, or it might take a couple of days.

In my experience, if you haven't heard back from a potential client in a week to ten days, they aren't going to hire you. However, there are exceptions to every rule o' thumb. I've had people surprise me by calling back a year later to give me the go-ahead. Some people just need more "process" time.

When I've been given the go, I collect half the design fee. The next day I send them a formal receipt that itemizes what we have just agreed to and the price, how much I have received as a deposit, their check number, and the date. On this document I list the deliverables and reiterate that the balance (specify amount) will be due at the design presentation meeting, date to be determined. I sign it and send them two copies—one for their files, one for them to sign and return to me. This serves as our agreement. I include a stamped, self-addressed envelope for the return copy. (I always include a stamped, self-addressed envelope when I'm looking for a signature or check.)

FIELD WORK AND SITE DATA

You've been hired. Now how do you start? When we're gardening and designing for our own places, most of us either put nothing on paper, or play with little bubble diagrams for areas we're reworking. Sketch a rectangle for the house, a line for a new border, a few plant symbols, then go out, buy plants, and put them in. Voilà, done. But now that you're a professional, you need to determine what visuals to use to convey your ideas to your clients.

The first step is field work. Once I'm hired, I return to the site, inventory or confirm existing conditions, take photographs and tight measurements, and if appropriate, take soil samples to send off to the local agricultural extension office for testing. It is while doing field work that I really bond with the property and am able to starting feeling the possibilities. I don't have to concentrate on clients or keep a thread of conversation going; I can just allow myself to Zen into the place.

I get measurements of the house, the property, and important elements on the property, including other structures, walks and drives, major trees, garden beds, pool, pole lamps, and so on—anything that is a significant component in the areas I'll be working design. I measure all structures to the half-inch and measure everything else to the inch. Sometimes I'll also want to have the site topography, which will give me the elevation changes over the property extents. You can learn to do topography yourself, or hire a surveyor or civil engineer.

When the job is large and complex, or if I know I'm going to be submitting plans to the conservation commission or needing permits (additions, pools), I'll want an electronic copy of a certified plot plan. Many clients will already have this from a recent home sale or an addition to their house. Ask them. If they have a printout, you can see who prepared the data in the title block. Call the engineers and ask for a copy, or if it was created on a CAD system and you have compatible software, ask if they can attach it to an e-mail. If the existing plot plan was hand-drawn (which means no electronic copy exists), you can still ask the engineering company for a copy. They'll either give it to you or let you have it for a nominal fee, like $10.

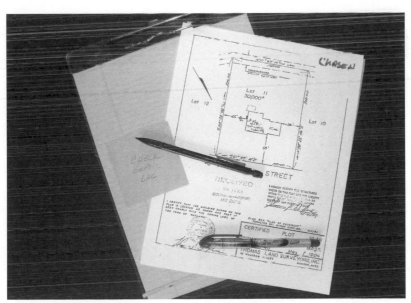

Sometimes only a simple, hard-copy mortgage plot plan is available, but this still gives you a good starting place for measuring the property. It can also help you locate property boundaries.

If you need a certified plot plan and one is not available, let your clients know that you will need to hire a civil engineering firm to create the plan. Call a local civil engineer, get an estimate (add your margin and project management time), and obtain approval from the client for the expenditure. Costs can range from about twelve hundred dollars to tens of thousands for larger properties, particularly if you need to capture a lot of topographic information.

TAKING MEASUREMENTS

Pick a nice day, and to make the job more pleasant, bring a pal. No, you won't need assistance, but it will make the task run faster. When I have an involved site to measure, I detest doing it alone. Sometimes friends have helped, or another budding designer, or occasionally my husband. Since my son was about five, I've often brought him along. He can hold the end of a measure, retrieve landscape pins, and crawl under shrubs easily. He has always made a good gopher.

First measure the house. If the clients have an up-to-date plot plan, or if you have had one made, your job measuring on-site will be much easier. Even if you are using an existing rough or dated hard copy to take additional measurements or put notes on, it will be a tremendous time-saver. Most plans will include a good footprint of the house, and it will be drawn to scale. From this you can easily locate major trees, fencing, septic distribution tank and cleanout covers, property lines, and, well, basically everything. You'll quickly get a feel for how much you need to include on a base map to create a good representation of the existing conditions.

I always make the house the "from" point for everything else in the landscape, so I start by measuring the house. It never fails to amaze me that I can measure even a very involved layout of a house, and when I input the dimensions into the CAD program—poof!—it comes together beautifully, sometimes within a quarter-inch. Ah, the wonders of geometry. Commonly it's more like an inch or two as a final gap, but I figure that's close enough for my purposes.

If you are starting with no plan of the property, measuring is still doable; it will just take a bit more time and patience.

As I walk you through measuring a site, assume for the moment that there is no plot plan, no site map, no reference document. It's just me, a clipboard, a pencil, and a pad of paper. I use the corners of the house as my reference points to plot nearly all of my other measurements, so the first thing I do is create a simple sketch of the house as I take a quick walk around. I also note the items I need to capture for my base map of existing conditions. Then I carefully measure the house. It will rarely be a simple square or rectangle, but it's easy to work with any structure, even one with weird angles. I measure decks, porches, and stoops, count stairs, and measure tread depths. I indicate where the bulkhead is and where the utility connections and hose bibs fall. All doors and major windows (like picture windows or bay windows) are captured. Once I have measured the house, I use ranges and swing ties to locate all other notable items in the landscape.

Using ranges off of the major architectural features of the house is a great way to locate things. Clean and simple. The range of the house is taken by running a tape measure down a plane of the building (kind of like mentally extending the wall of the structure) and measuring the distance from the corner of the building to the objects or points that fall

My measuring tools and marking paint at the ready in the back of my car. Yes, those are chopsticks in the pocket of the tote bag. They are cheap and biodegradable, and I often use them to mark edges of beds or indicate a line of site. In a pinch I can even use them to hold down the end of the measuring tape.

on that range of the house. I do this from all corners of the house and usually from the corners of any other building on the property. To take ranges accurately, make sure you stay right in line with the plane of the building façade you are using. You really cannot go more than an inch or two in either direction without knowing you are off of the range. Keep your tape measure straight, and avoid weaving in and out of shrubs. Once you have your range to the point that you need to capture, note the measurement. To indicate a range on my sketchpad, I draw a dotted line from the source corner to the object, and then write the measurement and the name of what I'm measuring, such as "prop" (property line), "fence," or "oak 12" (oak with a 12-inch-diameter trunk). Then I move on to the next corner. Some ranges give you a series of points—for example, 26 feet 4 inches to near drive edge, 39 feet 4 inches to far drive edge, 52 feet to property line. It's a super way to capture measurements.

Using swing ties involves taking measurements from two known points to locate an object relative to those points. This is an example of triangulation. I always take range measurements first, because ranges are easier to note and plot, and the more I can accomplish using ranges, the better. After the house is measured and the ranges are all noted, we're after notable items that do not fall on any range.

Swing ties allow you to locate any item on the property with precision. Given that you'll most likely be plotting a number of swing tie points, you need a way to keep your point notations clear. Say I want to locate a tree. I assign letters to the two points I'm measuring from—perhaps two corners of the house, labeled A and B. As I locate the tree, I measure from each origin point, A and then B, and put the corresponding letter plus the measurement in a circle beside an abbreviated description of the tree. For example, "oak 14 in.—A 31 ft. 4 in., B 43 ft." tells me that a 14-inch-caliper oak stands at the intersection of a circle 31 feet 4 inches from corner A and 43 feet from corner B. This is a simple way to give myself the data I'll need to draw the base map when I'm back home. Clear as mud? Really, it sounds complicated, but it's not.

Between swing ties and ranges, I locate everything on the property that I need to consider in the development of the design. Do I note every tree and shrub? Heavens no. If there is a wooded area, I may get positions on three or four major trees, then add tree symbols to the layout and note "wooded area" in the description. I do take my time and carefully locate large trees, particularly those that are in lawns or at property edges, and I take care to indicate exact dimensions of driveways, walkways, fencing, outbuildings, property lines, and major features (decks, patios, pools, and so forth).

Make sure to start creating your base map within a day or two of having taken measurements. You will be amazed at how many notations will make little sense if you let a week slip by. My preference is to measure in the morning and keep that afternoon free to input my base map. Once the base map is input, I can wait days, weeks, or months to start working the design, but the timing from measuring to base map creation is best when it is fresh in your mind.

PHOTOGRAPHING EXISTING CONDITIONS

A picture truly is worth a thousand words, and the arrival of digital photography has made our jobs much easier. You can shoot and shoot, and it doesn't cost anything but time. As I'm taking photos, I sit and ponder

When people look at their own homes, they often do not see the problems that are obvious to others. The photographs that you take can show your clients the "pain" in their landscapes, such as an unused doorway that is being engulfed by shrubs.

various view lines and get a good feel for the place. Shoot everything, because you will refer to these photos again and again as you design.

The pattern I use to photograph properties was modeled after the pattern used by my friend Mike Walsh of Horticultural Concepts. I photograph the approach from at least 100 feet or so down the street. This gives me a window on how the house works from a curb-appeal standpoint, and on how the drive and walkways function with the approach. Then I methodically take each side of the house and photograph a panorama (series of linked shots from left to right) *of* each side, and *from* each side. So I get each house "plane" and every possible view. In addition I take photos of major view lines (out major windows and doorways) and shoot details I want to remember—deck layout, rotten bulkhead, tree that needs pruning, wet area next to the foundation, peeling paint, missing downspout, great area for a hot tub, and so forth. Pictures often bring murky problems into high relief; they do not lie, and they often show clients what their eyes forgive every day.

I have client folders in the "My Pictures" folder of my computer. After I load the images, I arrange and rename them "Smith FH 1" and so forth (with "FH" meaning "front of house"). Sometimes I rename the detail shots by retitling each one, and other times I lump them as "Detail 1," "Detail 2," and so forth. Within each client folder I have subfolders for various photos: "Existing," "During Construction," "After," and "Best Shots." I keep the numbering convention roughly the same. This is a great way to keep photo files consistent, and it is easy to access exactly the shots you're looking for in just seconds.

When I am working the design, I often print out key photos I know I'll want to refer to frequently. If you don't want to waste the ink on your printer, find a retailer near you who offers quick turnaround on e-prints. They'll have a Web site where you load your selected images to print, and in an hour or two you can have the prints for about $0.12 to $0.25 apiece. Until just a few years ago I used to have to wait two to three days for conventional photo processing, so frankly I think this is incredible.

PREPARING A BASE MAP

Once you have collected measurements and photos, it's time to start your design work back at the office. Whether you are starting with an electronic version of the client's site plan, or drawing it yourself by hand, you need to map the existing conditions. If I have the luxury of being given an electronic copy, I first work on the drawing to portray the existing conditions based on the way I like to see them. I have a protocol that I use, with particular colors and symbols. I use Architectural units (feet and inches) versus Engineering units (tenths of feet), so I will convert the units if necessary. I verify a few measurements to make sure I didn't make some weird mistake on-site. Then I begin to add my landscape symbols and preferred embellishments until I have the existing conditions well represented. Only then do I resave the drawing and start designing the new landscape and garden possibilities.

If you have any background in drafting or graphic art, you will use these skills. If you don't have any existing drafting skills, you will develop what you need to. There are as many ways to get a concept across as there are designers.

When I used to hand-draw bubble diagrams, I would start with a large piece of graph paper, get the house outlined, and take it from there. I'd note items on the paper with my swing tie measurements and my

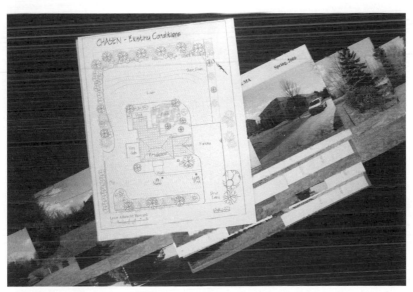

The design process begins with a map of the existing conditions and panoramic photos.

ranges, and then color in the outlines and symbols for everything. Lots of designers work this way. At a design seminar I attended, when the speaker asked how many people drew by hand, about 70% of the 150 people in the room raised their hands! Now that I design on the computer, I'm spoiled by the flexibility it offers and cannot imagine going back to hand-drawings. But remember that for most of the last five thousand plus years the people of the world have constructed amazing things, and nearly every concept and detail was hand-drawn. Consider Stonehenge, the pyramids of Egypt, Machu Picchu, the Hagia Sophia. All were initiated when someone drew something in the sand or on a parchment of papyrus. Incredible.

Several landscape architects that I know still only design by hand-drafting. They like the hand-crafted nature of the finished product (truly, they are gorgeous), and it is their way of putting a great deal of self-expression into the design and the proposed layouts.

Still other designers present their work as true art, using watercolors, oils, pastels, or pencils. Some layouts are whimsical, others clean and left-brained, and each is a personal expression of the designer. Obviously, a flair for the artistic is a requirement for this type of creation, but the proposed designs are unique and convey ideas beautifully. Some of the designs I have seen presented like this are exquisite enough to frame.

Then there are the less formal design layouts. Several of the most beautiful gardens I have ever seen were drawn on a lunch napkin, or so I was told. But it's a rare designer who can hold everything so clearly in their mind's eye, and it's a rare client who has the trust and vision to move forward with such a small amount of information.

Horticulturist and designer Gary Koller does simply amazing work. He puts nothing on paper but meticulously marks out the proposed changes in the space with paint, stakes, and string for the clients to walk through and experience.

Some designers, like Gary, have incredible and well-deserved reputations. This allows them more freedom in how they present ideas to clients. They come to the client with the highest credibility, and the trust is virtually immediate. A budding designer can aspire to this level of credibility, but achieving it will take years and lots of great work.

CAD

I design using a computer-aided design (CAD) program called AutoCAD. It's what most engineers and architects use, so we can share drawings. AutoCAD saves me time, but it is by no means a must-have to do garden and landscape design. It is arduous to learn and quite expensive (thousands of dollars). A myriad of other software packages out there can help you create wonderful landscape designs. Certain "homeowner" versions can cost as little as $50, and versions geared to professionals can run anywhere from a couple of hundred dollars to quite a few thousand. Google "landscape software" to find the plethora of options available, and try different Web sites to play with different products. You'll eventually find a program that works well for you.

In addition to designing with a CAD product, I use hand-drawing. When I prepare my layouts for presentation, I print them out in full color, enlarge them on an oversized color copier, and add hand-coloring and lettering to the layouts. This is unnecessary, but the layouts become more saturated, more beautiful, and more compelling as I embellish them. This process usually takes me a couple of hours, never more than part of a day, and I wouldn't say that any of my layouts end up being framable art, but they are quite beautiful. Bold color sells. I am also proud of the drawings I create, and that pride elicits a positive emotional response from the client, so taking the time to do these enhancements works for me.

DESIGN DEVELOPMENT

Now you have a base map of existing conditions and digital photographs of the site, and you've been turning over design possibilities in your mind. At this point in my own projects I sometimes study the photographs for several hours, making thumbnail sketches, adding notes, pondering options for various areas. Once some ideas are formulated in my mind, I start putting pen to paper (or mouse to pad). Here's where the fun begins.

But how do the ideas flow? Is it divine inspiration? Do we wait and mutter a secret mantra waiting for the ideas to come washing over us? Uh, no. Design is work. It is applied knowledge. If you sit around waiting for an idea to be channeled to you (thunderous sound effects), y'all are going to be waiting a long, long time.

People often think the creative process is mysterious, maybe even weirdly genetic. Well, there may be a genetic component, but mostly creativity is directed work. And sometimes, despite our facility with being creative, we can get stuck or not know where to begin.

Heuristics are practical principles that can help get you out of no-action mode, since half the battle is just getting moving. Personal development blogger Steve Pavlina (stevepavlina.com) offers his own fabulous list, "Thirty-Three Rules to Boost Your Creativity." Among my personal favorites is rule ten: "Cone of silence. Take a laptop with no network or Wi-Fi access, and go to a place where you can work flat out without distractions, such as a library, park, coffeehouse, or your own backyard. Leave your comm gadgets behind." Referring back to the principles of heuristics has helped me to be a more effective designer (and helped me get this book written!).

When I sit down to design, stuck or not, inspired or not, I start with the big stuff that really affects the function of the property. I start with the major hardscape and with the premise that form should follow function in nearly all hardscape design.

When contemplating a new design, consider how things function at the site. The process always starts with questions. What do you think of the approach? What do you think of the property as you come up the street? Do you know where to turn in? Does the driveway work okay? Does the client need additional parking or a turnaround? Can you see well enough to safely get in and out of the drive? How does the walkway connect the driveway to the house? Could the walk approach be more functional, more pleasing? How should guests enter, and how do we motivate them in that direction? Play with several layouts. How is the view from the street to the face of the house? Does the house show well? Can you see house numbers easily? Is the home visually well framed? If plant materials appear to be eating the house, what can we remove to make the home show better? What areas need screening from an unsightly view? Do we need additional privacy somewhere? Is there a visible utility area (garbage cans, hoses, electrical connections) that can be made more functional and attractive? How is the link from the client's preferred parking to the house? (It is unbelievable how many driveways are not even linked to the front door. No walk, no access, no view.

Dreadful.) Is the walk from car to house easy for toting bundles? How do utility companies access meters and fill pipes (propane, oil, water, meter readings)? Can the access be more practical, more attractive? How do the existing surfaces work or not work? (Rough stone walkways are not safe for people with difficulty walking. Gravel walks are not practical in climates where we shovel snow.) How does the mowing pattern work? Can this be simplified? If you're in a climate with harsh winters, how can we design the drive and walks so there is a convenient area to pile up plowed and shoveled snow?

You will have discussed some of these items with the client during your initial meeting and walkabout. But now as you actually take a microview of the elements of the property and get into the details of the design, you'll see far more ways for improvement both aesthetically and functionally.

As much as I design with a great deal of creativity, I also try to design a new landscape in keeping with the neighborhood. Of course any designer is expected to make great improvements, but remember that Versailles does not necessarily belong in Hoboken.

Once you complete the design, it will be time to create alternative versions. Giving your clients a range of design options is a major value-add to your service. It doesn't take much more time, but it will look to your client like it did. (The lion's share of my time is spent creating the base map and the first design. Additional design iterations are usually quick to complete).

You will find that one design can quickly morph into another. My designs are like an à la carte menu. I might present the designs as options one, two, and three, but the clients are free to take the walkway from option one, the driveway layout from option two, and the deck and plantings from option three. Usually, when the clients identify which treatments really appeal to them, we can make it work.

THE LAYOUT

Most designers work in plan view, or bird's-eye view, but there are other ways of viewing designs. Elevations are two-dimensional (2D) and show how something would look if you were standing in the space and looking at the designed object or area. Architectural drawings are drawn in elevations, as well as in plan view, so you can see the look of the building (elevations) as well as the footprint (plan). A north elevation of a house plan shows the north side of the building. Three-dimensional (3D) layouts are shown in elevation with perspective and dimension. Oblique layouts are also three-dimensional and show the design at an angle and with perspective.

I do all of my designs in plan view and then make thumbnail sketches of areas I want to detail in an elevation. Some designers are artistic enough to create elevations and perspective drawings, which are incredibly useful in helping a client visualize a design, but nearly everything starts with plan view.

If you are drawing by hand, make several color copies of your prepared base map so that you can play with them without ruining your original. If you are using your computer, save this drawing and copy the existing conditions so that you can play around with it. And play around is what you do. Look at the photographs, review your meeting notes, take a look at how the space is working, and determine what could work better. Start moving lines around. Don't be afraid to erase or undo—this is all part of the process.

Full property designs can take hours or days, depending on the complexity of the site, the scope of the work, and the amount you're getting paid. Truly, I can crank out a design in a limited number of hours—for a limited fee—that is similar to one I'll charge considerably more for. But the level of detail, the amount of consideration, the options I take into account, and the degree of illustration and preparation I'll bring to the presentation will be as different as night and day.

DESIGN PRESENTATION

Now you've made it through the design process. You feel good about the ideas you have articulated on the layouts. Time to turn these ideas into a presentation.

I employ a number of different tools for my presentations. I bring printed layouts of existing conditions, proposed design layouts, visuals that will help explain the design intent (photographs from books, for example, or the Internet), and a printed outline of the major points I will be making during our meeting.

For more extensive designs, I prepare a narrative. I actually don't know any other designer who does this, but here's my reasoning. The narrative serves as my notes and key talking points for the entire presentation, and it also acts as a leave-behind with the layouts, so the clients have all of the presentation information. Design presentations can be a little overwhelming for clients—lots of information in a concentrated amount of time. A narrative allows them to sit and review all the options at their leisure.

The client copy of the narrative is clean, of course. My copy will have notes in the margins for the design presentation, references to books I need to open at certain times, reminders about samples, and so forth. This is a presentation after all. I mention to the clients that they will have a complete copy of the design narrative at the end of the presentation. I explain that if I give clients a packet of written material at the beginning of the presentation, they invariably read ahead and can't pay attention to what I'm saying. I actually prepare a whole leave-behind folder that contains a clean copy of the narrative, key photographs, and small-copy versions of the design layouts.

I don't always bring props, but when I do they consist of samples of the stone I am recommending, or a bouquet of certain recommended

DESIGN CHECKLISTS

The day before a design presentation, run through a master checklist to make sure you have all the necessary information at hand. Also assure that you have props, if any, and books or photographs that you want to share with your clients. Taking a few minutes to make sure every *i* is dotted and every *t* is crossed will not only confirm that you are well prepared, it will also boost your confidence (and remind you of the dog's name—good move). Here is one example of a design presentation checklist:

- Layouts of existing conditions and each design option
- Photographs of existing conditions
- Notes from original meeting or consultation
- Books and photographs of design ideas and suggestions
- Samples and props, as required
- Leave-behind packet
- Invoice for balance due on the design fee

flowers (assuming the presentation takes place during the growing season), maybe a piece of fencing.

I start the design presentation by setting up all of my boards and information while everyone gets comfortable. Then I reiterate why the clients contacted me ("You called to ask me about a new walkway and garden for your front entry"). I walk them through the existing conditions on the base map and the existing conditions photographs of their property. This is about restating their "pain," as a friend of mine puts it. Their pain is the problem they brought you in to solve, but it is also the other places in the landscape that you have discovered could use attention. I point these out gently as I walk through the photographs.

Once we have reviewed the existing conditions, I start by unveiling option one. That sounds grand. I walk them through what this design suggests, the thinking that goes behind it, the features, and most importantly, the benefits. How will this design change the way they look at and live in their space? That's what will sell it.

Use your props when the time comes. When suggesting a bluestone walkway, bring up your small piece of bluestone and describe its characteristics. If your design includes granite steps, show a small piece of granite block and describe how it will be fabricated, "pencil edge with a thermal top, so it isn't slippery." A forecourt of brick? Bring a sample of the brick and a printout of the brick pattern you recommend. Most stone suppliers are happy to give free samples; otherwise you can buy them for just a few dollars.

On occasion, serendipity rules. It happened to be early summer when I was designing a "color garden" to surround an existing patio. This was the second home I was working on for this client, so she and I already had a good working relationship. To illustrate the brilliant, jewel-toned flowers I intended for her patio garden, I went into my own gardens and cut a generous bouquet that contained a number of the varieties that I knew she would like and that would grow well in her conditions. She was so delighted and excited that she didn't want to wait a year and decided to have the garden installed as soon as possible.

My excitement comes from sharing possibilities with clients, helping them to see their property in a whole new light. This excitement is contagious. Describe in detail how people will appreciate the new pocket garden you are proposing. Show beauty shots of some of the major flowering plants you intend to use. Present your ideas with confidence and delight. Reinforce that the new gardens will be beautiful, the new patio gorgeous and wonderful to enjoy on a warm summer evening. Smile as you introduce each piece of the design. You may be a designer, but you are in sales, too. You are selling your ideas as well as yourself.

At the conclusion of the presentation, ask for feedback. Usually you will have had plenty of dialogue, but you can reiterate. "So you like the proposed approach to the front door?" "You're excited about the sunny border in the side yard?" "What do you think about the selection of flowering trees?" "The forecourt in the front seemed like your favorite option." At this point I usually suggest to the clients that they take some time to review the various options together, and then let me know how they would like to proceed. To keep the process moving, I like to suggest a date a week or two out for them to respond to me with decisions. I also reiterate that I'm available to answer questions, clarify anything, or expand on a suggestion. This lets them know that I am responsive, there for them, and ready to move their project along.

At this point, if you haven't received the balance of your design fee, ask for it. I always bring my clients' updated "balance due" invoice with me. As I bring out the design invoice, I say, "Oh, and as we agreed, there is a balance of x dollars due for the design fee. I would greatly appreciate payment tonight." People are usually more than happy to give you the balance due. I am loathe to leave any design materials behind if I have not received full payment. Our design work is our intellectual property, and until the client has paid you, it still belongs to you. Once they have paid you in full, the design and information you give them is rightfully theirs, and they can install the design themselves, hire another contractor to build the design, or have you manage the construction process. They can also do nothing, which does happen. But do make sure you get paid for your design work.

Two shows on HGTV, *Landscapers' Challenge* and *Designers' Challenge*, offer a great opportunity to see how other designers present their work, including different types of layouts and presentation methodologies. On these shows, three designers present their ideas to clients looking to do landscape work or interior decoration and renovation. The clients choose the designer they want to work with, and the proposed work is installed. I find both shows incredibly informative. Some of the designers do not listen to the clients at all, and you can see how it bites them in the butt during the design presentation. One show introduced a lovely yard in the Southwest. The one critical criterion the clients set for the new backyard design was that they wanted to keep their magnificent palm trees. One of the designers came back with some great ideas, but during the presentation she said, "And we'll be removing these palm trees to make way for—." The clients immediately shut down and refused to listen to another word. The designer hadn't listened to their one request. Revealing, for sure.

My friend Mike Walsh does a multimedia design presentation. Gotta tell you, it's pretty impressive. He brings all of his equipment, which includes a laptop, glass-beaded projection screen, and LCD projector. The designs, the images of flowers and trees—everything is projected at about 4 feet by 6 feet. The presentation is stunning, and clients love it. Computerization coupled with creativity makes it all possible.

NEXT STEPS

I usually send an e-mail or note the day after the design presentation. I thank them for their time, briefly reference a couple of the high points from our exchange, and remind them of the date we've planned to reconnect. I also mail a receipt for the balance of the design fee.

Because design presentations are so information heavy, they can short-circuit some people, in which case there is an inclination to do nothing and decide nothing. Agreeing with them on a deadline and prompting them for feedback will keep the process moving. Several designers I know actually set up the follow-up meeting before they leave the design presentation. If clients know you'll be coming over next Thursday evening at 7:00, they'll be much more inclined to be ready than if you leave it open.

As I embrace my geezerhood (read: as I get older), I find I am less and less crazy about heading out for meetings at night. Too much going on. So I tend to be relatively casual about asking for client feedback. But when you want the process to continue on your timeframe, you need to take the wheel and drive. Set up a meeting to review feedback and to reach a decision on the course of action.

At the follow-up meeting, I usually review the boards briefly, and the clients usually punctuate the review with feedback. Then we identify what they want to accomplish *now*. Some people want to phase in landscape changes, while others want the whole banana. Either way can work beautifully. I have worked over a period of several years with many clients to phase in a total landscape change. This keeps me employed.

At this point we have an identified set of goals and a rough timeframe ("We want to do the patio, front walkway, and foundation plantings this year"). Now it's on to final materials selection, estimating, setting a timeframe, lining up subcontractors, and starting the work.

REALITY CAN BE STRANGER THAN FICTION

As you enter this world where garden designer and client intersect, you will be dealing with not only design issues but also your clients' personalities: their baggage, their marital health, their different styles, agendas, fears, wants, and needs. You are not just a designer and horticulturist but also a salesperson, counselor, negotiator, life coach, and friend. You'll quickly find that life as a garden designer is often stranger than fiction.

You will absolutely, positively never be bored meeting clients. Oh, some clients are boring of course, but if you like studying people you'll find even the boring ones compelling. My friends love the client antics that I relate. I'm careful not to name people or even towns for the most part, but oh, the stories! From the penny-pinching accountant to the flamboyant drama coach, from the spoiled-rotten newly moneyed to the plucky self-made artist, clients are a joy, a terror, a mystery, and an ever-unfolding drama. You will see people at their best and most gracious, and you will be equally appalled by exhibitions of selfishness and bad manners. My style is to work collaboratively. I become a part of my clients' lives as they become part of mine. We share joy, lots of laughter, and yes, even grief, though I try to stay away from the tears—at least I try to make sure I am not the cause of them.

THE ODD COUPLE

One couple I met with years ago were kind of a scream. Well, I think they're a scream now that I have nearly a decade of perspective on the situation and am no longer working with them. I was still pretty green in the business, and as they walked me around during our first meeting, the husband started talking about what he wanted and where the landscape work should head, and the wife started making faces behind him. For a while I tried not to notice. Then, as we continued walking, the wife started leading the conversation about the property, and the husband started making faces behind *her* back. Interesting dynamics, and trust me, I couldn't avoid noticing. At one point the wife took me aside and said, "He's crazy. Don't listen to anything he says. Just 'yes' him to death." I responded, "I'll certainly do my best to make you both happy." At the end of the meeting, the husband walked me to my car and said, "By the way, anything my wife says is nuts. Ignore her and work with me." I stood there, rather wide-eyed (I mean, how do you respond to that?), and reiterated, "I'll certainly do my best to make you both happy." At this point I wondered how the heck the design presentation would go. Eek.

The design presentation, in fact, was equally bizarre. They countered each other and parried back and forth with every option I presented, so I finally said, "I may not be qualified to work to bridge the gaps in your relationship, but I do think we can create a gorgeous patio planting that will delight you both." For a moment they looked at me like I'd struck them, but then, to my utter amazement, they both burst out laughing. Somehow this defused the tension they'd been creating, and we were able to move forward productively. Ironically, they were considerably less vindictive towards each other from that point on. Weird. Weird, but also instructive. Expect just about anything.

MARRIAGE, ON THE ROCKS

One couple I worked with had a new home on a lovely piece of rocky, coastal property. She would say, "Whatever. He doesn't need to know. Just do it the way we want it and bill me." Then I would do just that, and he would hit the roof when they got the bill. As we moved forward, I tried pulling him in on several landscape design conversations, but he'd always say, "I'm not interested. Just deal with Ann." As soon as I wanted to talk money, though, he dictated all kinds of opinions and whined about not being listened to. Charming to the last. We ended up building a lovely garden, deck, and patios around their home, but the process was agonizing. Hey, at least I didn't have to live with him!

HOT-BLOODED

One couple I worked with each had very different styles. She was rather laid back, and he was pure emotion. They'd argue intensely, then two minutes later kiss and hug. Delightful, but whew! One morning as my crew and I were working on the back screening planting, we cut through the invisible dog fence. Now, in many instances this is sort of unavoidable, so it happens a lot. We always repair them within minutes, and we had warned the clients that this would probably happen since we were using machinery in a tight space and putting in large trees right where the wires ran. Of course, the fence alarm tripped, and the husband flew out of the house like a storm of angry wasps. He raced to the back where we were working and stood there screaming, swearing, and looking like he was on the verge of a stroke. He refused to listen to my explanation or reassurances. When he spied the cut end of the dog fence wire, he grabbed it and started ripping the wire out of the ground—25 feet, 50 feet, almost 75 feet before he started getting into roots and the ripping became more difficult. After yanking nonproductively a few times, he screamed in rage, threw the wire down in disgust, and stormed back into the house. We stood there, all of us, dumbfounded. The wife, who was on the rear deck, had watched this entire tantrum with complete impassivity. As I approached her, getting ready to say, "Oh my gosh, I'm really sorry, we'll fix it momentarily," she cut me off with a wave of her hand, gestured dismissively towards the husband with her coffee cup, rolled her eyes, and said, "His mother was hot-blooded too." With that, she winked and walked back into the house.

See? Never a dull moment.

FEAR FACTOR

Clients can be gun-shy. Some people want a garden but are convinced that nothing will grow for them. When someone's first foray into gardening is energized by hope and great expectations but ends up being a total failure, they often figure they just can't do it. Our job is to convince them otherwise, and sometimes it can take some convincing. Convey to the fearful ones that you have the horticultural knowledge to know which plant belongs where, and that when you match up the plant to the right site, plants actually *want* to grow. Convince them to look out at the world, 'cause growing is what nature intended.

SERVICE YOUR CUSTOMER, NOT YOURSELF

Great gardeners have told me that there is no way they could do what I do. They insist they would get too frustrated by wanting to do *x* when the client wants to do *y*. My answer? This is a service industry. You present options and possibilities to the clients, and they decide what is right for them. Do I ever think my clients choose poorly? Perhaps. But it's their home, their lives, their landscape, and their money. It is appropriate that the final decisions are theirs.

DESIGN WITH MAINTENANCE IN MIND

One thing I always take into consideration when I design is maintenance. Always consider the mowability of any garden design, whether the client or a service will do the mowing. Shoot for well-defined areas of lawn with no obstacles. The lawnmower should not have to jump any major hurdles or hardscape to go from one area to another. Functionally and aesthetically, simpler is always better.

I always ask potential clients if they do their own yard maintenance or if they use a service. If they use a service, will their service handle weekly, monthly, or seasonal garden maintenance? Find out. If they do their own maintenance, how much do they want to putter taking care of garden beds? Design for the level of maintenance that your clients can handle. If you burden them with too much, the installation will quickly degrade and begin to look poorly, the clients will eventually become unhappy, and your reputation will suffer.

If you're not sure who will maintain the gardens, you can suggest someone. Early on, I maintained a few of my clients' gardens; this was a great way to augment my income, make the clients happy, and learn how gardens perform when they aren't being watched over every day. This practice helped me to refine the palette of plants that I make selections from when I design a garden bed or border. I now know several people who do perennial garden maintenance, so I can refer clients to them. (This is truly an underserved area. If you think you would like to do perennial garden maintenance, contact every designer in a 25-mile radius and offer your services. You'd be surprised at how much you might enjoy this and how good an income you can make. You might even hire someone to help you, and you can make margin charging for their time. Double income!)

DESIGN COLLABORATOR OR ORDER TAKER

I remember a certain design-related scene from the television drama *Judging Amy*. Maxine Gray (played by the inestimable Tyne Daly) was meeting with a landscape designer, Ignacio Messina (Cheech Marin). In her pragmatic, take-charge way, Maxine said hello, walked Ignacio to the backyard, and proceeded to tell him at length what she wanted and didn't want. She handed him a plant catalog, saying she had circled the plants she liked. When Maxine finally finished, there was a pause as Ignacio gazed deeply into her eyes. At length he asked why she had hired him, why she hadn't instead hired a high school kid to buy and plant whatever she wanted. He explained that he was a design collaborator, not an order taker, and suggested that if she were to hire him, he would create for her something of splendor, something that would speak to her soul.

I, too, am a design collaborator, working to create a landscape tailored to my clients, to speak to their soul. I am not an order taker. Many design shows have the garden designer take a homeowner to a nursery to "pick out" plants. On one show I watched recently, every time the client liked a plant, the designer would agree that the plant was lovely but then tell the client why she couldn't have it—wrong exposure, wrong moisture requirements, wrong aesthetic. Uh, you think? Choosing plants for a garden isn't the same as choosing a soap dish and toothbrush holder to go with the bathroom paint. I do not take my clients "plant shopping." I bring them images of the plant selections I have made for their gardens, selections based on what I have gleaned about them in our meetings—what they like, what they don't like, preferred colors, habit, textures, styles—combined with the cultural requirements for each area on their property. It is science plus nature plus art, with a dash of psychology.

I admit, though, that I have done something that at least resembles plant shopping: I have taken clients on a tree safari. I actually called it that. We were looking for the perfect large specimen tree to be the front focal piece in my clients' large, new front drive circle. I had preselected about a dozen trees, all of which I knew would look lovely and grow well in the chosen location. I had suggested we all make the final choice together. (When you're spending many thousands of dollars for one tree, you want to love it.) The trip was a smashing success. We selected one glorious, towering American beech. The clients were delighted to visit a big, impressive specialty tree nursery, and I was delighted that we all knew they'd be thrilled with the tree when it arrived. And they were. Happiness all around.

We all react, to a certain degree, to our clients' idiosyncrasies. I suppose they, too, react to ours. But they have hired you for your expertise, talent, and opinions. You are driving this process, and you are in control. Always bear that in mind.

CHAPTER SIXTEEN

Construction: Where the Shovel Meets the Load

YOU'RE OFF! AT LEAST ALMOST. You have a client, an approved design, a subcontractor or two—now what? The journey of a thousand miles starts with a single step, and so does a landscape construction project. Most construction is a fairly linear process. Take home construction, for example: foundation before walls, walls before roof, and so forth. Although parts of almost any project can be done in tandem, for the most part think logical sequencing.

Let's say you're establishing a front foundation planting with a new walkway, adding a couple of ornamental trees, and installing a new front lawn with an irrigation system. After calling your local dig hotline (always! see call811.com for a list of phone numbers) and protecting existing trees and other plants or areas you want to avoid damaging or compacting during construction, here is your process in simple terms:

1. Demolish the stuff that is going away. Remove all demolition detritus from the property and recycle or dispose of it appropriately. Identify where trenches and piping need to go to accommodate irrigation, lighting and electricity, drainage, and so forth.
2. Conduct the work that requires the most infrastructure and messing up of the surrounding area. In this case it is excavating and building the new walkway, which includes adding piping or conduit under the walk to accommodate future irrigation lines

and electricity. The conduit acts as sleeves or tunnels for the lines to run under the hardscape. (Remember to do this whenever you build a walk or driveway. Clients frequently need to run electricity, water, or drainage under an existing piece of hardscape, and ripping it up is usually not a good option.) Prep and install the new walkway.

3. Do a rough grade for the gardens, plantings, and lawn (primarily because the area is now a bit of a mess from the walkway construction). Major irrigation lines and heads go in at this point. Loosen up compacted soil.

4. Plant the largest plant stock, the trees, first, then lay out and plant the shrubs. Hand-grade the planting beds again, and lay out and install the smaller perennial stock and annuals. Complete the garden irrigation. Do a final grooming of the now-planted beds. Mulch.

5. Finish grading the lawn areas. Get the last irrigation pieces in— control boxes, lines, heads, drip, everything. Make sure it all works. Grade the lawn areas smooth, again. Now you can sod or seed the lawn. Tweak the irrigation, set the timing—good to go!

Before the work starts, protect existing trees from machinery that will be used during construction.

6. Add "jewelry"—pots, furnishings, birdfeeders, and so forth. If you are working drip irrigation into the pots, do it now.

Something to keep in mind: if any large, heavy stock, like a good-sized tree, will need to be moved over the new hardscape, consider popping it in before the hardscape is in place. If you are unsure of finished grade at this point, just move the tree into the space temporarily, and keep it hydrated until the walk is completed and the grade is established. If you must wait until after the walk is installed, either lift the tree over the walk, or put a piece of heavy plywood over the walkway and roll the tree in that way.

In simplistic terms, that lays out a construction process. The more complex the job, the more steps, but you can pretty much figure out that the pool needs to go in before you build the patio that's going next to the pool. It's all logical sequencing.

If I am doing an entire property, I prefer to start in the back and work forward. That way we're not messing up the front we've just finished as we're working the back. However, most clients want the front of their homes looking spectacular as soon as possible, so in many instances you will need to work from front to back, or work the entire property at once. Detailed planning and good communication will keep everything from blowing up in your face.

GOOD PLANNING EQUALS GOOD IMPLEMENTATION

When you're starting out, you'll be excited to get the first job that takes longer than a day or two. But soon your name will get around, and clients will ask for more and more, and in no time you'll be building driveways, pools, additions, and docks, and juggling multiple subcontractors and materials deliveries from all over. This takes more planning.

Planning is the most important part of the implementation process. It takes such a little amount of time and can prevent all kinds of construction snags. Spend an hour or two, put a calendar in front of you, and lay out what you think is going to happen and when. Recognizing that you do not have control over everything that could happen during the course of the project (weather delays, materials snafus, subcontractors taking longer or shorter than anticipated), you should still have a solid feel for who you expect to come on to the job and when, the points at which you'll need deliveries of materials, inspections (if any), and completion of milestones, particularly those that relate to expected payments from your client. Lay this out in a format that you can easily understand, and be prepared to share this "macro project timing" with your subcontractors. Get assurances that they will work with you to achieve your optimal timing on the various project pieces.

I had a wonderful manager at my first corporate job. He would ask me to map out the recruiting programs in terms of time and expense. Once I'd identified all of the parts and meticulously planned out the pieces, laid out the timeline, and estimated the costs, he would review it all, compliment me, and say, "Add 30% to everything, then publish it." Initially I couldn't see the rationale in doing this, but then we got into project execution. Time nearly always ran over, and costs frequently ran over as we inevitably added elements to the recruiting initiative. That 30% buffer assured that we always came in on time and on or under budget, so we never had to ask the powers that be to approve more expense dollars. So why am I telling you this? Wouldn't better planning have alleviated this? Yes, but we couldn't predict everything, and neither can

Demolition can look pretty scary, both to you and to the client. Reassure them that it will eventually look gorgeous. Then make good on your promise!

you. Always allow for some "slush" in your project planning. That way, if something slips by a day or two, the schedule can easily handle the delay and still complete on time. You will not have control over everything, but if you plan for some delays, you can absorb most of whatever comes along without blowing your completion timing—or worse, your client's patience.

SHARE THE GOAL

When I meet with my subcontractors, either to get a quote or to start off their piece of the project, I walk them through the whole job. The first step is to share the goal. I give them a copy of the design layout, take them around the site, and explain how everything will look and function when we're done. I talk about optimal construction timing, when I will need their contribution, what materials we have chosen that they'll be working with. You can share ideas on where materials can be temporarily stored, if necessary. Talk over how you want the job left each day (tidied, all trash removed, tools put away, caution tape used where necessary, and so forth). Communicating your expectations and understanding what we're ultimately aiming for can really help your subcontractors comprehend how their part of the project comes together with all of the other pieces. Sometimes they'll provide construction suggestions that are tremendously helpful. In fact, I often solicit their help. "Hey, Al, we need to trench from the house down to the lower lawn, but we can't get a machine in here. What do you think is the best way to do this?" Listen to your subs. I can assure you, for the first few years that you are doing this work, your subs will have built many more landscapes than you have. Take advantage of their knowledge and expertise.

When we all share the vision, it makes the collaboration more meaningful and ultimately makes the end results easier to achieve.

COMMUNICATING DURING CONSTRUCTION

I touch base with each sub every day they are working on the site. I often send a fax to my subs the night before, calling some things to their attention, noting any discrepancies, special requests, or questions I may have, and I have trained my subs to expect this. Providing some communication in writing is always good, too—a written document is usually easier to understand than a long voice message, and when printed it can be used as a checklist.

Clients are usually reasonable as long as they are kept informed about what is going on, what is not going on, and how timing to completion is being affected. I do this face-to-face, by voice, or by e-mail. For example:

Subject: Landscaping Update
Date: 12 April 2008
To: Sally and Jack
From: Love Albrecht Howard

Sally and Jack,

Hi! The project is coming along nicely. A few quick updates:

- The propane company called and the tank installation was rescheduled for three days farther out. Your gas guy is available, so no problem with this.
- The granite piece for the stoop is ready early and will be delivered and installed on Friday; footings will be poured tomorrow.
- Note that we will finish grading once the soil has a few days to drain since the recent rains. Then it will be three days to get the irrigation lines installed, the nursery materials planted, and the lawn seeded. "Instant landscape!" <Wink!>
- Monday we'll be finished with the masonry, so if you would kindly have the check for Payment 4 ready, I would appreciate it.

We're still on track for a mid-June completion as long as the weather stays on our side! As always, call or e-mail with questions.

Best,
Love

Yes, I really do write notes like that, winks and all.

Sometimes the news is not so good, and a face-to-face meeting is warranted. When we had an entire building project turned down by the town because it did not meet the side set-back requirements from the property line, this was a huge oops. The architect had screwed up by not checking the set-backs, and I had screwed up by not checking on the architect (after all, he was my subcontractor). Two weeks before we had planned to start, we had to go back to the drawing board, literally. Come to find out we could not build anything in that location at all. Talk about mortifying. So I met with the clients and explained the situation. I took personal responsibility and apologized profusely. They were royally angry. I also walked in with several other options for them to consider that would make the area usable without falling under the zoning laws or requiring building department approval. We ultimately found a fabulous solution, and the clients were delighted, but getting there was not without pain, suffering, and a serving of well-done crow.

Communicate early and often (daily!) with your clients, and you'll avoid most of the pitfalls that can derail a construction project.

SHOW UP

You need to leave your office to supervise landscape construction. I know designers who try to manage construction from their offices. They are available by phone for consultation, but they are almost never in the field. Consequently they have frequent redos and rebuilds, or things get finished that aren't completely to their satisfaction. Recognize that your vision is subject to others' interpretation if you are not there to provide direction and feedback. Your subcontractors will appreciate the time you spend on-site with them. When you check in on the site, they receive pointed direction and timely feedback, which helps them accomplish their work faster and better, with virtually no guessing. It's also an opportunity for you to say thank you as things come together. You don't have to be on every site every minute of the construction process, but you need to invest face time and get out there every day.

Showing up also proves to your clients that you are, indeed, managing the project. When they see you talking with and directing the subcontractors, checking over the materials, and working through small issues as they arise, they know that you are doing your job and that they are receiving the value they are paying for.

Unless there is a reason, you should have someone working the site virtually every business day during the entire construction sequence.

If there is progress every day, your clients will be much, much happier. There is nothing I hate more than a construction crew who shows up for two days, then disappears for a week. Also, unless you have previously discussed otherwise, your subs should be prepared to spend the entire day at the site. Clients hate to see subs arrive at 8:00 only to leave at 10:00 and not return. So do I. Make sure you have an agreement with your subcontractors that they work the job until their portion is completed. Structure your payment terms to support keeping them on-site and working.

HOW DO I BUILD THAT?

You may be asking, "Okay, plan, communicate, show up. Got it. But how do I *do* this? How do I actually build a landscape?" Right. How do you complete the work? Entire courses cover how to do construction, and I am not going to attempt Site Work 101 here. Trust me, you will grow into the knowledge as you do this. Just like I did, you will start off with fairly small projects, but as you take on larger and more complex landscape construction jobs, they will require more expertise and more problem-solving. You will rise to it. As you delve deeper into this business, you will learn to seamlessly direct all kinds of site work. The one critical thing to remember: rely on your subcontractors. You do not have to hold all knowledge of how to do all things. You will quickly learn which subcontractors grade the best, who are your best irrigation teams, who you call to install the plant materials, which masons are optimal for flat work, and which craft the best freestanding walls. I never have one subcontractor take care of everything. I rely on each sub's specialty to put the pieces together to make a gorgeous whole.

There are industry standards for various pieces of landscape construction, and some vary by geography. For example, how you best plant a tree in New England is pretty much how you best plant a tree anywhere. But how you go about building a new driveway in Texas is quite different from how you build that same driveway in Vermont. The penetrating cold and tough winters in Vermont require a deeper excavation and more involved base preparation than you would need in a warmer climate. Again, rely on the knowledge and expertise of your subcontractors. As you are learning, I suggest you only call on contractors with established companies that are known to serve your area. They know the special needs of your locale and will have been doing the work long enough and well enough to have a proven track record. After a few years you will be able to quickly distinguish between a contractor who is shorting the job and a contractor who is doing the job right.

TOOLS OF THE TRADE
Every profession has its requisite tools, and garden design is no exception. Here are the tools I recommend for both field and office, though these lists are by no means complete:

For data collection
Reel measures (50 feet and 250 feet)
Tape measure (25 or 30 feet—purchase a good make, brightly colored so it's hard to lose)
Digital camera (at least 4 megapixels of resolution)
Clipboard
Pens, mechanical pencils

For design
Computer
Landscape design software (from $50 to many thousands)
High-quality color printer
Scanner
Fax machine
12- or 18-inch rulers (Imperial measure)
12-inch three-sided architect's ruler, straightedges, compasses
Colored pens, markers, pencils, lots of stationery
Access to an oversized color copier (ledger- or poster-sized copies)

For daily site work
Food and water, water, water
Clipboard, notepad, writing implements (never leave home without these)
Boots
Clean shirt and socks in a clear zipper bag
One or two old towels

Pruners (invest in a really good pair, and keep them in a holster to avoid losing them or putting holes in your pockets)

Folding pruning saw (again, a good one)

Garden spade

Trowel

Work gloves (preferably leather)

Selection of screwdrivers, pliers, wire cutters

Hammer

3- or 5-pound sledge

Scissors (garden scissors work well)

A few spikes, some nails, selection of screws, zip ties in several sizes, twine, wire

Electrical tape

Duct tape

Heavy-duty contractor trash bags (use for trash or impromptu rain poncho)

Two 10-by-12-foot tarps (I spread these out in the trunk of my vehicle, and we often need to borrow one for use on the job site)

Six 1-foot and six 3-foot wooden stakes

Sprinkler head and timer

Landscape-marking paint

Colored landscape tape (several types)

Caution tape

First aid kit (first aid spray, saline solution for eyes, antibiotic ointment, instant cold compresses, Band-Aids, tourniquet, analgesic, small container of dishwashing detergent)

Rain poncho or rain outfit

Umbrella

Light sun hat

Sunscreen

Insect repellant

Hard to believe, but this whole list of items for daily site work won't take up all that much room in your car or truck. Why all of this stuff? Because in any given week, you'll use a bunch of these items. Really. And you'll be sure to need that odd thing right after you take it out, thinking, "I won't need *that*." So think like a Boy Scout and be prepared.

Remember to put your name on all your supplies, or dip tool handles in brightly colored latex paint to show the world that they belong to you. Tools are notorious for getting misplaced, buried, or forgotten. Know what you're using, and make sure the last thing you do before leaving a job site is check to see you have all your tools.

LAS MACHINAS

You'll need to develop a familiarity with the machines and power tools commonly used in our industry. You do not need to own any of this equipment. Either your subcontractors and suppliers will already have the equipment, or you will rent what you need for a day or two (work this into your pricing). Find local sources for tool, equipment, and truck rentals, and go introduce yourself. Get a brochure and price list from each, take a look at their equipment, and make a note of whom you can call for what.

A compact tractor comes in handy when unloading plant stock from a delivery truck, and is critical when we're unloading trees.

Auger, power auger. Large two-man "drill" primarily used to excavate soil to accommodate concrete forms for deck, porch, and outbuilding foundations.

Backhoe, mini-backhoe. Multipurpose tractor with a front-mounted loading bucket and rear-mounted digging bucket on the end of an articulated arm.

Chainsaw. Portable electric or gas-powered saw with teeth linked to form a chain. Used commonly in logging and residential tree work. Also the best tool to cut landscape ties to length.

Chipper-shredder. Machine that takes in wood and yard detritus and shreds it into small pieces.

Circular saw. Hand-held saw used to cut wood.

Cut-off saw. Hand-held saw used to cut concrete, asphalt, and various types of stone.

Disk or chain trencher. Portable machine used by irrigation companies to trench and pull irrigation lines through a landscape.

Dump truck. Heavy truck for carrying loose bulk materials, with a hinged bed that allows the contents to be unloaded onto the ground.

Excavator. Self-propelled machine with an articulated digging arm and an upper section capable of rotation. The excavation arm digs, swings, and discharges material without moving the chassis or undercarriage. Available with different-sized buckets to dig holes or trenches.

Forklift. Industrial machine with a power-operated, forked platform that can be inserted under heavy loads to lift or move them. Fork attachments are also available for most small tractors and backhoes.

Moffett delivery. Method of delivering stone and other palleted materials using a flatbed truck equipped with a Moffett truck-mounted, portable forklift. Moffetts can move materials where trucks cannot go. Suppliers call these Moffett deliveries, and extra delivery charges usually apply. Moffett is a trade name of Cargotec Corporation.

Plate compactor, plate vibrator. Heavy, vibrating "plate" used to compact soils, base materials, sand beddings, and pavers, to promote stability and longevity of masonry.

Reciprocating saw. Saw with multiple blade attachments to cut through almost anything. Most common brand is Milwaukee's Sawzall.

Rock hammer. Electric drill for stone products that drills as well as impacts to bite into stone.

Rototiller. Motorized cultivator that uses rotating mechanical tines to break up compacted soil.

Spider. Delivery truck accessory with an articulated arm that picks up large or palleted materials, like stone, from a flatbed truck, and can drop the materials by swinging over some obstacles.

Stump grinder. Portable or truck-mounted machine that removes tree stumps using rotating teeth.

Tractor. Wheeled vehicle used in many applications, often as a mount for other equipment.

Wet saw, diamond-blade saw. Saw that cuts brick, tile, and stone using water to cool the blade and reduce dust.

DUMP TRUCK SIZES AND LOAD CAPACITY

SIZE	SAND, STONE, OR LOAM LOAD	MULCH LOAD
"one ton"	3 yards maximum	8 yards maximum
six wheeler	8 yards	10 yards
ten wheeler	18 yards	20 yards
tractor-trailer/ eighteen wheeler	28 yards	30 yards

Probably the second most useful machine in landscaping, the mini-excavator is perfect for digging ponds, trenches, holes for new trees, and anything else that requires excavation up to about 6 feet deep.

STAGING THE WORK, PITCHING IN, AND GETTING DIRTY

I always help unload the delivery trucks. I indicate where I prefer the stock should be staged for installation, although the crews usually know where materials should go. If possible, plants should be put in the shade because they'll be less stressed until they are installed. The guys know to group them, in neat rows, by variety. This makes counting them against the delivery slip easier and simplifies the deployment. "Seventeen *Astilbe* 'Ostrich Plume' to the backyard, left section, eleven to the front under the oak." Make sure plants are well hydrated before they go in the ground, and if this requires two hours of hand-watering pots with a hose, do it. It saves the plants stress and can minimize or eliminate transplant shock and death. (If plants come in really dry, call the supplier and let them know that this doesn't make you happy.)

Stone can be stored almost anywhere, but make sure it is not a safety hazard. Also ensure it does not block the client's drive, house access, or any street traffic.

The plants are nearly all installed. We're now at the point when the clients return home and exclaim with delight. The beautiful new landscape and gardens are finally real.

If you can avoid storing bulk materials (loam, mulch, stone dust, gravel), do it. Have a delivery arrive the morning you need the material, and plan to use it all and clean up the dumping area before the end of the day. You won't always be able to do this, but bulk materials that sit around can soak up a lot of water in a rain, making them heavy and messy to move and use. They can also erode and create a mess, or can create a dust hazard. And they are just unsightly. Prepare accordingly.

I lay out all of the work; I do not rely on my subcontractors to do this. This means that I draw the lines for every walkway (with landscape paint or stakes and string) and outline every patio, every driveway, and every parking area. I work with the irrigation guys to determine the various zones of coverage, the type of irrigation (broadcast or drip), and where the valve boxes will go (so they are easy to access but not in the client's face). I mark every planting bed, set every grade, and place every tree, shrub, perennial, and annual for installation. Guess that makes me kind of obsessive, but I am always happy with the finished landscape, and I do

At the end of the day I might actually give myself
permission to take a few minutes and sit in my own garden,
reflecting on the day's satisfying accomplishments.

not have the expense, hassle, or embarrassment of redos. If I just handed planting plans to another landscaping supervisor, gestured to the plants, and said, "Go to it," I would have to be satisfied with the results when I later returned to the site. Or I'd need to pull stuff out and redo it. That is not in my nature. For me, the best surprise is no surprise, so I supervise closely. My clients pay me well for my time and expertise, and I give them great service and excellent value. The landscapes that are built under my supervision are built right and look beautiful.

This is definitely the fabulously fun part of the job for me. I enjoy the crews, I enjoy the work, I enjoy the dust and muck and noise and physical labor. I enjoy being an integral part of the transformation. Heading home at the end of the day, filthy, dirt-encrusted, tired, and sore, is a tremendously satisfying feeling. While it's fresh on my mind, I make notes about what construction will be happening the next day. Sometimes I phone my own voice mail and leave notes to myself as I'm driving home. When I arrive back at my home office, I get ready for the next day. I call or fax subs, note my deliveries, make sure I have all of the contacts and phone numbers I might need, and stage my car for the morning (remove trash, add supplies, and so forth).

Once that's all done, I get to take care of me. I drink a ton more water, put my clothes in the laundry, crawl into a lovely hot shower, and emerge tired but refreshed, ready to do it all again tomorrow. It's a good life.

CHAPTER SEVENTEEN

When Things Go Wrong

I T HAPPENS TO THE BEST OF US, despite our great intentions. Something goes wrong. It could be a construction snafu, a mistake on an estimate, a disagreement with a client. A key subcontractor could walk off the job, leaving you in the lurch. Your job could get shut down by conservation or zoning officials. Your acre and a half of grading and hydroseed could be flushed downhill by an unexpected summer rainstorm. You might have just finished the most glorious garden installation, and three days later your client wakes to find everything has been eaten down to nothing by deer. Maybe you just completed demolition for the largest masonry installation of your career thus far. The morning you start to lay stone, the tragedy of 9/11 happens and six of your eight masons are National Guardsmen who are instantly called up. All of these scenarios happened to garden designers I know. The last one happened to me.

How you handle situations like this will test your maturity, resilience, and problem-solving capacity. You *can* handle these situations. Keep calm and carry on.

THE BUCK STOPS HERE

The freedom you enjoy being your own boss is tempered by the fact that when anything goes wrong, the buck stops with you. It can be the fault of your subcontractor, a screw-up by your supplier, an unexpected weather disaster. Whatever it is, you still have to accept responsibility and think through how to fix the situation. It's up to you to make it right.

If you have a situation that you cannot readily see a solution to, reach out to your fellow designers. If you don't yet have friends in the industry, landscape blogs may be able to provide answers. If nothing else, people will sympathize, and that counts for something. Misery does love company.

SNAFUS

The project is going along as planned, then suddenly—disaster. A mistake is made, an unforeseen situation arises, a huge complication happens. What do you do? Don't waste time or energy trying to assess blame. The buck stops with you, remember? Take a deep breath and evaluate the situation. In the first twenty minutes you should be able to figure out what has happened and recognize how this affects the project. If you and your subs can also identify what you can do about it, great. But

Heavy rains cut deeply into this embankment and nearly undermined the new stonework, which made the clients uneasy. We stabilized the bluestone steps, then filled in and planted the banking. No more issues with erosion.

even if you don't immediately know the solution, you need to tell the client. Remember my communication mantra? You need to be completely transparent with your client. Let them know what has happened, and reassure them that you will take care of it. If you do not have a strategy to fix the situation right at that moment, if you need time to figure out the solution or if you need to bring in another expert to take a look, tell your clients what you are going to do and when it will happen, and reassure them that you will let them know what the recommendation is. This is the time to drop everything else and take care of the problem. Nothing confirms your abilities as a project manager better than how you manage to rectify a problem.

If the clients are not at home when the situation happens, depending on the severity of the problem, you probably don't need to upset them at work. But you should call and make them aware that a problem has arisen. "Bill, hi, this is Love. We've uncovered a problem here at the house. Nothing fatal, but I would like to meet you when you get home from work and walk you through how we're going to take care of this. When might you be available tonight?" Be proactive, positive, and professional. The client still might hit the roof, but at least you are being honest and managing the situation.

Here's how *not* to handle it. My sister-in-law and her husband planned to totally renovate and add on to their two-hundred-year-old farmhouse in Baltimore. They had an architect develop plans, they had the requisite approvals, and they hired a contractor and wrote him a large check to start. The first thing the contractor needed to do was remove the tiny, dilapidated covered porch off the driveway side of the house. Really, the whole thing was about 15 feet long by 4 feet deep, with slender upright supports and a sagging little roof. The total amount of detritus to be removed would barely have filled a pickup truck. The contractor used a large backhoe to start pulling the porch off the house. He did not cut the supports, nor did he cut the nails, bolts, or ties that attached the porch to the house. He just ripped the porch off—and promptly pulled that entire end of the house off as well. Well, he didn't pull it off completely, but he pulled it 6 inches away from the bottom sill and both corners of the house. The wall was still attached along the roof. When my sister-in-law and her husband came home, they found the wall half ripped away, the porch hanging by a thread, and no sign of the contractor. The contractor disappeared with their money and was never heard from again.

Obviously this is no way to handle business. Wonder why contractors get a bad rap? Some of them deserve it.

WHEN IT IS MY FAULT

If you or one of your crews has made a mistake, fixing that mistake will probably cost you money. Say you had a crew doing grading and the machine operator backed up too far and took out four sections of the new fence. That might cost you $1500 to fix, but it is just money. Call the fence company and have them come the next morning. Tell them you need to get the new pieces manufactured and installed as soon as possible, and find out how much it will cost. Then line up a painter to stain the new sections the day after they are installed. Let the clients know you have handled it, apologize again, and reassure them that it will cost them nothing.

WHEN IT IS NOT MY FAULT

Unforeseen scenarios can arise, particularly during excavation. At one point my crew and I were excavating for a large, new deck that was going to terrace down a small hillside. As we excavated for the footings towards the bottom of the hill, we uncovered an old septic tank that no one knew was there. Because of the height at which it was sitting, we couldn't construct the deck over it, so it had to be removed. We let the client know what the situation was, reminded them that it was outside of our contractual agreement, and gave them a rough estimate of the additional cost. (This generated a change order.) Demolition and removal of the tank cost a full day of labor for three men, plus a machine, trucking and disposal, and backfilling with soil. It also took about six hours of my time, plus margin. The clients ended up paying around $3500.

WHEN FAULT IS DEBATABLE

It was early summer, and we'd just finished regrading and seeding about two-thirds of an acre on a gentle slope in my client's backyard. At the end of the day, an unexpected and violent thunderstorm ripped through, dumping nearly 3 inches of rain in less than two hours. Some of the new grading and just about all of the seed went oozing down the hill, into the neighbor's side yard and driveway, and on down the street. Not good. Unhappy client, unhappy neighbor, and potentially unhappy city if any officials were to see eroded soil on the street or running into storm drains.

We couldn't get in there to regrade until the soil dried out a bit. Our solution was to immediately clean up the neighbor's property and the street—shovels, blowers, hoses, and crew to the rescue! After waiting a few days for the soil to drain, we returned, regraded the client's backyard by hand, top-dressed with several yards of additional loam, reseeded, refertilized, and hoped for a week of drier weather.

It cost about $2500 total for labor, seed, loam, and organic fertilizer. But the problem had been caused by an act of nature, so who should pay? Since this weather snafu could not have been predicted, and since I took care of the problem professionally and immediately, I added it

A manufacturing flaw caused some of the concrete pavers from this batch to crumble. The clients freaked, but we made a few phone calls and sent a few e-mails, and the manufacturer stood behind their product 100%. After we replaced the bad pieces and resealed the entire drive, it was gorgeous yet again.

to my client's final bill and explained that I was not charging for my time, just looking to recoup my out-of-pocket costs. Luckily my clients understood.

THE CLIENT FROM HELL

Most of your client relationships will be wonderful. Keep the communication frequent, open, and honest, and you will arrest almost any negative situation before it begins to fester. But there are times that, despite all of your hard work and good intentions, it can get ugly.

I have shared a few client mini-nightmares with you, but what do you do when the relationship degrades to an untenable level? Make sure you try to talk with them. Communication is critical, and if a client feels like they haven't been kept in the loop, they sometimes flip. At times people just need to vent and be heard in order to have their feelings validated. If this is the case, let them vent completely. During the rant, say nothing. Some just want you to know they are upset. Sometimes they want to hear, "I am sorry. What can I do to make this up to you?" And once they do, they chill.

If you have tried hearing them out, apologizing (whether they deserve it or not), sucking it up, and taking it, if you have attempted to work out a solution to make them satisfied and yet the client still refuses to be reasonable, what do you do? If it appears you are never going to reach a healthy equilibrium with a client, save your self-esteem, energy, and pride, and end it.

Resigning from a client is never easy. The right thing to do is to tell the client in person. If you are working with a couple, ideally they should both be there. (Warning: This might be the hardest thing you've ever done.) Sit down with them. This is a conciliatory posture and is much less confrontational than standing. Address them honestly, tell them that the relationship is obviously not working from either of your perspectives and that you think it best to end it. Let them know that you will leave the site clean and send them a financial reconciliation within two days. They may be completely flabbergasted. "We had no idea it was that bad. We don't want you to leave!" You need to assess whether it's worth it to make another try. Whether you give it another attempt, or cut and run, at least when you have sat with the clients face-to-face, they can never impugn your integrity. Conduct yourself like a professional to the end.

If you end it, your heart will tell you to get in your car and drive away from the clients and the site as quickly as possible. You have to fight this urge, because you need to tie up loose ends and exit like a professional. You'll feel so much better about yourself and the situation if you do. Tidy up and leave the site clean. Have your subs quickly finish what they are working on if they can complete the work in one day; otherwise, have them stack materials neatly, cover whatever should not get wet, clean up any detritus from the site, remove their tools, and leave. If the clients have paid for the materials that have still not been installed, leave them there. If the client has not paid for the materials (in which case, shame on you for getting behind on collecting payments) and if it will cost more to remove the excess materials than they are worth, leave them. If there is any area that is dangerous to leave unfinished, then fill in, protect, or otherwise secure the area. Remove any signage you or your subs have on the premises, take photographs of *everything* exactly as you are leaving it, and then enjoy a sigh of relief as you drive off into the sunset.

As soon as you return to your office, catch your breath and stop beating up on yourself. Now is the time to be proactive. Re-create a timeline of everything that transpired between the start of the job and your exit. Do it now while your memory is fresh. Document the work, reactions, conversations, e-mails, every piece of the project while it was under construction. This degree of detail can save your butt if your clients decide to take any action against you. Note that the sit-down resignation process will often avert any kind of legal action, because the clients will have seen that you treated them fairly and will feel like you listened to them. Lawsuits are frequently instigated by someone feeling as though they have not been heard. Yes, that may be stupid and juvenile, but it's real.

Take a look at the payment situation. If you are doing milestone payments, you should still be ahead of the money, and if the work hasn't been completed you may need to return some money to your client. If so, make sure you know what you owe your subs and suppliers, calculate what has been spent and what is still outstanding, and make sure you retain your portion of the fee that you have earned. Explain all of this in a detailed letter, make sure you include an apology for not being able to work together, wish them well, and enclose a check. Do this quickly and cleanly, within twenty-four hours if not sooner. Make sure to keep photocopies of everything, including the check. If they owe you money, do the same reconciliation, enclose it with a letter stating how much you regret that you couldn't work together, and ask for a final payment to cover your out-of-pocket expenses. Don't hold your breath at this point. You may or may not ever see this money. If it is not a huge amount, consider letting it go.

If the clients feel they were treated badly, or if they think the monetary situation was not in their favor (which is usually how they will feel, no matter how fair you were), they can take you to court. Make sure that if this were to happen you would be able to show your receipts for materials and labor, all of the communications you had with the client, the reconciled financials, a copy of any invoice for monies due or check for monies paid back, as well as the photographs you took when you left the site. If you can show that you conducted yourself professionally and in good faith, it will go a long way in any lawsuit.

One last thing. Once you have started to recover and gotten maybe a week's perspective, sit quietly, try to put the anger and resentment aside, and write down what you learned from this. Any "failure" you learn from is not true failure; it is a learning and growing experience. Do a little postmortem, and ask yourself some questions. Where did the job start to go sour? What was the first indication that the clients were unhappy, and what could you have done differently at that point? If you were the client, how would you have reacted to the situation? What would you have wanted your contractor to do? How can you prevent a similar situation from developing in the future? This can be an extremely worthwhile exercise, and spending the time to actually write it down can reinforce the lesson of it, and be cathartic as well. Define what happened, learn from it, then give yourself permission to move on.

TEMPERAMENT

If this job were easy, anybody could do it. At times it is really tough work—and I have held some tough jobs, so I am making a fair comparison. Are you wondering if you have the right temperament? I think I've drilled in long and hard that this job really isn't about the plants we so dearly love, it's about providing a service.

I know some gentle souls who are quite successful in this business. Just because you are sweet doesn't mean you can't do this. Like tends to attract like. One of my garden design friends is a darling, soft-spoken soul, and her clients tend to be equally sweet and gentle. I have a fiery, passionate disposition and tend to attract passionate clients. It makes for some great exchanges but can also be a recipe for disaster. I circumvent most potential conflict by being communicative and transparent, and by maintaining a sense of humor. I let the clients know just about everything that is going on so that they feel they are in the loop, understand I am in control of the project, and stay cool.

WARRANTEES, GUARANTEES

All of my subs who do hardscape installation guarantee their materials and workmanship for anywhere from one to five years. If I have ever needed some rework, I have always had complete cooperation from my subs. This is another reason to deal with established companies who plan to be around for a while.

My personal guarantees are limited to the plantings. I give my clients the option to purchase plant insurance. The insurance costs roughly 10% of the total cost for plants plus installation, and all plants—except for annuals and tropicals, of course—are included. There is no policy behind the insurance, there is just me.

A few years ago I completely renovated a gorgeous overgrown yard. The client adored me at first, but by the end of the installation she had turned on me. As I found out later, she was known for burning through subs and workers of all kinds. I never understood what I had done, or hadn't done, to make her so horrid to me. The installation was gorgeous when we were finished (even she admitted that), and because she had a collapsed timeframe, we did the install quickly (she admitted we did well with that, too). Everything settled in beautifully that summer, and the plants were guaranteed until June of the following year.

That winter we had one of the most bitterly cold winters ever. The temperature dropped below 0°F and sat there for days. For one week the high was 14°F, and the low was –16°F. Some local harbors even froze over.

As you can guess, that winter was particularly hard on plants. Most landscapers and designers said all bets were off and wouldn't guarantee anything, but I was determined to see it through. In the spring I went from client site to client site checking things out. For the most part the damage wasn't crippling. Even though I lost many mature shrubs in my own yard, most of my client sites fared okay. Except for one: yeah, the woman who detested me.

A section of her plantings were on the windy corner of the house. Between the bitter cold and the relentless winds, the broadleaf evergreens really took it on the chin. She called me that spring spitting mad and ready for a cat fight. I agreed I would come over and we would walk the property together. Dozens of shrubs were toast. I knew most of them would live, but they'd look scrawny for at least a year. Still, I stood by my guarantee. She didn't want the plants replaced, she wanted the money. Because it was her, and because I wanted this all behind me, I itemized the plants that looked miserable and gave her a check for the entire amount.

When I went by her home for the last time, I handed her the itemization and the check. She looked me straight in the eye and said, "Well, I must say, I heard that just about every landscape contractor and nursery reneged on their warrantees this year. But you stood by yours. I'll give you credit, you have a lot of integrity. You should be proud of that."

I was, and I am. My word is my bond. Yours should be too.

CRITTERS GREAT AND SMALL

Deer, rabbits, groundhogs, and gophers can do a number on a planting. When you are assessing a property, look for tracks, scat, and other signs of what critters you'll be dealing with at the site. One poor woman I saw on a gardening show said she often had thirty-five deer in her yard at a time. It looked like February in her yard in mid-June! Everything was nibbled down to the wood. Even the wood.

Rabbits are pickier eaters than other grazing creatures. They do love hostas, but with the exception of vegetable plantings, for the most part they leave much of the rest of the plantings alone (unless the plants you put in are flush with new spring growth—they really love those new shoots). Most of the rabbits found in my clients' gardens don't bother too much.

Groundhogs, also called woodchucks (or whistlepigs, for their shrill alarm whistle), are another story. These ground-burrowing squirrels can be big (4 to 14 pounds), they are entirely vegetarian, and they can mow down a new planting in the blink of an eye. I have noticed that aside from just about anything in my vegetable garden, they greatly prefer herbaceous perennials that are often listed as medicinals: echinacea, rudbeckia, valerian, and so forth. They have been known to climb trees and fences to get to food. I've seen them nimbly climb 5 feet of fencing to slip right into my vegetable garden. Annoying to say the least.

Tenacious little varmints, gophers can dig up a lawn or new planting faster than your landscape crew. Most "controls" resort to trapping or poisoning. Some deterrent suggestions are effective. One friend who tried the recommendation of putting mothballs down all the tunnel openings said it worked beautifully: the smell prevented *him* from going into his backyard for weeks! (The gophers, however, remained happy and completely entrenched.) Fencing is not a solution, nor is sending water or poisonous gasses into the tunnels. You are much more likely to damage yourself, the property, or the neighbors' property. If you have a client with a gopher problem, talk with them about what they are willing to do. Hiring a professional exterminator may be the best bet. You can also try electronic or sonic repellants, which are effective for some locations.

As a gardener you will probably know which plants are the most vulnerable to critter browsing in your locale. If you are designing a planting plan and you see signs of these various foragers, design your plantings to consist primarily of plants they do not care for. Although hungry deer will eat virtually anything, if other forage is available, for the most part the deer will not eat the varieties they don't particularly like. You know, kind of like humans at a buffet.

I am careful about the annuals I plant, and I ring a lot of the plantings I design with perennial varieties not preferred by gnawing critters, so animals often will not venture deeper into the bed or border. Ornamental grasses, daylilies, and many highly scented perennials like perovskias, salvias, and agastaches are almost never bothered by animals. Anything with volatile oils or milky sap are usually avoided, and succulents (*Sedum*) are nearly always shunned, although deer will tromp them into the ground when eating something else. Both bearded and Siberian iris are usually spared, as are furry-leaved things (*Verbascum, Stachys byzantina*) and poisonous plants (*Aconitum, Digitalis*).

There is a lot of information about critter- and deer-proofing to be found on the Web. Just keep in mind that no plants are 100% deer proof, and many deer-proofing products are stinky, annoying, unsightly, or need constant replenishment. You could actually supplement your design-build business by offering deer-proofing at regular intervals, though this wouldn't be my preference for making a buck.

I am completely against using the predator urine that is sold for this purpose. It is collected from caged wild animals, and the process is incredibly inhumane. Human urine works just as well (or just as poorly, depending on your particular experience), and you or your clients can volunteer to spill *that* around a planting all you want, assuming the neighbors don't cite you for indecent exposure. Any water-soluble, scent-based repellant requires frequent reapplication, to the point of annoyance, and many times won't work anyway. The rotten egg, oil, and garlic recipe (Google it) works, but it also really stinks. Scent-based repellants should deter the wildlife, not the people. I still think the best way to deter munchers is to choose plant materials carefully.

The only way to really stop deer is to fence the planting. Fencing to keep out deer needs to be 8 feet high and come to within 8 inches of the ground. To me, it isn't worth the hassle, so I design plantings that are full of plants deer do not particularly care for, then watch and see.

Winter foraging can be worse than the active growing season, as deer nibble down shrubs and mark their territories by slashing at trees with their antlers. I have saved several clients' shrub and tree plantings by installing a seasonal surround of layered monofilament (fishing line). The deer cannot see the line and are confused and repelled when they hit it. I put 8-foot metal gardening stakes 10 feet apart around large tracts of plantings, then run the monofilament around the entire area. I start the line at 8 inches, then run another at 2 feet, 4 feet, 6 feet, and at the very top. I remove this in late spring. You can barely see this during the winter months, and this treatment has spared woody plantings that had formerly been ravaged every winter.

Fair warning: even when you do all of the above, it is hard to stop a game trail. If your client has a well-worn path that is used regularly by these marauders, it will be difficult to persuade them to go another way. If you cannot plan the gardens to live with the critters, then tall, solid fencing might be the only solution. (Unless the clients are willing to consider getting a dog. Dogs work really well.)

Flocks of Canada geese are a terrible nuisance, and once again, we've done it to ourselves. These are magnificent migratory birds—flocks in perfect formation herald winter as they head 2000 miles to their southern feeding grounds. But in the mid-twentieth century when amnesty was granted to the Canada geese who had been kept in captivity for live decoying, it turned out they had lost the instinct to migrate. So they stayed around and had families. Big families. A pair of Canada geese can have three to twelve chicks per year. They reach reproductive maturity by age three, and their expected life span is twenty years. That's a lot of geese. The average Canada goose weighs 20 to 25 pounds, and each one can produce 4 pounds of slimy, gooey poop per day. That's a lot of poop.

Although the geese can be aggressive, particularly if they have goslings, the main annoyance is goose poop, otherwise known as goop. Dropped all over a lawn, goops do not dry out fast, they are gooey and nasty, and they are most unpleasant to step on.

Canada geese prefer open, grassy areas near a source of water. We have had great success keeping geese off client lawns by a number of methods. Motion-activated sprinklers, sirens, and other loud noises are of little use, since the geese get used to them quickly, and the noise is mostly annoying to the neighbors. Dogs work beautifully, particularly herding dogs like border collies and Australian shepherds. If your client doesn't want a 24/7 goose-chasing pet, however, they can hire services to come in several times per week, dogs in tow, to round up and scare off geese. Such services are pretty successful, though not as successful as a resident dog. We have also used low "goose fences" that deter the adults from coming up from the water source into the cultivated landscape. We construct the fencing about 18 to 24 inches high made of panels of unobtrusive dark mesh, and we provide a 5-inch open space at the bottom to allow turtles, snakes, and other critters an easy way under the barrier. Local conservation officials have been happy to approve this type of fencing, and it has worked beautifully to dissuade the geese from coming up onto the lawn.

Mice and voles do most of their damage to our plantings in the winter. In their subnivean habitat, small mammals like mice, voles, and shrews have an active winter life between the snow cover and the ground. The winter highways left by these animals can be easily seen when the snow melts down to about an inch. The damage comes when they tunnel into a crown of something they find delectable, like your client's favorite $50 hosta. They will eat out the entire crown of pips, leaving just the lower roots in a sad, empty, bowl-like depression.

The worst winter we had for vole damage here involved tons of snow. It was fabulous for the woody plants above ground but really bad for the herbaceous perennials. We lost dozens of hostas, and even hundreds of Siberian iris, which are usually a sure bet against critter damage. There isn't a lot you can do to end winter damage from these pests. If you're worried about some special hostas or tulip bulbs, plant them completely caged in hardware cloth (stiff metal with ½-inch openings). I have also heard that if you surround crowns or bulbs completely with builders' sand, voles will not tunnel through that, but I don't have personal proof that this works.

Other grand munchers include moose and caribou (elk). These large animals can eat a great deal of vegetation. My only advice is this: don't annoy any moose, particularly during rutting season. Let them eat what they want. If a herd of elk is threatening plantings, little will deter them, save stout fencing. Good luck with those!

Insects can also be quite the pestilence. The biggest nuisances in my area are the tree-munching caterpillars of winter moths, gypsy moths, and canker worms. Most trees can suffer 30% defoliation without suffering greatly. If the tree isn't stressed by other factors, like drought, extreme heat, or unusual winters, it should recover from the onslaught. I choose to let nature take its course most of the time, but the occasional intervention with a biological control can be warranted during extreme times. Learn to watch for signs of infestations that could cause long-term damage. After several years of drought, plus a few brutal winters, I feared I would lose the six 150-year-old white oaks that line the front of my property if there were yet another year of caterpillar defoliation. My favorite tree guy suggested a specific *Bacillus* product, and it worked beautifully. The trees got the break they needed, and we avoided killing everything around them.

Although some insects can be harmful, most are beneficial. Ants, for example, are one of the best soil conditioners on the planet, providing nature a much needed cleanup service; you do not need to kill them. Neither honeybees nor garden worms are native to North America. Categorically they are invasive exotics, but they do good things, so when you see them be grateful.

THE PLANTS WON'T GROW

What happens if you do an entire planting and nothing grows? Well, let me assure you that this doesn't happen. I mean, plants can die from lack of water or too much water, occasionally they can get a fungus or disease or be mown down by a munching critter of some kind, but plants don't just refuse to grow. They want to grow, and this is good, because it makes our jobs much easier.

Tell your clients this about plants: the first year they sleep, the second year they creep, the third year they leap. This is a really good rule of thumb with most perennials, woody or herbaceous, because the first year they spend time and energy getting acclimated to their new environment. As they do so, they are working to spread out their roots into the surrounding soil. Only when the plant has good roots and is well beyond the shock of transplant will it then push out abundant growth and flower with abandon. Patience is required for maximum payoff.

If a plant is truly languishing, there is a reason. Assuming the plant is receiving the amount of sunlight it needs, and isn't a full-sun plant that has been mistakenly popped into a dense shade garden, it is probably a water problem. You should be able to readily tell if the plant is stressed (or toast!) from too little water. And that's an easy one to remedy: water it. If the problem isn't too little water, it may be that the plant may be sitting in too much water. Either the irrigation is way too generous and isn't allowing the soil time to drain between watering events, or the plant is sitting in a particular spot that isn't draining. With the exception of water- or bog-loving plants, most plants do not like wet toes.

To check this out, dig up the affected plant. Are the root tips white? If so, that's a good sign. If they are beige to brownish, particularly if the ground is very wet or smells like a swamp, you have too much water and anaerobic conditions are probably rotting the roots. Now replicate your test hole several other places in the planting. If every hole has this same problem, check your client's irrigation schedule for this zone, and cut it back. If only the hole near the plant has the telltale signs of too much water, you might need to improve the drainage in that area, or even in the whole bed. If it's the whole bed, take out the affected plants, double-dig the soil to a depth of about 18 inches, mix in compost, and replant. Compost can fix nearly any problem soil. It helps sandy soils retain moisture, and it helps clayey soils drain excess moisture, all while giving new plants a great boost of nutrients.

It will be incredibly infrequent that the plants in your designs don't grow. Most often you'll have the opposite problem, with clients calling to say, "But the plants are all touching, and my gardens are overgrown!" I have had countless potential clients invite me to their homes to tell me their gardens are "overgrown," when really their gardens are positively glorious. That's when you teach people that having plants actually covering most of the ground is what we are going for. Having plants shade and cool the surface of the bed saves water, prevents many weed seeds from germinating, and looks lush and verdant. I love a dense, luxuriant planting.

So trust me, you are a horticulturist first and a designer second. You know how to garden. The plants in your designs will grow.

CONTINGENCIES

One thing I have worried about is what would happen to my business if I was severely injured or incapacitated—or heaven forbid, killed. I don't like to think much about it or feed the possibilities any energy, but, well, stuff happens. No one else is familiar with my business financials, no one knows what I am owed or by whom, nor does anyone else know what I owe my clients. If your garden design business has you working as a lone wolf, as I do, I suggest you find someone you can swap this information with, or set up a document in your computer and let the main people in your life know where the document is and how to access it. I just did this, and I'm sure I should have done it at the very beginning. Make a habit of updating this document every week, and maybe even e-mail it to, say, three main contacts. If anything were to happen, it would be great if my loved ones knew that the Martins owe me a milestone payment of

$16,000, the Sturretts owe me $1800, I need final payment of $2650 from the Rodricks, and I received a design retainer of $3200 from the Gordons and have not started the work. In a nutshell, those would be my receivables, and also what I owed back to any client. My husband, or other agent, would instantly know that my business needs to bill and collect a total of $29,450, and in the event I am incapacitated for some time, that he would need to refund $3200 to the Gordons. This would help prevent any undue financial hardship from falling on my family, since there would be supplier and subcontractor bills to pay. Your agent should also know how to refer business to someone who could, say, finish an install for a client you might have in the construction process.

In 2000 a friend of mine was hit by a car and nearly killed. He had severe brain damage and was not expected to live. His one employee at the time kept his installations going and the money flowing. My friend survived, and over time rebuilt both his brain and his life, and since his employee kept his business on life support, it didn't go under. It's always good to have backup, because bad stuff happens.

Conversely, what would happen if your client died? This is a singularly good reason for not working far ahead of the payments, particularly on a milestone schedule. It is also another reason for getting a signature on the original estimate, and keeping track of your payments to date. You can always hit up the surviving spouse or the estate for the outstanding monies owed, but you may have to wait a while for payment.

THINGS WILL GO RIGHT

If you call your local dig hotline (see call811.com for a list of phone numbers), work with reputable subcontractors, get permits for things that require permitting, keep getting your payments on time, watch the weather, and consciously think through the steps each of your projects will require, you'll avoid 98% of the problems that can hinder other garden design businesses. That means that the lion's share of your waking, working hours will go right. Sure there will be problems and little gaffes, but they just keep things interesting.

CHAPTER EIGHTEEN

The Business Grows

A NUMBER OF INDICATORS WILL TELL YOU when your garden design business is finally a viable entity. For me, one sign was that I had a steady stream of new client inquiries. I also felt like I finally knew what I was doing, even though I was still constantly learning. My jobs were profitable, and I was starting to make a tidy living. And finally, I had satisfied clients who were calling me back to do additional work and recommending me to their friends. I had started with a niche business, but the projects I was taking on were getting larger and more complex. I was a niche no more!

This is an exciting time, when you know this new life form, your business, is going to make it. Now the question is not whether the business will survive but whether *you* will survive. Steep learning curves, insistent clients, schlepping from one site to another, juggling subcontractors, managing money in and money out, being consumed by constant demands, wanting to be all things to all people while trying to maintain some balance with your personal life. Can you keep up this pace? The simple answer is, probably not.

THE SHORT-TERM FIX

As your business grows and you take on more, there will come a time when you have so much to do all of a sudden that you freeze like a doe in headlights. We've all been there. The way to move past this momentary inertia is to take one task that you know you can complete, and finish it. It might not be a critical task, it might not be something that needs to be done immediately, but it needs to be one that you can finish. Sometimes this is all that's required to snap out of a maxed-out stupor and function again, and this is so much more productive than laying your head down on your desk and weeping.

Another way to get a handle on overwhelming work is to make a list of all of your deliverables for the remainder of that week. Sometimes defining the work can help you to get some perspective on it. Then, live in the moment, and complete what you can. Don't think about everything that's trying to crash down your door. Instead concentrate on what you need to do today. Small steps will get you there.

After the crisis has passed and you can think again, the first thing you'll do is convince yourself that it wasn't all that bad and that you can handle it next time. Trust me when I say that this is complete self-delusion. Nearly every spring even we seasoned garden design professionals get into a couple of weeks or even months that are sheer insanity. We do get through it—whatever doesn't kill us makes us stronger, right?—but at what cost? You need to try to maintain some control and balance.

There comes a point when you cannot work any harder and need to work smarter. You either need to pace yourself, which will involve saying no to some of those demands coming at you, or rely on help from other people. It's time to soul-search a bit and ask whether you want to restrict your business growth or look to hire help.

RESTRICTING GROWTH

If you decide to restrict the growth of your company so that you can handle it all, you can accomplish this in several ways. You can go back to being a niche provider, and specialize in something you really love to do—say, water gardens. Then, only do water gardens. Oh, you wouldn't have to just design and build water gardens, you could also maintain water gardens, do season plantings around and in the water gardens, and create water gardens for other designers (be a subcontractor). This would maintain your income stream even in relatively tough economic times. Look at your business plan, review both the name of your company and how you are marketing your business, and rework everything to support your new goals.

You can restrict the geographic area you service. At one time I had clients from New Hampshire to Cape Cod, which was sheer insanity. The schlepping really did almost kill me, and what I realized was that the time I was spending on the highways of Massachusetts—whether I was traveling 70 miles per hour or 7 miles per hour—was time lost from my life. There's only so much you can accomplish from a cell phone. I knew that keeping up this pace would age me, as it had certainly aged my car. It also didn't make sense for me financially. If you look at the soft costs for servicing clients out of your general geographic area, it makes no sense. You lose hours of your own time, hours of crew time (and if you are paying them portal to portal, that is lost money that is hard to recoup, even though you charge the client for it), and you have increased fuel costs, additional wear on your vehicle, and major wear on your ability to endure. You lose patience with the job (and all of your other jobs) because of the long schleps and stress of being on time. Think hard about where you are willing to work.

You can become very selective about the clients you take, setting some criteria that every potential client needs to meet. I now only work with a

A wedding was to take place here in ten weeks, and we had to transform "rubble and weeds" into "wonderful." I called in a few favors and brought in a lot of help—and both the wedding and the site were huge successes.

client if I sense I will like them, if they are in my determined geographic range (which is way smaller than New Hampshire to the Cape), and if their project offers some interesting design and installation potential. This has cut my number of clients down by more than 50%, but I am making more money and enjoying the work—and my life!—more.

You can resign some of your regular annual gigs, assuming you have these, if they aren't profitable for you, are geographically undesirable, or require you to work with clients who are less than fun. How do you bid a client adieu? Be honest. Okay, if they are royal pains in the petoot, I do not suggest offering those particulars, since you do not want to burn bridges. In that case, embellish a little. Tell them you are centering your business closer to home now and will no longer be able to service their area. Or tell them you'll be working a large project (in the other direction) that will monopolize your time for the next two years. Yup, that's a white lie, but it works. Always tell them it was a pleasure working with them, thank them for any kindnesses, and then, aloha.

Not long ago I amicably divorced a client who was one of the most punishing people I have ever encountered. She had ripped my face off more times than I can count. (I realized early on that this was just her way, that she did this to everyone, but it was still hard to keep that in perspective.) I kept her because her next-door neighbor had also become my client, and I loved the next-door neighbor. So I guess I suffered with the pain in order to get the pleasure. Finally, it just didn't make sense to do their sites anymore; they truly were geographically undesirable, and I was tired of making the schlep. I respectfully resigned both accounts in the fall to give both clients plenty of time to find someone to do their patio and front porch plantings the following spring. The lovely woman was sorry to see me go, but amidst hugs and tears she was a doll and wished me well. The difficult client—well, you could have knocked me over with a feather, but she sent me one of the loveliest notes I have ever received. The note explained that I helped her realize her vision, that her gardens had never been prettier, and that I was always cheerful and funny and made her feel good about things. Wow. Could have fooled me those six or seven years when she was verbally flaying me alive.

If you do resign a client, it is courteous to make an effort to help them find someone else. You don't need to kill yourself to do this, but be ready to offer names of a few other designers that your soon-to-be-ex-clients could call. Make sure you clear this with any designer friends you are going to be referring them to, or at least give them fair warning.

A caveat. If you decide to restrict your growth, recognize that unless you are meticulous about it and strict with yourself, you will again get in over your head and be right back where you started. It is particularly difficult to say no when doing so means saying no to income. This may be a conversation you have with yourself every year for a few years, which may be the time you need to either get the no-growth thing right, or to admit that your company will be growing despite your best intentions and that it's time to look for help.

LEARNING TO ACCEPT HELP

I have been amused by the number of well-meaning friends and family members who have offered to help me with the administrative side of my work. Ha! That is the least of my problems. I always communicate with subs and clients, and stay on top of paperwork. Always. That is the easy, well-defined part of my job.

What I need help with is the schlepping and needing to be in two—or three!—places at once. Racing around to hand-select tree stock, find the right stone, choose the perfect paint color, check out annuals for next week's wedding planting, meet a client whose job is completed but they have a question—all the while knowing I need to check on a landscape crew doing plantings in one town, another team doing masonry at a different site, and an arborist doing tree work in still a third. How do you keep your projects on track while maintaining your sanity? This is project management at its most crazed. You spend most of the day roaming from job site to wholesaler site and back again, afraid each phone call will bring yet another task you need to complete or place you need to be. You are barely staying on top of things, and you know something critical is about to fall through the cracks. You recognize you cannot clone yourself, and there are no additional hours in the day, so what do you do? You get help.

I am a bit of a control freak—my friends call it The Virgo Curse—so detail and precision are important to me. If you are going to rely on another person to help supervise the work, the ability to trust and let go needs to be in your nature. Or at least you need to work on bringing this into your nature, as I have done. I have learned to let go quite a bit, but the parts of the job that require interpreting what the client wants (picking out large specimen trees, laying out the exact patio shape, selecting the three stone samples I need to bring to next week's materials discussion) still require my personal attention. The Virgo Curse lives on.

If you are hiring professional, proven subcontractors, you will have several talented crew chiefs in the teams you hire. Learn to trust them to make some decisions when questions arise. If you've walked them through the entire job at the beginning, they will understand your vision for the project and know how their piece fits into the whole. Still, a good project manager should check in every day and make sure everything's on track. This doesn't mean that I question crew motivation or throughput. My trusted crew members know the level of quality my jobs demand; they are motivated workers, and they see it through. But I wouldn't dream of leaving them entirely alone, because I wouldn't be fulfilling my project management responsibilities. I prefer to stay on top of things so that the project comes along exactly as I designed, and by doing so I assure that what is being built will meet the expectations I have set with the clients.

So am I the type of a person who can hire an assistant to make these calls for me, or am I a person who needs to rein in the work to maintain sanity? Currently I am the latter, but I am almost—almost—ready to hire some help. I can handle much more work than I could fifteen years ago, but there is still a ceiling to the amount of work I can take on, given the amount of personal attention I feel I need to give to every aspect of the job.

If you think you could work with a partner or could hire a project manager to supervise work under your direction, this may be your best next step. You will need to develop trust with this person, give them ownership and decision-making authority, and release some control. Having another "you" will leverage your time and talent, allowing you to take on and manage more projects at once. But developing this type of partnership and working relationship takes time. Minimally, this person will need to know horticulture, design, and hardscape construction. Together you will need to determine if this person can see things the way you need them to see things (project quality, design considerations, crew treatment), and of course the chemistry between the two of you has to work. If you want to broaden your reach and do more projects at once, keep your eyes peeled for good potential project managers who could grow into the role under your tutelage.

There's yet another good reason to do this: backup. If you are a lone wolf managing multiple projects, what happens if you get sick or break something? You can rely on your subs to a certain amount, but it might be nice to know you have backup. If you have a relationship with a freelance project manager, they could pitch in until you are back in the pink.

HIRING EMPLOYEES, INDEPENDENT CONTRACTORS, SEASONAL HELP

The U.S. Department of Labor provides comprehensive information on labor laws and definitions of types of employees, as does the Internal Revenue Service. The best way to assure your own peace of mind, as well as to stay out of prison (no, I'm not kidding), is to make sure you run your business by the books—the government's books. Pay strict attention to U.S. labor laws and rules set by the IRS. If you haven't already hired help to handle your company's accounting or taxes, look for outside expertise

I was the project manager hired by another designer
to work this oceanside installation.

as soon as you start hiring employees, because your bookkeeping will be much more complex. Professional tax assistance and professional legal advice on labor and tax laws are well worth the small amount of money they cost.

You can hire people to work freelance for you, which means they handle all of their own taxes and Social Security payments themselves. For example, when I manage a project for another designer, I am a professional working a freelance job, so I am their independent contractor. But the labor and IRS laws around working relationships are strict. Independent contractors use their own tools and equipment, work their own hours on their own schedule, are not directly supervised, and are assigned to a particular job. You hire Marielle Jones to supervise the installation at the Crowleys and to participate in the design development for the Griffins. You pay her an hourly rate or flat fee for the work you have defined for each project. In her spare time Marielle does not go to each of your installations and deadhead the roses. That would be outside the definition of "independent contractor."

It might be time to have a few seasonal or regular employees. You might need extra people just in the spring and fall when things are busiest. You might want a part-time office person to manage initial inquiries, orders, billings, and communications to free you up to spend more time in the field. You might realize that what you could really use is a person to do your layouts— based on your direction, of course. Or find a budding horticulturist who wants to do planting plans. There are many ways to help your business by hiring expertise, or by hiring people with strong potential and developing their talents.

Any potential hire needs to have a minimum skill set, certainly, but they also need to complement your personality. If I have two candidates for a position and their skills are about equal, I hire the one whose personality I think will fit in best.

You might eventually hire enough people to require an organization chart. First, congratulations! This will mean you have really developed a going concern. If your business is growing and has a dozen or so employees, make sure everyone knows who they report to, what their jobs are, and what the expectations are for their role in the company. They should be well versed in the company vision and mission, and should realize that everything they do should funnel positively into supporting the goals of the company. They should also know that in a small company pitching in and covering something that is not in your job description is just part of the scene. In turn, you have a responsibility to provide clear direction, communicate your expectations, be consistent, and provide timely feedback, praise, and constructive criticism. *The One Minute Manager*, *The One Minute Salesperson*, and a number of other *One Minute* tomes from the 1980s have been updated and reprinted and are useful resources. The really incredible message in this series is that timely, succinct, meaningful feedback—whether you are training a puppy, responding to your employee, or talking with your teenager—is incredibly valuable, whereas late or delayed responses are almost not worth your breath. Communicate frequently, clearly, and transparently with your employees. They are your clients, too.

EMPLOYMENT AND WAGES

Your employees should be working in the country legally. Since passage of the Homeland Security Act of 2002, penalties for employing illegal aliens have greatly increased. Make sure your employees are American citizens or have a current green card and Social Security card. Ask for documentation, make a copy, and check with U.S. Citizenship and Immigration Services.

Hiring "regular employees" is a whole new ball of wax. You are going to have a regular payroll, federal, state, and Social Security payroll taxes, unemployment insurance, workers' compensation insurance, short-term disability insurance, long-term disability insurance, health and dental insurances, retirement savings plans, and so forth. Hire an accountant and tax attorney, and consider signing with a payroll service to manage payroll for you. Hiring the expertise you need will free up your time to continue doing what you do best: running and growing your business.

By the time you start hiring employees, you will have been working in this industry for a while. You should have a good sense of what the prevailing wages are for various positions. Offer a competitive wage, not just to attract high-quality workers but also as a sign of respect and appreciation.

You might also consider a profit-sharing structure, which will make everyone—and I mean everyone—pay attention the bottom line. It's incredibly beneficial to have everyone care about both the large and the little costs. When my marketing agency started profit sharing in the early 1990s, the transformation was amazing and almost instantaneous. Hourly and salaried employees alike became focused on the profitability of every client and job. Billable hours became very important. Lights went out in unused offices. Employees avoided photocopying more than they had to, and quickly figured out that U.S. Postal Service mail costs less than courier or overnight services, faxes cost less than mail, and e-mail costs less than a fax and saves labor and paper to boot. People even started cutting sticky notes in half to save costs. And everyone drove less or hit two client sites in one trip. No one shorted the jobs, but we were all very much in tune with the bottom line. It mattered. The bonuses we started getting were an incredible incentive to keep on working hard to keep costs in line. Watching the costs on lots of little things really added up.

One of the designers whom I have managed projects for started a profit-sharing model several years ago. As much as I have always watched the bottom line, with this profit sharing in place I am even more careful about expenditures. Taking the extra effort to make sure the irrigation works perfectly the first time, checking calculations for bulk orders, pitching in with the crew to get it done in three days versus four, picking up supplies versus paying for delivery. Little items can save tens of thousands of dollars in a large installation. And if I'm likely to see a piece of that, I'm certainly going to watch costs that much more closely.

YOU'RE FIRED

If you have employees, you will inevitably have to let someone go some day. This is one of the hardest things you will ever do as a business owner or manager. If you have been communicating clearly and frequently with this person, it will come as no surprise to them that the end has arrived. Sit with them privately, and walk them through the problems with their performance. Ask them about the work, where it has gone wrong, why they are not happy. A key reason for someone underperforming is because they are unhappy in the job. If you do this right, the employee will effectively fire themselves, and the words "You're fired" will never have to leave your mouth. There never needs to be a huge fight, a

If your garden design business branches out to offer additional services like cleanups, there is a lot of extra income you can attract if you just know where to look. Many clients have no idea how convenient it can be to have you and your crew take care of so many of these "annoying" little annual tasks. Consider the following seasonal tasks as you think about what your services might grow to include:

SPRING CLEANUP

- Rake out leaves and other detritus, and dispose properly.
- Cut back dried stalks of herbaceous plants left for winter interest. Remove and dispose.
- Cut out broken or damaged branches of shrubs and trees.
- Trim and feed roses as appropriate for climate.
- Weed as you go.
- Remove containers of sand or ice melt and store for season.
- Clean out drains.
- Edge all garden beds and borders.
- Clean out around (unbury) all stepping stones and edges of walks and driveway.
- Insert staking systems for plants that topple (peonies, for example).
- Remove stakes or guy wires left for winter support on new trees.
- Clean out water features as appropriate. Install and test pumps; set up timer as required. Install tropicals. Feed hardy lilies.
- Clean out birdfeeders and birdbaths; refill.
- Top beds and borders with compost.
- Clean out and turn vegetable garden. Add generous top-dressing of compost.
- Mulch beds and borders.
- Blow all porches and doorways clean of detritus.
- Check exterior lighting; replace dead bulbs. Clean all light fixtures from grime and dead insects.
- Check conditions of welcome mats; suggest replacements if necessary.
- Clean out gutters and downspouts.
- Remove and dispose (or store) leftover holiday decorations.
- Remove winter materials from pots, loosen and amend remaining soil, add climate-appropriate annuals.
- Bring out stored pots; clean, loosen soil, amend, plant with appropriate annuals.
- Wash down stone walks to remove winter sand and detritus.
- Check and clean patios.

- Carefully check structure of decking and determine whether deck needs power washing, staining, repairs.
- Remove, clean, and store snow shovels. Empty gas from snow removal equipment; clean and store for warm months.

SUMMER CLEANUP
- Check out property and gardens.
- Deadhead and weed as required.
- Replace spring annuals with summer annuals.
- Check under eaves of house and outbuilding for wasp and bee nests; remove as appropriate.
- Check soil to see if watering level is on target.
- Clean out collected detritus from water features.
- Check plants in pots; trim, deadhead, or replace as required.
- Clean out birdfeeders and birdbaths, then refill.

FALL CLEANUP
- Rake out leaves and other detritus, and dispose properly.
- Cut back dead foliage of herbaceous plants. Leave appropriate stalks standing for winter interest.
- Weed as you go.
- Clean out gutters and downspouts.
- Clean out drains.
- Remove, clean, and store any plant stakes.
- Check exterior lighting; replace dead bulbs. Clean all light fixtures from grime and dead insects.
- Remove tired materials from pots, loosen and amend remaining soil, add greens or other decorations for winter. Or remove selected pots; clean and store for winter.
- Clean out water features as appropriate. Remove pumps from smaller features; clean out and rinse clean. Store indoors for winter.
- Clean out birdfeeders and birdbaths; refill. Make sure birdseed is stocked.
- Blow porches, walks, doorways, and the drive clean of detritus.
- Position containers of sand with scoops for winter traction.
- Bring out and clean snow shovels. Position to be at the ready for the first snow.
- Make sure snow removal equipment is clean and in good working order. Fill with fresh gasoline.
- Install snow stakes to guide plow or snow removal contractors around perimeter of drive.

drawn-out screaming match, or an audience, unless the employee drags the problem in front of other people.

A few other cautions about terminating someone. You should have documented problematic issues over a period of time. Date them, and maintain a log. Share this with the employee, because it shows you're not just fabricating grounds for termination. You should have already had conversations with them about problems as they came up. Document those conversations as well. And never fire someone on a Friday. Doing it earlier in the week allows the person to return home, cool off, and start doing something proactive about securing new employment the very next day. It is when people have a weekend to obsess over it that anger and depression can set in.

THE EMPIRE STRIKES

You could end up creating a successful business that grows into a large design-build empire. Great oaks from little acorns grow! What types of positions might there be? Do some snarfing around on the Web. Look up "landscape design" or "landscape architecture," and you'll find links to some really large firms, with positions ranging from owner or manager to sales or new business development, creative team (landscape architect, landscape designer, garden designer, architect), CAD draftsperson, civil engineer, project or construction manager, receptionist, office manager, bookkeeper or accountant, laborer, maintenance, and installation specialists (irrigation, masonry, carpentry, plumbing, lighting, pools and spas, and so forth).

TO GROW OR NOT TO GROW

When you are trying to decide between growth or no growth, look at your business as well as your personal life. You may find that not growing is the right way to move forward, so that you can keep enjoying what you are doing and keep it manageable. Or you may realize that you would love to head up a good-sized design group and forge ahead with confidence, adding new clients, new employees, new challenges. On to the future: grow, grow, grow!

CHAPTER NINETEEN

But Am I Any Good?

WILL MY WORK BE GOOD ENOUGH? When will I know that my design and installation work is good? Well, first off, good enough for what? Good enough to make your clients happy? Good enough to get you additional clients? Good enough to make it into a magazine? Good enough for you? I think you will be amazed at how good your work can be when you are following your passion. Once you have some basic design principles under your belt and leverage that with your horticultural knowledge, you cannot help but create landscape transformations that your clients will love and that other people will want. But will these landscapes be good enough for you? That is another question. When is our work good enough to satisfy *us*?

You would be surprised to know how many successful people suffer from the imposter syndrome, characterized by feelings of inadequacy and the fear that you are living a life, working a job, or receiving accolades that you secretly don't deserve. I have heard musicians, artists, writers, physicians, and lawyers talk about this hidden fear. After the elegant and talented Nicole Kidman received an Academy Award, she was asked whether she could relax now that she had received unequivocal proof that she was an amazing actress. She said no, not at all, adding that she always feared someone would leap out at her on stage someday and scream that she was horrid, and that it would be true.

Every person I have heard share this same kind of fear is very good at what they do. The irony does not escape me. But when we compare ourselves to the best, the crème de la crème, we know we still have a long way to go. We are always asking, "When will I be good enough?" And you know what? That is a good thing. We should always have goals.

Imposter syndrome or not, at some point you will just know you are doing good work. For me, I was receiving constant inquiries from potential new clients. My existing clients were passing out my name to their friends and families, telling them I could make their properties beautiful and more valuable, and bring them so much more pleasure from their homes and gardens. My projects were getting larger, people trusted me to take on some huge initiatives, and I was starting to make a good income. I was working my proverbial cojones off, learning like crazy, and living the dream. I had arrived.

Part of what it takes to get good is putting in the time. One project completed successfully does not an expert make. Twenty projects completed successfully, well, that's a start.

A charming folly in Ellen Lathi's gardens, staged for a magazine photo shoot. I greatly admire Ellen—and her glorious gardens—a perfect example of the crème de la crème to which I aspire.

Malcolm Gladwell's *Outliers* is a book about exceptional people, people who are highly successful, people who have become famously rich and live at the extreme outer edge of possibility. Gladwell explores how they got there, what made them, how they made themselves. The one piece of information that really spoke to me was what he calls the Ten-Thousand-Hour Rule. Gladwell contends that the key to success in any field is not talent, intelligence, or luck (although a certain amount of those certainly helps), but work. Success is realized by practicing what you do and getting better and better. Twenty hours of practice a week, each week, for ten years. Ten thousand hours of practice. Gladwell also points out that it is never too late to start, and he references several internationally famous people (Alfred Hitchcock, Paul Cézanne, Robert Frost, and others) who started practicing their craft in their fifties but still made it to the top echelon of practitioners in their respective fields.

What does this tell you about garden design? As with any other profession, pastime, or passion, it is your commitment to doing the work that will make you successful. It's akin to the old joke, "How do you get to Carnegie Hall? Practice, practice, practice!"

I have put in my ten thousand hours and then some. My work is accomplished. I am paid well for it. I am not Bill Gates or Martha Stewart, but I guess you could say I am living proof of the Ten-Thousand-Hour Rule.

It is never too late to start a new career or craft and become very good at it. You might always harbor some doubts about your abilities, but these doubts shouldn't stop you from pursuing a dream. On the contrary, they should keep you hungering, reaching, stretching to push yourself beyond your comfort zone, and they should make you grow and help you to ultimately reach that goal.

YOU ARE WORTH MORE

A couple of years after a friend of mine started doing design and installations, she asked, "Love, do you actually make any money at this?" I looked at her like she was crazy and said, "Well, Hon, I don't just do this for my health. Of course I make money at it!" At the time, she was barely breaking even. I eventually sat down with her and took a hard look at her numbers. The bottom line? She wasn't charging enough. It can be extremely hard to look at yourself and your work and put a price tag on it.

As you contemplate pricing and fees, margin and markup, you are probably formulating an idea of what you'd charge for your services. Whatever that dollar figure is, I'm here to tell you that you are worth more.

One of the largest mistakes designers make is to dramatically undervalue their services. The killer is, they have no clue they are undervaluing themselves or their work, but they know they are not making any money. And lots of these designers have been working in our industry for years, so this is not just a newbie phenomenon. Many of them forgive this. "Oh, I love my job, so it doesn't matter." Sure, you love your job. You're realizing a dream to be able to work with plants and gardens for your livelihood. But your livelihood needs to be, well, lively. Vital. Substantial.

At first you will be grateful for every job. You might even be grateful for jobs that just break even. Get over this. And if you have jobs on which you are losing money, stop! You need to make a living, and not a paltry one. I am appalled when I see designers virtually give away their work. Yes, we all pay our dues and make some mistakes, and initially you will be learning on the job and spending too many hours on various tasks. Initially you can be a bit more generous with your time versus your billable

I neither design nor install gardens for free, unless it's here in my own gardens.

hours. But that doesn't mean you should be giving away your services. Unless you are doing a job pro bono, charge for it. And even if you are doing a job pro bono, it's okay to make some margin on the materials and subcontracted services.

Stop and take a close look at each job and do a profit-loss analysis on each one. You don't need a degree in economics or mathematics to do this; we'll keep it simple. Take the gross amount of monies—the price—you are charging the client for their project. Subtract the costs of all the goods and services you have purchased for the project. The total is your gross profit. This is not your personal profit, it is your businesses profit. Now subtract your fee or hourly charges. The number you have left is the net profit for your business. Depending on how you have structured your margin share and fees, this net profit amount should run anywhere from 10% to 50% of the entire price for the project. Of course, to get a net net you need to subtract all of your operating expenses (phone, car, rent, utilities, supplies, and so on) from this, but this little exercise gives you a window into your pricing structure and helps determine if you are charging appropriately. Here's the quickie formula:

Total price of project	$75,000
Less goods and services	− $55,000
Equals gross profit	= $20,000
Less your fee	− $8,000
Equals net profit	= $12,000, or 16%

Where you come out on the net profit percentage is a factor of how good you are, as well as what the market can bear. It is true that if you are not charging enough, your clients will not value your service. I would much rather be known as expensive but worth it than really good and cheap. Follow the money.

Your fees and profits should increase as you get better. Like any professional, the more you do what you do, the more skilled you become. The more skilled you are, the more your services are worth—and the more you should reap reward from your hard work. I know, I know, you love the fact that you're a garden designer so much that the money doesn't really matter, right? Bull. You are good at what you do, and you deserve to make a living. Heck, if you can, go for the gold and get rich!

CHAPTER TWENTY

Exiting Gracefully

O LD GARDENERS NEVER DIE, they just go to seed. As much as you love what you are doing, there will come a time when you'll be ready to work less. This doesn't necessarily mean leaving the business or quitting, but it does mean ramping down. I guess you could say that I've been ramping down for a couple of years now. My business has grown to the point where I don't need the geographically or emotionally undesirable clients in order to stay afloat, so I have amicably divorced a number of clients who have fallen into those categories. It is very freeing.

Is it silly to talk about the end of your business in a book that is focused on starting, building, and growing it? No, because the smartest of the smart always have an exit strategy.

One designer I know entered this business by starting up a "better" maintenance company. Her crews do the mow and blow thing—a highly competitive, price-driven market—but she also maintains properties using sustainable, no-chemical practices (a differentiating factor in the marketplace), and her crews do perennial garden maintenance, pond maintenance, and even keep clients' pots looking scrumptious year-round. She'll have your deck power washed, your house painted, or your car detailed—just phone her. This is a fabulous, all-inclusive maintenance company. Through her maintenance work she has also built a viable design business, which supports not only her but also another full-time designer and project manager, an office support person, and a part-time CAD draftsperson.

So why keep the maintenance? For one, it covers her cash flow. She always has money coming in. Her maintenance clients frequently turn into design clients when they need a new walkway, foundation planting, or water feature. Additionally, she has trained her crews to do installation as well as maintenance, so she has a knowledgeable group to pitch in on installations if she needs it. Lastly, she knows she will retire at some point, and she wants a business that is saleable. A stand-alone designer, or even a small company with a couple of design associates, is more challenging to sell. If you don't offer a continuous service, your design clients are mostly one-shot projects, and there isn't much continuity that you can bank on for continued income. My friend designed her business this way from the beginning. She thought through the various options open to her in the industry and designed her exit strategy while developing her business plan. When she is ready to get out, she will have a well-established maintenance business with a terrific client list that will be very, very saleable. She might sell it for two to three years of her gross receipts, along with selling the used equipment and tools. That isn't chump change.

You'll eventually reach a time in your life when you're ready to make a big change. You might want to spend more time on personal undertakings and less on client projects. As a person with a garden design business, you actually have more options than you might imagine. You can ramp down your work, which will allow you to enjoy more "me" time while maintaining an income stream and keeping your finger in the business pie. You can repackage your design business and do something similar but not quite the same. You might have the option to sell your garden design business, bringing you a sum of money that can help fund your future. Or if you don't want to go through the headache and hassle of selling your business, you might decide that you've enjoyed the run and are just ready to stop. All of these options are best pursued when you have thought about it beforehand and allowed yourself the appropriate lead time to put everything in place. Above all, realize that it is okay to have new goals that are different from what you wanted five, ten, or fifteen years ago. Feel free to reinvent yourself and your objectives. We change, and so does life.

If you decide to ramp down, you can go about this in all the ways described in chapter 18 under "Restricting Growth." Additionally, you can offer to consult. Maybe your favorite part of the job is talking the garden and design talk. A designer I know decided that the physical demand of design and installation would not be sustainable as she got older, so she morphed her business into a consultation-based enterprise. She meets with clients, assesses their existing gardens, offers suggestions for improvements, and charges for her time.

SELLING YOUR BUSINESS

So you're ready to make a really big change. If your garden design business has been a success, you have probably poured most of your time and energy into it. You might have trouble imagining your life without your business, like it's a part of your family. But still you ask, is it time to sell? This could give you instant freedom and a chunk of income for your well-deserved retirement.

Selling your business is a one-shot, make-or-break deal. You only get one chance to put a price on your years of effort and sign it all over to a buyer. You'll come out way ahead if you take the time to understand the steps required. You need to ask yourself what you need to get from the sale, and you need to be able to articulate your priorities. Do you want

You might actually enjoy lounging on a chaise instead of only planting around them.

Plan ahead. Smart owners start getting their companies ready to sell as early as three years before they want to sell. This will help you maximize your window of opportunity.

Put your team in place. You may not need a team of dozens to sell your business, but you should minimally have an accountant, a lawyer, a business appraiser, a tax expert, and a business broker looking out for your interests. If you are selling to an employee or family member, you should at least have the business appraised, an accountant should review the business records, and a lawyer will need to draft the sales contract. The other party should employ an accountant to review the books and a lawyer to review the sales terms. Family or not, everyone should be careful to cover their own butt.

Keep meticulous, updated records. Make sure your sales and tax records are up to date, and have a detailed business history and sales portfolio. Your financial advisor should take an active role in keeping your books perfectly maintained.

Price your business accurately. Hire a professional small business appraiser.

Hire a small business broker. This person will act as your agent and work for you. Small business brokers usually work on a commission basis, but they frequently get you a larger dollar amount for your business, which is often more than the amount of their commission. Interview several and ask for references. This is a critical decision, so make sure you have the right person acting on your behalf. The chemistry should work.

Keep growing. Your business is being valued and carefully observed. You want to show that it is a viable, thriving entity, so showing growth, even modest growth, during the year or two or three that you are getting ready to sell will illustrate to buyers that your business has great upside potential.

Sell yourself. The impression you as the business owner make to the buyer is as important as your business itself. You are the best promoter for your business. Your knowledge, enthusiasm, and passion will be contagious and can motivate a buyer better than any broker.

Update or create operating manuals or protocol lists. You want your business to succeed even without you. Make sure you have documented how you and your employees do things. If the new business maintains the same standards that made you successful, they are more likely to be successful, too.

a block of cash, or can you self-finance your buyer for three to five years? Do you want to serve in a transition role during the first several years of the new ownership? Do you want a guarantee that your two employees be kept on for a period of time? You need to think about the structure of the deal you will propose.

You also need to identify your optimal timing. Selling a business can easily take two or more years. And you'll need to rely on outside expert help. When you're an entrepreneurial spirit, it can be hard to admit that you need to look outside yourself for advice about your business, but this is one time you should seek it. You may be an expert in your business, but you are not an expert in selling your business.

From the time you start to think about selling your business all the way through to the sale, you need to pay meticulous attention to your business and your books. Your records will be under scrutiny by your own experts as well as by the buyer and their agents. You'll need to work twice as hard to keep your business going and healthy, while at the same time wading through the unfamiliar territory of interviewing and choosing experts to help guide you through this process.

How do you determine the value of your business? Rely on a professional business appraiser. Presumably a lot of what you will be selling are intangible assets, which are also called "goodwill" or "going-concern" values. Selling a business that is based on intellectual property is very different from selling a business that has inventoried assets, a definable product, and a customer base with years of sales continuity. Business appraisers have a number of ways to establish value on major aspects of your business. The value they determine will be a starting point for your negotiations with potential buyers.

CLOSING SHOP

Unless we die with our work boots on—taken out while planting that maple with the 1000-pound root ball—we garden designers will usually close up shop at some point. When it's time, you might say to yourself, "This is the last year, then I'm retiring to my own gardens." When you are ready, and you have decided you don't want to bother with the hassles and uncertainty of selling, then go ahead, shut your doors, and prepare to remember your business fondly. Inform all your clients whom you've worked with in the previous five or so years that you will no longer be doing design or installation. This might be the time to craft a lovely letter-to-my-former-clients that speaks to how you have valued them and your relationship all of these years but are looking forward to enjoying gardening in your own landscape again. Thank them for the opportunity to work with them, and for their referrals, and wish them well.

Remember to shut down your Web site, or at least add a visible note to your home page saying you are no longer accepting clients or are retired. Change the message on your answering machine.

But wait! On the other hand, you could shut your doors while helping to open them for other up-and-coming designers. You might be able to turn the seeds cultivated from the success of your business into a continued stream of income. Consider working out an agreement with another designer or two or three whom you know and respect and who are in the prime of their work lives. These other designers could follow up on inquiries that come in from your Web site or from continued client referrals (in which case, don't shut down your site or tell your clients that you've retired). If the designers to whom you've referred your inquiries get hired for the design work, you can be paid a referral fee, say two to three hours of their billable time. Yes, you would need to have a relationship based on trust, but this could work nicely for both of you. You could also think about serving as a consultant for them. They can do the legwork, and you can work with them to carve out some hardscape designs and planting plans. This will keep you working and enjoying the business, but you won't have the schlepping or the work that bothers your hands, back, and knees. You'll also be paying it forward, since you'll be an invaluable role model and source of inspiration as you guide the next generation of garden designers.

QUIESCENCE

When our business, like our garden, has grown, blossomed, and then set seed, dormancy follows. Whether you sell the seed or let it scatter with the four winds, the question that faces you now is about tomorrow. Will the dormant season last forever, or will you have an epiphany and develop a fresh passion for something new? Only time and your own personal experience can tell you that. You might just take pleasure from years of true retirement, enjoying what you want to do, when you want to do it, and gardening as much—or as little—as you like. Or you might reinvent yourself, leveraging your talents. Maybe you'll teach gardening and design. Maybe you'll become a mentor to other designers. Maybe you'll start a blog or publish a regular column. Or maybe, just maybe, you'll write a book. It could happen.

The garden in spring.

The garden in winter. Life, too, is a cycle.

A Final Word of Encouragement

DESPITE MY WHINING about various aspects of this business, I wouldn't trade what I do for anything. I love what I do, I love the process of transforming space, and I love the people I work with. All the designers I know are generous with their knowledge, with their time, with their laughter. We have a great time doing what we do.

As you continue to ponder your options, take a few steps towards making a change. You don't have to quit your day job, but set aside an hour or two to research courses and volunteer opportunities available in your area. Sign up for a horticultural design class. Attend a locally sponsored seminar on building walls. Network with the professionals giving the course and talk with the people attending. Teach preschoolers how to plant sunflowers. Design and install a vegetable garden at a nursing home. When you branch out beyond your own yard, you'll get a little taste of what it's like to do this for a living.

Working with plants, creating beauty, being your own boss—it's a good life, and it might be the right life for you. If you made it through this whole tome, you have tenacity, that's for sure. That's certainly a prerequisite for this job. You also must have some whisper of desire inside of you, encouraging you to try something different. If you do, if you decide to try this profession, at least you will go into it with a little more information than the average plant-loving Jane or John who decides, "I want to be a garden designer."

Whatever you decide, whether you choose a life that is one with the soil or one that stays cleanly away from the garden design business, my final advice to you is the same. Laugh every chance you get. Drink plenty of water. Check for ticks. And always call before you dig.

Now go forth and conquer!

RESOURCES

American Horticultural Society (AHS)

ahs.org

The oldest national gardening organization in the United States dedicated to gardening education and awareness. A network of experts and budding gardeners sharing information and experiences from all over the world.

Association of Pool and Spa Professionals (APSP)

apsp.org

International trade association for the swimming pool, spa, and hot tub industry, promoting best practices through education, certification, standards, research, and safety.

Association of Professional Landscape Designers (APLD)

apld.com

National organization with state and regional chapters, providing great information, education, national conferences, local seminars, certification opportunities, and networking for professional garden and landscape designers. If you join no other organization, join this one.

Better Business Bureau (BBB)

bbb.org

National organization with local chapters. Network of businesses with performance ratings for use by consumers and professionals.

Beyond Pesticides

beyondpesticides.org

Searchable database listing hundreds of common pesticides. Includes comprehensive data on ingredients, mode of action, exposure symptoms, primary toxicity, downstream toxicity, and environmental persistence.

Chamber of Commerce

chamberofcommerce.com

National organization with local chapters. Excellent networking, help, and advice for small businesses.

Dark Sky Society

darkskysociety.org

Resources, news items, and links to local initiatives to reduce light pollution. (This organization is separate from the International Dark-Sky Association.)

Environmental Protection Agency (EPA)

epa.gov

Government organization with local offices in each state.

Garden Writers Association of America

gardenwriters.org

National organization of professionals who write about horticulture, gardening, design, lawn care, and the environment.

Internal Revenue Service (IRS)

irs.gov

Useful information on personal income taxes and business taxes.

International Dark-Sky Association (IDA)

darksky.org

Comprehensive Web site on Dark Sky initiatives and actions happening globally. Free e-newsletter, links to local Dark Sky initiatives, and information on how to choose lighting fixtures in keeping with Dark Sky protocol.

Perennial Plant Association (PPA)

perennialplant.org

Great Web site with useful information and tips on perennials, including new introductions and the PPA's perennial plant of the year.

Pesticide Action Network (PAN) **Pesticide Database**

pesticideinfo.org

Searchable database listing thousands of pesticides, rated by toxicity.

Seedland

lawngrass.com

A phenomenal wealth of knowledge on turf grasses. The Web site lets you quickly see what turf grass zone you fall in, and you can click on your state and learn about the various turf grass varieties that perform best in your area.

Small Business Administration (SBA)

sba.gov

Government organization that helps small businesses. Great Web site. Many offices across the nation.

The Underground

theunderground.pbwiki.com

Online network for gardening professionals in the Northeast (Connecticut, Maine, Massachusetts, New Hampshire, New Jersey, New York, Pennsylvania, Rhode Island, and Vermont). Great question and answer sharing.

United States Department of Labor

dol.gov

Government regulations on labor, hiring, firing, insurances, and so forth.

RECOMMENDED READING

Allen, Debbie. 2008. Five mistakes to avoid when selling your small business. http://retail.about.com/od/exitstrategies/a/selling_mistake.htm.

Avent, Tony. 2003. *So You Want to Start a Nursery.* Portland, Oregon: Timber Press.

Blanchard, Kenneth, and Spencer Johnson. 1982. *The One Minute Manager.* New York: Morrow. Honest, immediate feedback is the best way to communicate with your employees, subcontractors, and clients. (Not a bad way to communicate with your spouse or children, either.) Very effective management principles articulated in a digestible format.

Bradley-Hole, Kathryn. 2000. *Stone, Rock and Gravel.* London: Cassell.

Build Easy. 2008. Deck anatomy. www.buildeasy.com/fp_decks_anatomy.html.

Carson, Rachel. 1962. *Silent Spring.* Reprint. New York: Mariner Books, 2002. Widely credited with launching the environmental movement, Carson's message is as timely today as it was in 1962.

Centers for Disease Control and Prevention. 2008. Learn about Lyme disease. http://www.cdc.gov/ncidod/dvbid/lyme/.

Centers for Disease Control and Prevention. 2008. Rabies. http://www.cdc.gov/rabies/.

Centers for Disease Control and Prevention. 2008. Rocky Mountain spotted fever. http://www.cdc.gov/ticks/diseases/rocky_mountain_spotted_fever/.

Chapple, Renee. 2008. Design the right pool for your family. http://miami.about.com/cs/shoppingservices/a/pool.htm.

Consumer Product Safety Commission. 1998. CPSC reminds residential pool owners and parents of precautions to prevent drownings of young children. http://www.cpsc.gov/cpscpub/prerel/prhtml98/98124.html.

Consumer Product Safety Commission. 2008. Spas, hot tubs, and whirlpools. http://www.cpsc.gov/cpscpub/pubs/5112.html.

Dirr, Michael A. 1997. *Dirr's Hardy Trees and Shrubs: An Illustrated Encyclopedia*. Portland, Oregon: Timber Press. My tree and shrub bible. I have two copies and both are in shreds from constant use. Great photography accompanies extremely useful plant descriptions, including ornamental characteristics, growth habits, hardiness, and cultural preferences. Dirr offers the positive attributes for each species and many varieties, as well as the negatives, which is equally useful for the designer to know.

Dirr, Michael A. 2002. *Dirr's Trees and Shrubs for Warm Climates: An Illustrated Encyclopedia*. Portland, Oregon: Timber Press. Since I do not live in a warm climate, I don't have this book. But if it is half as good as its colder-climate counterpart, those of you living in the southern tier of the United States or a similar climate should find it an incredibly useful resource for your garden design business.

DiSabato-Aust, Tracy. 2003. *The Well-Designed Mixed Garden: Building Beds and Borders with Trees, Shrubs, Perennials, Annuals, and Bulbs*. Portland, Oregon: Timber Press. Great design principles and captivating plant combinations engagingly presented by a masterful plantswoman. Inspiring to any gardener or garden designer.

Eck, Joe. 1995. *Elements of Garden Design*. New York: Henry Holt. Writing for serious gardeners, Eck beautifully articulates the theory and practice of garden design and the art of fine gardening.

Eck, Joe, and Wayne Winterrowd. 1995. *A Year at North Hill: Four Seasons in a Vermont Garden*. Boston: Little, Brown. A month-by-month chronicle of one of the most beautiful and beloved gardens in North America, this book is for every earnest gardener and garden designer who wants to be inspired anew.

Grant, Elaine Appleton. 2008. Q&A: Selling your business without going crazy. www.usnews.com/articles/business/small-business-entrepreneurs/2008/02/26/qa-selling-your-business-without-going-crazy.html.

Home Decks. 2008. Anatomy of a deck. www.homedecks.com/deck-glossary.php.

International Dark-Sky Association. 2008. IDA practical guide. Introduction to light pollution. http://data.nextrionet.com/site/idsa/Practical%20Guide-Light%20Pollution7-28-08.pdf.

Lewis, Sanford, and Paul Schramski. 2008. *The Truth About Cats, Dogs, and Lawn Chemicals: Community Action Toolkit*. Boston: Pesticide Watch Education Fund and Strategic Video.

Lewis, Sanford, and Paul Schramski. 2009. *The Truth About Cats, Dogs, and Lawn Chemicals*. Boston: Strategic Video. Eighteen-minute documentary.

Lipkis, Andy, and Kate Lipkis, with TreePeople. 1990. *The Simple Act of*

Planting a Tree: A Citizen Forester's Guide to Healing Your Neighborhood, Your City, and Your World. Los Angeles: Jeremy P. Tarcher.

Nelson, Lewis S., Richard Shih, and Michael Balick. 2007. *Handbook of Poisonous and Injurious Plants*. Second edition. New York: New York Botanical Garden, Springer. Every designer should be familiar with the possible toxicity of the plants they specify. This is a superb reference.

Outdoor-kitchens.org. 2006–2008. Outdoor kitchen design guide. http://www.outdoor-kitchens.org/.

Pausch, Randy. 2008. *The Last Lecture*. New York: Hyperion. Vision, encouragement, and ethics on how to run your life and how to conduct yourself in business. A quick read that could change your entire life for the better.

Pavlina, Steve. 2008. Thirty-three rules to boost your creativity. http://www.stevepavlina.com/blog/2007/05/33-rules-to-boost-your-productivity.

Plymouth Quarries. 2008. *Paving Patterns*. Hingham, Massachusetts: Plymouth Quarries.

Reed, David. 1998. *The Art and Craft of Stonescaping: Setting and Stacking Stone*. Asheville, North Carolina: Lark Books.

Stewart, Martha. 2005. *The Martha Rules: Ten Essentials for Achieving Success as You Start, Build, or Manage a Business*. Emmaus, Pennsylvania: Rodale. Very accessible information on the entrepreneurial process, particularly valuable as you start or build a business.

Tukey, Paul. 2007. *The Organic Lawn Care Manual: A Natural, Low-Maintenance System for a Beautiful, Safe Lawn*. North Adams, Massachusetts: Storey. The definitive guide to no-chemicals lawn care.

Turn the Corner. 2008. Proper tick removal. http://www.turnthecorner.org/proper-tick-removal.htm. Lyme disease support and information.

WaterPartners International. 2008. Elementary curriculum unit 2.0. "Water is life." Global water awareness mini-unit. www.water.org/FileUploads/WPElemCurric2_0.pdf.

RECOMMENDED PERIODICALS

Architectural Digest (architecturaldigest.com). The quintessential word on architecture, interior decorating, garden design, and exquisite interior and exterior furnishings, with spectacular photography and comprehensive information on preeminent homes worldwide. Indispensable.

The Avant Gardener. This eight-page newsletter from Horticultural Data Processors is the most valuable publication I receive each month. Easily read, strangely all green, and delivers more succinct and timely horticultural information than any other publication. The only periodical I keep and file, highlighted and flagged with Post-it notes.

Fine Gardening (taunton.com/finegardening). A beautiful, instructive gardening publication useful for any gardener or designer.

Garden Design (gardendesign.com). Offering a worldwide perspective, this magazine delivers dramatic, inspiring examples of garden and landscape design, integrating gardens with beautiful homes, and stunning treatments and accessories.

Horticulture (hortmag.com). This magazine formed the foundation of my horticultural knowledge. Unparalleled information and photography for advanced gardeners or garden designers.

Martha Stewart Living (marthastewart.com/living). Decorating, homekeeping, gardening, furnishings—every trend in interior and exterior design is covered in this gorgeous monthly publication.

Meredith Publishing Group (meredith.com). A large multimedia company, Meredith publishes a wide spectrum of special-interest magazines about home, family, and gardening under its *Better Homes and Gardens* brand. The gardening magazines are well worth getting for their inspiring photography alone. Show a client one photo of a perfect patio with planted pots, and you can instantly sell that concept in your design. Available on newsstands. Seek out titles such as *Country Gardens, Deck, Pool, and Patio, Garden Ideas and Outdoor Living, Nature's Garden, Outdoor Rooms,* and *Landscape Solutions*.

Organic Gardening (organicgardening.com). Published by Rodale, this magazine brought the organic movement to the United States and the rest of the world. Invaluable information for those who want to "do it greener."

This Old House (thisoldhouse.com/toh/magazines). This how-to magazine about home renovation offers not only compelling before and after stories but also accessible information on gardening, exterior design, and reworking space.

ACKNOWLEDGMENTS

I WANT TO THANK Mike Walsh of Horticultural Concepts for giving me my first opportunity for a freelance collaboration with a "real" designer, and for sharing so much of himself and his proven techniques for working in this business.

I am grateful for my friendship with Nancy Lattanzio of Lattanzio Landscapes, whose perspective and brilliantly ironic commentary never fail to make me roar with much-appreciated laughter.

A special thanks to Jonathan Nagler of Plymouth Quarries for sharing with me so much more than I ever imagined about stone, brick, pavers, and masonry, and for his witty retorts and laughter. Additional thanks to John Devine for allowing me to photograph his wonderful, historic, stone-y site.

Jill and Lee of South Shore Mulch and Loam are wonderful, responsive suppliers. I thank them for allowing me to pick their brains and for graciously coming through on all of those obnoxious orders when I needed materials in, you know, like half an hour.

My thanks to Jeff Smeed of That Bloomin' Place for his fabulous plants, his support, and for always being quick to share a hug, a story, a coffee, a kvetch.

Thanks also to the wonderful, knowledgeable, accommodating crew at Sylvan Nursery, and a big thanks to Neil Van Sloun for always being there with a smile (as well as great Hosui pears, winter squash, and luscious leeks).

Derek Stearns and Dean Marsico of Stearns Stonework are such joys to work with—professional, dedicated to creating quality work with timeless beauty, and the most uproariously comedic gentlemen who ever worked with feathers 'n wedges. Or a microphone. They are rock stars, indeed.

I offer my heartfelt appreciation to Peter Wells of Presidents Landscape and Design. He and the "A" Crew—Al Borges, Angel Santiago, José Santiago, and Joe Borges—have been the muscle and the backbone of building my business success. They've all enriched my work and my world.

I owe a great deal to Eve Goodman, my editorial clock-watcher, and Mindy Fitch, my editor. These talented women kept me on track, motivated, and succinct, proving once again that any endeavor truly does take a village. We started this journey as bicoastal coworkers—I am delighted that we're finishing as friends.

A special thank you to Tony Avent of Plant Delights Nursery for writing *So You Want to Start a Nursery*, a shining example of a primer for wannabes.

Finally, my deepest gratitude to Tom Fischer of Timber Press for dreaming up the idea for this book and then asking me to write it. That really blew me away (and still does). From the first time we met at *Horticulture* magazine, I always wanted to work on a project with Tom, even though I figured it would probably be something like repotting our orchids together. Thanks for thinking bigger than that, my friend. I am eternally grateful.

INDEX